Date Due

JUL 12 '62		
DEC 20 '63		
MAY 7 68		
APR 29 '70		
PRINTED	IN U. S. A.	

TEACHING MUSICIANSHIP

TEACHING MUSICIANSHIP

A Manual of
Methods and Materials

HOWARD A. MURPHY

Teachers College, Columbia University

1950

COLEMAN-ROSS COMPANY, INC.

44605

To
John Winter Thompson
Knox College, 1890-1938
Great teacher, musician, and friend

ACKNOWLEDGMENTS

The author gratefully acknowledges criticism of the manuscript by Professors Lilla Belle Pitts, James L. Mursell, Charles Leonhard and David Barnett.

In addition, he is indebted for permission to use the material on orchestration (Professor Ernest Harris), college harmony survey (Professor Frank W. Hill), Rochester Plan (Howard Hinga), corrective listening (Professor Elizabeth Kaho), common-tone modulation (Professor William S. Newman), keyboard analysis of piano literature (Charles Walton), use of mood effects (Charles D. Arnold), summary of chord function theories (Dr. Israel Silberman), material on teaching children (Mary Lenom); as well as the Leonhard and Walthall doctorate studies cited in the Selective Bibliography, and the Zimmerman dissertation referred to in Chapter I.

CONTENTS

FOREWORD

The purpose of this book is to clarify the premises and the procedures for the development of musicianship through an understanding of musical structures. It is based upon a belief that understanding is essential to true musicianship and that it is best developed through an organized study of music itself.

Though the word functional has been worn smooth by usage, yet in the truest sense such a study is functional if it makes more meaningful music heard, performed, or written. With this objective in mind, the teacher becomes a guide through literature rather than a taskmaster through a textbook. The clarification of experience that leads to understanding is the primary function of the teacher—not the development of techniques. Art cannot be reduced to a set of formulas. To teach technique without understanding is to fail as a teacher. Skills and insights are interactive: their separation is fatal to learning.

The acceptance of these premises will affect all teaching of musical structures, simply because the emphasis will be shifted from the acquiring of skills to an understanding of music from which techniques will naturally result. Music and "theory" have had little relationship. The practice of composers apparently contradicts many textbook maxims. This dichotomy is both needless and useless. Our business as teachers is to explain music, not textbooks. When we do so, the chasm between theory and practice will be bridged, but not before. The first question is what does the student need to know for an understanding of music, and the second, how can he learn it from the practice of composers? In answering these questions, we as teachers must stress realities, not theories, and help the student to discover for himself the answers. Probably the best learning is indirect in the sense that it originates with the learner. As Pope said—

"Men must be taught as if you taught them not;
And things unknown proposed as things forgot."

31 January 1950   HOWARD A. MURPHY
New York

INTRODUCTION

Chapter I

BASIC PHILOSOPHY

I

In all methods of teaching, two questions are paramount—*why* and *how*. Too often undue emphasis is laid on the latter, whereas the former, in reality, is the more basic of the two. Hence discussion of methods must begin with their underlying and implicit philosophy.

The only valid reason for so-called "theoretic" instruction is to explain the structure of music for appreciative, expressive, and creative purposes. This is a fundamental need of the listener, teacher, performer, and composer—so essential, in fact, that it is the logical core of any type of rational music instruction. Its central purpose is the development of musicianship, which may be defined as the ability to deal effectively with musical problems through insight into musical texture. It is the conscious understanding of the organization of music.

The organization of musical practice presents both general and specific problems. This is true of all the arts but especially of music because of its unique technical difficulties. A child can express himself spontaneously through singing an original song, but the symphonic composer requires years of study for an equally satisfactory expression. This is not true, in the same degree, of the other arts. There are many more amateur painters than composers, because the basic techniques of painting are simpler than those of music. Great composers are rarely entirely self-taught, although all have learned much through experience. Thus it is essential, first, that the technical aspects of musical structure be organized with special care because of their unique difficulty, and second, that the learning of these aspects should be directed primarily toward a real understanding of music. "Wisdom is the principal thing; therefore get wisdom: and with all thy getting get understanding."

Since, then, this understanding is an essential need of all connected with music, two questions arise: *first*, is this need being met by present practice in theoretic instruction, and *second*, if not, how can the need be met? A recognition of the underlying reason for theoretic instruction leads to a very simple conclusion: namely, that the most effective approach to the understanding of music is through the organized study of music itself. This proposition appears to be self-evident, yet it has been almost entirely neglected in the past. Its acceptance largely negates present practices and explains, in part at least, their relative failure, for if the goal of theory teaching is to develop musical insight, surely this is best accomplished through a study of musical practices.

II

As regards the first question, criticism of present methods is due to their failure to promote musical growth or to achieve a functional understanding of musical structure. The word "theory" itself describes the prevalent emphasis with devastating accuracy. The materials used are principally artificial "exercises" unrelated to living music and consequently of no musical value. The methods tend to be mechanistic and without sufficient diversity of approach to insure a complete picture of musical structures. Emphasis is laid primarily on written skills and sight singing without due recognition of the vital role of ear training, keyboard harmony, analysis, and creative work. Furthermore, if presented, these aspects usually are isolated as separate courses rather than combined into a single unified course. Such arbitrary divisions tend to obscure basic concepts common to all areas, and to present a confused and often conflicting picture of musical structure as a whole.

In addition, theoretic instruction is usually delayed too long. Even a child should understand, in his own terms, the structure of music he plays or sings. Yet how often such instruction is not given until the college level—when it is usually too late to be effective. Understanding music should be a process of continuous growth from the child's first contact with music. But whenever introduced, such instruction, to be effective, must be in terms of the musical background and the maturity of the student. Failure to consider these factors is one of the chief reasons for the widespread musical illiteracy existing among students today.

Any teacher familiar with the field is aware of the non-functional character of "theory" as commonly taught. A thousand cases attest its impotence to vitalize music. How frequently during entrance examinations a student admits previous theoretic study which has been forgotten because it was never used. Such a statement is an indictment of the student's previous non-functional training based upon "theory" rather than practice. The blame, however, does not rest entirely with the "theory" instructor. Teachers of applied music seldom relate music structure to the student's repertoire. It is the exceptional teacher who questions the student regarding the key, form, and harmonic content as related to performance. Yet these are all vital elements of musical understanding without which performance sinks to the level of parrot-like repetition. Failure on the part of the instructor to teach understanding as well as technique may be due to personal musical deficiencies. Musical feeling is based on knowledge as well as upon intuition. The head as well as the heart must interpret. While the appeal of music is primarily sensuous, it is also intellectual through the understanding of structure, and any approach that ignores this fact, either in the classroom or studio, is inadequate and incomplete.

III

It is evident, then, that the aims, procedures, and outcomes of current "theoretic" instruction are open to serious criticism, and recognition of this fact brings us to the second question—how can the need be met? The answer is contained in music itself—by a realistic and rational organization of musical experiences relevant to practical needs. These "experiences" lie in six major areas or avenues of learning: writing, reading, listening, playing, analyzing, and creating. The areas may be likened in function to the fingers of the hand. Maximum effectiveness demands their correlation—the insight and skills derived from them being integrated parts of a unified whole. Like Roman roads, these avenues of learning all have a common objective: musical insight.

Further, all learning should be based upon practice as found in music literature. *Practice always precedes principles*. To ignore these facts is to continue the present schism between "theory" and music.

Often texts perpetuate "rules" that have no basis in practice. Codification frequently results in stratification. Only by constant reference to living music can instruction be validated and freed from artificiality. Music itself is the ultimate authority, not in an arbitrary sense but in the sense of proved practice. Textbooks should illustrate music—not music textbooks.

General principles can be derived from living music without fear of contradiction. Skeptics who infer that composers are a law unto themselves and differ so widely in practice that no valid principles can be deduced from their practices are simply not informed. Exceptions undeniably occur, but throughout music literature, whether in design or texture, run consistent threads of practice that may serve as a basis for instruction. Bach did not contradict Handel's practice, and Chopin and Wagner are remarkably consistent in technical details. The truth is that one sees what one wants to see, as in the familiar definition of optimist and pessimist in terms of the doughnut. But for educational purposes one must recognize the circle of similarities, not the hole of differences. To assert that the divergencies in individual practices are so wide as to preclude the formation of general principles is not only pessimistic but untrue. Mountains and valleys fail to alter the essential rotundity of the earth—human nature strikes an average in spite of individual differences, and the same is true of human beings working in the arts. A man is the product of his age and creates as such. A comprehensive study of the art of a given period will reveal more likenesses than differences. These similarities can be stated as *general principles* valid for that period. The vast majority of sonata-allegro movements have only two genuine themes. [1]* The seventh of a chord does "resolve" downward; "the sun also rises" —even on a cloudy day. To quibble about exceptions is to strain at a gnat and swallow a camel.

Music has a well-nigh universal appeal. Students like music as much as they dislike "theory." It does not have to be "sold" to them. Liking is the first step toward understanding. Three principles are involved in the selection of music for instructional purposes. First, the music used must be suitable for the student's background, interests, and maturity. This is self-evident and requires only good judgment in application. Second, the music used should be the best on any given level, and third, it should be chosen to widen and deepen the student's knowledge of music literature. Begin on his level and lead him to a higher one. All functional music is "good," although sometimes in a

---

*Notes to Chapters I-XI will be found on pp. 224-225.

non-musical sense. On the other hand there is a world of music which is truly "great," and it is the privilege of the instructor to help the student to discover, explore, and understand this world for himself. Upon utilitarian standards, Johann Strauss was as "great" a composer as Chopin, since both wrote very effective waltzes; but obviously, in the broader sense, Chopin was the greater creator. It is essential that this distinction is clear in selecting music for study or for performance. Use music commensurate not only with the immediate but with the potential capacities of the student. Too many school programs compromise with what is believed to be the students' tastes. Careful selection of material is especially important in the teaching of musical structure, since only the best models are desirable. The practices of a Beethoven are superior to those of a Sousa; Bach's chorales are a better text than Gospel hymns, irrespective of their religious value.

IV

Furthermore, organization is essential for instruction. Random sampling may be good statistics, but it is poor education, except in the most general sense, simply because it is not efficient.

When the student is encouraged to wander unguided through the forest of musical literature, he is quite apt to be confused by the differences of the individual trees. The wise teacher will proceed from general principles to specific exceptions, and not be lured by the phantom of "freedom" to aimless comments on differences of procedure found in music. In other words, he will *organize* these observations of real music into recognizable paths of practice that will guide the student through the jungle of literature.

Naturally these general practices found in literature must be evaluated, although even raw statistical data is illuminating. But these patterns of practice, once determined by observation and refined by evaluation, are the most rational basis of instruction for the average student. True, composers expanded traditional techniques through aural perception, but they did so on the basis of past practice, not of vague intuition. The romantic conception of a composer working in an artistic vacuum according to the dictates of his genius is neither realistic nor accurate.

In regard to organization, it has been stated that student's interest should be the determinant factor rather than the proved practice of composers. This is a very loose and questionable type of organization if followed literally. Interest is a condition of learning but hardly the sole basis for organization. Heterogeneous class interests do not comprise a practical pattern of learning. Interest is the spark which sets the engine in motion, but, once started, the engine runs logically, not haphazardly. Even methods courses are not organized on an interest basis! The organizational focus on interest also stems from the notion that attitudes are more important than knowledge. *Both are important*, and again it is the question of the doughnut or the hole. Certainly in technical courses skills cannot be slighted, since they are the beginning, not the end, of wisdom. Interest is essential as a condition, but learning grows from doing.

Considerable emphasis has been laid on the use of musical experiences as a basis of instruction and of the desirability of organizing these experiences into function patterns, because of the prevalent fallacies that composers' divergence in practice is too wide to determine trends, and that even if possible, organization of them nullifies teaching by reducing it to meaningless generalities. Undoubtedly there is some truth in both objections, but ultimately they are questions of degree, not of kind. Life is exceptional as well as learning, but both must be organized to function effectively.

V

Granted, then, that present methods of "theoretic" instruction are ineffective, and that the solution lies in a functional organization of practice as found in standard literature, let us consider the six areas of learning mentioned above.

In doing so the function of skills must be clearly recognized. Rightly used, technical facility is the best means of gaining insights. [2] As previously stated, we learn by doing, not by appreciating, and learning is essential to understanding. This is one of the pitfalls of extreme "progressive" teaching—the hope that skills may be somehow by-passed, and that appreciation will lead directly to understanding. Such a hope is obviously futile in teaching applied music. How can it be valid in relation to the study of musical structures? Should not skills be regarded as the second essential link in the learning sequence connecting appreciation and insight? Otherwise the outcome of the study is very apt to lack focus and precision. The student "understands" the principle of modulation, but cannot identify or use the chords involved; or he may "know" the German Sixth but be unable to spell or sing it. Such understandings or learnings are very superficial indeed. *Skills are tools of insight*, not objectives in themselves, and as such should be neither stressed nor neglected if true functional learning is to result. It is dubious if real insight can be attained without some measure of skill. Skills are the wings that lift the student from the appreciative to the understanding level.

Of the six areas of learning, writing has traditionally received primary emphasis. However, with the growing emphasis on musicianship, the other areas have received more attention. Actually none can claim primacy—all should be utilized from the first contact with music. This point is of vital importance and its neglect is the root of much of the failure of current practices to promote musical understanding. It is difficult to achieve a balance between these six avenues of learning—there is a natural tendency to emphasize one at the expense of the others. For example, it is often stated that the written approach has been so overstressed that it seems proper, in the light of contemporary educational theories, to minimize its value; or again, ear training is so difficult for many students that its neglect is readily rationalized. Further, not all students play the piano—to the consequent detriment of essential keyboard experience—or relatively few students possess creative ability and hence all should not be expected to compose, and so on *ad infinitum*. Also, the instructor often stresses what is of interest to him rather than what is of value to the student. A thousand excuses can be found for omitting one or more of these vital areas. But if genuine learning is to take place, *all phases must be included*, and the neglect of any one of them weakens and vitiates the program proportionately.

Hence, any real educative effort must utilize and equalize all techniques in order to present a comprehensive and adequate description of musical structure. All parts of the musical body must be developed for perfect health. Some parts will require more training than others, but if all phases are integrated from the beginning, the objectives will be realized most completely.

In passing, it should be noted that early training also is of the utmost importance. Nothing is more frustrating to the student and disheartening to the instructor than to find mature students baffled by simple probems that could readily be solved by musically trained children. Take the case of the twelve-year-old boy who excelled in an advanced college harmony class simply because his first piano teacher taught him to *think* music as well as to play it. Probably one of the chief reasons why "theory" is disliked is because it is usually a case of too little too late. When structure is properly taught *from the beginning*, the student is never aware of any distinction between "theory" and music—the former is only a rational explanation of what he hears and plays. All of which strongly suggests that even the child should understand, in his own terms, the structure of all music he contacts.

VI

Finally, a clear understanding of the specific objective of this new integrated approach to musical understanding is essential. The use of music as a basis for instruction and a complete renovation of procedures alone are not sufficient to achieve the desired goals. Conventional "theory" cannot be reformed. What is needed is a wider concept whose primary objective is insight through skill applied to practical situations. Skills become means, not ends. Learning grows from liking and this new approach would probably begin with "appreciation" and lead, through techniques, to understanding. Contrasted with the conventional "theory" course, it would move from the general to the specific by dealing with structure primarily in terms of musical needs. Such an approach would be definitely experimental but, for that reason, all the more challenging. Its success would depend upon clear objectives, adequate technical equipment, and constant resourcefulness on the part of the instructor.

To summarize briefly: the true aim of "theoretic" instruction is to promote an understanding of music through a growing awareness of musical structure in terms of musical needs. Failure to achieve this goal is due to the schism between "theory" and music, and its remedy lies in the functional study of music literature through the writing, reading, hearing, playing, analyzing, and creating of music by the student in relation to his interests, maturity, and background.

In subsequent chapters the six areas of learning will be discussed in detail, including their integration and evaluation, followed by a consideration of the requisite training for teachers and of the role of the teacher as musician and educator.

PART ONE: THE STUDENT

Chapter II

WRITING

OF the six avenues of learning listed in Chapter I, writing has traditionally taken precedence on the general premise, presumably, that music is seen and not heard, and consequently that literacy should be the first consideration in music study. Both the premise and its conclusion are false because music is *heard*, not seen, and because literacy is only a part of the total musicianship expected today. As a matter of fact, it has been pointed out that none of the areas of learning have any defensible primacy. To begin with any one of them alone would be analogous to training a single finger before the whole hand. However, since writing is the most familiar approach, it will be discussed first, irrespective of its relative importance.

I

The preliminary fundamentals of music—called rudiments—usually include an explanation of musical notation, and the construction of scales, key signatures, intervals, and chords. The *corpus* of facts is known also as "theory," pure and simple—although actually it is neither. Rudiments are usually administered to the hapless student in large doses of little educational value. The whole process, often lasting a year, is purely intellectual, without any reference to or use of real music. It is a grim endurance test which only indifference or resignation can make endurable. What makes this state of affairs peculiarly unfortunate is that it constitutes the student's first contact with the structure of music. After such a beginning, it is a miracle that there are any students in first-year harmony classes!

But the whole approach and method change when *music*, not "theory" is taught. How can factual material such as rudiments be taught from music? Simply by singing a familiar song, *The Star Spangled Banner*, for example, and then by analyzing what the symbols mean in terms of the sounds sung. Such a simple procedure will explain staff, clefs, [3] note values, key signatures, whole and half-steps, accidentals, diatonic and chromatic progressions, time signatures, slurs, and ties. All these facts are either present or implied in this song. It is a springboard from the known to the unknown—from the familiar world of melody to the unfamiliar world of music structure. It also illustrates the principle of giving factual knowledge only when needed to explain a given situation. Here lies one of the major fallacies in the conventional method of teaching rudiments prior to musical experience. Hundreds of meaningless facts are to be learned before there is any need for them. True, all will be used eventually. Why not defer learning them until the time of need? When will the need arise? When the facts are necessary to explain the music being studied. This concept of "felt need" aroused by curiosity about music heard is basic, and will revolutionize teaching procedures from the lowest to the highest levels. The concept is equally effective applied to key signatures or fugal answers.

The only prerequisite for harmonic study is notation—the staff, clefs, note and rest values, bar lines, and time signatures. As we have seen, these can be learned from a comparison of the sound and the sight of a familiar song. Scale structures, key signatures, chords, and intervals may be learned as a part of regular first-year harmony: the intervals to differentiate chord quality, and scales and key signatures through modulation, that is by identifying the new scale and its key signature when a modulation occurs in the music being studied.

Let us consider briefly the reason for and methods of presenting these elementary facts as a part of harmonic study rather than of rudiments. Applying the principle of *learning through need*, it is obvious that only a few essential facts regarding notation are required to begin the study of musical structures. The teaching of *all* the scales, intervals, and chord structures previous to musical experience, even of the "theory" textbook type, is both unnecessary and unmusical in the literal sense. Our objective is, or should be, to *teach music*, not "theory." What *need* has the beginner to know the signature of G♯ minor, or the construction of a doubly augmented fourth? Obviously none. Yet weeks are often spent cramming such irrelevant facts into his head when he is supposed to be learning about music! Even if mastered, such knowledge is soon forgotten because it is unused.

How then can scales and intervals be presented in a logical musical sequence, assuming a knowledge of notation? *First*, in regard to scales: the piano keyboard suggests a solution. Its consecutive white keys form the scale of C major. This scale does not have to be taught: it has no signature and all chords in it can be formed by using alternate white keys without any knowledge of intervals or of chord quality. Here is a known tool which will unlock the structure of music. Begin with the examination of simple music in the key of C major—or transposed to it—and continue using only that key until the student has sufficient *musical* background to assimilate other keys. How can these be taught—by learning the circle of keys? Definitely not—the student becomes aware of other keys and their necessary signatures through *modulation* discovered in the music that he examines. When a change of key is felt, it is time to explain that change and to learn the scale and signature of the new tonality. This is a radical but logical departure from accepted practice. Furthermore, it is impossible to delay the consideration of modulation until all diatonic chords and keys are "learned," since modulation permeates all music from the simplest to the most complex and consequently must be reckoned with early in harmonic study. When a passage modulates from C major to G major, the time has come to explain the structure of G major and its signature. All scales except C may be discovered thus through modulatory examples, so that by the end of the course the student has become familiar *through experience* with all tonalities.

The teaching of the minor mode requires special comment. There are many theories regarding its origin and various forms, and it presents unusual pedagogical difficulties. In the first place, the minor mode should be taught only after the student has learned and used the major mode in a number of keys. This is a sharp contrast with the usual procedure of teaching all the minor scales before the major scales have been used. Second, the parallel or tonic-harmonic minor scale should be taught first *for purely aural reasons*. Again this is at variance with the usual practice of teaching the relative relationship first. To justify the introduction of the minor mode through the tonic rather than through the relative minor, it is necessary to consider the nature of tonality and how it is best apprehended. Tonality may be defined as the relationship of a series of tones to a central tone known as the keytone. It is perceived *aurally* by the effect of finality which the keytone gives as the center of the key. Granted that this theory of tonality is correct, it is obvious that two scales having a common keytone are more closely related than scales having different keytones. Hence, C major and C minor are actually two forms of the C tonality, since they both revolve about the tone C. What are their differences? Simply that when the third and sixth degrees of C major are lowered by one half-step, the scale becomes C minor. Irrespective of tradition and historical development, this is what the ear *hears*. No aural similarity is apparent between C major and A minor because of their differing key centers. Remember that music is heard, not seen. In relative major and minor scales the ear does not *see* the similar signature, but only *hears* the differing keytones. The usual minor signature is "borrowed," for convenience only, from the corresponding "relative" scale. Consequently, the *parallel*, not the relative, relationship of the minor scale to the major is the one which coincides with aural experience. It is interesting to note, in passing, that such a conception recognizes only a change of mode, not a change of key, between C major and C minor. The corresponding minor of C major is C minor rather than A minor. As usual, music literature, not theory texts, substantiate this viewpoint. In contrasting the two modes a composer uses the parallel, not the relative, minor in the majority of cases. (See the ending of Schubert's *Serenade*, the *Andante* from Beethoven's Second Symphony and innumerable other passages in music literature.) This concept of the parallel or tonic minor has decided pedagogical advantages, as will be seen in the discussion of music reading (page 46) and keyboard harmony (page 81). It simplifies and clarifies the whole problem of minor, making it perfectly clear and reasonable—because audible—to the beginner.

After the harmonic minor scale has been heard and learned as a variation of the major scale built on the same keytone, the melodic and natural minor forms should be presented in the same manner. In doing so, the approach should again be aural—not "theoretic." Play a passage which should use the melodic form of the minor scale, but do so *without* the necessary accidentals, and have the student determine *by ear* what accidentals are required. Then draw the obvious conclusions regarding the structure of the scale. The natural minor scale can be learned similarly. This will naturally involve a discussion of the medieval modes—an important area seldom treated in textbooks. Some knowledge of the modes is essential, however, since modal characteristics are found in both folksongs and in the music of great composers.

One important point in the teaching of the three forms of the minor scale should be stressed, namely, teach all forms as variations of the major mode, irrespective of the location of whole and half-steps. Nothing is more confusing or futile than the attempt to teach the minor mode as a variable series of whole and half-steps, or worse yet, as a combination of tetrachords. The step-wise pattern will take care of itself when the aural comparison with the major mode is the basis of construction. One of the stumbling blocks for the student is the usual reference to key signature or to intervallic relationships. Concentrate on the major form which is thoroughly familiar and the minor variants will be clear. This point cannot be overemphasized.

Naturally, all the minor scales and keys are learned, like the major ones, by an examination of modulatory passages, but only after the student is familiar with all except the enharmonic major keys.

Second, in regard to the teaching of intervals as music: intervals are obviously difficult to present musically, since little music is predominately intervallic. Here again the question should be raised as to the real utility of intervals. A knowledge of them is unnecessary in scale structure since it can be explained by the white keys of the piano later reduced to whole and half-steps. Contrary to general opinion, neither is a knowledge of intervals necessary for music reading, as will be shown later. What, then, is the functional use of a knowledge of intervals? *Simply to determine chord quality*. Once this function is recognized, intervals are easily taught *as parts of chords* when it becomes necessary to distinguish and identify chord color. When does this necessity arise? Only after a considerable chord vocabulary has been acquired through use. This point will be discussed in connection with the order of chord presentation, but for present purposes it is sufficient to state the principle and apply it to the learning of intervals.

Intervals determine chord quality. The first step is to hear large and small thirds as parts of major and minor triads whose fifths are constant, and large and small fifths which occur in the dominant seventh chord. The small fifth in this chord results in a small chord-seventh. *All other intervals can be derived by inversion*. The thirds and fifths are eventually named in relation to the major scale of the lower tone— a known norm. The designation "perfect" is difficult to explain, but may be justified by the fact that in perfect intervals each tone belongs in the scale of the other tone, in contrast to the major intervals whose upper tone only is found in the scale of the lower tone. Another characteristic of perfect intervals is that they remain perfect when inverted. Minor intervals should be taught as being one half-tone smaller than the corresponding major interval—*not* as belonging to the minor scale of the lower tone. Thus, C—E♭ is a minor third because of its size, not because it is 1—3 in the C minor scale. This approach is obviously sound—since a minor second is not formed by the first and second degrees of the minor scale.

However, it would be wrong to assume that the teaching of intervals as parts of chords tends to minimize their importance or to make superficial their learning. Once the principle of their function as harmonic "color tones" has been established, all intervals should be found, identified, and thoroughly learned. The harmonic approach also is most useful in certain rare cases for which no real reason is usually given: for example, in the case of doubly augmented or diminished intervals which are found in the augmented $\frac{6}{5}$ chord (German Sixth). Such a chord built on A♭ would be A♭—C—D♯—F♯. Here we have a functional example of the doubly augmented fourth —from A♭ to D♯. By inversion the doubly diminished fifth, D♯—A♭, is obtained. What better explanation is needed for such abstruse and rare intervals? This impinges on the whole problem of the spelling of music, discussed on page 55, but for the present it solves a difficult point in regard to the teaching of intervals.

Considerable time has been spent in a discussion of the teaching of scales and intervals, not only because of their vital importance but because there are no areas which are taught so mechanistically and unmusically. *All* facts regarding musical structure can and must be related to living music if musical growth is to be nurtured and musical understanding achieved. This is a basic principle. Scales and intervals, indeed the whole of rudiments, are no exception to it. Until this principle is accepted and put into practice, rudiments will remain an isolated mass of meaningless facts which repel rather than attract the student. The simple is always more difficult to teach than the complex, because of limited background: scales often present more problems than symphonies, and so it is essential that rudiments, the basis of instruction, be treated as *musical* experiences, not as "theoretic" facts.

II

Following rudiments, the teaching of four-part vocal harmony usually has been the next step toward musical literacy. In fact, it could be said that for most students four-part writing *was* "theory" in the accepted sense unless they were talented or courageous enough to venture into the jungles of counterpoint and composition. The reason for this approach probably was due to a feeling that four-part writing epitomized all written techniques, and, once mastered, would provide the necessary foundation for more advanced study. While undeniably this training had some merit, it is clear, in the light of our premises, that to begin harmonic study with four-part writing was to practically insure its failure. The reasons are obvious: musically, it is one of the most difficult types of writing and, furthermore, one remote from ·the interests of the average student. Is it really expected that a beginner be interested in connecting the I and V chords in root position for mixed voices? What would be the musical value of such a task? Is the bulk of music written for mixed voices? These questions alone expose the fallacy of this approach.

It is essential, before suggesting a solution of the writing problem, to make very clear a basic approach in all class instruction: namely, base each recitation on a specific musical example and begin by performing and analyzing this passage. *Aural experience precedes analysis.* Draw from class comments the desired inferences and conclusions. Avoid facts before feeling. It is essential that technical facts be deduced from the music heard. Discussion should clarify music, not vice versa. This is in direct opposition to the usual "theoretic" approach, in which facts are stated first and music is sometimes used to illustrate them. The simple procedure of beginning each recitation with music, not "theory," will revolutionize attitudes and outcomes. It should be stressed, however, that the examples used be both significant and interesting musically—preferably thematic—drawn from the best sources suitable for the student's background and interests. Frequently inconsequential or meaningless fragments are quoted which defeat the educational purpose. Here the point is to find examples which are both interesting and pertinent; that will expand the student's knowledge of literature, and be of lasting value to him long after the specific technical point involved may have been forgotten. No example, however *apropos*, is good unless it fulfills these larger requirements.

To return now to the question of how to introduce writing. One solution is to begin writing, not for four voices but for one. Capitalize on the student's inherent creative ability by having him set short poems to music. In other words, *begin with a single vocal line and gradually add the other three*. This procedure has obvious advantages. It frees the student at the outset from clumsy and unmusical four-part writing and permits him to acquire gradually the necessary musical background for such a task. For the present, specific details of melody writing may be deferred until Chapter VII on creative writing, and we shall continue with a consideration of multi-voice writing.

The addition of a second voice (mezzo soprano) will come considerably later and may be introduced in several ways. One of the best is to have individual students sing a lower part by ear against a melody played or sung. This develops an aural awareness of linear relationships. Another method is by singing and inventing rounds or canons (e.g., *Three Blind Mice*). This will also give an opportunity for a discussion of polyphonic texture. In both cases the individual lines should be stressed, not harmonic background. The approach should be more linear than vertical—every effort being made for the independence of each part through *hearing*.

The subsequent addition of the third voice (alto) will lead naturally to the male voices, since the alto usually can be rewritten on the bass staff as tenor or baritone. Here, for the first time, the harmonic background is considered, and the vertical concept takes precedence over the horizontal.

Note that four-voice vocal writing should be presented only when the student has fairly comprehensive harmonic vocabulary and has developed real musical discrimination. To handle four voices musically is so complex that it is unreasonable to expect beginners, with limited background, experience, and vocabulary, to do so successfully.

The traditional method of teaching part-writing was *figured bass*, but since it is no longer necessary in the playing of accompaniments, its functional value has diminished considerably. Certain other values, however, do remain. The student should understand and use its terminology which is universal. In addition, he should be able to add the inner voices when the soprano and figured bass are given. Needless to say, such drill material would be derived from literature and hence will contain non-harmonic tones, which are almost entirely lacking in much figured bass material. There is also value in the completion of a passage in which the soprano and unfigured bass are given. Both these types of completion problems stimulate choral thinking, but the use of figured bass alone—that is, without a given soprano, is of very little value to the average student.

Obviously, the most important skill to be developed in four-part writing is the harmonization of melodies. Musical values rather than routine techniques should be stressed; expressive harmonic values emphasized and the whole process raised from a mechanical to a creative level. The following procedure is suggested:

1. Sing or play the melody.
2. Identify the cadences and form.

3. Determine an essential bass using only the first, fourth, and fifth scale steps. (One or two bass notes for each measure will be sufficient.) Test by singing while melody is played.

4. Work out complete bass line, making it as melodic as possible. (One bass note for each beat. Do not harmonize all melodic pitches.) Test as above.

5. Add complete alto, then tenor, and sing in four parts.

Note that the above procedure differs somewhat from the usual one, in which each chord is chosen and completed before passing on to the next chord. However, in harmonization, it is essential to proceed from the whole to the parts. Determine first the broad, over-all effects; then work out the details as outlined above.

One determinant factor in melody harmonization, implied but not stated above, is the principle of *harmonic rhythm*, which is an adjustment of the number of chords used in harmonization to the tempo of the melody being harmonized. In other words, the faster the tempo the fewer the chords, and vice versa. Even a cursory examination of music will show the basic nature of this principle. Yet it is scarcely mentioned in harmony texts [4] and rarely, if ever, applied in practice. Its neglect is one of the reasons why students often fail to harmonize a melody musically. Of course, its application implies a thorough knowledge of non-harmonic tones, since obviously in many cases not all the tones of the given melody will require a separate chord. In general, the working principle for melodies in moderate tempo is to assign a chord for each pulse: for example, two chords to a measure in duple meter and three in triple. Even artificial, unmusical textbook exercises can be improved if this principle is followed. It will be noted that indirect reference was made to it in the outline of vocal harmonization given above, but it applies with equal validity to the harmonization of instrumental melodies.

As regards the all-too-familiar "rules" of voice leading, it should be remembered that they are only amplifications of two fundamental principles:

1. Hold the common tone in the same voice if it is present.

2. Move in contrary motion to the nearest position of the next chord if there is no common tone.

The basic principle of doubling chord tones may be summarized thus: double the bass note in all chords that require doubling, except in the first inversion of triads; in them, any other tone than the bass may be doubled.

These statements are *principles* rather than "rules," *and should be so called*. Technical points of this type are best stated broadly and then adjusted to individual cases. In cases of doubt, refer to the best musical practice, not to textbooks. (See page 14.)

This closes our discussion of four-voice vocal writing, since it is seldom practical or necessary for the average harmony class to write for more than four voices. However, an excellent discussion of the technique of writing for five or more voices may be found in Goetschius, *The Materials Used in Musical Composition*, pp. 244-245.

III

Instrumental writing, particularly for piano, is an important activity which should be introduced from the outset, although it is often delayed or omitted entirely. The reason for its early inclusion is the fact that it is in many cases a technique closely related to the interests of the student, and because its technique is in general much simpler and more easily mastered than the involved procedures and prohibitions of four-part voice writing.

The piano, as a harmonic instrument, naturally takes precedence. The piano keyboard should be taught to all students as a part of rudiments and is consequently known when writing for the piano is begun. The tonic and dominant seventh in the key of C major undoubtedly will be the first chords to be used by the student. The function of the accompaniment figure should be discovered from music and applied to single melodies requiring only these chords. Probably the first accompaniment figure used will be one in $\frac{6}{8}$ in which the tones of these chords are arranged consecutively rather than simultaneously. The procedure follows in general the one suggested above for four-voice vocal writing, thus:

1. Sing or play the melody.
2. Identify the cadences and form.
3. Determine the harmonic background as outlined by melodic steps, general effect, and the cadences, using only one or two chords to each measure.
4. Sing the bass while melody is being played or sung. (Women— melody, men—bass.)
5. Sketch in the chords for the left hand in "block" form, that is, in close position.
6. "Break up" the chords in left hand into an accompaniment figure.

Example 1 outlines this procedure, thus:

Ex. 1

This procedure is entirely within the capacity of both pianists and non-pianists.

It is most important that, after the first rough draft of one accompaniment is written, it be made practical pianistically by adjustment to the natural position of the hand. Otherwise the student's first attempts may be awkward and poorly written. For example, the clumsy distribution in Ex. 2 (a) may be improved by omitting the chord-third in the dominant as in (b), thus:

Ex. 2

Such guidance is the instructor's responsibility, and, if not assumed from the beginning, results in bad and careless left hand patterns. The objection to (a) above is not only the parallel fifths, but the inept chord positions. The guiding principle here is that since all accompaniment figures are essentially part-progressions heard consecutively, the common tone (G in this case) should be kept, for smoothness, in the same "voice" as in vocal writing. This is not mere pedantry, but is based on the practical hand position involved. Too often instructors ignore this point, on the theory that it is better to allow students to write badly than to inhibit them by too much guidance. Strange to say, this attitude has little defense in the teaching of language. Apparently the arts are a paradise for students who resent or avoid discipline. If the "common tone" principle is applied from the outset to instrumental writing, the student will be prepared for its use in vocal writing. While it is true, on the whole, that instrumental is freer than vocal writing, nevertheless its fundamental techniques are similar and should be learned as such.

Another point about the writing of accompaniment figures requires special comment, namely, the treatment of the chord-third, which should never be written below small C (second space in bass staff) because of the resultant thickness in chord texture. In seventh chords, also, it often may be omitted effectively for better hand position, since the dissonant chord-seventh appears to compensate for its omission.

These related points, hand position and the omission of the chord-third, are only several of many which contribute to effective writing of accompaniments. Through wise guidance, the student should be aware of them and use them from the beginning if he is to master this technique. As suggested, the responsibility for their application depends upon the musicianship and good sense of the instructor. In this, as in all cases, discipline is the basis of freedom, but it should come from within, not from without.

Another essential feature of writing an accompaniment figure is that it remain *uniform in design throughout the composition*—especially in harmonizing short melodies. All harmonic progressions can be reduced to consistent accompaniment figures. Examination of literature shows that the design of accompaniment figures is seldom changed during a composition. This is a difficult point for the student to grasp, since his natural inclination is to alter the figure when it fails to adjust readily to the chord progression. Yet regularity of pattern is almost as important as it is on wallpaper or fabric. Ex. 3 illustrates this point:

Ex. 3

The point is, that in elementary writing, the initial pattern should be retained unaltered. Mendelssohn's *Spring Song* or Bach's Prelude I, Book I, of the *Well Tempered Clavier* are excellent examples of this principle, exceptions to the contrary.

Harmonization for piano should continue *throughout* the student's training. A knowledge of piano is an aid to the understanding of music and can be developed by writing for it. [5] Many and varied types of accompaniments in either hand should be used including those invented by the student.

Writing for other instruments, especially the student's own medium, also is valuable and should be encouraged. However, since the only other harmonic instruments are the organ, harp, and accordion, discussion of writing for instruments other than the piano will be postponed until the section of this chapter on creative writing.

A discussion of the principles of modulation common to all types of writing as well as to keyboard harmony will be found in Chapter V, pages 87-89.

IV

The study of counterpoint is justly and universally regarded as essential for potential composers, and as highly desirable for serious students of music. This is because musical texture today is either harmonic, contrapuntal, or a mixture of both, and hence the knowledge and use of these textures are necessary for a comprehensive understanding of existing musical structures.

Their basic concepts are entirely different since harmony stresses the *vertical* and counterpoint the *linear* relationships of tones. Historically the linear concept is the older, but for the past two hundred years the two textures have been so intermingled that today pure examples of either are comparatively rare. A brief historical survey may aid in orienting the problems of teaching counterpoint.

Until 1600 music was predominantly polyphonic and vocal, but with the rise of homophony and the development of solo instruments in the 17th century the new vertical concept of music affected its texture. Hence there exists historically two types of contrapuntal writing: the *vocal* polyphony of the Renaissance period culminating in Palestrina, based entirely on intervallic relationships, and the instrumental polyphony of the late Baroque, represented by J. S. Bach and based essentially on chordal relationships. To further complicate matters, a third artificial type arose, known as strict or *academic* counterpoint. This variant was an effort to systematize the early vocal polyphony and first appeared in Fux's *Gradus ad Parnassum*, published in 1723. The Fux treatise purported to reproduce Renaissance practice, but actually it was only a rough approximation of it. He divided the free flowing rhythms of Palestrina's school into five species or types, the first four according to the number of notes written in the counterpoint against a unit of the given melody or *cantus firmus*. The fifth species was a combination of the preceding four with some new rhythmic figures. Of course such a procedure was contrary to Renaissance practice, since the rhythms were never thus divided arbitrarily. Further, Fux added a number of restrictions not found in literature. The final touch of artificiality was the fact that no examples from literature were or could be quoted, since the system was largely theoretical. However, the work was used extensively for over a century and is still the model for many contemporary texts. Many famous composers studied it, which accounts for the fact that free examples of the various species—even in combination—can be found in such non-academic composers as Schubert and Rossini.

Which of these three types of counterpoint (vocal, instrumental, or academic) should be taught? All have relative merit, depending upon the object in mind. Academic or strict counterpoint is the type most widely taught, largely for traditional reasons. Its advocates argue that being vocal, analogous to four-part harmony, it is the basis of written techniques: that it is well organized for instruction, and that it has produced satisfactory results. On the other hand, much of its material is remote from musical practice and its methods are so mechanistic that its pedagogical value is highly suspect. In other words, its rating is low when challenged by our initial questions of *why* and *how*. While acceptable, it is definitely the least satisfactory of the three types.

The decision between vocal and instrumental counterpoint is more difficult, but again must be solved primarily in terms of objectives. A potential composer definitely should have *both*, but for the average student of musical structure a knowledge of instrumental rather than of vocal counterpoint is more urgent in terms of the music which he hears or performs. However, it is undeniable that, on the college level, some technical acquaintance with Renaissance literature is desirable, and for this reason it is suggested that one half-year of each type be offered in lieu of a complete year devoted to either type. Of course, in a professional music school both types should be offered for at least a full year.

Several compromises have been tried. For example, strict counterpoint has been taught coincidentally with harmony for a period of two years. However, little musical transfer is apparent and it is impossible to make a real tie-up with literature. Again, some American texts attempt to "modernize" strict counterpoint by relaxing some of its maxims. This practice is particularly pernicious, since it tries to straddle several fences without marked success in surmounting any. Finally, four-part harmony has been approached through two- and three-voice "free" counterpoint. Using this approach, four-part counterpoint becomes four-part harmony. [6] This last device has much to recommend it, especially in the training of composers. However, it might be open to criticism on the ground that, since little musical literature is contrapuntal in origin, undue stress on the linear concept of music distorts the whole picture proportionately.

The teaching of strict or academic counterpoint requires only brief discussion. Instruction beyond three voices is of doubtful value for the average student. Mixed counterpoint—a combination of species in various voices—is highly questionable. In two voices a counterpoint should be added both above and below each *cantus firmus* assigned. In three voices, the cantus firmus and moving counterpoint should appear once in each voice, the other voice being in first species, thus providing three solutions for each cantus. Use the C clef for the cantus and keep all writing within vocal range. Some semblance of musicality may be invoked by using familiar melodies (e.g., *Old Hundredth*) as a cantus firmus, analogous to the practice of Renaissance composers in writing Masses.

In teaching strict counterpoint, some contact with music literature may be made by analyzing music of the Renaissance period, for example, a Palestrina Mass, especially one which has been recorded. It is also interesting to have the class sing the work before hearing the recordings. The instructor should be warned, however, that Palestrina's procedures will not coincide with those taught in class—perhaps a desirable point—and furthermore that the analysis of such music is difficult and requires considerable background in the music of the period.

Application of listening and reading can be made by introducing the new species through dictating and singing examples to be considered. The cantus firmus of problems to be solved in class may also be dictated and sung rather than copied. The completed problems should be sung in parts by the class, both to test the solution by ear and to emphasize the fact that, however dry and academic, the result should have musical value. The practice is also one which stresses the necessity of keeping within the normal vocal range. Test all examples used in class by singing.

A practical application of contrapuntal principles may be made by adding descants to chorales, hymns or part-songs. Begin by giving all four voices to which the descant is to be added: later have the student add the inner voices as well as the descant. This is an excellent bridge between counterpoint and harmony and also serves as a review of the latter. In doing so it is essential that the four-part harmonization be complete in itself—independent of the descant. It should also be stressed that the descant is an independent fifth voice, and as such can form no parallel fifths or octaves with any of the four voices. Many violations of this principle can be seen in published descants, although such laxity is no more effective musically in five voices than it is in four. Descants are of various types: a simple, unadorned melody with few, if any, rests; a melody which imitates or is derived from a motive of the real soprano, and finally, a melody on an independent motive, often containing a number of rests or long held notes. Naturally these types intermingle. *Avoid excess ornamentation* and keep within a reasonable vocal range. In order to preserve the vocal line, the descant sometimes crosses the real soprano. The descant should be written freely, not in accordance with the rules of strict counterpoint. Again, test results by class performance.

The teaching of vocal counterpoint of the Renaissance period has been revived within recent years, and the present trend is entirely toward it and away from strict counterpoint. There are a number of excellent texts on Renaissance counterpoint in which teaching procedures are adequately outlined. Needless to say, it is based entirely on *practice*, and a course in it should be enriched and supplemented by both a visual and aural analysis of much literature of the period. It offers peculiar advantages for creative writing, since the student can learn to understand the idiom by writing music in it. True, music of that period is alien to present styles, but perhaps for that very reason students would profit by becoming familiar with it. At least it would make obvious the common fallacy that Bach was the first great composer. Naturally, all said above regarding the use of dictation and music reading as class procedures on teaching strict counterpoint applies here with equal force.

Free counterpoint is undoubtedly the most functional of the three types of polyphonic study, since it is the one used in the bulk of music heard today. A course on free counterpoint should be organized around the invention and the fugue, and should include a thorough analysis of Bach's *Well Tempered Clavier*. It could also include chorale harmonization, in which the melody is placed successively in the bass, alto, and tenor voices. The value in such work is that it provides a link between harmony and counterpoint, and gives the student clear perception of the chorale idiom as contrasted with other four-voice writing. (29).* Furthermore, the Bach chorales are examples of a fusion of the harmonic and contrapuntal textures, and while studying chorale harmonization *contrapuntally*, the class should sing a number of Bach chorales, noting their characteristic idioms.

Other procedures are helpful. Have the students play selected preludes and fugues from the *Well Tempered Clavier*, each student playing a single voice-part. Three or possibly four students could use one piano, or better yet, two at each piano if more than one instrument is available, in which case each voice-part may be doubled in the octave. Follow this performance by playing a recording of the same composition. It is also possible for the group to sing a fugue in four parts, e.g., Fugue No. IX in Book II, or to have some played by string quartet, as No. VII, also in Book II. Encourage the students to copy at least one four-voice fugue in string score, indicating its struc-

*Numbers in parentheses refer to the Selective Bibliography, pp. 249-262.

ture. And finally, recorded vocal and instrumental fugues from standard literature should also be played and discussed to show that the fugue is a living, expressive idiom, not a dry academic exercise.

Definite suggestions for planning a course in free counterpoint will be given in Appendix II, page 239, but at present it will be sufficient to suggest that such a course be concluded by the writing of a three-voice instrumental fugue on a real subject, and a four-voice vocal fugue on a tonal subject. Both fugues should contrast in mode, meter, and tempo. In the vocal fugue, write the words under each voice, in order to focus attention on the problem of words and the vocal line.

V

Finally, orchestration and arranging are important written skills, particularly on an advanced level. Work in these areas involves considerable creative ability (Chapter VII, page 117) but here the highly specialized skills required seem to justify a discussion of orchestration and arranging. As for prerequisites—the more training in fundamentals and counterpoint, the better, although surely a background does not always insure adequate preparation. Here, as always, judgments are dependent upon objectives, and it is quite possible that a student with a good harmonic training can achieve excellent practical results and develop his own musicianship in the process. Hence it is difficult to set up prerequisites in terms of courses when the objectives include musical growth as well as technical skills. However, work in these areas would certainly require a good ear, imagination, and a working knowledge of harmony, form, and if possible, counterpoint.

Orchestration is tonal painting, and while precise technical knowledge of the ranges and uses of the instruments is indispensable, such knowledge alone will not insure effective orchestration. The texts can only supply information; it is the function of the instructor to stimulate the creative imagination of his students. Development of the ear is of primary importance, not in the sense of formalized "ear training" courses, but in the practical sense of aural discrimination. This implies not only the ability to think music, but also a sense of instrumental color and its use in relation to the context.

This conception of orchestration is very different from that of the typical course offered which increases the student's knowledge of instruments and their use without giving him the skill to orchestrate effectively. Failure to achieve satisfactory goals technically and musically is due to a variety of causes, chief among which are the stress on factual knowledge regarding instruments rather than upon creative imagination, and "a theoretic" and intellectual approach, rather than a functional one, based upon the hearing, *through actual performance*, of the material scored. This hearing is greatly aided by use of a large opaque projector in which scores, either printed or in manuscript, can be seen by the entire group while being performed (see page 38).

For example, a particular problem is approached first through the mental *image* of the score, followed by a mental *hearing* of this image. The passage in question is then immediately performed by a group of players and a comparison is made between the images and the actual sound. The same process is repeated with different chord spacing or distribution, and the two versions compared and discussed by the group. By this means tonal thinking and imagination are definitely stimulated and developed. Technical facts regarding the characteristics of the instruments, transpositions, and bowings are not neglected but are introduced when needed in connection with the score at hand. This demonstration-lecture is followed by testing, analysis, and criticism of each student's score for each assignment.

This, in brief outline, is a method for the functional teaching of orchestration and arranging: the underlying philosophy implemented by practical procedures. So treated, orchestration and arranging are two of the most useful and effective means of developing musicianship through tonal painting.

VI

One question constantly arises in connection with all written work: should the piano be used while writing? The answer is both yes and no. Yes for checking and no for actual writing. The practice of composers varies on this point. Bach regarded the use of a keyboard instrument during composition as a sign of musical imbecility. In his later years Beethoven was of necessity independent of the piano, although before his deafness became total, he often improvised before composing. Mozart did not use the piano while writing, but he also liked to kindle his imagination by improvisation. On the other hand, Wagner says in one of his letters to Mathilde Wesendonck that he cannot begin Act II of *Tristan* because his piano has not arrived! This statement, however, must not be taken too literally, for he composed so rapidly that he could not have accomplished what he did had he been fingering the piano with one hand and writing with the other. But after all, it is the result, not the process, that counts. However, for the student the reverse is true. Growth comes through effort and hence the process is important for him. The student should use the piano as little as possible. Certainly simple chord progressions in four voices can be written without its aid. Students, working under pressure, often rely too much on the piano. Better do less and do it mentally. Use the piano only when necessary to check completed work.

Vocal, pianistic, contrapuntal, and orchestral writing have been discussed at some length, since they are the media for the learning of structure through writing. We now turn to the various methods of evaluation of the student's written work, which is one of the most difficult and complex problems that the instructor must face.

VII

Organized learning is dependent upon intelligent criticism: otherwise it degenerates into a mere disorganized trial-and-error sequence. This is not to deny the value of *guided* experiment, but in the teaching of specific skills the margin of experimentation is necessarily curtailed somewhat, and the learning process is probably best implemented through assigned problems whose solution needs wise evaluation.

There are a number of methods of criticism whose effectiveness is partially dependent upon the size of the class. Traditionally, the instructor "corrects" the student's work outside class and returns it with solutions and written comments. This method is efficient but not always educative. In a large class it is often unavoidable, but when used should always be supplemented by thorough individual and class discussion of the points involved. Frequently one criticism will be common to many papers, in which case it certainly should be discussed by the group. Furthermore, it is desirable that the instructor work out solutions using the student's data. When properly handled, this method of criticism, though hardly ideal, can be helpful to the group as well as to the individual student involved. In either case, the suggestions must be helpful and tactful. The two defects of this method are first, that it may become routine and mechanical, and, second, that the student may not grasp the full import of the criticism, since he was not present when it was made. Both of these objections can be partially met if the papers are adequately discussed when returned to the student in class. A helpful device to aid objectivity in grading is to have written work identified by an assigned number rather than by the student's name. This device is most practical in large classes for which the instructor has an assistant who can return individual papers to their owners without the instructor knowing their identity. In discussing the papers, the instructor refers to them by number only. This promotes objectivity both in grading and in making public criticisms.

A much better method, in a small class, is to group the students around the keyboard, play each exercise, and have immediate criticism by the group as a whole led by the instructor. This is an ideal learning situation and, when properly handled, can produce excellent results. Here again criticism must be pertinent and tactful. Usually the group is more blunt than the instructor cares to be, but fortunately group judgments are more readily accepted than individual ones.

A third method is to have students evaluate each other's work after exchanging papers. Such a procedure is possible in either a large or small class. It has decided advantages if used *occasionally*, but it is slow and cumbersome, and the papers eventually must be evaluated by the instructor. A variation of this method may be applied to problems worked in class. Certain students are assigned to solve the problems on the blackboard while other students act as critics. When the work is completed, the student-critic plays the passage on the blackboard and evaluates it. If any points are omitted, the instructor, of course, completes the criticism. This procedure could be varied by having the second student act as instructor by helping the first student solve the problem. Doubtless there are many variations of these three methods which will occur to a resourceful instructor.

A fourth method of criticism involves the use of a large size, opaque projector. [7] The student's score is placed in the projector for performance and criticism by the entire class. If the score is long, it is written on only one side of the paper, and if more than one sheet is required, two or more sheets can be joined together by means of transparent tape. This, however, would be unnecessary for the average short harmony problem. The advantages of this system are obvious. The music can be played or sung by the entire group and then evaluated immediately by both group discussion and the instructor's comments. Special effects and changes can be heard immediately, thus making clear the value of the suggestions. This method is undoubtedly the best of the four discussed. It is adaptable to any size of class and combines the advantages of the other methods. Its use should both promote discrimination and simplify the whole problem of the criticism of written work.

However, the fundamental problem of evaluation, namely, *criteria*, remains irrespective of the method used. On what basis should the material be judged? This question raises a crucial point indeed—and one which is basic to the teaching of music structure, since the

validity of the whole body of "theoretic rules" is involved. Two
sharply conflicting points of view emerge from any attempt to set
up criteria for evaluation. The first accepts textbook dicta and applies
them strictly; the second questions their validity on the ground that
composers never wrote according to "rule." In support of this second
view is cited Beethoven's impatient declaration, when parallel fifths
were pointed out in his work, that he "made the rules," in other
words, that he was a law unto himself; or Haydn's remark that the
"sole authority" of value in music is "the educated ear," and that he
has "as much right to lay down the law as anyone else." Schumann
agrees in principle when he avers that what sounds right, is right.
Statements like these support both the student and the instructor who
are often justly irked by the pedantry of textbook prohibitions.

But, upon closer examination, can these statements be taken literally at their face value? Are all composers iconoclasts who succeed
only by defying accepted practice; are they ignorant or scornful of
orthodox techniques? The answer is emphatically no. To accept such
a viewpoint uncritically and without reservation is to negate the function of education, and reduce the creative process to an afflatus independent of organized knowledge and learning. As a matter of fact,
neither viewpoint is entirely correct. Composers are human beings and
as such may be either radical or conservative, regardless of their
relative talents, although many were considered radical in their day.
Furthermore, no composer works in a vacuum: he learns the fundamentals of his craft from the past and pushes on into the future. Few
great composers were entirely self-taught: both Mozart and Mendelssohn had a thorough conventional training which apparently did not
inhibit or hamper them as creators. In the light of these facts, it is
impossible to accept the theory that organized training is detrimental
to the growth of creative ability. All that can be said is that certain
kinds of training are distasteful and possibly detrimental to certain
types of composers, irrespective of their native abilities. It is a truism
that any musical talent must be nurtured on the practice of the past.
The skeptic errs in inferring unorthodox training from revolutionary
practice.

We must conclude, therefore, that to totally ignore generally accepted "theory" is at least as questionable as to adhere to it slavishly.
Further, the "iconoclast" viewpoint is open to question on still other
grounds. Does the *practice* of great composers contradict "theoretic"
principles, and if so, to what degree? The answer is to be found in
music literature: the composer's practice often contradicts specific
"rules" but not general principles, simply because these principles are

based upon the practice of his immediate predecessors from whom he learned. His apparently radical departures from precedent are like the waves of the sea which do not affect the level of the ocean. *Principles are organized practices.* The distinction between "rules" and principles may appear somewhat tenuous, but it is real, nevertheless. The "rule" prohibits parallel fifths—the principle affirms the independence of individual voice lines.

The question naturally arises as to whether divergent practices are sufficiently consistent to be reduced to general principles. The answer is emphatically in the affirmative, provided the essential factor of *style* is considered. Actually, style is the core of the whole problem of codification and evaluation of practice. (128).

Now style is a difficult and elusive element in any of the arts. It is relatively easy to recognize, but correspondingly difficult to define or to isolate. Style is largely determined by two factors: the musical material available when the music was written, and the taste and ability of the composer. Hence it may be roughly defined as the totality of technical devices characteristic of a given period and creative artist. Sachs finds that it has oscillated between two shaping trends—the classic and static as opposed to the baroque, romantic, and dynamic, although he warns against the danger of accepting unreservedly this terminology which is capable of many meanings. (124). Yet in spite of the intangibility of style, it is the essential criterion in judging techniques, simply because its constant fluctuation alters the validity of these techniques. In other words, changes of style cause change of technique, and these variations in style constantly make obsolete or acceptable various expressive devices. An excellent example in music is the attitude toward parallel fifths, which were "in style" during the period of *organum,* subsequently lost favor, and only recently have been accepted again. Obviously they are right or wrong only in terms of style or usage. This is a further confirmation of the statement made above regarding the validity of principles deduced from practices. It is obvious that composers' practice agrees with the style of their period, since their works determine the style.

To return to the use of parallel fifths: a certain type of student or instructor will point with glee to a pair of parallel fifths discovered in Beethoven's work, and conclude that since he has found one pair, all "academic" prohibitions are removed, and that parallel fifths may be written henceforth, in the name of freedom, with complete impunity and ineptitude. Such an attitude reveals abysmal ignorance as regards both style and its relationship to technical training. Exceptions of this type can be found in the work of all composers from Bach to Brahms, but they are *stylistic impurities* because of their rarity. It is a faulty philosophy that encourages "freedom" in the learning process *before* recognized practice is understood and assimilated; that permits inexperienced students to use chords in chorale harmonization that occur only half a dozen times in the *371 Chorales* of Bach. *Exceptional use by masters does not justify continual use by students.* Such deviations from the norm should be encouraged only when the student has harmonized at least three hundred and seventy-one chorales himself! But students, alas, too often take advantage of all exceptions in their first chorale. They are "exceptional students" in the wrong sense of the term.

Granted, then, that principles are based on practices as found in literature, and that these practices vary from one period to another, what is the implication for criticism of student work? Obviously, that it must be evaluated in terms of the practices of the tradition in which it is written. Nothing is right or wrong *per se*. No passage can be right "theoretically" and wrong musically. A student writing in the 18th-century tradition is limited by the techniques of that period. Thus, in a closing cadence, the 1^6_4 chord would be used, a device that would be avoided as a cliché if written in a contemporary idiom.

Such a criterion is far removed from the practice of condemning parallel fifths because they sound badly, or of permitting them because they occur once in Bach's *371 Chorales*. Students presumably are learning the idioms of the music that they hear and perform, that is, the music of the Baroque, Romantic, and Classic periods. They are not learning the practice of the 10th or of the 20th centuries, at least not until prepared for advanced study. It is of no benefit to the student to encourage, in the name of freedom, experiments in contemporary idioms when he neither understands nor can use the language of Brahms and Wagner. This aspect of teaching will be referred to again in Chapters VII and VIII on creating and planning, but for the present it is sufficient to repeat that all written work should be evaluated in terms of its stylistic or traditional characteristics.

In closing, one other aspect of evaluation should be noted. Since all problems to be solved are drawn from literature, the instructor should play the composer's solution and compare it with those written by members of the class. These solutions should be discussed, followed by an identification of the composer's solution. Such a procedure helps the student to understand some of the reasons for the composer's choices, and should prove a stimulus to his own thinking and writing.

Obviously, care must be taken not to give the impression that the original version is the only or perhaps even the best solution. In most cases it will prove to be so—but the student must be convinced for himself of the reasons for its superiority, and certainly not be made to feel that the composer is always right and that he is always wrong. This procedure can foster interesting group discussions and should, if wisely used, develop standards of taste and judgment. It also may relieve the instructor of making value decisions arbitrarily, although sometimes they are necessary. Naturally any passage discussed, either by group or instructor, should be heard as well as seen. It is also essential that it be identified by title and composer for future reference.

VIII

This concludes our discussion of written skills—the methods of presentation and evaluation. Specific applications to various levels, from elementary to graduate school, are beyond the scope of this book. However, a few general principles may be suggested:

(1) Writing is the most exacting of the six basic skills and consequently its introduction requires thorough preparation.

(2) Writing should be introduced through a single vocal line and simple piano accompaniments.

(3) Each recitation should be based on a specific example from literature which is first performed and analyzed.

(4) Once introduced, writing should be neither stressed nor minimized in relation to other skills. In other words, writing should not progress *beyond* other skills—especially listening and playing.

(5) Writing should utilize the vocal and instrumental resources of the class and be tested in class performance of written work.

(6) Writing should become a *natural* means of expression, comparable to the writing of language. It should never be mathematical or purely intellectual.

(7) In writing, *style* is essential. To write, ignoring style, is both academic and unmusical in the literal sense.

From these general principles application regarding specific levels can readily be made, provided the basic *why* be answered before the perplexing *how*. Writing is one of the two aspects of literacy, and hence it is essential that its basic techniques be fully mastered as an important part of general musicianship. In the next chapter we shall consider the other aspect of literacy—the ability to read music and reproduce it vocally.

Chapter III

READING

Broadly defined, reading and writing are the two aspects of musical literacy. Writing has been discussed, and we shall now inquire into the purposes and methods of teaching music reading—or "sight singing" as it is usually called. Neither name for the process is entirely satisfactory, but a definition of purpose may aid in classifying it.

I

The immediate purpose of music reading or "sight singing" is dual: to learn to read music *silently* and to reproduce it *vocally*. The selection of descriptive names for these two related skills depends upon the relative emphasis given to each. Each is important, but as a means of musical growth the ability to read mentally takes precedence, and consequently the term *music reading*, with its educational implications, is probably preferable to "sight singing." The ultimate purpose, common to all skills, is of course the acquisition of musical insight.

Why is this training of the inner ear of *primary* importance? Simply because the vocal reproduction is merely the echo of the silent sound (that which is heard silently). [8] In other words, *hearing precedes singing.* Composers, singers, and string players possess a keen sense of pitch relationship derived from the inner ear, but in others it can be developed considerably. It has many uses based on its independence from physical sound. In this respect it corresponds to the silent reading of language. How many musicians can read Schumann and Shakespeare with equal facility and pleasure? Is the greater difficulty of reading music silently a valid reason for failure to do so? This ability to *think music* is essential to real musicianship—and its importance and cultivation cannot be exaggerated. It means hearing with the eye.

On the other hand, the ability to reproduce vocally what is heard mentally is also of great practical importance. Special training is often required to control the voice, not so much for tone production as for physical coordination. Frequently students protest that they can hear but cannot sing a passage. This failure is primarily due to faulty coordination rather than to a lack of vocal ability, and hence some system must be devised which translates sight into sound.

One of the basic objectives of music reading is to develop a sense of relationship between the pitches sung. Two systems do so by assigning a meaningful syllable, letter, or number to each pitch sung. A third system relies on a strong sense of tonality developed by rote without the use of individual pitch names. All systems are merely teaching devices and should be abandoned, like crutches, when the objective is achieved.

It is sometimes stated that any system that works is a good system and hence that attempts to evaluate them relatively are academic and futile. However, choice of a system is a genuine problem that cannot be evaded through ignorance or indifference. It is not sound to accept uncritically any system that promotes musical insight, however ineffectively and inefficiently. This indifference to evaluation of method seems as questionable regarding music as it would be if applied to language. Unfortunately, techniques of music reading lack the wealth of psychological confirmation that has revolutionized the teaching of language reading. Nevertheless it is both desirable and possible to draw certain general conclusions about the relative merits of these three systems.

The whole problem of music reading is exceedingly complex and includes many psychological as well as musical factors. But the present discussion is concerned only with musical evaluation, not with psychological or historical backgrounds. It is also limited to the three systems cited above and attempts no résumé of all systems extant.

The solfeggio system is the most widely used. In it the pitches are named in two ways, depending upon whether the first syllable (*do*) is stationary or movable. In the first case, the pitch C is always called *do*, irrespective of the tonality; in the second, C is given a variable syllable in relation to the prevalent tonality. The "fixed" or immovable *do* is most used in Europe, while the variable or movable *do* has been more popular in England and America.

The weight of tradition behind the use of syllables is tremendous, principally because of their long use as *vocal* tools by singing teachers who followed the Italian *bel canto* methods. As a result, syllables have acquired an almost cabalistic significance, both vocally and educationally. There is no magic in them. Objectively considered, they are only a system of artificial syllables. But for many they constitute the only true method of "sight singing." Undoubtedly, solfeggio is a successful system—but is it the best system? Recognizing its success, yet at the same time ignoring its tradition, let us attempt to weigh some of its merits and deficiencies.

Certain values are common to the use of syllables, numbers, and letters: all teach pitch relationships, focus attention on specific details of pattern, and in doing so, promote tonal and mental insights. These values are often cited as arguments for the use of syllables, but obviously they are common to the use of numbers and letters as well. This being the case, what are the unique values of the solfeggio system?

The first unique value of syllables is that they are the best vocally, although this claim is somewhat dubious. Second, that they provide for extraneous accidentals. Third, the "fixed" *do* is useful in singing atonal music for which a sense of absolute pitch is essential. Fourth, that the greatest facility is developed by their use.

Let us examine these claims. It is true that the syllables are easily sung, but not invariably so, as witness the use of *mi* for a high E, whose vocal production is very similar to and equally difficult as that of the letter E. Furthermore, it is pointed out that syllables can be altered to agree with accidentals, yet these chromatic alterations are ignored, and the letter C is sung as *do*, irrespective of whether the indicated pitch is C, C♯, or C♭. Such usage in reality negates a sense of absolute pitch, which is one of the arguments for using fixed *do*. As for the utility of the fixed *do* in singing atonal music, surely relatively few students will ever experience this need, and if they do, their facility will make any system superfluous, or they can learn the music by rote. Finally, it is claimed that syllables promote exceptional ease in reading. If so, this facility is probably largely due to long and intensive training, true of any system. The success of the fixed *do* in Europe is undoubtedly based on this factor and also on the fact that syllables are more functional there in the sense that they, not letters, form the musical alphabet, at least in France and Italy.

Undoubtedly the best use of syllables is Curwen's *tonic sol-fa* adaptation for amateurs whose primary interest is ability to read a single vocal line. This use is functional since it by-passes complicated problems of notation, but skill is emphasized to the detriment of musical comprehension. For this reason it is hardly adequate for the serious student who wishes to understand the structure of music and who, consequently, must master notation, however difficult.

If syllables are used, the best case can be made for employing the movable rather than the fixed *do*, simply because it promotes a relative sense of pitch. Since the essence of music is relationship, it is more important to know how a pitch sounds in regard to other pitches than to be able to identify a particular pitch by name. In other words, how a tone acts is more important than what it is. Actually though, pitches can be identified specifically, even when heard relatively, if the key is known.

The use of the movable *do* in the minor mode is troublesome. One of the most flagrant examples of the misuse of syllables is the practice of basing syllables on the relative rather than on the parallel relationship of the two modes. This results in calling the tonic of a minor scale *la* instead of *do*. The aural and psychological fallacies are obvious: *la* has presumably been established as an active tone, when suddenly, for no conceivable reason except similarity of signature, *not of sound*, the student is asked to hear *la* as an inactive tone—and still worse, as the key center! Such a procedure is contrary to aural perception, psychology, and common sense. The tonic of a minor scale should be called *do*, as in major, and the other syllables altered accordingly. The only possible justification is for the use of melodies in the Æolian mode, which apparently use the major and minor modes interchangeably.

Modulation also raises a problem when either syllables or numbers are used. Modulatory procedures will be discussed in connection with the use of numbers and letters (page 49). With either the minor mode, modulation, or both, the essential point is to promote a legitimate and logical sense of tonality, regardless of any particular system, and that is precisely what syllables often fail to do in these instances.

The basic objection to the solfeggio system is that it often fails to stimulate, and in many cases actually retards musical growth. [9] Many reasons can be cited in support of this statement.

Syllables are, in effect, an artificial language superimposed upon music and have absolutely no function aside from "sight singing." In this country there is little transfer to actual music, since pitches are named by letter and not by syllable. Furthermore, the syllable names connote no sequence psychologically as do the use of letters and numbers. Hence both the syllable names and their order are both entirely arbitrary and artificial. None of these objections are applicable to the number-letter system. Let us consider these points in more detail.

There is no question as to the artificiality of the syllable names. Their origin was fortuitous as regards singing and therefore they cannot be regarded as a carefully planned educational device. Dependence on syllables is a serious handicap in harmonic study, since they apply solely to a single melodic line. When once learned, the student must always translate them into letters in order to think vertically. Our whole system of pitch identification is based on letters, not syllables. The argument that they are more easily learned on the elementary level than other systems lacks any logical support, simply because the order, as well as the nomenclature, is arbitrary. The sequences *a—b—c* or 1—2—3 recall familiar successions, but *do—re—mi* connotes no imaginable order until it is so learned. Surely the establishment of a feeling for pitch relationship is sufficiently difficult without the additional handicap of new syllables in an unknown order, which must be translated into letters for instrumental or harmonic use. Viewed thus, a more inept system could scarcely be devised.

In addition, syllables are widely disliked by students. (127). This aversion is due probably both to the inherent weakness noted above and to the essentially routine manner in which syllables are often taught. However, meaningless repetition of artificial sounds cannot be blamed entirely on the instructor. It is inherent in the system. Unfavorable student reaction is a very serious criticism indeed since it strikes at the root of good motivation. This means that too much time is used in learning syllables which should be used to better advantage musically. Certainly no other system could take more time than is consumed by syllables.

To summarize: from what has been said it seems reasonable to assume that the solfeggio system fails as the best means of teaching music reading and apprehension, since it actually does nothing, with the exception of adaptability to accidentals, that cannot be accomplished by other simpler and more functional systems. Awareness of pitch relationships, structural details, and the development of musical insights—all can be achieved through the use of numbers and letters, or by a purely musical approach with little or no formalized drill. But perhaps the most conclusive reason against the use of syllables is the difficulty of interesting the student by this approach. He intuitively resents their essential unmusicality. All these reasons substantiate the statement that syllables tend to retard rather than to promote genuine musical growth.

II

After syllables, the staff letters and scale numbers are the most widely used. They correspond respectively to the fixed and movable *do*. Obviously the letter-number system has many advantages as device to teach the reading and thinking of music. First, they constitute a *known* succession of symbols. Even to children, consecutive numbers and letters represent a familiar sequence of related units. No meaningless syllables, artificially related, need be learned. Signification is already established, ready for use. Second, this familiarity with letters and numbers enables the learner to apply old concepts to new situations. Abstract relationships acquire concrete meanings. There is a definite reason why a—b is an upward or 3—2 a downward progression. The old concept helps the new. Third, the learner becomes familiar with standard music terminology. Intervals and chords are identified by using letters and numbers. Keys and scales have letter names. It is impossible to discuss music without using these terms. Fourth, letters and numbers are an excellent introduction to instrumental music. Through a knowledge of their use in vocal music the transfer to instrumental music can be readily made. They form a natural bridge between the two types. The first two reasons, which involve moving from the known to the unknown, are psychologically sound, and the third and fourth reasons—standard terminology and its use in broader study—are equally valid musically. Together they make a very strong case indeed for the use of letters and numbers.

Furthermore, these four advantages are unique to the letter-number system. It is said that syllables are more singable, but actually, letters can be sung with equal facility, and numbers present no serious vocal difficulties. If so, the only real advantage of syllables seems to be that they can be adjusted to accidentals foreign to the key. In some instances this flexibility may be of real use. It is true that accidentals cannot be sung with numbers and can be used with letters only for non-rhythmic drills, but by the time accidentals appear frequently, the need for any system as a crutch should be past.

A word should be added about the modulatory use of accidentals in both systems. Since modulation is essentially harmonic in nature, it is often difficult to determine from melody alone precisely at what point the change of tonality is made—if indeed it does change. But it is necessary to do so exactly if a true sense of tonality is to be preserved. This is one of the dangers in the use of either syllables or numbers. Too often, real modulations are disregarded by treating the accidentals as if they were chromatic pitches of the previous key instead of diatonic steps in the new key. In general, accidentals related to the cadence are modulatory while those found elsewhere are transitory. In many cass it is difficult to make a clear cut decision, but all doubtful cases should be tested harmonically. Even so, awkward transitions often result, which only confirms the statement made above that any system is only a crutch to be abandoned as soon as possible.

In consideration of all of these factors, it is dubious whether the chromatic flexibility of syllables outweighs the numerous advantages of the number-letter system. Tradition is the greatest obstacle to a just appraisal of syllables, and when it is ignored and reading is regarded as a method of developing musical thinking rather than of good singing, the weight of evidence points to the superiority of numbers and letters over the solfeggio system.

III

Many other methods have been tried, but the most promising—because of its essentially musical nature—is the so-called Rochester Plan. It recognizes the fact that while reading is not the chief purpose of the public school music program, it is one of the spokes in the wheel and as such should receive adequate consideration. Too often an excess of technical paraphernalia stands between music and the student and stifles, if not all but blocks, his musical instincts. Students struggle with syllables (a new foreign language), the learning of tonal names, and the fixing of pitch names. There is drill and repetition to make the tonal name immediately suggest the tonal pitch. Rhythm is approached arithmetically, ignoring the basic rhythmic experiences as manifested particularly in the natural and spontaneous activity of children. Harmony in part-singing is too often a linear process rather than a feeling for harmony through the ear—something quite natural to many if rightly approached. (See discussion of two- and three-part writing, page 26.)

It is an imposed technical approach from the adult viewpoint of what children should learn, rather than from the viewpoint of how children learn. Many natural aptitudes are never recognized. Children are so busy learning crutches and props about music that they seldom hear or see what music really is.

The first approach to music in the primary area is one of musical orientation—of developing a feeling for music which is basic to later skills. Through varied singing, rhythm, and creative experiences is developed a feeling for melody, form and design, key center, and basic rhythms.

Reading is delayed until the third grade. The first reading concept is the "up and down," the "high and low" of melody related to the "up and down" symbols on the page. First reading songs are built on the scale line and are strong in form and design so that musical feeling may act as a support to interval reading. Intervals become part of melodic compulsion rather than isolated tones. Intervals in scale line (line to space or space to line) are known as "steps." Numbers are used to reinforce pitch.

The key chord is taught as a unit (space—space—space—line, or line—line—line—space) and reinforced through its scale numbers. Later, intervals of a third related to tones and to the key chord are learned and are called skips of a third. All intervals are sung, written, and played on a xylophone or tone bells. In reading new material the emphasis is placed on singing the song with the words first.

The problems of rhythm are approached entirely through physical response—"Walk, run, slow." Rhythms are stepped, clapped, or executed on percussion instruments. In doing so, children are not confronted with a new problem or process, but are expressing rhythms that are innate through natural child activity. Names and arithmetical values easily attach themselves later through experience to that which is unknown.

In the singing of part-music, it is the feeling for harmony that must be strengthened through considerable experience in rote singing of part-songs rather than through immediate line reading. Harmony is a phase of musical talent not always correlated with ability to read a tonal line. Part-singing involves a certain ability to "catch on" or "make up"—that is, over and above note reading. Greater progress in actual reading of part-music is noted where there has been a rote experience—a harmonizing period with material that features the natural harmonies of thirds and sixths, and simple passing tones.

Enjoyment and satisfaction are key words in a school program. Its purpose is not the accumulation of skills and techniques for future need in adulthood. It is the daily joyous response that would build the happy acquaintance with music throughout life.

While the Rochester Plan is oriented for use in the public schools, it obviously has many implications for teaching on other levels. It deals realistically and musically with the problems of reading, and proves conclusively, by long use, that it *is* practical to teach reading without dependence upon a mechanical system. It should be noted, however, that numbers are occasionally used to clarify pitch relationships. Staff letters are also a natural outcome of this musical approach. The plan as a whole is an outstanding example of the promotion of musical insight and understanding through learning to think and to read music phrase-wise rather than note-wise. It validates the psychological fact that reading skills are best promoted by a general approach from which gradually emerge specific details. The Rochester Plan is neither random nor mechanistic. It embodies the best features of exploration with the advantages of organization. It may be likened to a free body based upon a well articulated skeleton.

In connection with teaching reading without the use of a mechanical system, the writer recalls a statement made to him by Marchant, organist of St. Paul's Cathedral in London. It was assumed that the choir boys learned to read by the traditional English *tonic sol-fa* method, but Marchant stated positively that no system was used. The boys learned simply by following the up and down movements of the notes on the staff.

One other approach to reading on the elementary level should be briefly noted—that of using simple flute-like instruments. This disposes of the problems of vocal production, especially with adolescent boys, and obviates the use of any intermediate system, since letters are taught directly. It suggests the preliminary use of toy percussive instruments in the earliest stages, which can be replaced later by instruments of more definite pitch. This instrumental approach has been successfully used in the rural schools of Delaware.

Analogous to pitch relation methods, there are a number of highly organized and somewhat artificial devices for teaching rhythm. The term itself is used somewhat loosely. Actually, time in music may be divided into two elements: *meter*, which is the regularly recurrent pulse or accent sometimes called the *Takt*, and *rhythm*, which is the breakdown of the meter into smaller units represented by individual note values. Meter is the more basic of the two. For present purposes, it is unnecessary to discuss the physical and psychological bases for our perception of the temporal element in music, but it is pertinent to distinguish clearly, for pedagogical reasons, between these two aspects of musical time. Apparently meter is more easily "felt" than rhythm probably because, since Gregorian chant, meter is fundamental. The obvious implication is that meter should be noted first—a variant of apprehending the whole before the parts. But though necessary, this is a somewhat superficial and obvious approach. Furthermore, time is so intimately related to tone that to treat them in isolation is to distort their total effect. This isolation from tone is the chief criticism of toneless rhythmic drills, or any system which stresses rhythm as separate from pitch. Hence rhythm and pitch, like eyes or legs, must function as a duality, and any attempt to teach them separately is doomed to failure.

IV

Having reviewed various systems of teaching reading, let us consider some specific classroom activities and procedures. First, as regards objectives: it is of the utmost importance that reading be approached musically and be so organized as to focus on tonal designs rather than on single pitches. In other words, reading should be phrase-wise, not note-wise: musical insight, not "sight singing," should be the goal. If so, probably the whole process would be clarified both by silent reading and by some writing. Analysis should precede singing. This suggests the complete integration of the six avenues of learning to be discussed under Planning in Chapter IX. Remember that the ultimate objective of reading is the ability *to think music* and by so doing gain insight into its structure and meaning. Vocal reproduction of the score is only a confirmation of the ability to read it, and hence is essential to insight.

In order to check on this ability to first think and then reproduce music, it is essential that all recitation be both by the individual and by the group. If group singing is used exclusively, there is no check upon individual progress. However, the balance between the two types of recitation must be carefully maintained—otherwise class time will be wasted and the weaker students will develop a feeling of inferiority. One solution is to have an individual begin the passage and the group complete it. Many other similar devices can be worked out by the experienced instructor.

There are two types of classroom activity in music reading: functional drill and the actual reading of the score. They will be considered in that order, which naturally is the order of presentation rather than of importance. Wishful thinking to the contrary, it is very difficult to dispense entirely with drill. It has been suggested that the student be assigned material to be used outside of class for study, analysis and self-evaluation. This is a constructive idea which may be applied to a limited degree. (See Chapter IX, page 196, on self-evaluation.) Its full application is hampered by the difficulty of getting student cooperation. On the whole, students simply do not study or practice music reading assignments outside of class. For some obscure reason this is peculiar to reading, possibly because of the wide-spread feeling among students that "sight singing" should be treated, according to its title, as a laboratory course. Whatever the cause, instructors will attest the fact. For this reason some drill in class is essential. What types of drill are desirable? The answer is, of course, those types that are functional. They may be introduced either at the beginning to check on basic structural knowledge, or may be used later to clarify and perfect specific points in the material being read. When possible, the latter procedure is preferable.

Scales, intervals, and chord progressions are basic structural material that may be checked by preliminary drills as follows:

1. All types of scales may be sung without rhythm, using letters with the required accidentals. This drill can be applied to major and minor scales, either by beginning each on its tonic, or by beginning all scales on the same pitch, irrespective of the tonic. This latter device develops a feeling for tonality, and should be sung using first numbers and then letters. For example, if the pitch C is chosen, it is 1 in the scale of C major or minor, 2 in the scale of Bb, 3 in the scale of Ab, and so on. Each one of these complete scales should be sung, beginning on C. In the study of chromaticism it is most important to emphasize the fact that a chromatic scale is spelled according to the prevalent tonality, thus, in major:

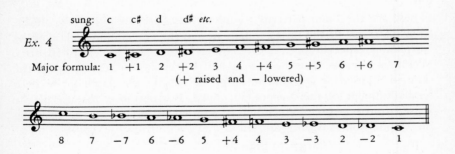

Applying this formula to the chromatic scales in the keys of B and D♭ major, we have:

Ex. 5

In minor, the alterations differ somewhat, thus:

Ex. 6

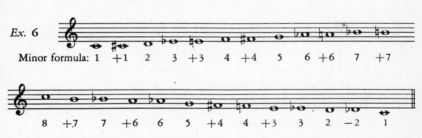

These are the basic patterns found in literature, despite many deviations. The use of the raised fourth step in the descending scale may be surprising, especially as it is often given in texts as a lowered fifth step. Yet it is obvious that the lowered fifth step is too remote from the key to be used. It is found in only one chord—the dominant seventh embellishment of the Neapolitan chord. Furthermore, the use of the raised fourth degree descending is attested by usage, as, for example, in Mendelssohn's *Spring Song*:

Allegretto grazioso

Ex. 7

The spelling of the chromatic scale raises the whole question of spelling in music, which is of vital importance in the study of chromaticism. This is not the place to discuss it fully, but suffice it to say that *music is always spelled according to its meaning in relation to context, not to its sound.* This principle is illustrated by the fact that in Beethoven's C♯ minor String Quartet, Op. 131, the leading tone of the key is, of course, spelled B♯, even for the cello, although C is the lowest string on that instrument. This embodies the whole principle and is worthy of serious consideration.

Aside from the teaching of spelling, the singing of the chromatic scale is an excellent pitch and consequently *ear* test. At the beginning it will almost invariably be sung out of tune—especially in the ascending form. But if a new scale is assigned each week—possibly the major for one term and the minor for the next—marked improvement should be noted by the end of the year.

2. Intervals may be drilled by singing them in relation to the prevailing tonality rather than to the scale of the lower tone. "Absolute" intervals are of very little practical use. On the other hand, "relative" intervals are of the utmost importance in developing a sense of tonality. In fact, the absolute quality of intervals is seldom heard against a tonal background. Thus, all thirds in the key sound alike, irrespective of their actual size, and hence should be practiced up and down the scale using numbers and letters (the latter with accidentals), thus:

Ex. 8

sung: { 1 - 3, 2 - 4, 3 - 5, *etc.*
       { c - e, d - f, e - g,

The same drill may be applied to all intervals up to and including the octave. Similar drills can be invented from material studied to promote facility.

3. The most important type of pure drill, however, is concerned
with chords. *From the beginning,* chords should be sung as arpeggios
using only letters with the necessary accidentals, thus:

Ex. 9

sung: c - e - g - c - g - e - c   g - b - d - g - d - b - g *etc.*

This type of drill is invaluable in teaching the specific spelling of
chords, which are often conceived generally in numerical terms.
Students who can sing the pitches easily on a neutral syllable often
find difficulty in doing so using letters and accidentals. This points to
a definite lack of precision in *thinking music,* which should be reme-
died. Assign chord progressions from the music being studied. This
drill is particularly effective in understanding modulation. The chord
progression to be sung should modulate, using the particular chromatic chord being studied. Thus, much of the mystery and consequent
uncertainty of modulation will be dispelled.

However, it should be emphasized in connection with all these
pure drills that their use is only justified when they contribute to
specific musical insights. *They are means, never ends.* Failure to regard
them so is fatal to functional learning. They must mean something
to the student. Hence, the suggestion that they be derived, as far as
possible, from material being studied. The instructor must constantly
answer the question *why* as well as *how* a specific point is to be taught.

Furthermore, these drills need not be isolated from the actual
reading of music. Their principles can be applied to the solution of
specific difficulties encountered in reading. For example, sequential
drills can be invented using the pattern of a difficult passage, which
will become easier when heard duplicated on different pitch levels.
Obscure harmonic progressions are frequently clarified by singing the
chords in arpeggio form: singing the chromatic scale helps to correct
intonation, and so on. Apparently such a use of drill is more functional
than when it is used alone. Yet there is a place for both uses to be
determined only by existing needs. Drills are tools and need no defense when used as such.

The second type of classroom activity is the actual reading of the
score. Needless to say, the music studied and read must be living
music, not artificial exercises, if the objective is an insight into music,
not into textbooks. This point is basic, and when accepted in practice
will revolutionize teaching procedures. Two types of material from
literature are available: either music with or without words. Let us

consider the latter type first, since it corresponds most closely to the conventional "sight singing" exercise.

It might be argued that a genuinely musical approach to reading would use only vocal literature having words, and eliminate both wordless singing and drill. However, singing without words can be justified, like drill, because it is organized experience directed toward a specific end. But there is an additional reason: it offers the possibility of contact with a much wider range of music than purely vocal works.

Obviously the widest choice is possible in selecting wordless music for reading. At present, probably folksongs are the largest source, but there is no reason why the entire range of literature should not be used. In fact, representative choice is essential if the student's background is to be broadened and enriched. The material also should include the use of the C clef, especially on the third and fourth lines of the staff. Knowledge of the alto and tenor clefs is essential in reading score—an activity of music reading on the college level. (See Chapter IV, page 93.)

In singing without words, either syllables, letters, or numbers may be used, but it is strongly recommended that a *neutral syllable*, such as *la* or *loo*, be substituted as early as possible. Singing should be preceded by a structural analysis of the melody—cadences, form, use of figures, modulations, and so on. It is often advisable for the class to read the melody silently before singing it. The accuracy of this process may be checked by asking the class to change unexpectedly from thinking to singing at any point. Naturally a fixed *tempo* must be set and maintained to insure a uniform rate of silent reading.

How is a steady *tempo* to be secured in reading? By having the student "conduct" as he sings. This physical expression of the meter helps the performer to sing more rhythmically (or "in time," as the saying goes) because he establishes and maintains the beat, and naturally it is difficult to disagree with himself. The practice also serves a secondary purpose of teaching the proper conducting motions for each meter. Students often find it difficult at first to sing and conduct simultaneously, but once mastered, the final result more than justifies the effort involved.

Turning to music with words, there is a vast quantity of material available not only in standard collections for school use but also in vocal and choral literature. This second source is naturally the more important since much music for school use is on a par musically with the textbook exercise, having been written to solve specific musical or educational problems. Only one "school series," to the writer's knowledge, is based entirely on music literature. This is curious, since those most opposed to drill *per se* will use drill material sugar-coated with words. In a reading class the rational solution would be to use material both with and without words—especially on the college level. In this case the music with words should be a well-known choral work of appropriate difficulty, e.g., Haydn's *Creation*, or works of similar caliber. Recorded works are preferable, since the class should hear a good performance of the portions studied. Out-of-class study assignments are a good preparation for class performance, but considerable time should be given to actual sight reading. Solos are useful for individual recitations, the choruses being sung by the group. Time permitting, the use of a student conductor and accompanist adds interest and value to the class performance. Study of a standard choral work also offers opportunity for comment on various aspects of structure which aid in gaining musical insight. In fact, there are so many oportunities in such a situation that the instructor must select carefully which to use or he will scatter his energies. This is in sharp contrast to "sight singing" classes devoted entirely to the mastery of solmization rather than the development of musicianship.

It is well known that Robert Shaw, the choral conductor, picks his chorus first for knowledge of "theory," then for ability to "sight read," and lastly for voice. When singers fail in the musical requirements, they learn them by systematic study. His chorus sang Bach's *Passion According to St. Matthew* from the miniature full score, which uses the C clef for the tenor, alto, and soprano parts, because he "wanted the altos to know what the oboes were playing." In other words, the relationship of each part to the whole was vitally important even to the extent of learning to read a new clef. These are practical, not academic, requirements made for the greater effectiveness of his chorus. Why cannot the music reading class be regarded essentially as a chorus whose objective is musicianship through the study and singing of choral masterpieces? Such a conception would change for the better many current classroom procecures.

To summarize: music reading may be defined as the acquisition of musical insight through the development of the ability to think music and to reproduce it vocally. Silent reading is given precedence because it is a prerequisite for vocal reproduction. For either, a sense of pitch relationship is essential. This sense can be developed in many ways: solmization, letter-numbers, the Rochester and the Delaware Plans, and many others so little used that they were not discussed. Judged on musical grounds, all had values—some more outstanding than others. But it was stressed that any formalized system, such as syllables, letters, or numbers, is only a means to an end, and that skill is the intermediate link between appreciation and insight. Although the reading of the score is of primary importance, any new experience should be prepared by analysis so that the first attempt at performance is successful. The function of drill is to clarify problems, and a number of functional drills were suggested. The experienced instructor will be able to devise many others pertinent to specific problems, situations, and levels. Preparatory drills may introduce the reading of the score—either with or without words. The value of the latter is that it simplifies vocal problems and provides oportunity for using all types of music literature. Reading with words should utilize standard recorded choral works, which offer endless possibilities for insight into structure and for musical growth. It is of great importance that the student should conduct all individual or group singing, since bodily participation clarifies rhythmic problems. Recordings are used to summarize and focus class discussions and learnings. And finally, music reading should be conceived in terms of *musicianship*, both as the means and as the objective.

Such over-all conceptions and procedures elevate "sight singing" to the status of a musical experience and activity by putting music first and adapting technique to it. The watchword is *technique for music*. Desirable outcomes are attainable in reading, as in all other avenues of learning, when music itself is the focus of study.

Chapter IV

LISTENING

I

LISTENING is undeniably the sole basis of musical experience. There is ample confirmation of Mursell's statements that "in a certain sense listening is the primary type of musical activity" and that "hearing is the very center of musicianship." Yet, this simple fact, so pregnant with implications for teaching, has been either consistently overlooked or neglected in the organized study of musical relationships. This is curious, considering the wide-spread agreement as to its validity. Educators pay it lip service in theory but disregard it in practice. Few "theory" courses are centered on listening. A thousand alibis are offered for its neglect. In fact, the traditional focus of "theory" was almost entirely on writing. As noted previously, "theoretic" study meant four-part vocal writing—a kind of mathematic puzzle totally divorced from listening. But the inescapable conclusion is that effective study of structure must be, in a very literal sense, "sound" instruction. It must be the cultivation of intelligent listening.

For present purposes it is unnecessary to examine the psychological bases for the primacy of listening or the various types of responses to it. All that is required are a few simple criteria as to its use and its relation to the educative process called "ear training," for want of a better term. Actually there are dangers in the separation of listening and "ear training," since both are concerned with the aural understanding of musical structure. As Mursell points out, listening is the general and "ear training" the specific development of intelligent hearing. What are some of the basic assumptions for educative listening?

(1) Listening, in all degrees of intensity, is a *mental activity* dependent only in a very general sense upon actual physical hearing. This is shown by the fact that animals "hear" as well as humans. In fact, it is known that certain animals hear much more acutely. But for animals musical sounds are totally without musical meanings. Only through mental activity do musical sounds become meaningful. The mind selects, organizes, and clarifies what no human ear receives. "Ear training" is mind and sense training. The ear catches aural sensations but the mind evaluates, discriminates, and identifies what was heard. *We hear with our ears, but we listen with our minds.* It is a combination of intuition and knowledge. It includes remembering what was heard in the past and anticipating that which is to follow, i.e., listening is memory plus anticipation plus critical discrimination. It is hearing the present in relation to the past and the future. *These considerations imply that listening can be improved and developed consciously.* Aside from comparatively rare physical or psychological defects, there is no such thing as "a bad ear for music"; there are only untrained minds.

(2) "Ear training" should be regarded as intensified listening for all rather than as a separate skill for the select few. Naturally the degree to which listening can be intensified will vary widely with individuals, but the basic assumption remains true. Efforts to develop organized listening often fail here, either because this fact is doubted or because its implications are not sufficiently realized or executed. It is true that some students have more difficulty than others in learning to hear consciously, but this very limitation makes more urgent the necessity for developing their powers to the utmost. The ear is truly the gateway to musical enjoyment and understanding, and should be open to all to the fullest extent of individual capacity.

With these assumptions in mind, the following criteria may set up for teaching of listening:

1. *Listening should be enjoyable.* This is a primary consideration in the choice of material. Obviously, it should be drawn from the best musical literature consistent with the student's background, interests, and maturity. This point has been previously discussed (see Chapter I, page 15), but in addition it should be noted that enjoyment is

dependent as much upon the enthusiasm, knowledge, and skill of the instructor as upon the material selected. It is a truism that enthusiasm is contagious. Fire begets fire, but unless the zeal of the instructor is enriched by true insight and the skill for imparting it, he will kindle no responsive 'flame in the student. Enjoyment is dependent also on the attitude of the student as well as that of the instructor. This involves all the psychological factors necessary for learning, such as readiness, "felt need," etc.

2. *Listening should be exploratory.* Through it students should discover wide areas of music literature previously unknown to them. Further, the discovery should be specific as well as general. Details of structure should emerge naturally from repeated hearings and be formulated into clear statements of musical practices by members of the class. The learnings should be cooperative. These outcomes are related to the selection of material discussed above. On the whole, students have the impression that "theory" is a body of artificial rules unrelated to practice—as indeed is often the case. There is no more effective means of establishing functional principles from practice than by *hearing* them in operation. Indeed, one of the objectives of true listening is to promote insight into the composer's choice and treatment of his materials.

3. *Listening should be focused.* Obviously all details of structure cannot be grasped simultaneously. In any listening, certain elements of the music are unconsciously isolated for attention. This principle must be recognized through using what is often called "directed listening." In general, listening may be directed to any of the many aspects of music, but in a listening class the attention should be focused specifically on definite elements—the harmony, melody, rhythm, form, or style. Too often a class is told simply "to listen" to a passage without being directed to listen specifically. In other words, *selective* listening is what is required for definite results.

4. *Listening should be functional.* The primary objective of ear training is to develop musical insights through increased aural sensitivity to musical relationships. It is only another approach to the training of the inner ear discussed in the preceding chapter. To function successfully this aural awareness must be applied to specific musical problems of appreciation, performance, and creation. Like all skills, it is a tool with which to fashion understandings. It is meaningless without practical application, and all efforts to develop aural awareness must be appraised in these terms.

II

Having discussed the nature of listening and suggested some criteria for its use, what specific procedures promote its growth?

Probably dictation is rightly regarded as the principal device through which aural senstivity is developed. But to justify such a statement it is necessary to define "dictation" rather precisely. By dictation is meant the ability to recognize and identify specific elements of music aurally without reference to the score. It is analysis by ear rather than by eye. As indicated above, this is primarily a mental ability and as such is open to all in varying degrees.

There are two broad types of dictation—oral and written. The first is general, the latter specific. Both may be given on various levels. Oral dictation is apt to deal with the extensive "over-all" initial impressions while written dictation concentrates on specific details. However, they overlap in certain respects. Either may be relatively general or specific. Since the usual "directed listening" of appreciation courses is a kind of oral dictation in which the verbal response is often lacking, it is the most familiar type and will be considered first.

1. *Oral dictation* may range from "directed listening" to quite specific recognitions. Even in an appreciation class some verbal response by the student is desirable. These responses may quite properly be in non-technical terms. But in a class focused on musical structures, the responses should be more technical in nature. Oral dictation has many levels progressing from the general to the specific, which may be classified thus:

(a) Identification of the form as a whole. Here the purpose is to distinguish the total pattern through focusing attention on cadences, repetitions, and similar definitive points.

(b) Differentiation between consonance and dissonance. This is of primary importance and requires considerable practice. Begin by playing a simple series of chords in which other factors help to make the distinction clear. Emphasize the contrasting concepts of rest and activity, tension, and relaxation. Use both familiar and unfamiliar music.

(c) Distinction between the major and minor quality of fundamental triads. Here again work slowly with material described above. The concept of chord "color" can be used to advantage. Often the difference between major and minor qualities can be grasped by a comparison with a familiar chord of known quality, as for example, the arpeggios at the opening of the *Star Spangled Banner* or the *Andante* of Haydn's "Surprise" Symphony, both of which are major. The minor variation of the Haydn theme may be too unfamiliar to serve, and if no other example can be found, the test may be applied negatively, that is, any sound which is *not* major must be minor.

(d) Recognition of inverted major and minor triads. This distinction seems to be particularly difficult. Frequently inversions are confused with minor, and patience and skill are needed to establish the distinction. Possibly the first step should be to use only one quality at a time—major fundamental and inverted forms followed by minor.

(e) Recognition of inverted seventh chords. Concentrate on the dominant seventh quality and deveop a feeling for inversion in general before attempting to distinguish specific inversions. Show how the bass of each inversion moves into the tonic.

(f) Combine (c) through (e) above, naming only quality or color and fundamental or inverted form of the chord. Sometime during the process the part of the chord in the melody (i.e., root, third, fifth, or seventh) should also be identified.

(g) The final step in chord recognition is to return to (c) above and attach specific number and letter names to all chords through (f).

Obviously this is quite a comprehensive procedure, moving from the general to the specific. Applied to a simple phrase, it enables the student to identify all the chord qualities orally. However, it should seldom, if ever, be used in its entirety at one time, and then only to clarify doubtful points. Its chief value is that it gives specific ways for hearing the various harmonic elements in a phrase. It is a kind of emergency kit to be used as need arises.

The melodic line may be analyzed in detail also—but only after the general design is apprehended. Melodic analysis is chiefly concerned with patterns—sequences, repetitions, chord skips, and the like. The class should in all cases sing the melody from memory before discussing details of its structure.

Oral dictation serves two purposes. It may either be used in place of written dictation or it may serve to introduce it. In actual practice it can also be used effectively during written dictation to clarify specific points or as a basis for class discussion. Students should be encouraged to verbalize their reactions and arrive at group decisions. This perhaps is the chief educational merit of oral dictation. Frequently, musical insights are reached most readily by group discussions, and the wise instructor will utilize oral dictation for this purpose.

2. *Written dictation* is the most exacting type of listening. Its function is to confirm aural impressions. It offers conclusive proof of their accuracy. In other words, writing is the strongest reinforcement

of listening. It is the direct opposite of group-discovered insights. Through it the individual alone masters simultaneously the techniques of both hearing and writing and in doing so acquires a unique understanding of musical texture and organization. The dual aspects of this skill constitute its greatest value and greatest difficulty. For these reasons, its validity as a means of musical growth has been questioned. But after all, literacy means more than the speaking and reading of a language. It includes writing it as well. Real mastery of a foreign language presupposes the ability to write it from dictation. And music is a language. Certainly professional musicians, at least, should attain written mastery of it, and even for the average student moderate skill in written dictation is desirable. The truth of the matter is that its difficulty is an argument for, rather than against, its mastery, since proficiency in it is an accurate measure of musical literacy. If it is questioned, it must be on other grounds.

Perhaps the most cogent argument against written dictation is that the time required for it exceeds its value. This is actually a variation of the "difficulty" argument, and stems from the belief that insights can be acquired without tehniques. The argument is that time spent on written dictation could be used more profitably in general, rather than in specific, learnings, and further, that the procedures and devices of written dictation tend to become stereotyped, academic, and unrealistic. Undoubtedly both of these objections have some validity, but when the unique values of written dictation are considered, its merits far outweigh its faults. Perhaps the best answer is that when effectively used as a tool it has unique values for promoting insights, but if treated as an end in itself, it can retard rather than promote musical growth.

The controlling principles of written dictation may be summarized thus:

(a) *Its growth should parallel that of other skills.*
This is in line with the general theory of integration, but it means specifically that in written dictation the same material should be presented at the same time as in the other avenues of learning. The reason is obvious—only by simultaneous timing can the full value of written dictation be realized. Beginning with rudiments, written dictation should crystallize and focus learnings. But here again the familiar "difficulty" argument appears to block progress. Written dictation, we are told, theoretically should parallel other phases—but it is more practical, in view of its difficulty, to permit it to lag behind written work. Such a compromise admits the impotence of the instructor, not of the student. If lack of background really necessitates a slower pace

in written dictation, then the *tempo* of instruction in other phases should be adjusted to meet this need. Written dictation is one of the most reliable gages of insight, and as such should be kept at the growing edge of learning.

(b) *It should be presented as a unified whole.*
Music is heard in its entirety, although composed of various elements which often receive special attention. Play the entire passage first for the general effects and record them, then concentrate upon specific elements. For example, decide upon the form, meter, and type of melodic and harmonic progressions before writing any of them; then concentrate upon the notation of the component elements. These general decisions may be reached either individually or by group discussion. But this unified approach has a further implication: namely, that *all* elements should be notated in order to clarify the initial impression. This means that a passage should not be dictated only for chords, melody, or rhythm, *but for all three in succession.* It is unrealistic, psychologically and musically, to give specialized drill in any one aspect. The only exception to this procedure is in very elementary work for children who have not as yet learned the concepts of harmony with its "bass line." But even beginners should be taught to hear and write these as components of the whole as soon as possible. From the first lesson in harmony there should be no specialized drills in chords, rhythm, or melody. Certainly high school or college classes should react to the total situation rather than to parts of it. Yet textbooks are filled wih specialized drills of various types! There is undoubtedly a very limited use for such drills as special needs arise, but they have no regular place in the *schema* of functional teaching. [10]

(c) *It should be based on musical literature.*
This proposition should be self-evident, since music, not "theory," is being studied. As in other areas, the use of literature is essential because it presents real, not artificial, problems for solution. The problems in literature differ both in type and frequency from those of textbook exercises. For example, a well-known theme seldom contains all the uses of the $\frac{6}{4}$ chord as in textbook exercises. The result is that exercises simply do not prepare the student to cope with musical problems. Not only is the transfer from text to music negligible in quantity, but it is of the wrong quality. This may be the origin of the idea that composers constantly "broke rules." If they broke rules, they established practices. For these reasons, students trained to hear textbook dictation exercises have trouble transcribing real music of much less actual difficulty, since they miss the academic clichés and familiar

patterns. Now real music has style but, if it is great, no clichés. It follows its own inner and unique law of sequences, and it is precisely this characteristic of real music that makes its use for dictation difficult yet imperative. Here is the core of the educative process: to gain insight into musical structure through its reproduction. This is not a mechanical process but an act of re-creation, and music literature is the food upon which it is nourished.

(d) *It should develop musical memory.*
One of the values of written dictation is the cultivation of memory as a means by which musical designs are apprehended. Memory is essential to the understanding of music since it is a temporal act. The development of memory is one of the major objectives of written dictation, yet it is at the same time one of the most difficult to achieve. To do so, it is essential *that all dictated material be memorized and written phrase-wise.* (For details of procedure, see page 70.) However, since writing itself is also difficult, it is desirable to separate the two skills by dictating familiar music, thus eliminating temporarily the problem of memorization. Students respond favorably to familiar music. It acts as an anchor in the sea of sound. It is a useful device for beginning a recitation, since it promotes confidence. Once the known passage is recorded successfully, the following unknown passage loses some of its mystery. The transition to completely new material can, of course, be made through a partially known passage. As his memory strengthens, the student should be able to recall, both orally and by writing, more structural details. In other words, memorization brings into increasingly sharp focus outlines of musical patterns and in doing so enables the student eventually to grasp the total design.

III

The general principles of written dictation are relatively few and readily stated, but the specific procedures are more difficult to classify, due to their variety and complexity. A few, however, can be indicated. For convenience only, they will be divided into those on the elementary, intermediate, and advanced levels. Discussion of melodic and harmonic dictation separately will in no sense negate the statement made above regarding the essential unity of written dictation.

1. Let us first consider, then, melodic dictation on the elementary level. Here it is desirable to break down written dictation into its component parts. Probably rhythm, as the most basic, should be notated first. Announce the key and play the melody with an accompaniment

to establish the meter. Children can usually determine meter in terms of walking (duple) or dancing (triple). The instructor then gives the unit of rhythm. Next, prepare the staff by ruling off four measures with the pulses indicated by dashes, thus:

Ex. 10

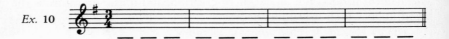

The rhythm is then sketched by placing a dot for each beat under the proper dash. For *Ach du lieber Augustin* the pattern would be written, using a slur or long dash for the held pitch, thus:

Ex. 11

or:

This rhythmic sketch can either be made while the tune is being played or from memory. The melody should then be memorized and checked by singing before the scale numbers are added below the rhythmic sketch, thus:

Ex. 12

The melody should be sung, using these numbers, and repeated immediately with letters. The instructor then announces that the melody will be written in a quarter-note rhythm, i.e., in $\frac{3}{4}$, and the student does so.

When the melody is written in $\frac{3}{4}$ it should immediately be copied in other triple meters, such as $\frac{3}{2}$ and $\frac{3}{8}$. This is necessary to establish the fact that notes are *relative*, not absolute, in value. Too often children are taught that "the quarter-note gets one beat," to the detriment of accurate rhythmic conceptions. *It is impossible to determine aurally the unit of note value*: all triple meters sound precisely alike. It is curious how persistent is the myth that different note values have different connotations! Choice of note values is purely arbitrary according to musical practice. One only has to listen to a concert to recognize this fact. Beginners should immediately become aware of the aural identity of time signatures belonging to the same meter. Note values differ visually but not aurally. *Tempo*, not value, is the determinant factor.

The next higher level to the procedure outlined above is to dispense with the rhythmic sketch and begin by memorizing the melody which is tested by singing. The pitches are then written directly on the staff with *slanted strokes* written in the rhythm of the melody, thus:

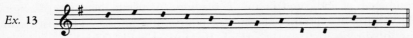

Ex. 13

Next, a stem is added for each beat, again written in the melodic rhythm, thus:

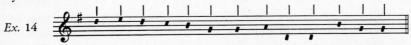

Ex. 14

Finally, since the meter and unit of rhythm are known, bar lines are inserted before each strong accent and the note values are completed.

The value of this procedure is that it utilizes the rhythm to aid in placing the pitches on the staff. Frequently, students pause to round and perfect each note-head, and in doing so forget the melody. This procedure insures getting the note-heads on the staff before the melody is forgotten. This device can be used advantageously on any level.

Careful analysis of structure (use of figure, sequence, repetition, and type of melodic progressions) aids greatly in both memorizing and writing. For example, this simple folksong may be analyzed thus:

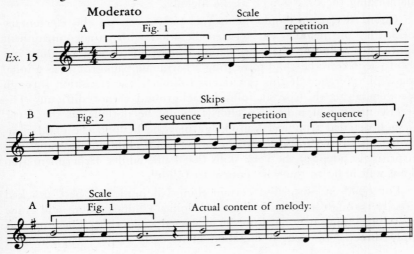

This is a miniature three-part design (A—B—A): a symphonic micro-cosm! Show how the melody grows from two small figures. Such analysis can profitably be applied to all levels.

As memory is essential to written dictation, it is appropriate to consider other devices for its cultivation. For example, after a phrase is played, have the class sing the melody silently, *conducting as they do so*, before singing it audibly. This ability to *think* music is invalua-able and has been discussed previously. Thinking and singing may be combined, as indicated in music reading, by using them interchange-ably (without warning) during the course of a phrase. The instructor simply directs the class to think or sing at will. Thinking may be made more concrete by *visualizing* precisely how the melody would look if written on the staff. In doing so, all details of staff and notes should be clear to the mind's eye. Children often prefer to close their eyes to aid mental sight. Visualization is an excellent device, but it is not an easy one and requires considerable concentration. The ear must learn to see as well as to hear.

Memory may also be developed by writing short one- or two-measure figures *after only one hearing*. Begin with short, simple patterns which gradually increase in length and complexity. Many more devices can be developed by the resourceful instructor, such as singing only the pitches on the accented beats, singing only the essential figure whenever it occurs in repetition or sequence, and other means of emphasizing essential structure characteristics of the melody. Nat-urally all thinking and singing should be done *in tempo* as the students conduct. All these devices can obviously be applied to memorizing the bass as well as the melody.

Chord dictation should be begun early even on the elementary level. Play all melodies for written dictation with an accompaniment figure, not only for the clarification of the meter and rhythm, but also to accustom the child to hearing a harmonic background as a tonal frame of reference. If this practice is followed, the transition through the general to the specific chord background is not difficult. The precise naming of individual chords should be optional at this level, as such detailed technical knowledge may be beyond the child's im-mediate need or capacity. On the other hand, children are sometimes surprisingly adept at the very skills that baffle adults. Experimentation alone will indicate the wise course to follow.

For children especially, certain things in music are best attacked directly through hearing, feeling, and doing. Understanding will come later. Everything new need not be explained at the time. These notions apply directly to written dictation in its early stages. Apprehension often dawns gradually, like the day, and the wise instructor will confidently await this increasing light.

2. The above procedures carry over to the intermediate level of written dictation in modified forms. Isolation of special rhythmic and pitch problems should drop out as facility increases, the general practice being to note the melody in its entirety after memorization. *The basic learning sequence is to listen, discuss, write, and check.* The precise order in which the melody, bass, and name of chords are written is immaterial, although this particular order seems logical. The bass should be written phrase-wise like the melody. Often it is helpful to sketch in the cadence and other essential points first. In naming chords, identify the quality first, using plus (+) for major, minus (−) for minor and a check (√) for dissonance. Both the chord number and letter names should then be added. Capital letters may be used for major chords, and small letters for minor. It is important that chords be identified by both number and letter, as numbers primarily indicate external relations, and letters the internal construction of the chord. In choral dictation, the writing of all four voices is much too difficult to be done on intermediate levels.

Meters, like note values discussed above, are relative in the sense that the time signature does not always designate the true meter. The Beethoven *scherzi* are outstanding examples of meters whose sound differs from their appearance. Although written in $\frac{3}{4}$, they sound in $\frac{6}{8}$, $\frac{9}{8}$, or even $\frac{12}{8}$. In other words, each visual measure is only a beat in a large aural measure. This fact has an important bearing on both dictation and analysis. In both, of course, it is essential to distinguish the real meter *by ear*, and the student should be made aware of any metric discrepancies. In this connection it is desirable to dictate melodies, using the less familiar time signatures—$\frac{6}{4}$ for $\frac{6}{8}$, $\frac{4}{2}$ for $\frac{4}{4}$, and so on.

A word is required regarding the media of dictation. The piano is almost invariably used, but through recordings other media should certainly be employed if the aural experience in the classroom is to prepare the student for listening in the concert hall and school auditorium. A chord sounds entirely different when produced by a piano, orchestra, or chorus. A melody followed with ease when sung may be quite difficult when played on a violin or oboe. Furthermore, use of recordings makes available a wide range of music literature in its original form. Surely this fact alone would suggest the use of other media in addition to the piano. Many excellent examples come to mind: the bass "motto" at the beginning of Schubert's "Unfinished" Symphony, the clarinet theme in Weber's *Der Freischütz* Overture, Brahms' song, *The Smith*, and dozens of other examples. The Bach chorales are available, to mention only one example of choral literature. There is a wealth of material which is easily found and readily available. Here is an excellent opportunity for a direct "tie-up" between "theory" and music. In selecting recorded music for written dictation, however, it is essential that the passages chosen are short, simple, and significant. Songs should be used in their entirety whenever possible. The careful study and writing of complete songs can be a rich musical experience. Probably time will permit only the writing of the melody while the bass and harmony will be sketched. It is highly desirable also that dictated material be utilized in other ways: for example, transposed in keyboard harmony, arranged for mixed voices, or analyzed in detail. Further, the addition of the inner voices of dictated choral material can be given as a written assignment. There are many possibilities for such integrations.

The manner of playing the piano for dictation is important. The tone should be clear and distinct, never hard or forced, and of *mezzo forte* intensity. Use very little pedal. Play in a moderate, even tempo: slow enough to make details clear but too rapidly to permit writing during performance. Play musically with no distortion or exaggeration of accent. The passage to be memorized should first be heard in full for recognition of meter, cadences, and form. Repeat in phrase units for the memorization and writing of the melody, bass, and chord qualities and names. Complete one of these elements for the entire passage before concentrating upon another. The melody should always be heard *with its accompaniment* or chordal background, never alone. Test memorization by singing before writing. It will be necesssary to repeat each phrase for clarification of details. When doing so, the student listens, analyzes, and memorizes, *but does not write*. Only during the notation of chord qualities and names should writing and playing be simultaneous. For repetitions, play the entire phrase, not a particular chord, measure, or melodic figure. Probably the greatest student difficulty in taking written dictation is memorization, and failure to do so adequately results in furtively writing each note as it is played, and in requests for repetitions of isolated fragments rather than of the complete phrase. This difficulty can be lessened by careful, clean, musical playing. Obviously, the manner of performance is one of the crucial points in written dictation, and as such should receive careful consideration by the instructor.

3. Written dictation seldom goes beyond these intermediate levels because of the limitations of time and background. However, in music

schools on the graduate or postgraduate levels there is a legitimate place for advanced written dictation. Such dictation would include more difficult material including possibly the introduction of some contemporary music. It is a curious fact that "theory" courses seldom explain music written later than the mid-19th century. Even the attainment of this point is rare, as shown by the fact that the majority of students can neither hear, write, nor understand the twelve-tone tonal chromaticism of Chopin! The reason for this lag is, of course, the fact that the understanding and application of musical organization is delayed too long: that students are well advanced in the performance of music before considering its structure. This point has been previously noted. How often students attempt to write in contemporary idioms when they are unable to grasp the harmonic idiom of *Parsifal*! This gap between the past and present may be partially bridged by advanced written dictation. Such a course may well be set up in such a way as to provide a summary of style and harmonic vocabulary, beginning with modal influences and ending with Debussy, Strauss, or Sibelius. It should include dictation of the Bach chorales, writing all four voices—the upper three in the C clef. Naturally more difficult recorded music will be used. The emphasis will be on general questions of style, texture, and form. Scores should be consulted for the study of orchestral works, and the whole course oriented toward *general musicianship*. The extent of such a course will depend on the musical maturity of the student, the ingenuity of the instructor, and the time available. When properly organized, it should be the consummation of all previous aural experiences, and serve to round out, summarize, and integrate many phases of previous study.

IV

Three new types of dictation require special comment: contrapuntal, "corrective," and analytic dictation. All three have distinctive values and techniques which promote the musical growth of the student, and for this reason merit careful consideration.

1. When sounds have been heard simultaneously, the traditional emphasis of written dictation has been primarily harmonic, but such an emphasis ignores a large quantity of music of contrapuntal texture well within the range of the student's aural experience, at least on the college level. Consequently it seems reasonable to meet this need by organized linear listening. The approach must differ from that for

vertical listening, since the element of chord quality or "color" is entirely lacking. It is, in fact, an extension of melodic dictation and should be treated as such.

The material used can be drawn from Carroll's *First Lessons in Bach*, Books I and II, the Bach *Two-Part Inventions*, and, on the advanced level, Bartók's *Mikrokosmos*. Rounds and canons are also useful.

The manner of dictating contrapuntal material differs radically from that used for chords. First, the entire passage should be played, and second, it should be subdivided into short one- or two-measure fragments which are played *only once* to insure linear rather than vertical listening. This point is important, since repetitions would permit the writing of the two lines separately, thus defeating the purpose of hearing both lines simultaneously. Should the task prove too difficult, the interval relationship of the two voices at the beginning of each measure or other accents may be pointed out. In fact, it is desirable to have the initial interval identified before playing the fragment.

Contrapuntal dictation is suitable for all levels and should be introduced as early as possible. It introduces the student to a new concept of tonal relationships, full of unique and challenging problems, but the reward in terms of understanding is well worth the effort involved.

2. Another new type of written dictation, which, for want of a better term, might be called "corrective listening," has been recently developed. (195). It is organized on the principle that one of the most practical uses of aural sensitivity is the detection of errors in music heard. This is a perfectly reasonable assumption which has many implications for teaching. Obviously conductors constantly are required to do this very thing in rehearsals, but it also applies with equal validity to any musician who is called upon to make decisions involving the eye versus the ear, as for example, the teacher of applied music or music education.

This discrimination is developed through a comparison of the printed score with what is heard. The first approach is through intervals. Ten harmonic intervals are written on the blackboard, and the class is told that the lower notes would be played as written, but that some of the upper notes might be changed. The students are confronted with an entirely new problem, that of deciding if what they hear is what they see. When such an experiment was tried, it was found that the class as a whole scored lower on the recognition of these ten intervals, which were both seen and heard, than they did on the writing of ten similar intervals dictated in the traditional manner.

The results of this trial were so suggestive that a series of mimeographed sheets of music were prepared involving melodies, chord progressions, rhythmic patterns, and harmonizations of simple melodies for piano. These sheets were studied silently by the class in order that the students might first hear mentally the sound expected. The students then made corrections or changes on the sheets as the music was played, both as printed and with slight variations. The students agreed that this new approach was more difficult than the traditional one. If any difficulty was experienced with the association of sound and symbol, the sight of a possible notation added to the confusion. However, the students agreed that the problem was practical and more closely allied to the work that they expected to do in music.

As the work was continued, together with the traditional approach, improvement was noted in both the old and new way. Later a second-grade piano book was used to check the music as played. Some students became very adept in hearing changes, not only of the melody but also in the spacing of the chord-tones, as well as in the phrasing and the inner voice patterns. These results seemed to justify continued training in musicianship by practice in hearing more music from notation.

This "corrective" type of written dictation has much to recommend it when used in conjunction with the traditional method. It is, in reality, the reverse of that method, since it proceeds from the sight to the sound rather than from listening to writing. It can readily be applied to music literature as indicated above. The interval approach is perhaps questionable (see page 23), though it does have the merit of simplicity. Broadly considered, it is an interesting and functional approach which has many possibilities for increasing the acuity of listening.

3. Finally, analytic dictation is the broadest and most general approach to the problem of listening. Its objective is a grasp of formal structure through "directed" listening to recorded music. While in some respects similar to the typical "appreciation" class, it differs from it in two important respects. First, it is primarily concerned with *form* or design in music, and second, it involves the notation of these designs by a set of artificial symbols. [11] Thus, though it is concerned with aspects other than form, attention is focused on the various recognized designs from the simplest to the most complex. Notation is confined to the recording of these designs which may be indicated in detail or quite generally, depending upon circumstances. The simpler part-forms should be outlined specifically in terms of cadences and relative

lengths of parts. On the other hand, the larger forms need only to be sketched unless precise analysis of certain portions is desired.

All dictation is done by the use of recorded music—a means of increasing the student's familiarity with literature, as noted previously. However, if the group was sufficiently large and diversified, some of the material could be presented by members of the group. But it is always questionable whether the diversion of interest from the music to the performer compensates for the increased interest in a "live" performance.

There are a variety of reports that could be assigned for study and self-help outside of class. These might consist of an analysis of music heard in concert or by radio, of music in the student's repertoire, or of assigned recorded music. The first two would be individual projects and the last a group activity. The reports should be written in case evaluation is desired. However desirable for the student, individual projects in this type of class are problems for the instructor. In order to criticize each report even superficially, he must have either great patience and ample time, an encyclopedic memory, a vast library, or preferably a combination of all three! Otherwise, how is he to cope with the variety of forms submitted? But there are very real values in individual projects of this type if the instructor is sufficiently rash or courageous! The third method offers a reasonable compromise, since the recorded music will be chosen by the instructor for the group. It has the additional advantage of supplying a practical basis for group discussion. As an over-all term project the student might find a new example of all the forms discussed and submit a written analysis of each.

Analytic dictation, or aural analysis as it might be called, has many obvious values. Its approach is musical and less technical than that of written dictation. Furthermore, it eliminates entirely the problem of notation and hence is less exacting. On the other hand, it does develop the musical memory, since aural apprehension of design is dependent on this faculty. Like "corrective" listening, though, its value is supplementary. To use it as a substitute for the usual type of written dictation described above would be very questionable indeed. But it might well perform the same function on the college level that was suggested for the advanced written dictation class in a professional school: namely, to summarize and integrate past learnings. It can be a very fruitful exploration of musical literature and, if properly presented, should result in broadened and enriched musical insights.

V

Several salient conclusions may be drawn from our survey of the functions, types, and procedures of organized listening. The objective of listening is to develop aural awareness of musical structures for practical purposes. The means by which this objective is realized is the trained ear. This training involves discrimination in hearing, association of the sound and symbol, and the analysis of what is heard. The important point is to *apprehend the music* rather than to put it on paper. This must be constantly stressed, since students are apt to confuse the end with the means in written dictation.

Basic assumptions of educative listening included its mental basis, and hence its practicality for the many rather than the few. It was suggested that listening should be an enjoyable, exploratory experience focused on certain aspects of music and capable of being applied directly to specific musical problems and situations. The two general types of listening, oral and written dictation, were then considered with their specialized techniques on the elementary, intermediate, and advanced levels. And finally, three new approaches to listening (contrapuntal, "corrective," and analytic dictation) were discussed and their place in the curriculum indicated.

In conclusion, it should be pointed out that there is no music without sound and there is no sound without the ear. But the ear alone is not sufficient—it must be the *listening ear*, or as Haydn truly said, "the only arbiter of music is the trained ear." Perhaps the most surprising fact about many musicians, professionals and students alike, is that although they hear music, they simply do not *listen* to it. This is the purpose of "ear training"—to transform hearing into listening. It is hearing plus recognition. Ear sensation is paramount in any musical situation, and hence music must be approached through the *ear*, not through the eye.

to transpose accompaniments, to improvise for group activities, and to read vocal or instrumental scores. This is an impressive list of music needs that are met by keyboard study. On the other hand, the need for figured bass reading is questionable, and hence it should be included only on an advanced level if utility is one of the accepted criteria.

Obviously other criteria could be applied, but those cited are a sufficient basis for a discussion of the various skills involved and their application on three levels of achievement. Let us first consider keyboard study for the pianist in these terms.

III

1. On the elementary level all musical learnings should be transferred to the keyboard *beginning with rudiments*. Everything written should also be played. The location of the various octaves on the staff should be transferred to the piano, as well as reading in the alto clef, depending upon the maturity of the student. Later, scales and basic chord types can be added. Keyboard and written skills should be acquired simultaneously: do not allow the keyboard application to "lag."

Before specific drills are discussed, two important points should be considered: requirements of student performance and role of drill in keyboard study. As regards performance, two requirements are basic: first, the maintenance of an even, steady *tempo*; and second, the independence of the eye from the keyboard. The first is necessary to overcome the natural tendency to stop or hesitate when in doubt, but the *tempo* should be maintained irrespective of errors. Finish the progression, however imperfectly, then repeat for correction. The second concerns the practice of looking at the keys while playing. This too is a natural tendency, but it must be overcome. Facility will never result from keeping the eyes glued on the keyboard. The analogy with typewriting is obvious: students learn on a "blind" machine so that the relative position of the keys will be memorized. The same principle applies to the piano, as all teachers will testify. In other words, keyboard harmony is essentially a *mental*, not a physical activity, and as such should be done without visual reference to the keyboard. Cases have actually been known in which a student's keyboard facility *improved* by practice away from the keyboard! Virtuosi learn music thus while traveling.

This mental aspect of performance also gives an important clue for the correction of errors—particularly in playing chords. If the student has difficulty, have him name the chord by letter and quality (G major) *before playing it and without looking at the keyboard*. In other words, the abstract mental concept of the chord should be absolutely clear before it is made concrete on the keyboard. Above all, the student should never "hunt" for the right notes by ear and sight. Such a procedure is both fatal and futile because it blocks basic mental concepts.

Before consideration of specific skills, the place of drill in general should be mentioned. Functional drill is used, as in other areas, to clarify specific problems. Limited chord drills for the group and individual aid in learning harmonic vocabulary or modulatory devices. These chord patterns, in phrase form, can be embellished with non-harmonic tones or broken up into pianistic figurations, and then repeated in the opposite mode if feasible harmonically. They can serve also as a basis for improvisation, the student reproducing them in various styles of composition: the march, the waltz, the barcarolle, etc. Sequential chord patterns likewise develop a sense of harmonic relationships. Limited use of both these types of drill is desirable on all levels.

Naturally the functional skills at the beginning are fewer and their application more simple than on the higher levels. They include:

(a) *Harmonization*, which probably should be restricted to the harmonic background whose chords are "blocked out" by the left hand, that is, played in "close position." Simple piano accompaniments such as the following can be employed:

Ex. 16

(b) *Transposition* should include: (1) playing familiar melodies by ear, either with or without an accompaniment, and (2) shifting to a key of the same letter *but different key signature*. Music within the reading range of the student, e.g. Schumann's *Happy Farmer* in F♯ major, instead of F major, and music from the student's repertoire can well be used for this purpose, but there should also be opportunity given for transposing new music in this manner.

(c) *Improvisation* offers an opportunity for self-expression, which is desirable on any level. Begin with unaccompanied melodies in both strict and free form. The addition of the harmonic background or accompaniment figure in the left hand will depend on circumstances.

(d) *Reduction* of piano compositions to their essential harmonic progressions is an excellent device for showing how the music is organized. It should be applied to both familiar and unfamiliar material. Either the melody may be played by the right hand and the chord reduction by the left hand, or as understanding grows, the melody also may be reduced to essential progressions. Here again the precise application of this device is determined by the teaching situation.

In general these four skills, together with the keyboard application of rudiments, constitute the practical extent of keyboard on the elementary level. Experimentation will widen or narrow its application, *but the essential point is that it be applied.*

A word should be added in regard to playing by ear mentioned in (b) above. The value of this type of "ear training" has been recognized only recently. Melodies alone can be played entirely by ear, but when chords are added, the harmonization should be checked with the music, memorized, and then transposed by ear to various keys.

2. The intermediate level offers a wider opportunity for keyboard learnings because of the increased background, maturity, and interests of the student. A summary of the skills on this level would include:

(a) *Harmonization* now can be definitely divided into (1) chord style and (2) piano style. In the former, the chords are played by the right hand and the bass by the left hand. This style is used to harmonize choral material. Piano style reverses the procedure, since the chords are played in figurated form by the left hand while the melody is played by the right hand. As in written work, it is well to precede harmonization by an analysis of the salient features of the melody including the cadences, consequent form, and harmonic background. Remember the learning sequence previously cited: listen—think—act—check, which simply means that any act should be preceded by an analysis of the situation and followed by an evaulation of results.

(b) *Transposition* of the accompaniments of standard songs is the most practical material on this level. Have the melody sung or played during the transposition to approximate a "real life" situation. However, orchestral scores could also be used by having the parts written for transposing instruments played in concert pitch. (See Chapter V, page 86.) The choice of material naturally depends upon the class. *Major and minor seconds and thirds are the most practical intervals to assign for transposition.* The best method of transposition is by the use of clefs (see page 91), but its complete application requires special training. It can be applied partially, however, through an exchange of either the treble or bass clef, thus:

Ex. 17

Hence the use of the bass for the treble clef automatically transposes the right hand up a third (from C to E), leaving only the bass note to be consciously transposed. The reverse is true when the treble clef is substituted in the left hand for the treble clef: a downward shift of a third (C—A) results. Of course the utility of this device is limited to these particular intervals, but it illustrates the principle of transposition by clef. The best alternative is to rely on the linear motion of the outside voices, the new key signature and the general harmonic background. *Think the specific interval of transposition only for accidentals contrary to the key signature.* For example, in transposing a passage in C major, containing an F♯, up a major second to D, all pitches would be read one letter higher, relying on the new key signature of two sharps for necessary accidentals except in the case of the foreign F♯, which would be read as a *major second higher,* i.e., as G♯. But this is the only interval that would be read so specifically: all others would simply be read a second higher.

The utility of transposition has sometimes been questioned—especially for the music educator. Yet one of the most successful junior high school teachers known to the author uses it daily to adjust the *tessitura* of the printed song to the vocal range of her classes. She is not only an excellent musician but she is able to use her techniques functionally. *One uses what one has*—but, on the other hand, personal deficiency in a skill often leads to disparagement of it. This may be one of the causes for the wide-spread criticism of "theoretic" instruction.

Continued "transposition" by reversal of key signature only is recommended. Have the student play a composition from his repertoire in this manner. The result will show clearly his grasp of tonal relationships. This device is related to the once-despised practice of playing "by ear," which has recently returned to favor. Both are a very practical kind of keyboard "ear training." (See below, page 90.)

(c) *Improvisation* is one of the most fascinating yet difficult aspects of keyboard work. It offers the best opportunity for controlled creative expression. Imagination, technical equipment, and memory are its essential requirements. During performance an even, regular *tempo* must be maintained, as in all phases of keyboard work. All improvisations should conform to a recognizable formal design, and in the beginning be based on a predetermined harmonic sequence. The initial steps may be outlined thus:

(1) Play chord phrase in "block" form—the chords played by the right hand.

(2) Break it up into various rhythmic patterns.

(3) Add melody based on original or suggested motive with accompaniment played by the left hand.

In planning the harmonic background, *aim for the cadence*. Its plan may be sketched using only one chord to each beat, either placed before the student or memorized, thus:

Ex. 18

This chord plan may be original or taken from textbook exercises which give only the soprano and bass. This somewhat formalized approach is desirable only as a means of making improvisation concrete and definite. As skill increases, it should be gradually abandoned.

A motive may be assigned to give material for practice outside of class, but in class the motive should be varied in order to prevent the student from simply memorizing his "improvisation." For example, an assigned motive could be varied thus:

Ex. 19

Obviously this alteration of the given motive requires considerable ingenuity on the part of the instructor, but it is necessary in order to preserve the spontaneity essential in true improvisation. The typical pattern of the motival development of a phrase is as follows:

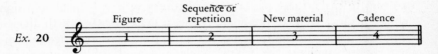

Ex. 20

Naturally this pattern can be infinitely varied, but its basic outline conforms to musical usage. It is of great value in aiding the student *to think concretely.* Aimless wandering is the bane of improvisation, and any device which helps to overcome this tendency is of value.

The first form used is naturally the repeated phrase, followed by the parallel, then the contrasting period. Using phrases or periods as units, the song forms are easily improvised next, the simplest being the incipient three-part form consisting of a period, and two phrases for each part respectively. Note that in such simple three-part forms it is essential to end part II on some form of the dominant chord. The motive of part II is usually the same as that used for part I. The two-part form should be employed next. In it both parts end with a perfect authentic cadence. The motive of part II is usually new, although related in style to that of part I. Both parts may have a similar ending. (See Schumann, *Album for the Young,* Op. 65, No. 4. This composition in A—B form also admirably illustrates the difference between a repeated and a double period.) The various extensions of form may be added gradually.

In improvisation, care must be taken to keep the expression as free as is consistent with the use of a given motive and predetermined harmonic scheme. Many devices are useful for preserving spontaneity. Perhaps the simplest is to continue the improvisation of unaccompanied melodies entirely free of restrictions of any kind. The breaking-up of a series of chords in arpeggio form, four or five octaves, is also helpful. In doing so, the two hands are used alternately, thus:

Ex. 21

A third device is to improvise freely on a given rhythmic pattern, as is usually done in teaching improvisation for the dance, or for the various physical responses to rhythm used on the elementary level. In order to make these patterns more concrete, it is helpful to assign definite styles, such as the march, the waltz, etc. A fourth device consists of one student playing a simple predetermined accompaniment figure, such as the waltz, while a second student improvises melodies over it. If there is an instrument available for each student, this is an excellent preliminary device for the entire class. Half the class plays the chord background while the other half improvises individually different melodies. Of course this is only possible when the melodies are limited to chord tones. Begin with very simple melodies—first one note to each measure, then two, and finally three. The subdivided beat may then be introduced on each beat until all three beats consist of two notes. Eventually complete freedom may be given provided the melody consists only of chord tones in quarter- and eighth-note values. This is the limit of group performance. If the procedure is continued further, the melody with non-harmonic tones must be improvised by only one student accompanied by the remainder of the class.

Three general points regarding all improvisation must be constantly kept in mind: (1) that the student play in a regular tempo; (2) that he repeat immediately and precisely the improvisation played in order to emphasize that memory is essential, and (3) that he be given increasing freedom as skill develops. The stress placed on improvisation will vary with conditions, but some work should be done in it since it performs the functions of creative expression, functional use of material, and the training of memory.

(d) *Score reading* has obvious practical values and may well be included as part of keyboard work, especially as it is easily integrated with other phases of structural study. The reading of vocal scores probably comes first, as it is easier than orchestral reading and more widely needed. It can be linked to music reading through the use of the same material. It should include the reading of both assigned and new material in a moderate, even tempo. Orchestral reading can be linked with listening through using whatever symphonic score has been chosen for aural and visual analysis. Begin with relatively simple material, such as Mozart's *Eine kleine Nachtmusik*, and his G minor Symphony, K. 550. Schubert's C major Symphony (No. 7) is an excellent introduction to the full score, since all the instruments are written in C, thus eliminating the necessity for transposition. For skill in reading the transposing instruments, first assign groups of them alone, for example, the brass or woodwind. If the classroom is equipped with multiple pianos, divide the class into string, woodwind, and brass groups for the performance of the complete score. Ability to read the complete score is thus developed gradually. Study of the score may also be integrated with transposition. Assign only short passages of eight measures or so for study outside of class, but do some sight reading in class. Ability to play both vocal and orchestral scores has many practical and musical values, and some experience in it should definitely be a part of keyboard study.

(e) *Modulation* is for many a *terra incognita*, glimpsed but never explored. Probably no phase of harmonic study is more important or less mastered. Yet its principles are simple and their application relatively easy. There are two reasons for its present unsatisfactory status: its introduction is delayed too long, and its principles are not clearly stated or understood. As regards the first reason, modulation is an essential and ubiquitous element of harmony, and as such should be introduced as soon as the student's harmonic vocabulary is adequate. Secondly, its basic principles must be simplified and clarified.

Fundamentally, modulation may be approached either through the common-chord principle or through emphasis on the first chord of the new key. The first stresses the chord of departure, the second, the chord of arrival. Both have unique value, but the second seems preferable in many respects for practical purposes, and so will be considered here first. The validity of modulation, as contrasted with chromaticism, is largely dependent upon cadential confirmation of the former. That is, a new tonality is best established by a strong cadence in it, usually the perfect authentic cadence. Consequently the essential point is not so much the *departure* from the old key as the *entrance* into the new one, which is confirmed cadentially. Now the strongest confirmation of any tonality is the cadential pattern I_4^6-V_7-I, and hence this pattern is the simplest and most practical for keyboard use. Employing it, the modulatory scheme is as follows:

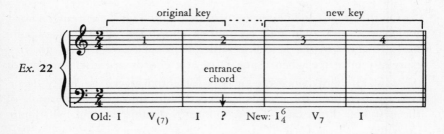

Ex. 22

This pattern can be used for all types of modulations on all levels.

It gives the student a definite and practical *picture* of the process, which may be varied at will. The two tonalities are sharply contrasted and the effect is conclusive. It is strongly recommended as a means of avoiding modulations that have neither formal symmetry nor harmonic consistency.

Further discussion is necessary regarding the common-chord and the entrance-chord approach to modulation. Specifically, the common chord is either a diatonic or a chromatic chord that has a function (though different) in both the old and the new key. In many cases the common-chord concept is helpful in apprehending the actual relationship of keys in terms of their harmonic identities and differences. This point is seldom made sufficiently clear. There are four types of common chords—diatonic, chromatic, bi-modal, and enharmonic. To illustrate: each major triad obviously belongs to the keys in which it functions, as the I, IV, and V in the major mode, and as the V and VI in the minor mode. Similarly, each minor triad functions as the II, III, and VI, and as the I and IV in the major and minor modes respectively. *Hence each major and minor triad occurs in five different tonalities*, and consequently can be used as an entrance chord to four of them. (Experiment by having the student resolve each type to all possible keys.) These diatonic relationships provide for modulation to nearly related keys, and the distant keys can be reached through a chain of these dual relationships; that is, C through G through D, and so on. The same principle applies to all types of diatonic chords as well as to major and minor triads. But these chords may be diatonic in one key and chromatic in another, in which case the common-chord principle is extended. In addition, the mode of either key may be changed, adding new possibilities, and finally the chords may be spelled enharmonically. These four applications of the common-chord concept obviously cover all types of modulations, and are of great value in thinking key relationships.

On the other hand, attention may be focused on the entrance chord, which may or may not be a common chord as well. This viewpoint *looks forward* to the new key rather than backward to the old. It is especially effective when using chromatic chords as embellishments of the new I_4^6 chord. Since the function of chromaticism is chiefly decorative, many chromatic chords lead very easily into cadence formula of the new key. For example, the dominant, diminished, and half-diminished sevenths, as well as the augmented $\frac{6}{3}$ and $\frac{6}{5}$ and the Neapolitan Sixth chords are all used in this manner.

In using the formula given in Ex. 22 (page 87), it is best to assign a definite chord to be used, preferably the one under immediate consideration, regardless of whether the common-chord or the entrance-chord approach is adopted. Both concepts are helpful and should be used as needed. The modulatory pattern should be broken up into piano syle, either in arpeggios or in a definite rhythm or style, as suggested above.

There are other modulatory devices more used in writing than in playing, except on an advanced level. These include modulation through a *common tone* (a favorite device of Schubert), the *chromatic inflection* of one or more tones of a chord (the fundamental C major chord changed to a D♭ dominant $\frac{4}{2}$), and *cadential modulation*—that is, the assumption of a new key by simply beginning on its tonic after a perfect authentic cadence in the old key. The reader undoubtedly can recall many examples of these types. In practice all types may overlap somewhat. In attempting to define types of modulation, it is important to remember that progression to a *new key center* is necesssary for a modulation. Hence C major to C minor is merely a change of mode, not a modulation.

In conclusion, there are two important general concepts regarding modulation that need to be made clear to the student: first, that all keys are equidistant, technically speaking, and hence may be reached with equal ease; and second, that it is essential to look *ahead* and determine the entrance chord rather than to memorize a particular formula for each type of modulation. Once more it is urged that modulation be introduced early and clearly in keyboard study because of the vital role it plays in harmonic relationships.

(f) *Reduction*, either of piano compositions or of vocal or instrumental scores, aids in achieving insights into musical organization. It is especially helpful to use material selected from the student's repertoire as well as material for the entire group. The process consists simply in reducing the chords and melody to a series of essential chords in "block" form—either with or without rhythm. This reduction may be on several levels. Probably it could begin with the playing of all chords, gradually eliminating more and more until only the basic skeleton remains. The student should name the chords as played, both by number and letter, and identify all non-harmonic tones. This is a very practical means of understanding harmonic and structural relationships—for example, part II of an A—B—A form may be found to be only an expansion of dominant harmonies. Such *keyboard analysis* also aids in memorizing, since it provides a broad rather than a narrow view of harmonic progression and formal structure. A fairly extensive harmonic vocabulary is desirable as a prerequisite for this type of study.

(g) *Keyboard dictation* may be accomplished by having a student repeat *by ear* any material played by the instructor or fellow students. This is primarily a classroom activity rather than an assignment for out-of-class study, but its value justifies including it in the present discussion of keyboard techniques. Probably the simplest procedure is for the instructor to play a simple progression of three or more chords and ask for it to be repeated. Should the first student fail to do so, other students try until a correct repetition is played. Results vary: sometimes it will be necessary for the instructor himself to repeat the progression, while at other times a correct repetition is played by the first student. If the latter is true, the instructor should use the same progression again, with slight variation, for the next student. This parallels the procedures suggested for oral dictation (Chapter IV, page 63). It may be varied by having the students dictate for each other, or by having an improvisation repeated by another student.

3. The advanced keyboard application of musical structures will naturally use the skills and techniques discussed in (a) through (e) above, but in extended and intensified forms. As in advanced written dictation, the material should be selected with reference to bridging the academic gap between the classical and the contemporary idioms. The following expansions or additions of skills should be made:

(a) *Harmonization*: add a study of the unique idioms of chorale and figured bass harmonizations, and possibly of chorale figurations.

(b) *Transposition*: introduce transposition by use of movable clefs. (See page 91.)

(c) *Improvisation*: extend improvisation to include the larger forms. Add the variation principle as one of the best means for understanding and manipulating form.

(d) *Modulation*: connect two choral numbers or songs using one of their motives—either the closing motive of the first or the opening one of the second. This skill is obviously related to improvisation.

(e) *Score reading*: read the Bach chorales and choruses from his larger works in vocal score, using the C clef for the upper three voices. This skill can be integrated with (a) above. Continue the facility to read orchestral scores on the foundation laid on the intermediate level.

(f) *Reduction*: extend the keyboard analysis through blocking chords to include orchestral scores. The relation to (e) above is obvious.

(g) *Keyboard dictation*: extend dictation to be repeated by the student to include idioms of the late 19th and early 20th centuries. Such a course on the graduate or postgraduate level would serve as a summary of preceding learnings and, through highly specialized techniques, should insure proportionate insights.

The above discussion outlines briefly the various skills which may be developed in keyboard study. The large number and variety of approaches make careful selection by the instructor essential. Actually, an entire course could well be given on any one of them, particularly on the advanced level. The instructor must choose those which he feels to be most needful for a given situation, bearing in mind that, generally speaking, the more varied the approach, the broader the resulting musicianship will be.

IV

Two specialized types of keyboard instruction remain to be considered: the teaching of transposition by means of movable clefs and the acquisition of musical insights by the keyboard analysis of piano literature. Both have been subjects of organized experimentation and for this reason deserve consideration and evaluation.

1. The teaching of transposition through the use of movable clefs is not a new idea. (115). It is the traditional European method whose value is attested by long and successful use. The reason for its success is undoubtedly due to the fact that the clefs, *not the notes*, are transposed, which simplifies the process considerably. In other words, clef transposition enables the student to play the notes as written, altering only the accidentals in accordance with the new key. Once the clefs are learned, this procedure is much more logical than the usual methods of transposition. The specific details of the procedure may be summarized thus:

(a) *Uses of clefs*: the G, F, and C clefs are in general use. The G clef may be placed on the first or second lines, the F clef on the third or fourth lines, and the C clef on the first four lines of the staff. Thus c′ (middle C) may be written in the following ways:

Ex. 23

In this example, no. 1 gives the same reading as no. 8 and consequently is not used in transposition. No. 1 could also be written using the C clef on the fifth line, but the F clef on the third line is more practical.

As used for transposition at the keyboard, these clefs designate the letter names but not always the octave pitch of notes. Thus the C clef will simply locate C, but not necessarily c′. The player must play it in the proper octave.

The following table indicates the clefs required for transposition to any interval:

Interval		Upper staff clef	Lower staff clef
Up	2nd	alto	mezzo soprano
"	3rd	bass	baritone
"	4th	mezzo soprano	soprano
"	5th	same as down a 4th	
Down	2nd	tenor	alto
"	3rd	soprano	treble
"	4th	baritone	tenor
"	5th	same as up a 4th	

Note that adjacent clefs are always used (the alto and mezzo soprano for up a 2nd), but in reverse order, i.e. the *upper* staff using the *lower* clef, and *vice versa*. Using this table, the first two measures of *America* would be transposed up a 2nd from G major to A major, thus:

Ex. 24
alto clef
mezzo soprano clef

The signature of A♭ major would be visualized for transposition to that key.

(b) *Treatment of accidentals*: visualization of the proper clefs and key signatures will result in the desired transposition, provided accidentals do not occur in the music. General principles have been worked out for the treatment of accidentals. These principles may be summarized thus:

When transposing:		*Accidentals before*:
Up	major 2nd	F and C are raised
"	minor 3rd	B, E, and A are lowered
"	major 3rd	F, C, G, and D are raised
"	perfect 4th	B are lowered
"	augmented 4th	F, C, G, D, A, and E are raised
Down	major 2nd	B and E are lowered
"	minor 3rd	F, C, and G are raised
"	major 3rd	B, E, A, and D are lowered
"	perfect 4th	F are raised.

In general, transposition by clef is most useful to professional accompanists and orchestral players, although the music teacher in the schools could use the skill to advantage. However, its full application to music education is limited by its highly specialized and complex nature. Undoubtedly all musicians should have a reading knowledge of alto and tenor clefs, and such skill could be developed by pianists through transposition as well as by score reading.

Aside from the practical value of transposition, it has the additional value of emphasizing and reorienting tonal *relationships*. The ability to think and perform tonal patterns from all pitches is certainly of great value educationally and amply justifies any course in transposition, irrespective of "practical" application.

Finally, a knowledge of the clefs is of value in score reading, not only for reading the C clef used, but for reading the parts of transposing instruments. For all these reasons some practice in the use of clefs for transposition is desirable, and the most immediate, practical, and musical application appears to be to the piano, as outlined above, either in complete or modified form.

2. The second type of specialized keyboard instruction—the keyboard analysis of piano literature is organized for the teaching of structural knowledge via the keyboard for interpretive purposes. Its central idea is that genuine musicianship is a prerequisite of good performance, and that this musicianship can be promoted through analytical keyboard study of representative compositions selected from piano literature. This is a thoroughly sound and practical idea, first, because it is a musical approach, and second, because it can be readily organized and implemented. Its underlying assumption has been previously stated: namely, that the basic approach to music study is through music itself. Analytic keyboard study represents the core of functional teaching by the exploration, analysis, and application of the principles

of structure to be found *in the literature of the student's own instru-ment*. Such a procedure should greatly aid intelligent performance. It could also be applied to the literature of other instruments. The details of procedure may be summarized thus:

(a) *Structural design*: recognition of the over-all structural design as related to performance.

(b) *Tonal design*: recognition of general key scheme with reduction of portions to essential harmony in block form—a study of the function and specific use of chords in context.

(c) *Harmonic vocabulary*: a more detailed study of diatonic and chromatic harmony of the compositions as pertaining to the style of individual composers.

(d) *Memorization*: the technique of memorizing based on (a) and (c) above.

(e) *Transposition*: practice in playing selected passages in other keys both by sight and by ear.

Such a class would be suitable for rather advanced piano students with some previous background in harmony and form. The study outlined above would be focused on intelligent musical performance. It might also serve as a brief survey of piano literature showing the relationship of style and composition techniques. Properly presented, such a study of the basic repertoire in any field should vitalize both performance and structural study.

V

Keyboard study for the non-pianist presents unique problems. Undeniably it is of great value musically for him both to play the piano and to have some keyboard application of structural principles. Frequently both of these activities are neglected entirely. At least three solutions of the non-pianist's keyboard problems are possible: piano instruction alone as a secondary subject, some keyboard harmony in the "theory" class, and a combination of piano instruction and keyboard harmony in a single class. Let us consider each of these solutions.

1. As stated above, piano instruction is often given to the non-pianist individually as a secondary subject. This procedure is open to serious criticism, since it often fails to give keyboard facility or to promote musicianship. It tends to become almost entirely a mechanical study of note values and fingerings: first, because little time is spent on it, and second, because the emphasis is almost entirely on technique.

Too often the non-pianist spends a whole semester attempting to learn one of the Bach *Two-Part Inventions* for the final examination! Properly taught, such a course could have value, especially if the repertoire were slanted toward the student's interest: for example, simple arrangements of fragments from orchestral works, [12] or piano accompaniments for singers and players of solo instruments. Such consideration of the student's interest would aid greatly in providing effective motivation, which is often conspicuously lacking. But even if secondary piano lessons functioned properly, keyboard application of "theory" would still be omitted, unless the piano teacher had unlimited time and an enlightened concept of teaching.

2. The second solution, that of including some keyboard harmony in the "theory" class, is of vital importance, irrespective of whether the non-pianist has any regular piano instruction or not. *This keyboard need is primarily the responsibility of the harmony teacher*. Explain the piano keyboard in teaching rudiments, and immediately apply these facts to it. For example, have the student locate specific pitches in the various octave groups. As scales, intervals, and chord structures are presented, each student should demonstrate his understanding of them on the keyboard. If necessary, scales may be picked out by one finger, chords played with one hand only, but in all cases *use the piano to change abstract facts into concrete, tactile realities*. In harmonizing melodies, the melody should be played or sung while the non-pianist plays the harmonic background of I, IV, and V, using only one or two chords to a measure. In some cases, he may even learn to harmonize folksongs, playing the melody with the right hand and the harmonic background with the left. If harmony is taught in a separate class, the keyboard application will of course be limited, but even so, rudiments and all diatonic and chromatic chords should be transferred to the keyboard by pianists and non-pianists alike. In practice, however, both the piano and "theory" teacher often are delinquent as regards the non-pianist. In these areas he is the "forgotten man" who "slides through" piano and keyboard training with a minimum of instruction and profit. The pianist is fortunate that his instrument is also the best for musical growth, but for this very reason, the non-pianist's piano and keyboard problems merit special attention.

3. Such consideration is the purpose of the third solution mentioned above: the combination of the teaching of performance and keyboard skills in one class which would supplement *but not supplant* the regular "theory" class. After rudiments, this class would be concerned with development of the ability to read music, play simple compositions, harmonize folk melodies, and play by ear. The principles of

form would be recognized and the entire approach would be musical rather than technical. This solution has many obvious advantages: group activity, practical objectives both from the standpoint of achievement and of use, and emphasis on musical rather than technical growth. Its execution would require a piano for each student, a condition that will be discussed below. Its success, as in all teaching, would rest ultimately on the instructor. Its dual purposes would require equal emphasis: it must neither be a class-piano course with a few scraps of "theory" added, nor a keyboard class that neglects piano techniques. Naturally to obtain this equality of emphasis, extensive content must be curtailed. It can include neither as much piano technique nor keyboard harmony as a class devoted entirely to one or the other. But the values obtained by such a compromise outweigh the loss in each area, and when broadly considered in terms of musical growth and insight, it offers the best solution to the problem of giving the non-pianist both types of keyboard facility.

VI

Finally, the question of proper equipment underlies all teaching of keyboard skills both to pianists and non-pianists. Most classrooms are equipped with only one piano. However, the growing emphasis upon class-piano lessons has made it necessary for each student in the group to be provided with his own instrument. Multi-piano equipment is almost a necessity, especially in certain devices used in keyboard instruction. Its advantages are obvious: continuous *group* participation, more variation of class techniques, and more attention and interest from the student, to mention only a few. In fact, one is almost tempted to say that the individual learnings are related, if not proportionate, to the number of instruments available to the group. The cost of equipment should be considered in relation to the number of students served, especially since it can be used both by the regular keyboard classes and special class for non-pianists described above. Much of the discussion in this chapter is predicated on the availability of multiple pianos. Their use should be seriously considered in organizing any program of music instruction in which interest and efficiency are regarded as conditions of a good learning situation.

This concludes our survey of keyboard study. The need for it is general and individual achievement is in terms of keyboard facility. Its growth—especially for pianists—should parallel that of other skills. Its basis is musical literature and its immediate objective the solution of practical problems. Specific procedures on various levels for pianists were discussed, including two specialized aspects: clef transposition and keyboard analysis. For the non-pianist who needs both performing and keyboard skill, the best solution appeared to be a single additional class combining these related skills. The use of multiple pianos was urged for maximum interest and efficiency in learning, irrespective of the student's pianistic facility. Considering the many phases of keyboard study and the heterogeneous group of students who need it, perhaps its chief value is that it transmutes abstract facts into concrete realities and thus promotes, to varying degrees, a better understanding of the nature of music.

Chapter VI

ANALYZING

ANALYSIS is basic to musical understanding. It is implicit in performance and is also the means of clarifying musical relationships for the listener, teacher, and composer. Its objective is the explanation of musical structure in such a way that insight results. Its means are the ear and the eye focused on specific relationships. In this sense all study of music is analytic.

There are of course many types of analysis—harmonic, contrapuntal, formal, stylistic—none of which, in classroom practice, should be divorced from a real performing or listening situation. In other words, specialized courses in any type of analysis are questionable—the only exceptions being either non-technical appreciation courses or highly technical advanced courses. For the average music student, analysis should be part of a simultaneous mental and physical approach to music. Specifically, there is no need for a separate course in harmonic analysis or the song forms if the course in writing—creative harmony or what you will—is properly taught. It is a mystery how harmony can be taught *without* analysis of it or of the compositional forms in which it occurs. This of course involves the problem of *integration*, to be discussed later (see Chapter VIII, page 144), but the application cited above is sufficient for the present. Recognizing this essential unity of living music, let us consider some types of analysis.

I

Harmonic analysis is concerned with the structure and function of chords. There are four outstanding tonal theories as outlined by Riemann, Schenker, Hindemith, and Schillinger. Their respective positions may be summarized thus:

1. Riemann explained harmonic phenomena in terms of "tonal functions of chords." These functions he limited to the tonic, dominant, and subdominant: all chords belonging to one of these three groups. This theory simplified classical harmony and rendered unnecessary complicated chord structures, although it by no means solved all problems.

2. Schenker advocated a linear approach to chord formation, to harmonic relationships, and to form in general. His theory was based on three propositions: (a) that classical music was organized primarily on the horizontal progressions of the outside voices; (b) that this two-voice outline determined the general design of the movement as well as the details, and (c) that form, as well as harmony, was dependent on this two-voice outline which differentiated musical phenomena according to structural purpose.

3. Hindemith's theory is essentially one of tension between chord-groups whose non-invertible chords included seconds and fourths as well as thirds. Chord connections were based on a new theory of root progressions in relation to the two-voice framework formed by the outside voices, and to harmonic fluctuation or variation of chord tension. This system rationalizes much puzzling practice in contemporary music, while at the same time it strongly affirms the principle of tonality in the use of the twelve-tone scale.

4. Schillinger formulated a method primarily to aid composers. He proposed to expand musical resources by an application of mathematical possibilities to rhythm, melody, harmony, form, and orchestration. In harmony he developed new scales, chords, and techniques of harmonization. Æsthetically he proposed the use of a scale of tension and a psychological dial of emotions. In form he suggested basic thematic patterns and designs to insure coherence. The technical devices offered by Schillinger are very comprehensive and are of great value in the mechanical organization of musical resources. They are to be used as tools, however, not as substitutes for creative imagination.

II

How can these four systems of harmonic analysis be used by the

student? All are useful, but of the four a combination of Riemann and
Schenker seems most practical for the music of the Classic and Romantic periods. One modification by Wedge is important: namely, the
theory that *chromatic chords are best regarded as embellishments of
diatonic harmonies.* This theory is definitely related to the Schenker
conception of essential and non-essential chords. The whole problem
of chromaticism requires careful consideration.

There are three theories of chromaticism: first, any interval may
be altered in any chord; second, certain intervals may be altered in
certain chords, and third, chromatic chords form groups of harmonic
entities that are purely decorative and hence non-essential in function. Let us consider each in turn.

1. The first theory, while theoretically true, is too broad to be of
practical value. Music is a language that grows by *usage*, not by invention. Chords, like words, appear for expressive reasons. They may
be "coined," but only through the creative process. There are very few
instances indeed of the general acceptance of either artificial chords
or scales. The "mystic chord" of Scriabin and the whole-tone scale of
Debussy are isolated exceptions. The one hundred and thirteen theoretic scales of Busoni have never been used for the same reason that
Esperanto has been a failure as a language. Invented scales or chords
are interesting for experimentation but only when used by a master.
Furthermore, if general usage as found in literature is the basis of
study, obviously such structures will not be found. The student should
understand and use the standard vocabulary thus derived. It is a waste
of time and effort for him to try to discover or to invent "new" chords.
Pedagogically, the concept of the free alteration of any chord interval is confusing because of its vagueness, and as indicated above, does
not conform to practice. For both of these reasons, the practical value
of this theory is very doubtful indeed.

2. The second theory of limited alteration has been the most widely
accepted in the past and has proven its worth. It is much better than
the first theory, because it is more definite and hence can be classified
more readily. In it, each chromatic alteration in the chord is indicated
by the corresponding accidental written below the Roman chord
symbol. (See Ex. 25 below.) This makes possible classification into
general types of alteration, although the symbolization fails to indicate which type. Actually it is an outgrowth of the old thorough or
figured bass system. However, it has serious limitations: it implies
that diatonic and chromatic chords are equal in function, and its
symbols *for the same type of chromatic chord* often vary with each
key. In other words, the symbols express adequately neither the func-

tion nor the spelling of the chromatic chords. This means that the student learns a variety of spellings for one function—hardly a desirable procedure. For these reasons a better system of identification is required.

3. This improved identification is furnished by the third system, since it indicates precisely both the notation and function of the chromatic chord similarly in all keys. As stated above, it regards decoration or embellishment as the essential function of both harmonic and melodic chromaticism, and it symbolizes the chromatic chords in relation to this function. Precisely, chromatic chords are regarded as general applications of specific diatonic progressions whose harmonic function relates only to its chord of resolution, not to the tonality as a whole. On this basis, harmonic chromatic embellishments may be classified in the following groups:

(a) *Dominant chords* (X triads and X₇)
This is by far the most common type and is based on the diatonic progression $V_{(7)}$-I. It assumes that if the tonic chord can be preceded by its dominant or dominant seventh chords, then any major or minor triad may be preceded or embellished by its own dominant seventh chord, thus:

Ex. 25

Here we have the principle of all chromatic embellishing chords. The symbol X is arbitrarily used to designate the dominant seventh chord which is regarded as an independent chord-type, irrespective of tonality, and hence it is symbolized consistently. Such a concept obviously simplifies many aspects of chromaticism, but its chief merit is that it confirms the aural impression. All analysis should conform to the aural impression, since *music is heard, not seen*. The inversions of the dominant seventh, of course, may be similarly used and notated.

Formerly such a progression would have been analyzed as a series of so-called "next related" modulations to the key in which each dia-tonic chord is the tonic. But here again the ear protests. None of these tonalities are confirmed cadentially. Modulation may be likened to the establishment of a tonal home in a new harmonic community. These progressions merely *pass through* the new point of repose. Such a con-cept radically reduces the number of modulations recognized in analy-sis by reducing them to chromatic alterations or embellishments of the prevalent tonality. As noted above, this relates the theory of chromatic embellishments to the Schenker system of analysis previously dis-cussed.

A rarer type of dominant embellishment is derived from the deceptive resolution of the dominant chord ($V_{(7)}$-VI). This explains the step-wise dominant embellishment whose root is either a whole or a half-tone below that of the diatonic chord. It is usually found only in fundamental positions.

(b) *Diminished seventh chords* (O_7)

This type is based on the diatonic progression VII_7-I and VII_7-VI_6 in minor, and provides for the step-wise embellishment of major or minor triads by a diminished seventh chord on the same or an adjacent bass tone. Its use necessitates an understanding of the true nature and con-struction of the diminished seventh chord.

A diminished seventh chord is made up of equal intervals—minor thirds. For this reason its inversions are apparent only to the eye, not to the ear, since all inversions have the same intervallic structure and consequently sound alike. This curious fact has an important implica-tion for its spelling: namely, any diminished seventh chord may be spelled upward from its bass tone *in minor thirds* in relation to its chord of resolution. For example, in embellishing the C major chord by a diminished seventh on the same bass tone, the diminished seventh would be spelled upward in minor thirds from C as C - E♭ - G♭ - B♭♭. But this would "contradict" the spelling of the C major chord, hence the diminished seventh would have to be respelled or "corrected" for its chord of resolution as C - D♯ - F♯ - A. The following example makes this difference clear:

Ex. 26

Note that all the tones of the C diminished seventh chord, except the

C, are neighboring tones of the chord of resolution, and as such must be spelled with different letters. From this fact may be deduced the basic principle of chromatic spelling: namely, *spell each chromatic chord in relation to its chord of resolution by using the same letter for the same pitches and different letters for different pitches.* In other words, chromatic chords are spelled in relation to what follows, not to what precedes them. Chromatic chords have a future but no past! This is a general principle that is particularly useful in the spelling of diminished seventh chords having actually both an aural and a visual root. Thus in Ex. 26(*b*) above, the D♯ is the "eye root," but the C is the "ear root" from which the chord is heard and spelled most practically.

Hence, in analysis a diminished seventh chord is best named *from its bass tone as root*, regardless of its visual inversion. This device greatly simplifies the recognition and writing of diminished seventh chords. The following example illustrates the use of the diminished seventh to embellish the series of chords in Ex. 25 above:

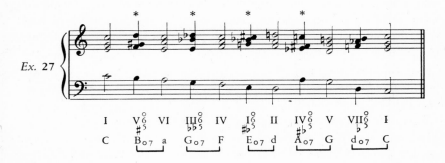

The greater simplicity of the second system of notation, disregarding the Roman numerals and accidentals, is obvious.

The diminished triad in the first inversion is occasionally used as an embellishing chord. Its origin is, of course, the VII6-I progression in both modes, and its use parallels that of the dominant triad or its inversions.

(c) *Half-diminished seventh chords* (Ø7)

The half-diminished seventh embellishment stems from the VII7-I progression in major. It is largely used as a cadential embellishment of the V or the I⁶₄ in the major mode, although it is sometimes used as in the opening of Tchaikovsky's B♭ Minor Piano Concerto, Op. 23:

(d) *Augmented chords* (†)

There are two types of embellishments containing augmented intervals: the augmented dominants (†X *or* †X7) and the augmented sixths (†6, †⁶₄, †⁶₅). The characteristic interval of the first is an augmented fifth, while that of the second is an augmented sixth. The augmented dominant chords are formed by raising the fifth of a major triad or seventh chord used as an embellishment. This type of course can only embellish major triads. Even the III chord in the harmonic minor is best regarded thus.

There are three chords in the second type—the well-known augmented sixth (†6) or *Italian Sixth*, the augmented ($^6_4$) or *French Sixth*, and the augmented (†⁶₅) or *German Sixth*. They are quite similar in construction, all dominant seventh in quality, each differing from the others by only one pitch. Their respective names and constructions are easily remembered when they are written over the pitch C, thus:

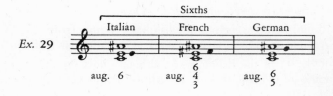

The German Sixth is also known as an enharmonic dominant seventh embellishment (X7en). The French Sixth sounds like a V_3^4 with a lowered fifth. All the chords of the augmented sixth are best spelled, like diminished seventh chords, *intervallically* as though their bass tones were the roots of the chords. This spelling makes them independent of the accidentals in the prevailing key. They are named only by letter, not by numeral.

  . (e) *Enharmonic chords* (en)
There are a number of chromatic embellishments that are spelled enharmonically in accordance with the general principle of spelling given above, the most frequently used being the dominant seventh in the third inversion (X$_2^4$en). It is generally used cadentially, as in the following example from Barnby's part-song *Sweet and Low*:

Larghetto

Ex. 30

$$X_2^4$$
en

This chord is actually the third inversion of the X7en or German Sixth.

There remain three other types of chromatic chords which cannot be classified as embellishments, because they are not chromatic extensions of diatonic usage. They are:

  (a) *Borrowed tones*
These chords retain their diatonic functions but *are "borrowed" from the opposite mode*. In other words, they are due to a temporary interchange of mode. The *tierce de Picardie* is an historic example. They are symbolized by either Roman numerals or letters.

  (b) *Change of quality*
This term refers to certain changes not readily explained either by change of mode or dominant embellishment. The quality of the III chord is changed from minor to major in this passage from Verdi's *Il Trovatore*, thus:

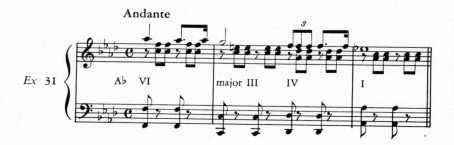

Ex 31 { Ab   VI   major III   IV   I

(c) *The Neapolitan Chord* (N)

This chord is interesting because of the speculations regarding its
origin. It is usually found in the first inversion (N6), although the
fundamental position (N8) can be found, and the second inversion
(N$^6_4$) very rarely. Two explanations have been made regarding its
source: first, that it is a variation of the cadence formula II6-I$^6_4$ or
V in minor, with the fifth of the II6 lowered one half-tone; or
that it is a Phrygian cadence with a Picardian third. The following
example illustrates both, thus:

Ex. 32

II$_6$ I$^6_4$

Such is the typical chromatic vocabulary until the close of the
Romantic period. Beginning with Chopin, its use was so free and continuous that it almost became a separate system which might be termed
the tonal use of the twelve-tone scale. In this scale, chords built on
each semitone of the octave were regarded as valid members of the
prevalent tonality. The tonality, though greatly expanded, was preserved through the emphasis on the tonic and the dominant elements—
the only anchors in a sea of chromaticism. Tonal relationships were
clarified by sequential passages—as for example, the beginning of the
Liebestod from Wagner's *Tristan*, which is a series of sequences in
rising minor thirds—Ab - Cb (B) - D - F, returning to Ab. The entire
passage remains in Ab major and is an excellent example of the tonal

use of the twelve-tone scale. In the 20th century the tonic and dominant anchors gave way and the use of the twelve-tone scale became
entirely *atonal*. The point in our discussion of analysis and the embellishment theory of chromaticism is that *this theory enables us to
cope best with the tonal use of the twelve-tone scale*. Roman numerals
are helpless to indicate the broad, over-all tonality, but letters and the
use of generic symbols for chromatic chords solve the problem very
well indeed. The analysis of a page of Wagner's *Parsifal* or Franck's
Symphony will prove its value. The fact is that after 1850 the old
numerical system of identifying chromaticism simply did not function. The symbolization became too involved to be realistic aurally.
For this reason alone it is important, in teaching harmony, to name
chords *both* by number and letter from the beginning. Gradually, as
chromaticism increases, letter should supplant number names.

This concludes our summary of the third system of chromaticism,
that of embellishment, and of its application to music of the Classic
and Romantic periods. Wedge developed it most consistently, though
both Piston and Chapple use the general principle. Broadly speaking,
it offers the simplest and most practical explanation of chromaticism,
because it agrees with aural impression, and offers a consistent and
logical system of symbolization that is uniform in all keys.

III

Contrapuntal analysis is of equal importance to harmonic analysis
discussed above. Here the attention is focused on the linear rather than
upon the horizontal aspects of music. Since this is true, contrapuntal
analysis is more concerned with the style of writing and the so-called
contrapuntal "forms" than it is with the combination of tones at any
given point. However, there are a number of contrapuntal *devices*
which merit individual attention. They may be summarized thus:

1. *Inversion* is the process which reverses the direction of each interval in a melodic line—the size, but not the quality, of the interval
remaining constant. Inversion may be used in two ways: (1) a simple
reversal of each interval in its original order, (2) the reversal of the
intervals when the melody is played backwards, that is, in retro-
gression. The latter process results in a retrograde canon. Both types
are illustrated below, applied to the first phrase of *America*, thus:

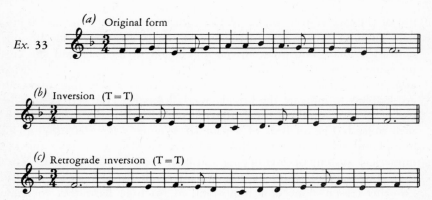

Ex. 33

(a) Original form

(b) Inversion (T = T)

(c) Retrograde inversion (T = T)

Inversions may be constructed, beginning on various steps of the scale. In (b) above, each tonic note of the original is answered by the tonic in the inversion, hence T = T. Other inversions are obtained when the tonic of the original is answered by the mediant or the dominant of the inversion. (T = M or T = D.) The best form is T = D, since its harmonies correspond most closely to that of the original. The Bach fugues abound in all these types of inversion, although the retrograde type is rare.

2. *Augmentation and diminution* refers to the doubling or halving, respectively, of note values in a melodic line. Here again the Bach fugues furnish many examples. Two famous ones occur in Wagner—the augmentation of the Day motive in Brangaene's Warning in Act II of *Tristan*, and the diminution of the Meistersinger motive beginning the Eb major section of the overture of that name.

3. *Stretto* means literally pressing on or forward and refers to the overlapping of the subject in two or more voices. Like inversion, it may occur in any pitch relationship. Again, see Bach fugues.

4. *Canon* is a strict and extended application of the stretto principle. It may occur at any pitch or rhythmic interval. A *round* is a canon in the octave—the other voices entering after the completion of the first melodic figure or phrase. All rounds are canons but not all canons are rounds. The principal theme of the *Finale* of Franck's Violin Sonata is a good example of canon; also the subordinate theme in the first movement of Beethoven's Fourth Symphony.

5. *Combination of themes* is a common device. The return of the principal theme, combined with the King David motive and the Prize Song in Wagner's *Die Meistersinger* Overture is a famous example—but there are many others: for example, see Mozart's F major Piano Sonata, K.533, first movement, or his G major String Quartet, K.387, *finale.*

6. *The Fugue* and *Invention* are styles of composition rather than forms. The fugue was originally canonic. The distinction between them relates to their subjects: the fugue subject is answered only in the fifth, while the invention's subject may be answered either in the octave or the fifth. The fugue also is more complex and highly developed than the invention. Bach wrote his two- and three- part inventions as preparatory studies for his sons.

7. *Chorale figuration* is a species of contrapuntal variation woven around a chorale melody which may or may not be embellished. Bach's Chorale-Preludes are examples of this *genre*.

8. *The Basso ostinato* is a short bass figure, one or two measures in length, which is repeated continuously throughout the passage or composition. Järnefelt's *Praeludium* is an example, as are also the Crucifixus from Bach's *B minor Mass*, and Dido's Lament from Purcell's *Dido and Aeneas*. When the recurrent bass figure is lengthened to eight measures, the composition using it is called a *Passacaglia*.

These are the eight principal contrapuntal devices and stylistic forms of purely polyphonic texture. However, the harmonic and polyphonic textures are so often intermingled that the best examples frequently occur in homophonic works. Contrapuntal analysis is necessary for the understanding of many works in standard literature. Yet too few musicians are familiar with polyphonic devices and forms. Pages of Schumann, e.g., *Träumerei*, Op. 15, No. 7, or *Nachtstück*, Op. 23, No. 4, are full of polyphony. It is essential that the instructor understand both harmonic and contrapuntal devices in order to explain musical texture clearly.

IV

Recognition of musical designs or forms is probably the most neglected area of "theoretic" instruction. Curricula are constructed with no reference to form—books on æsthetics ignore it—lectures are given on various periods in music with a superficial reference to the rondo as a simple form, as though it were any less complex in structure than the sonata-allegro form! Yet the principles of form are relatively few and simple, however varied their application.

Possibly one reason for this neglect of form is a feeling that designs differ so widely that generalizations are futile: that each compositional design is a unique product of the composer's *dæmon;* furthermore, that analysis destroys rather than enhances enjoyment; that to pull a rose apart does not contribute to its understanding. These are

case it is a fascinating and essential field of study for the music lover, creator, and performer.

V

Beyond musical form or design is the vast, misty Valhalla of musical study and speculation known as style. It was mentioned in Chapter II, page 40, in connection with criticism of written work, but not fully discussed. But in a work on teaching methods, adequate discussion is hardly appropriate, even if it were possible. If a definition were hazarded, it might be that style is the sum of technical skills, individually used to produce a unique whole. Style and content are often separated, and there are many strong reasons for doing so; yet the essential unity of any art work makes the distinction between them difficult at times. All that need be said for present purposes is that style is both individual and collective: that is, it belongs at once to the composer and to his epoch, and that the ultimate goal of all textural and formal analysis is a recognition and appreciation of style.

It is interesting to speculate on the factors that make style a reality irrespective of the difficulty in defining it precisely. Why does Beethoven sound like Beethoven and at the same time like a German composer? Unknown music heard on the radio can often be identified as regards style with considerable accuracy. What makes this possible? Undoubtedly the first requirement is a wide general knowledge of all phases of music literature, and second, considerable specific technical knowledge regarding the idiom of various composers and periods. Certainly a sense of style is most desirable, and should be cultivated to the utmost. So all analysis should be focused on stylistic factors— the unique way in which a composer expresses himself. In teaching form, begin with broad generalities gradually refined to specific details. Draw stylistic conclusions from all data and endeavor to wrest the secret of style from music heard either in or outside of class. Once analysis is thus oriented, it becomes one of the most potent factors of genuine understanding and growth.

VI

Analysis may be both aural and visual, but analysis by ear is much the more musical and realistic approach. It should be supplemented and amplified by examination of the score. One of the best means is a combination of the two methods—the reading of the score during performance. Let us consider the possibilities of each type.

1. The chief merit of visual analysis is its precise and definite quality. Unfortunately for many, the eye is the most reliable source of musical information. However regrettable, this dependence on the eye is natural, since it presents the entire picture while the ear records only a fleeting moment. Furthermore, our visual background is music is much broader than the aural, although this condition is being equalized by proper training. But for all its usefulness, the eye is not always reliable. The look and the sound of music do not always agree. Composers attest this fact: Schumann admitted that the score of *Lohengrin* sounded much better than it looked, and Verdi, when asked to give an opinion regarding a score, said that he could not tell whether it was good or bad music unless he heard it! If composers are partially dependent on the eye for evaluation, what of the struggling student?

There is no doubt about the fallibility of visual analysis. Tonal combinations that appear to form chords often contain non-harmonic tones. Schoenberg is responsible for the amazing theory that all intervallic combinations form chords. [13] In other words, all tones are harmonic: non-harmonic tones do not exist! Such a theory would name the following combinations of neighboring tones from Mozart's G minor Symphony, K. 550, first movement, as a "chord":

Ex. 34

This can only lead to the utmost confusion, since the number of such combinations is limitless and defies classification. Ignoring the forest, it focuses not only on the trees, but even on the branches. It contradicts aural experience through intelligent listening.

In a lesser degree, erroneous analysis is often made of chords containing one or more non-harmonic tones. For example, the use of the *échappée* at the cadence is sometimes analyzed as part of the chord, thus:

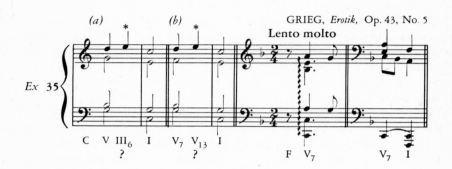

Ex 35

Only a "theorist" would name these combinations as a III6 or a V13 chord. Yet they may be found in texts as examples of the use of the III6 as a substitute for the V at the cadence! Such an interpretation results from purely visual analysis and is contrary to aural perception and common sense.

Another case in point is the naming of all dominant discords above the V7. The V9 only exists when its root progresses—usually to the I chord. The V9 when followed by the V7 is merely an appoggiatura over a V7 chord. Furthermore, the higher dominant discords exist only when there are more than four voices, since in less than five voices too many chord intervals must be omitted to identify the chord as other than a V7 with added non-harmonic tones.

All these instances should make one wary of depending entirely upon sight in harmonic analysis, but this is true regarding the analysis of form. Music is fluid and free and cannot be subdivided continuously into neat four-measure phrases. A composition in a rapid tempo may consist of only one phrase or period, as witness the second prelude in Book I of Bach's *Well Tempered Clavier* or Chopin's B♭ minor Prelude No. 16. Expansions may be tremendous, as in *Siegfried*, where one hundred and thirty measures occur between the cadential I⁶₄ chord and its resolution! The eye is helpless in analyzing such music. Hence, visual analysis should be used with caution, preferably as a check on what is heard.

. 2. Enough has been said above to indicate the prime importance of aural analysis. The chief reason for this is first, because "the educated ear," according to Haydn, is the sole arbiter of musical practice, and second, because aural analysis best approximates actual musical experience, either in the home, concert hall, or classroom. Ultimately, the structure of music is how it sounds to the listener or performer, so that all efforts to understand this structure must be based on hearing.

Several media are available for this study—the piano, phonograph, or radio, all of which have unique advantages. The first two are useful because the performance may be stopped at any point and passages repeated for clarification. On the other hand, the radio gives a complete, continuous performance that gives the over-all view of the composition. Radio listening is more difficult because of its relentless continuity, but this very difficulty is a challenge. Probably the best procedure is a combination of all three—especially applied to the same composition. The playing of doubtful passages on the piano is most helpful, since the listener is the performer as well. Next, the recorded version of the passage should be heard, and finally the passage, when clarified, should be incorporated into the complete radio performance if possible. Piano and recorded performances can be used in group analysis, since they combine the advantages of all three media. The radio is best used individually for listening outside of class.

3. For real growth, however, the best method of analysis is a combination of aural and visual impressions gained by reading the score during the performance of the composition. Here sight corroborates sound—to the clarification of both. The merits of this point cannot be overemphasized. With the score in front of him, the student can follow in detail the unfolding of the design. Obscure or doubtful points are clarified by the double points of reference, and the student gains immediate and vital insights into the organization of the score that would require much more time using either method alone. Of course the ultimate goal is purely aural analysis, but this skill must be developed gradually through both the ear and the eye. This is a strong argument for the student building a representative musical library in order to be able to follow all types of music heard on the radio. In fact, class analysis should be the motivation for extensive listening outside of class. The student should be encouraged to listen, score in hand, to as much music as possible. The radio is not the only source of this out-of-class listening. Much can be learned by taking scores to concerts. The point is to develop in the student awareness of musical structures wherever heard. Only then can structure become a reality—a vital and integral part of music itself.

VII

While formal analysis, as indicated above, should be a part of all music study, mention should be made of a recent specialized approach to the apprehension of form. This is the class in aural analysis or analytic dictation mentioned in Chapter IV, page 75. The class has two objectives: to present an outline of the principal musical forms, and to do so aurally—the designs being recorded by a set of arbitrary symbols. Thus it combines analysis of form and written dictation, although the latter is in modified form since it dispenses with notation. The class is organized around "directed listening" in class, supplemented by assigned listening outside of class. It should be a survey of the whole range of musical literature with emphasis on style as well as form. As suggested in the previous discussion, the assignments for study may be either drawn from music heard in concert or on the radio, selections from the student's own repertoire, or pertinent material selected by the instructor, that will serve as a basis for subsequent group discussion. The course may be conducted on any level indicated by the needs of the particular situation: that is, it may stress either the technical or the appreciative elements of the music studied. If properly organized and taught, such a course can fill many needs. It can serve either as a general introduction to music or as a summation of previous technical learnings, depending upon the emphasis given. But as stated before, it may represent either extreme, but never the mean. It should not be used as a substitute for regularly organized courses in listening. In all cases it should be as free and exploratory in nature as is consistent with its aims.

To summarize: analysis is an integral part of musical learnings, and as such should not be studied separately except in special cases. Textural, formal, and stylistic analysis were discussed, and appropriate procedures for their teaching suggested. A class in aural analysis or analytic dictation was described as a new approach to the problem of the understanding of form and style. Apprehension of form will grow gradually through the use of both the eye and the ear, separately and in combination, but eventually the ear must be the sole arbiter. Again we are brought back to its primacy as an agency of musical learning. Structural study is one of the six avenues of learning and only "theory," *but not music*, can be taught without parallel analysis as a means of musical insight.

Chapter VII

CREATING

I

THE word *creative* has become a semantic battleground. It has as many meanings as usages. Definitions range from Mursell's broad concept of "recombining familiar elements in a new way" to the narrow dictionary definition of "the production of a work of thought or imagination, especially as a work of art." In seeking for agreement one is reminded of Humpty Dumpty in *Through the Looking Glass*, whose words meant just what he chose them to mean, "neither more nor less." And this is apparently true in the present instance. Any action or reaction, however trivial, may be considered creative if it reorganizes past learnings. The better the individual learns, we are told, the more creative he becomes. Apparently this means that all savants are creative geniuses! The truth is that the sharp edge of meaning has been so dulled by usage that the word must be redefined and the edge resharpened to make it serviceable. For present purposes, musical creativity will mean specifically—and narrowly—*the expression of personal feeling through written tonal and rhythmic configurations*. In other words, it refers only to the various levels of composition rather than to generalized concepts of personal initiative or creative living. It is regarded as an activity rather than as an attitude.

The function of creative writing, as defined, is primarily self-

expression, but it can serve a secondary purpose as a means of promoting musical insights. It is a truism that we learn by doing not only
the possible but the impossible. Creative activity is often regarded as
belonging only to the fortunate few, whereas it is the possession of the
many—since all possess the spark of expression in varying degrees.
This is meant in the literal, not the general sense. There is no means
better adapted for learning the relationships of music than the discovery of them through use in composition. Furthermore, the sense
of satisfaction from self-expression is an impetus for learning that
cannot be ignored. For all these reasons it is important to utilize
creative activity as a means of understanding musical relationships.

II

Granted these premises, what are the basic requirements for creative expression? Two educational ones are paramount—an adequate
background and a functioning technique. However, these are co-exis-
tent requirements, not prerequisites. Both can be developed during
and through the creative process itself. Of the two, background is the
more general and difficult to define. It consists in a thoroughly assimilated, subconscious feeling for musical relationships based upon
wide contacts with music. Its possession enables the student to exercise
initiative and to make effective choices. Background is needed as a
starting point. Creative expression often begins with imitation and may
end with originality. Children learn thus, and a composer's "first
period" is usually reminiscent of his predecessors. The imitation is, of
course, quite unconscious—certainly not deliberate. But it does exist
and it grows naturally from background. However, this essential background does not mean a stereotyped set of musical patterns to be
copied, but rather a rich subconscious reservoir of musical experiences
which stimulate expression. It is the soil from which the tree grows.
To carry the analogy further, the other basic requirement—technique—bears the same relationship to creative expression as the sap
does to the growth of the tree. It is the means by which the background is used for growth. It transmutes the background into new
forms of expression. Technique should result from a desire for better
expression. Creative work without technique is ineffective and disorganized. This implies that, to be functional, technique must not
only be motivated by need, but that it must be forged *during* the
learning process as a tool of expression. In other words, technique is
the way by which specific problems are solved, and it is capable of

generalization only after the solution has been reached. It then becomes crystallized experience—available for the solution of similar problems.

The perplexing problem of the role of technique in guiding creative expression can only be solved adequately in terms of objectives. If the writing is to be purely recreational, very little technique is required, but if the purpose is educative, considerable technique is necessary. In other words, the more serious the effort, the more technique is needed. Children and amateurs require little, professional students of music more, and embryo composers most. This view is readily accepted in connection with applied music—piano for example—but is often seriously questioned as regards composition, as though it were a mysterious process independent of technique. Determine the objectives of creative expression and its technical requirements are largely implicit. Skills are essential to expression. Their importance is determined by the objectives and the maturity of the participants. The problem of technique in creative expression should neither be stressed nor minimized but faced objectively without educational qualms.

Considerable confusion exists between the terms musical composition and creative writing or expression and their relation to the study of "theory." Few music students have the maturity or technique for musical composition, in the strict sense of the term, but all have sufficient imagination for creative writing on some level, however immature, which may develop into true composition. This creative ability can be utilized to organize and clarify musical insights at all levels—it is one of the most effective means of teaching the organization of musical structures. Techniques develop by solving problems, some of which may be creative in nature. Failure to use creative expression as one of the avenues of learning is one of the basic errors of conventional teaching. It is quite unnecessary to complete "theoretic" study before beginning creative writing. The two processes—apprehension and application—should be inseparable. In fact, in many cases they are identical. To "understand" the function of a chord should imply the ability to use it creatively or otherwise, and conversely a good use of the chord shows an "understanding" of its function.

This conclusion leads naturally to the question of what emphasis should be given to "theoretic correctness" in creative work. Here again it is a question of objectives and of the maturity of the student. As stated previously, serious *musical* criticism is based primarily upon style. Of course personal and psychological considerations are always present to a degree, but if the student's work is to be judged musically it must be in terms of the techniques of a particular style or idiom. Why should ineffective expression be encouraged under the name of originality any more in music than in English? The real trouble lies in the attitude of many instructors who feel that "theory" is unrelated to practice. A typical instance is that of the instructor who, after teaching the uses of certain chords, advised his students to "forget them when composing"—or of the counterpoint teacher who merely directed his students to "give the alto a good time!" Imagine a vocal or instrumental teacher who consistently advocated ignoring breathing or fingering for freedom of performance. *Writing is based on technique as truly as is physical performance,* and to ignore or minimize this fact is to strike at the very root of effective expression. Consecutive fifths, like bad fingering, should be corrected if inconsistent with the idiom used. This is not pedantry but common sense, and the *laissez-faire* attitude toward technique in writing has done as much harm as false emphasis on "correct" procedures. Of course, in criticizing, one must be sure that the technical criticisms are validated by practice and are not simply artificial textbook "rules"—which leads us back once more to music itself as a criterion of judgment. Most of the objections to technical criticism of creative work are based upon a confusion between real principles and arbitrary rules. The instructor must be able to recognize this distinction through wide experience and an *educated* ear. He must *guide* the student's experimentation in tone, rhythm, and form if learning is to be fruitful and efficient. He must help students to find the *best* solution of their problems, not simply a solution, however original but imperfect. So conceived, technique is a vital element in creative expression and can well serve as an agency of learning and growth.

One point in connection with the role of technique in creative writing has been suggested but not emphasized, namely, that the specific procedures naturally vary with individuals. The role of technique is always commensurate with the background, interests, and maturity of the student. Children require a different treatment than adults—more can be expected from professional music students than from amateurs. No set pattern can be followed for all, but all should be guided to the best expression of which they are capable—and not be left to flounder in a chartless sea of meaningless experimental sonorities.

III

With this understanding of the function and basic requirements of creative writing in mind, let us consider its place in the regular "theory" class. At the outset it must be clearly understood that only the skills involved in creative expression can be taught—never the creative act itself. The imagination may be stimulated and discrimination refined, but, as Goetschius says, "The life-breathing attribute of emotional passion cannot be acquired." In other words, while all individuals are creative to a degree and can acquire technique and discrimination, only a few are capable of becoming composers in the true sense of the term. Composers are born, not made. This fact shapes class procedures.

Creative expression is a means of musical learning applicable to all levels. From the beginning, experience should be transmuted into expression. This is often done through rhythm bands, and when the level of writing is reached it may be introduced through the setting of words to music. Song writing offers many advantages as the initial step in creative writing. First, words provide an emotional stimulus, and second, they clarify many organizational problems. The poem must have both literary and musical value as well as emotional appeal. Many poems are unsuited for musical setting. Furthermore, the melody should enhance the meaning of the words and not merely agree with them metrically. The use of words helps to solve both temporal and structural problems. The scansion of the poem determines metrical and rhythmical values and also the form. The automatic determination of these factors simplifies compositional problems, since initial creative efforts are apt to be disorganized without the underlying word pattern. Also, the organization of words is a readily understood parallel to that of music, and thus through words the beginner absorbs general principles of organization without feeling that they are arbitrary or restrictive. These songs should be unaccompanied in order to focus on specific problems of expressive meaning, time, and form.

Creative expression "controlled" through use of words should be supplemented by the writing of free melodies for those instruments played by the members of the class. Much group learning can result from such an activity. These instrumental melodies may or may not conform to the formal patterns dictated by use of words. However, it is desirable that there be some transfer as regards organization so that the student's instrumental writing gradually acquires structural logic from the patterns used in songs. Both vocal and instrumental melodies should be performed in class and evaluated by the group.

Creative writing should parallel harmonic study as well. There is no reason why the student should not learn to use the material studied in class, but on the other hand, experimentation with material not yet discussed should by no means be discouraged. As facility increases, compositions can be written for groups of instruments played by class members, or a soloist or singer can write a melody which could be harmonized by a pianist in the class. This latter type of activity will inevitably involve valuable discussions between the co-composers. Thus, in the best sense, creative writing is a process of self-education, motivated by real desire for and interest in self-expression.

Experimentation with contemporary idioms is a perennial problem on higher levels. Students hear these idioms everywhere and naturally try to imitate them without a mastery of basic techniques. Adequate criticism is made within the framework of a particular period or idiom, as has been suggested previously. The wise instructor will evaluate efforts to write in current idioms on this basis, but at the same time will develop in the student an understanding and mastery of earlier and more fundamental techniques. A real understanding of Wagner is essential to the comprehension of Webern; Debussy and Ravel explain many of the devices found in current popular music. Few students develop far enough to have an adequate basis for the study of contemporary techniques. Any work in this area is consequently experimental and superficial, and will be encouraged by the wise instructor only in exceptional cases. The "theoretic" understanding and appreciation of contemporary idioms is very different from possessing the requisite background or skill for their manipulation. If the student has real talent, he will develop an original and personal idiom through a mastery of past practices and the exercise of his own creative ability. Furthermore, present practices are so varied and contradictory that only a recognized composer who uses them is qualified to teach them. In brief, then, modern devices should be evaluated objectively in terms of style, but their use should be discouraged without an adequate technical background *both* by the student and by the instructor.

From the above discussion it is clear that creative writing as a means of musical learning should be an integral part of any regular "theoretic" instruction on all levels. No longer is it to be delayed until the study of harmony and counterpoint is completed. Some form of creative writing should parallel all "theoretic" study. Make it functional, individual, and continuous—an activity that vitalizes and personalizes written musical expression.

A word should be added regarding the composition class *per se*. In colleges or music schools where creative writing is done on the lower levels, much can be accomplished in a class devoted entirely to composition. Usually, however, such a class attempts to cover too much ground. Better results would be obtained if the area of study were limited, for example, to the variation form. The techniques of composition are best learned through the writing of this form, since the principle of variation is basic to all writing. Such a class should be selective—admission being based on objective evidence of marked creative ability and intelligence. There is a place for such specialization on the upper skill levels, but in order to function properly it must be professional in attitude and demand a high level of performance. It is the level at which real composition emerges from creative activity or expression.

IV

In addition to correlation with a planned learning sequence in a regular "theory" class, creative writing also can function through emphasis on two special aspects of music—mood and style. The development of creative writing through a consideration of mood and style has been carefully studied and the following summary of the procedures and results may be of value.

1. *The Use of Mood Effects in Musical Composition.*

(a) Theory class analyzes by ear many types of music for mood effects. Check-list helps clarify the contribution of the following musical elements: tempo, intensity, pitch, melody, meter, style, harmony, mode, rhythm, and timbre.

(b) Students survey available library recordings through individual projects, reporting their mood reactions. Such a listing later offers good material when concentration on specific mood is desired.

(c) From check-list results, summarize specific elements of music which appear most effective in creating certain well-defined moods.

(d) Analyze a play which the school will produce, to determine moods required for incidental music.

(e) Study those musical techniques needed to write simple music appropriate to the moods required by the play. Correlate analysis through hearing and score-study of music known to create the moods wanted. This procedure helps to clarify the means used by recognized composers in producing specific emotional responses.

(f) All students write themes in a small part-form for the different moods needed in the incidental music, incorporating the mood-elements determined by earlier study. Choose the best themes and divide remaining work into individual projects (i.e., for overture—transitions, codettas, development, and coda; and development of themes in entr'actes, transposition of themes, copying of parts, etc.).

(g) Arranging could be done by members of an orchestration class or by members of the "theory" class—again probably best handled as individual projects.

(h) Prepare and perform the music with a student orchestra and student conductor when the play is presented.

Such is a brief outline of the project which was used to supplement a regular "theory" class. Step (c) above was implemented by a comprehensive Chart of Musical Moods on a tension-activity scale. The music written for the play (*Outward Bound* by Sutton Vane) was remarkably effective and well written, and amply demonstrated the value of this approach. The success of such a project naturally depends upon careful preparation and intelligent guidance, but granted these prerequisites, it is reasonable to assume that the "mood approach" is valid musically and educationally. It should be stressed that this approach is experimental and is not a substitute for organized instruction, but is to be used as an additional means of stimulating and freeing creative effort. Furthermore, the concept of assigning definite meaning to music is debatable.

2. *A New Approach Through an Extensive Study of Style.* (128).

Somewhat related to the stimulation of creative expression through a reproduction of mood effects is the study of *musical style* as a motivating force in the teaching of music theory in general and of composition in particular.

The concept of style as a tool of learning has wide implications for the whole field of "theory" teaching, but we shall be concerned only with its use in guiding creative expression. Thus, the harmonic vocabulary acquired by the student should be understood both from the standpoint of structure and from its use in a particular period. When both harmonic structure and usage are understood *from the analysis of literature*, the student can apply this material to specific styles of composition for various media. This approach stresses the *extensive* study of style as a foundation for later intensive study— possibly on a graduate level. The student is led to discover needed techniques and criteria in the music with which he is familiar either through performance or hearing. Thus musical structures and their stylistic use become real and functional because they explain certain phases of the student's own musical experience. More concretely, this means that the student first analyzes, then uses in composition, technical procedures found in familiar music. Style is set up as the criterion of usage, and techniques are applied to this end.

But the idea of style includes the characteristic musical expression of both the period and the media. This approach is concerned with both aspects. Hence the student discerns both how music was written in a certain era and how it was written for different media. Instrumental, choral, and vocal techniques of writing are differentiated, and the student learns how to balance the temporal and technical aspects of style.

Achievement of this balance requires careful planning by the instructor, combining flexibility with precision and experimentation with definite goals. The procedure might be roughly summarized as *exploration, generalization, and application,* the precise sequence of learning being dependent upon group interests and needs guided toward a desired goal. The areas covered in such an approach would include elements of form, song, choral and piano writing, structural devices, stylistic characteristics of various period from 1600 to the present, modal music, and unique scale structures (72). These elements of style would be studied concurrently with the acquisition of the standard harmonic vocabulary and be applied immediately through creative writing.

This approach has much to recommend it. Educationally it is sound because its motivation is excellent, its goals are desirable, and the means of achieving them are practical. It proceeds from general concepts to specific instances. It is a good example of the integration of creative writing and regular "theoretic" instruction. And finally its approach, being based upon music literature, is musical. Its weakness lies in the danger of loose organization and lack of focus, which may result only in a mass of unrelated facts about music rather than a clear cut explanation of it. But this danger is inherent in any approach that is also flexible enough to encourage initiative and experimentation, and such a weakness can be easily obviated by intelligent guidance. Its advantages as a means of motivating and stimulating composition are obvious, since it encourages creative rather than "theoretic" musical thinking.

In considering the relation of style to creative writing, the importance of a broad, general approach should be stressed. Much of the value of a stylistic approach is lost when it is restricted at the beginning to one style, however important. A striking example of this narrowness is to be found in the exclusive use of four-part vocal writing in teaching harmony, but it applies equally to the concentration on a particular period irrespective of the number of media employed. Such specialization is suitable only for advanced study. At the beginning, study or creative writing should embrace more than one period and medium simply because a single one gives too narrow a segment of musical experience either for complete understanding or expression. So in creative writing the student should have as a minimum an adequate understanding and use of the techniques of the Classic and the Romantic periods (1750-1900), since the bulk of the music that he hears falls within this span. This does not mean, of course, that he will not explore both backward and forward beyond these limits—but it does mean that the idioms of *both* these periods, as the basis and core of his early musical experiences, must be assimilated first.

V

Creative writing may also be stimulated by special projects either connected with or independent of the learning sequence set up in the regular "theory" class. The writing of music for a play production discussed above is an example of the former—although the study of mood effects could be used without the incentive of a play. On the other hand, the writing of the incidental music for the play might also be independent of the theory class or of a study of mood effects.

The treatment of creative writing on a project basis falls into two general categories—curricular and recreational. By the first is meant projects connected with some particular area of study, either musical or otherwise. The second consists of writing music for school uses. Let us consider some of the values and procedures of each.

1. *Curricular Projects* could be related to numerous areas of study. Since many phases of human life are reflected in music, these human experiences may in turn be creatively expressed in music. History, English, languages, and the social sciences all supply excellent opportunities for musical expression. The music of an historical period, of a country, of a particular group—all offer stimulating suggestions for creative writing which could be utilized if instructors in those areas were interested in making the correlation. Undoubtedly such projects would require the cooperation of the music teacher as well, but the results would amply justify the effort involved. For example, during the study of the Revolutionary period in American history, music of that day could be performed, supplemented by an original setting of a short poem of the period or of a characteristic dance. The original composition need not and indeed should not be elaborate, but it would reflect the spirit of the times. The idea could be presented as being similar to that of writing music for a documentary film. Perhaps such a suggestion may seem impractical for the average history class—yet surely the history and music departments could cooperate in a joint project that would involve creative writing.

The field of music itself is rich in possibilities—for example, music of a particular period, composer, or medium could be illustrated by original compositions based on a recognition of style. Imitation is one means of learning, and some great masters—for example, Dvořák and Rimsky-Korsakoff—have deliberately imitated national styles. Most student writing is unconsciously imitative and there is no reason why some of it should not be consciously so to a limited degree. This writing could be done quite independently of formalized "theoretic" instruction, in which case it might conceivably lead to a desire for directed technical learning.

2. *Recreational Projects,* however, offer by far the greatest opportunity for spontaneous creative expression through writing music for school use. School songs and marches are perhaps the most obvious, but original or arranged dance music, Christmas carols, and any music for special occasions fall into this category. Incidental music for a play production has been discussed above—and the next step in this direction naturally would be an original school play with songs or even a complete operetta. To write and produce a complete dramatic work is a major task—but it has been done successfully, with satisfaction by the performers and with great credit to the school. Such an undertaking is a group activity—and the various tasks are divided among members of the group—one writing the melody for a song, another harmonizing it, and perhaps a third doing the orchestration. Obviously it also requires the cooperation of many groups outside of the music classes. For this reason, the composition and performance of a cantata may be more practical. In any case, the musical objective of such projects is the stimulation of creative expression through writing music for social use. A band march, a choir number, or a school song will all attain this objective if the music teacher has the vision, initiative, and skill to use the resources at hand.

VI

One more approach to the stimulation of creative writing remains for consideration—the so-called "laboratory method." This consists in setting aside a weekly period during which students at any level may bring their compositions for criticism. The project is informal, the student being entirely free as regards attendance and type of composition submitted. At the end of the season a short program is presented consisting of the best compositions submitted during the year.

In one instance known to the author the age level varied from
children to adults, and naturally the types of compositions submitted
were equally diversified.[14] On some days the workshop was crowded
while on others only two or three students appeared. Some attended
regularly, others occasionally, and a few came only once.

The compositions submitted ranged from rather aimless little melodies harmonized entirely by one chord to elaborate chamber and
orchestral works in score. The evaluation of such varied material
naturally presented many problems. The first criterion was musical
logic or continuity. This involved problems of style which were discussed according to the maturity and background of the composer.
Music being studied was often used to illustrate the technical points
involved—an eight-year-old can grasp structural principles quite readily from material in his own repertoire. Harmonic criticisms were
adapted to the technical age of the composer, while structural principles such as length of phrases and types of cadences were treated
as factors of continuity, balance, and style in general. An effort was
made to base all criticism on musical rather than technical grounds.
Naturally there was no formal instruction—all learning being concomitant.

The results of this experiment in the guidance of free creative
expression were most gratifying. The workshop drew from all levels.
The attendance, while irregular, was sufficiently consistent to show
that the class met a real need—that of writing freely without technical
restrictions. The annual composition program gave an added incentive and significance to the work and helped to maintain standards
through competition.

Naturally a composition group of this type functions best when
the participants are concurrently developing skills and insights in
regularly organized classes. Learning based entirely on experimentation is a slow and inefficient process. On the other hand, such a
project can release potential creative ability to a degree impossible
in an organized learning sequence, and for this reason deserves serious
consideration. It is essential, however, that the criticism of compositions submitted be definite and constructive and also tend to emphasize rather than minimize what is learned in the regular "theory"
classes. In other words, it should create a desire for more technical
skill on the part of the student—not a feeling that it is a useless
restriction. This "felt need" may be aroused if the critic can successfully steer a middle course between the Scylla and Charybdis of
formalism and freedom. Above all, the atmosphere of the workshop

must be kept informal, tolerant, and helpful in order to maintain a climate favorable to creative expression on any level.

VII

And finally, what external means can be used for the stimulation of creative writing? Out of many possibilities three are outstanding: performances, competitions, and organized groups. All appeal to the competitive spirit and satisfy the craving for recognition that is so essential in creative work. Let us consider briefly how these means can be utilized.

1. *Performances* of student compositions can be divided into two types: those of compositions written for and performed in class, and those chosen for public performance regardless of origin. As suggested before, creative writing done in the class should be performed before the group and criticized by it. The advantages of such a procedure are obvious. Students derive satisfaction from a group-hearing and learn much from the comparison and evaluation of individual work by all. Creative assignments should use all the instrumental and the vocal resources of the group. Principles of good practice will be validated by hearing. The reasons for criticism and suggested changes may be clarified better thus than by any other method. Such a procedure aids in lifting written techniques from the "theoretic" to the practical level.

The public performance of superior student work also stimulates creative writing. This may be done either through the performance of single compositions on general musical programs or by giving a concert devoted entirely to original student works. Both procedures are good. On the high school level a school song, a choral composition, or a solo work by a student might well be included in a general assembly or concert program. In addition to compositions for groups in colleges and professional schools, student recital programs offer an excellent opportunity for the performance of solo works. For example, a student composer might offer or be asked to write a work for another student—or might perform an original work on his own program. In fact, both cases occur frequently—especially in professional schools.

A concert devoted entirely to student compositions is one of the most effective means of stimulating creative writing activity. Such a concert, consisting of works by members of composition classes, has long been a feature in conservatories and colleges. It is an essential part of a functional composition course since it serves to demonstrate competence similar to student recitals in applied music. For this reason it is to be hoped that the practice will eventually be followed as widely by music departments of liberal arts colleges and universities as by professional schools.

A broader type of composition concert is that which features original works by all students regardless of "theoretic" affiliations. Probably the program is best selected on a competitive basis by a competent jury consisting of faculty and students. The program would include both assigned and "free" compositions judged entirely on merit. This type of program provides for general participation in creative and performing activities. As an annual event at the end of the school year, it dramatizes creative writing. The closing date for submitting compositions should be announced months in advance, and should be arranged so as to allow sufficient time for the selection and planning of the program. This type of activity can well be sponsored by student organizations with faculty advice and guidance. The concert itself should be on the same level of importance as other concerts or dramatic performances. The number and quality of compositions submitted for such a concert will be most encouraging. A large proportion should originate outside "theory" or composition classes and exhibit a wide range of style and media. The program should be highly selective, excluding popular songs and arrangements of various types and encouraging serious, original music from all available resources. Technical skill, while desirable, need not be mandatory, but on the other hand neither triteness nor eccentricity should be encouraged. Here again the nature of the program will be determined by objectives—but it is to be hoped that on the college level, at least, the same standards will prevail in the selection of a composition program as in the selection of any applied music program where arrangements of folksongs and jazz numbers would not be included. In other words, ideally the student composition program should represent serious creative efforts comparable musically to other college programs. In some cases such a program has been given annually for over twenty-five years.

The type of program described above is equally practical on either high school or college level, although the details of procedure will naturally vary with the level. It is probably the best means of stimulating creative writing outside the classroom, since it is open to all, is competitive in nature, and offers the incentive of public performance.

2. *Composition contests* also are effective means of promoting creative writing. Many are sponsored annually by various organizations for a variety of purposes. The student composer has less chance of success in this field, due to professional competition, unless the contestants are limited to specified groups. The rewards usually are in terms of publication rather than of performance, although they may include both. On the high school level definite efforts have been made through professional organizations and publications to provide for the nurture and recognition of creative writing.[15] Through these agencies much creative ability has been discovered. In one national contest over five hundred compositions by high school students were evaluated. These were classified in ten categories. The compositions submitted exhibited a wide range of technical and stylistic competency, but there were a surprisingly large number which successfully met exacting standards. The results unquestionably demonstrated that creative musical ability is widespread among high school students and requires only encouragement to develop significantly. The same condition probably exists on the college level, although composition has not been promoted through contests on that level except by musical fraternities or sororities whose memberships are naturally limited. In any case, composition contests of all types and on all levels serve a useful purpose and the student should be encouraged to enter them whenever eligible.

3. *Composition societies* are of two types. The first is a student group, self-organized for the performance and discussion of their own compositions. This is a very valuable activity, comparable to debating, literary, and dramatic clubs in both high school and college. Probably it functions best when entirely free of faculty advice or direction unless requested. Here student-composers can work out their own salvation by mutual criticism. Such an activity should by all means be encouraged and supported. The second type includes many national and local societies for the performance of native works either by amateur or professional composers. While geared more to the adult rather than the student-composer, they nevertheless do offer some opportunities for the mature student, especially in professional schools, and he should certainly join one or more of them in order to maintain contacts with creative groups after leaving school.

VIII

Creative writing, in the above discussion, was defined as musical.

Chapter VIII

PLANNING

I

Organization is essential for successful teaching. The learning sequence is the framework of instruction. It is concerned both with ultimate goals and the means for their achievement. These two aspects of organization are so interdependent that their separation is neither desirable nor practical, because the quality of the end results can never rise above the quality of the means employed. For this reason, means and ends are of equal importance, though it is sometimes stated that "the directional goal process assumes a superiority over fixed-end goals." (112).

It is questionable whether desirable means alone will produce desirable results, for undue emphasis on means may rob results of concrete value. Of course, the reverse is also true—fixed-end goals lose value when achieved arbitrarily or mechanistically. Because of the failure to recognize the inherent parity of means and ends, much futile argument has developed around the learner vs. the subject-matter centered curriculum. Education is an orientation to living through the establishment of patterns of action, feeling, and thought based upon knowledge of our cultural heritage applied to the present and projected into the future. It includes facts as well as feelings, learnings as well as attitudes, and to stress either one at the expense of the other is to distort proportionately the function and meaning of education.

There are two theories of planning based upon the relation between means and ends. If fixed-end goals of "content" are stressed, the planning will be logical and impersonal—"the subject matter being selected and organized *before* the teaching situation." On the other hand, if the means are emphasized the planning will be psychological and personal, "the subject matter selected and organized cooperatively by all learners *during* the learning situation." Both procedures are doubtful because neither one will result in the optimum of functional learning or of personal growth. The first is too rigid—the second too free. Used alone, neither one provides sufficiently for both techniques and attitudes, skills and insights, to achieve alike personal satisfactions and concrete results. Yet some organizational plan is essential. How can this paradox be resolved?

The practical solution depends on the teacher's ability to recognize and coordinate the best features of both theories. The primary responsibility for instruction rests with the teacher, not with the student. If the student is actually qualified to determine the learning sequence, he has no place in the class. The notion that an ignorant but interested group can learn efficiently by an exchange of ideas is fallacious. The blind cannot lead the blind. Group learnings are only valid when directed and focused by a leader of superior background and knowledge. To him alone belongs the primary responsibility for planning the learning sequence. To do so he must think in terms both of the sequence as a whole and in parts. The broad general objectives should be determined first and the details then worked out in relation to them. Thus, in a very real sense, the first step cannot be determined until the last step is known. But this plan, though predetermined without cooperative action, is by no means a rigid, impersonal blueprint to be executed exactly at any cost. Rather, it is a preliminary sketch to be modified, when necessary, by the specific learning situation. The instructor's flexibility and resourcefulness are based on the existence of such a plan, not upon its absence. Alteration of a preconceived course of action is implicit in adaptation to a particular situation. In teaching, anticipation is as important as improvisation.

What is suggested then is a practical general plan subdivided into specific units of work that will be modified as occasion requires. It will evolve gradually, its details becoming clear and its procedures more definite in proportion to background and experience of the instructor and the amount of thought that he gives to it. When it is ready for use, details should be clear—but the procedures not rigidly fixed. As the course proceeds, new ideas will emerge and be incorporated. Evaluate each new unit in terms of the preceding one, and, in the actual presentation of the material, use improvisation to meet unexpected or novel situations. Such planning is very different from day-to-day improvisation, overnight preparation, or rigid adherence to the details of a previously used outline. In life we plan for more or less routine days yet often each is unique. The same is true of teaching. It is as futile to have no plan as to adhere rigidly to a preconceived one—perhaps even more so, since there is, after all, more similarity than difference in both teaching and life.

II

The teacher's plan is *a plan for learning* in reference to the learners, the material, and the time involved. As suggested above, all these phases are best handled through long-term planning which will give the proper emphasis and perspective. Specifically, this means that an entire year's work should be outlined well in advance in considerable detail—beginning with general objectives which will suggest specific steps for their achievement. Obviously no course will be successful if the instructor possesses only the minimum of knowledge and background for the course. Furthermore, an instructor fails who does not amplify and enrich the textbook used. To teach is to illumine the subject, which means that the instructor must be constantly acquiring an ever wider background to supplement the text material. Some general principles for planning may be summarized thus:

1. *A teaching outline should have definite focal points based on the context used.* Even a rich context may be ineffective because it is simply a mass of unrelated detail. Teaching is organized learning, and without focus is ineffective. It is not enough to expose students to good music: the experience must be made meaningful by context and emphasis. Teaching, like art, is selective—and the function of the teacher is to choose suitable material and to make it significant for the end in view. Above all, the focal points should be provocative and stimulating.

In passing, it should be noted that too much material is always better than too little. The best can then be selected. It is also desirable that the material used represent a cross-section of music literature, and not be concentrated in special areas, such as piano, vocal, or orchestral compositions. One of the desirable outcomes of "theoretic" study is a wider knowledge of the best in music literature.

2. *The time element in planning is also of great importance.* It is one of the best reasons for long term planning, since only through

determining in general the material to be covered in a year can the content of individual units be approximated. Careful consideration must be given to the general rate of speed, time required for assigned work, reviews, and tests. These problems can only be answered by experience, but in general it is safe to assume that any given operation will consume more time than is anticipated. In other words, allow ample time for every activity. Much good teaching is negated by speed on the part of the instructor. Students must be shown *how to work* efficiently. One hears constantly of hours being spent on assignments where minutes would have sufficed. Education is training in thinking.

3. *Courses should be so planned as to promote self-evaluation.* The whole question of evaluation will be treated at length later (see Chapter IX, page 196), but for the present it should be pointed out that formal tests are only one means of determining progress, and that the well-organized course will provide opportunities for the student to become aware of his strengths as well as his weaknesses. Self-evaluation is probably more acceptable psychologically than that made by the instructor, and for this reason alone opportunity for it should be included in planning through the setting up of practical problems and other self-checking devices. Group evaluation of work is also useful in this connection.

4. *Finally, planning must be in terms of the group concerned.* The teacher should learn to know the group in order that it, in turn, may learn from him. This is practical common sense, not impractical theory. It neither negates previous planning nor leaves the content of the course to be determined by the whims of the group. It simply recognizes the fact that meaningful learning is dependent on the cooperation of the learner and that this is best secured through an understanding of him. It is in this sense that the learner has a share in planning the course. His needs, desires, and reactions should be among the determinant factors in planning. The wise instructor will mold his preconceived plan to fit each particular group. The extent of this adjustment will depend upon many factors, too numerous to discuss here, but in general it should remain within the framework of the instructor's leadership. Of all group contributions, those of the instructor should be the most unique and valuable to justify his position of leadership. If students can discharge his function, the class may as well disband.[16]

In connection with planning in terms of a specific group, the age and maturity level of the group must also be considered. A "theory" course on the secondary or high school level will be organized with less technical emphasis than one for the liberal arts college. Again, courses in professional schools will differ from those in teachers colleges. However, one reservation must be made: all courses, on whatever level, should teach specific techniques suitable for that level, not merely generalized concepts without concrete applications. Whether the student is five or fifty, his study should give him definite technical skills adapted to his needs and his maturity. Too often secondary and high school "theoretic" instruction evaporates into vague "appreciation" because nothing concrete has been taught. Why not teach the "appreciation" of mathematics? Undoubtedly it would be beneficial, but so is the ability to use mathematics. After years in the secondary school, students reach high school without any real technical knowledge of music. The time to teach technique is when the student is so young he does not know it as such! If it is possible in other subjects it can be done in music.

In elementary schools the first contacts with music naturally should be concerned with basic orientation, but even here the child can learn such technical facts as contribute to this end. Gradually, *through experience*, the structure of music becomes clearer until, when junior high school is reached, the student has considerable insight into the organization of music and ability to handle basic technical problems, such as reading and notation. Such a background would enable the senior high school to carry on serious musical programs either preparatory for college, professional study, or for intelligent amateur enjoyment of the best in music throughout life. Instead, many students reach high school without even the ability to read music, due to the notion that technical knowledge is, in some mysterious way, inimical to enjoyment. True, not all desire or need to learn to read or write music, but certainly *the opportunity* should not be denied to those who wish to do so, and the whole program should be so oriented as to increase, rather than lessen, interest in technical aspects of music.

Indeed, many of the crucial problems of teaching "theory" in college or professional school arise precisely from this lack of background which should have acquired in childhood. A parallel exists in the learning of a foreign language, which is much more readily acquired by the child than by the adult. College students often grasp with difficulty elementary technical concepts that children learn readily under proper conditions. Hence, in planning, it is vital to make provision for some technical achievement at *all levels*, from kindergarten to college, if musical insight is ever to rise above the level of superficial "appreciation." This fact has long been recognized in other fields and deserves thoughtful consideration as regards music. It is sometimes argued that high school and even college students have not sufficient background for a systematized study of structure, but if such is the case, it is due to faulty training, not lack of intelligence or maturity. The technical aspects of music assuredly are no more difficult than those of mathematics, if as much so. The student who can master long division can harmonize a melody or write a song, if properly trained—and even enjoy doing so! For maximum enjoyment, music must be more than an emotional or social experience. Remarkable results have been achieved with average children under expert guidance. Let us not deceive ourselves by shifting the blame for poor results to the child's immaturity or the difficulty of the subject. One cannot gather grapes from thistles, but one can make the thistles bloom.

III

The principle of differentiation first appears in planning courses for liberal arts or teachers colleges and for professional schools. The "theory" course in a liberal arts college should certainly stress cultural as well as technical aspects of music. Music should be presented as one of the humanities, emphasizing the historical importance of figured bass, for example, and the influence of related arts. On the other hand, courses for professional needs, either as teacher or performer, would naturally stress more immediate and practical problems. Thus, arranging for various vocal or instrumental groups would receive more emphasis than figured bass. Score reading of all types, transposition, and the detection of errors in group-performances would all receive attention, as well as technical and æsthetic discrimination in the selection of music for performance. These are practical problems which confront the teacher and performer.

All technical "theoretic" training for the professional, either teacher or performer, should begin with a preliminary year of basic general study before differentiation for particular needs is introduced. Specifically, this means that the first-year course would provide a general structural background for subsequent specialization. In the second year the work could be differentiated for pianists, singers, conductors, and instrumentalists. If so, the work in this second year would be oriented to the special problems of the various fields of professional activity. However, the continual emphasis should be on *musicianship*, developed through an understanding of tonal relationships used for expressive and creative purposes and implemented by functional techniques. Beyond the second year the work naturally becomes increasingly specialized, until, on the graduate level, it is entirely devoted to special problems of style, technique, or composition. The planning of a curriculum to achieve these goals is a challenge and a joy that compensates for the labor involved. In doing so, the teacher is richly repaid, both by the students' and his own musical development.

However, it should be clearly understood that specialization, even on the graduate level, is difficult unless techniques are absorbed from the first contacts with music. In fact, the division of music into so-called "theoretic" and practical aspects retards musical growth on all levels. Knowing and doing are but halves of the whole, and emphasis on either results in distortion. Understanding is not something to be added *after* the experience of hearing or performing: it is part *of* the experience. The recognition of this basic fact, with its implications, would revolutionize not only the teaching of "theory" but of music instruction in general; for it means that *music* as related to playing, singing, listening, or creating, would be taught, not simply piano, voice, appreciation, or composition. This orientation solves many problems that beset teachers in all areas. Thus musicianship becomes the center and core of the learning process from which other activities radiate. Applied to curriculum planning, this implies that the focus will be primarily *musical rather than technical*: that objectives will be set up in terms of insight *through* the acquisition of technical skills rather than mastery of the skills *per se*.

IV

Two general principles for planning emerge when musicianship is regarded as both a means and as an end: first, music literature as the source material of learning, and second, full use and integration of the six avenues of learning, discussed in Chapters II—VII inclusive. Both concepts have been considered previously, but they should be reviewed in terms of curriculum construction before the problems of planning individual courses are raised.

The use of music literature as the source material of instruction is essentially a radical yet reasonable notion. Its acceptance shifts the implicit emphasis of teaching from "theory" to practice, from skills to music. But its application in turn will require musicianship on the part of the teacher based upon real interest in musical relationships. It is a truism that learning is dependent on curiosity.[17] Without it teaching becomes static and the results negative. The teacher, then, must have a constantly widening knowledge of music literature if he is to really teach music and not simply facts about it. The acquisition of this knowledge is not an unwelcome task to the music lover: it is the inevitable result of genuine interest in music. All musical experiences contribute to it—all music heard and performed furnish data. The only problem is to record and organize these varied musical sources for teaching purposes. To do so requires the building of an adequate library, patience, enthusiasm, and insatiable curiosity. Once the basic premise is accepted and applied, the teacher will be overwhelmed by the quantity and quality of material available.

But the use of music literature for instruction suggests new patterns of organization and learning sequence. Even a cursory survey will reveal differences between practice as found in literature and "theory" as taught in textbooks. One of the most obvious and suggestive is the relative importance of technical facts as determined by use-frequency in literature. This notion has been chiefly applied to the harmonic vocabulary but it is equally applicable to all technical data. It is, in fact, the most rational basis of organized instruction, once primary goals have been determined; and is practically mandatory, if music, not "theory," is to be taught. Let us consider more precisely the underlying philosophy and its application to the teaching of harmony.

The order of chords, as usually presented, consists of fundamental triads, chords of the 6th, six-four chords, fundamental 7th chords, their inversions, and 9th chords. This sequence has no basis in music literature. It is purely arbitrary—based upon a logical rather than psychological arrangement of material. For example, composers very rarely use fundamental triads exclusively—yet the typical text devotes considerable space to them, before more practical material is presented. If, then, this sequence is faulty, what sequence should be used? Manifestly the sequence of chord-frequency to be found in music literature.

The idea of *chord-frequency* is not entirely new. Certain texts have deviated from the usual order of chords cited above, apparently because of a growing skepticism regarding its validity. But thus far few have abandoned it completely and based the presentation entirely upon use-frequency. (106). This is somewhat curious, since the idea has long been basic in the teaching of languages. It seems obvious that the most important vocabulary to teach, either in music or language, is the one most used. Furthermore, acceptance of music as a basis of instruction makes it almost mandatory, since the student, in order to function successfully, needs to learn first the chords that he encounters most frequently in literature. Nevertheless, the idea has aroused some opposition, partly from sheer inertia, but also because of doubt as to the existence of a clear order of frequency and of its practical teaching value if such an order can be established. Both of these objections merit examination. The pattern of use-frequency for diatonic chords has been validated by extensive research. Such a pattern *does exist* in music of the 18th and 19th centuries. It is possible to list the ten most frequently used diatonic chords within this span. The second objection, that of teaching value, seems to be the crux of the matter. The bases of the opposition are varied. Apparently some defenders of the *status quo* have a lingering desire to progress logically from what is regarded as the simple to the complex. Others take the opposite view by criticizing the approach as too mechanistic, on the theory that any organization is bad organization. Here, however, only the *degree* of organization is actually involved, since some planning, however loose, is essential for teaching. Still others maintain that the use-frequency sequence is actually more difficult to learn since the chord-forms are not presented in the logical order of their structure. This is the only objection that deserves serious consideration. Are chord-forms more difficult to understand and use when presented in the order found in literature? The answer is emphatically in the negative. A moment's reflection will show that the problem of writing *musically* for fundamental triads alone is much more difficult than that of using inversions and dissonances. And once more we are brought back to the primacy of *musical* over "*theoretic*" problems. "Theory" is not a *corpus* of technical facts to be learned as rapidly and painlessly as possible and then to be forgotten when "real music" or composition is studied. Properly taught, *it is music,* and any educational approach to the art that separates the two is open to very serious question. Why learn "traditional harmony" in order to forget it? Music today is the sum of all previous techniques extended through experimental practice, and any valid theory of music education must recognize this fact. In the light of this conclusion, *the basic criterion of pedagogy is its musicality*. For this reason, the principle of chord-frequency offers the best compromise between the prevalent arbitrary logical pattern and the mere random sampling of harmonic effects.

In concluding our discussion of musical literature as the basis of instruction, one essential corollary of the principle should be stressed, namely, that the music used should coincide with the student's musical contacts. In other words, *it should be a cross-section of 18th- and 19th-century music literature for all media.* This breadth of selection is especially desirable in fundamental courses. Concentration upon a particular period or medium is appropriate only in advanced courses. Since the bulk of music heard and performed by the student was written in the period between Bach's birth and Brahms' death, this body of literature is the logical basis of instruction below the graduate level, but without stress on any particular portion or medium. The undergraduate student requires *a working knowledge* neither of Renaissance nor of Impressionistic techniques. Understanding of them is the function of survey courses, not of the undergraduate "theory" class.

The application of this corollary entails, *from the beginning,* a careful balance between instrumental and vocal writing using examples and problems drawn from all media. It does not mean concentration upon four-part vocal writing of a particular period, nor the aimless sampling of literature from Palestrina to Prokofieff, ignoring temporal and stylistic sequences. Group education must be organized for practical reasons, and *it is the function of the instructor to provide organization that will result in progressive clarification of the music studied.* The process of education is one of gradually emerging insights and understandings. Skills sharpen these insights, but skills must be sufficiently developed to perform this function. It is futile to expect a student, without adequate technical preparation, to be able to write any specific type of composition merely from a classroom analysis of its structure. As well expect a beginning pianist to play a concerto from an explanation of the technical problems involved! True, we learn by doing, but by doing well, not badly. The philosophy is admirable—but the application faulty.

Hence, in the use of musical literature, we are confronted with two extremes of procedure: one that uses all types of literature in any order as a basis of instruction, expecting students to be able to reproduce these types after classroom analysis of them, and the other that emphasizes one particular period of literature using one medium exclusively. Both are obviously deficient in terms of a well-rounded and consistent use of literature. The first, by emphasis on general knowledge without adequate technical foundation, tends to superficiality and faulty techniques. In learning, generalizations are good beginnings but poor endings. The second, through premature specialization, fails to give the general, over-all view of literature and the techniques of various media. Truly the whole is greater than the parts.

The rational use of literature, as indicated above, would appear to be a compromise between these two extremes of generalization and specialization. What the *undergraduate student* in any type of school really needs is first, an explanation of the music he hears or performs, and second, an adequate concept of the whole range of literature during the 18th and 19th centuries. If he is brought in contact with music beyond these limits, the explanation of it properly belongs in *survey courses*. He has neither the time nor the skill to master other techniques adequately. If he tries to do so, the result tends to be a smattering of ignorance.

Such a philosophy recognizes the educational value of both Renaissance and contemporary idioms. But why attempt to write in either of them if the student cannot analyze or imitate the idiom of *Parsifal*, for example? Musical techniques follow natural laws of development. No period is independent of its past, and it can only be adequately understood as a part of an historical sequence. Time for instruction on the undergraduate level is limited, and hence should be concerned with the contents of the circle of common musical experience, not with either one segment or its periphery.

The graduate level is the appropriate field for specialization. Here specific periods, media, and techniques can be fruitfully studied upon an adequate intellectual and technical basis. In fact, it is only on this level that the student has the requisite maturity and background for such intensive study. Many problems of curriculum planning will be solved if this essential point is understood and applied. But adequate undergraduate preparation is implicit in such a principle. Graduate instruction must not be hampered by students lacking essential background whose foundation should have been laid in the elementary school. Today there is an alarming tendency to reduce graduate study to an undergraduate level, particularly in respect to skills. It is the responsibility of the schools to train leaders as well as followers—and training for leadership can only be functional if the graduate student is a superior student with adequate preparation.

V

The second general concept derived from the primacy of musicianship is that of the integration of all avenues of learning. Similar to the use of musical literature and chord-frequency, this concept has been applied for some time, though rather negatively. In general, "theory" courses fall into two patterns: either the written harmony class, which includes some "ear training" and keyboard harmony, is supplemented by classes in "sight singing" and analysis, or all these phases are taught quite independently in separate classes. Obviously both patterns leave much to be desired. In the first, the emphasis is usually placed on written skills, and the aural and keyboard applications are apt to be very superficial or spasmodic. In the second, too often each instructor goes his own way, and the student receives a very confused and contradictory impression of musical structure and of the purpose and use of skills.

The logical solution is, of course, the integration of written and keyboard harmony, music reading, dictation, analysis, and creative work in a single large class, or "workshop," taught by one instructor. Such a class would meet at least four, possibly five, days weekly *to give a unified concept* of musical structure for practical, creative, or cultural purposes. The class can be organized on two bases: either the various aspects of "theory" may be taught at regular periods, or all phases can be so integrated that no special time is assigned for any one. Both plans have advantages. The first is more easily administered and guarantees equal emphasis on all phases. Integration is secured through a unity of presentation and material used. Special problems can be carried over from day to day and solved in a different area from their origin. The skilful instructor can develop a high degree of interrelationship between each recitation during the week. The second plan, however, has distinct advantages through its flexibility. Immediate application of principles can be made to all phases of work. In it there is no artificial separation of means. It provides a genuinely unified study of structure. However, certain dangers should be noted, principally a difference in emphasis, either individually or as a group. That is, it is quite easy to spend more time upon one phase than upon another, sometimes for apparently valid reasons. Thus the end-results may vary in achievement. This is a crucial point indeed, since the whole theory of a varied approach rests on the parity of all phases. In other words, writing, reading, listening, playing, analyzing, and creating *are all of equal importance;* and any procedure which produces imbalance between them is questionable. This lack of balance can occur quite as readily with individual as with group achievement, and it is equally deplorable in either case. This is not to disregard individual differences—for no teacher expects all students to be equally proficient in all areas—but it does recognize the basic premise that achievement, whether of the individual or of the group, should be relatively uniform in the six avenues of learning. In general, however, the second plan offers better opportunities for musical growth than the first, although both are far superior to the majority of current procedures.

If these are the educational advantages of a unified class, what are its practical aspects? Two problems arise immediately—personal and temporal. The first is undoubtedly the most troublesome for many reasons, primarily because of the difficulty of finding one instructor capable of teaching all phases equally well. However, this is a practical, though hardly valid, reason against such a plan, and only emphasizes what has been said before regarding the prime importance of functional musicianship for instructors as well as for students. But there are other personal difficulties. Even if a competent instructor were available, there may be many staff members who have specialized in one phase for years and who consequently would oppose any change in the curriculum, either from sincere professional reasons or because it would imperil their position. This is the most difficult problem in connection with reorganization, and it is best met realistically by accepting the *status quo* and by making changes as expeditiously as circumstances permit. A sweeping reorganization in the face of faculty opposition is rarely, if ever, justified, and then only because of proved incompetency on the part of those involved.

The second problem—that of fitting a unified class into the existing schedule—is much less difficult. In fact, it may solve some more troublesome problems, since it serves to unify the whole program. Naturally any schedule must be planned around such a class, as it should meet at the same hour daily. The primary consideration here is one of educational and administrative efficiency; this being the case, the objection of possible inconvenience to the students need not be taken too seriously.

One point regarding the programming of a unified class needs clarification. Specialized keyboard application for non-pianists is provided elsewhere, as stated in Chapter V, pages 94-96. Consequently they participate only in the *general* keyboard activities, and do not register for the full number of credits or attend all recitations of the unified class. For this reason it is necessary to indicate, in organizing the course, the keyboard recitation from which they are excused. Hence, even in the most flexible and unified learning sequence, some specific time must be allotted for keyboard harmony which non-pianists do not take.

Somewhat related to this adjustment for non-pianists is the possible differentiation, in the second year of college or professional study, between the work of students having different performing media. After the first year it is highly desirable that "theory" be adapted to the students' area of specialization. This can be done in two ways: either by varying the class assignments to meet individual needs, or by setting up separate classes for pianists, singers, and instrumentalists. The first solution is troublesome, especially in large classes, and the second is impractical in many cases. Probably this is one of those ideal adjustments that must be made gradually as circumstances permit.

One other type of unification requires passing mention, namely, the consolidation of all instruction in written harmony into one large class for each level, while the criticism of assignments is done in a second small class by a different instructor. Thus the student receives two hours weekly of instruction in written harmony, instead of one hour, as is customary. Theoretically this appears to be an excellent device, but in practice it reveals several deficiencies. In the first place, instruction may be more efficient in a group of sixty, but it cannot be as thorough, due to the lack of personal contact with the instructor and the size of the class. Second, the change of instructors in the two classes does not always promote learning. Third, teachers of the small groups sometimes are less capable than the large-group instructor. And fourth, and most important, the psychological effect on the teacher of the small group is bad. He has no responsibility for planning or for instruction, and consequently is relegated to a secondary role which is apt to be keenly felt. The criticism of the students' notebooks tends to become a routine task that offers little or no opportunity for personal growth or initiative. The situation is not challenging and as such is bad educationally. Hence, from the standpoint of both the learner and the instructor this device is somewhat questionable, although under ideal conditions it has merit. It is a technique of mass education—a tendency too prevalent in our schools today.

VI

The discussion in the two preceding sections—of music literature as source material and of the place of the single unified "theory" class in the curriculum—has prepared for a detailed consideration of the planning of specific courses on various levels for differing situations. This problem will be approached through the six avenues of learning, but it must be repeated that such an approach is for convenience only, and in no way negates what has been said above regarding the value of integration. In fact, the discussion will conclude with definite suggestions for integration. It should also be noted that the discussion is focused on *planning*, not teaching, which was treated at length in Chapters II—VII. Specimen outlines of courses will be found in Appendices I and II, with typical assignments for them.

1. WRITING

1. Writing includes all levels of structural study from rudiments to composition. Planning of written work is best conceived in terms of these levels, thus:

(a) ELEMENTARY SCHOOL

A simple, general treatment of rudiments, principles of form, and creative expression, largely for purposes of orientation. Rich musical experience *from which* technical facts are derived Optional experience in notation.

(b) JUNIOR HIGH SCHOOL

Clarification and extension of work on the secondary school level, including use of primary triads and dominant seventh chord in the major mode.

(c) SENIOR HIGH SCHOOL

Elective classes giving a general survey of harmony and harmonic techniques, the emphasis being primarily on diatonic forms but including a few of the most used chromatic chords. Achievement in two years should be sufficiently concrete to enable superior students to enter the second-year harmony class in college. The work should include vocal and instrumental writing and arranging adjusted to the performance level of the group.

(d) LIBERAL ARTS COLLEGE

First Year: diatonic harmony (Classic period).

Second Year: chromatic harmony (Romantic period).

Third Year: vocal and instrumental counterpoint (Renaissance and Baroque periods).[18]

Fourth Year: orchestration, composition, or a combination of both. These technical courses would also be open to non-music majors having adequate background. The emphasis would be on music as a fine art with its cultural implications. Should be supplemented by a survey course of music literature.

(e) TEACHERS COLLEGE

Same as the first two years of (d) above but with emphasis upon practical teaching problems. Non-music majors would require less intensive courses similar to (b) and (c) above. Both types of students should have a supplementary survey course of music literature, and a course in "theory" methods should be given for music majors. Orchestration and arranging should occupy the third and final year for music majors.

(f) PROFESSIONAL SCHOOL

The conservatory offers the best opportunity for the training of very young students in musicianship. Here the complete integration of all phases of "theory" is most natural and most effective. Hence, in considering the curriculum for the professional school, all the work outlined for students of elementary and high school age is given below for the six avenues of learning, although they are listed separately for convenience. Awareness of musical structures should begin at the earliest age with a feeling for rhythm developed through various percussion instruments, preceding the study of a major instrument, and with considerable physical response by walking, running, skipping, and clapping. Reading and writing are approached through the informal analysis of familiar folk melodies which also serve as a basis for creative work. All technical facts are derived from the music sung and analyzed, and then applied as needed to the various techniques of expression. The material covered may be summarized thus:

Elementary level

Written work: rudiments, use of all triads, the V_7, the I_4^6, and the II_6 for melody harmonization in instrumental styles.

Dictation: response by singing, playing, or writing. Notation of rhythm, melody, bass, and name of chord—both separately and in combination.

Keyboard harmony: use of all chords listed in (a) above for harmonization and improvisation in period and small A-B-A forms.

Music reading: singing of folksongs with words, and chords with letters and accidentals.

Analysis: form, cadences, chords, and non-harmonic tones of all material used.

Creative: use of all material learned in period, A-B-A, and variation forms.

High School Level

Extension of work as presented on the elementary level to
include all diatonic harmony applied to both instrumental
and to four-part vocal writing.

It should be stressed again that all the above material *is
presented in a single class* through a complete integration
of all these techniques. The work outlined will occupy
approximately eight years. Much has been accomplished in
a number of schools following this plan. Children and
young people respond intuitively to music, and when these
insights are a part of musical experience *from the beginning*, skills are acquired naturally and almost unconsciously.
In fact, the fatal separation between "theory" and music
never occurs, and the student's insights and skills keep pace
with his progress as a performer. Here is the secret of
teaching musicianship: *to make it a vital element of all
musical experiences from the outset.*

The program outlined above covers all work up to the
college level. Consequently, subsequent statements regarding the curriculum of the professional school will assume
this background and begin on the college level.

College level

Same as (d) above, but with emphasis on professional
problems, supplemented by two years' survey of music literature, the first general, and the second devoted to the
student's area of specialization. A course in the teaching of
"theory" should also be offered.

(g) GRADUATE LEVEL

Genuine specialization should begin at this level, but too often
undergraduate achievements vary so widely in different schools
that much previous material must be reviewed before the student is prepared for real graduate work. However, *no graduate
credit should be given for making up these undergraduate
deficiencies*, as is sometimes done. Appropriate graduate studies would include skill in:

the Bach chorale idiom

the 19th-century twelve-tone scale

artificial scales   for all

contemporary idioms   media

the larger homophonic and polyphonic forms

five to eight-voice polyphony.

In reference to the above, several points should be noted. Contemporary idioms should be included only when *both* the student and the instructor are properly qualified. Such work should be as definite and precise as strict counterpoint, and not simply be aimless experimentation in dissonant sonorities. *The larger homophonic and contrapuntal forms are suitable only for graduate work.* It is both ludicrous and pathetic to find undergraduates who have had a year's course, or possibly only a semester, in composition in which they have written one example of every form from a phrase to a fugue! On the undergraduate level, knowledge of these larger forms should come from analysis, not writing. The small song-forms alone require at least a year of intensive practice. Nothing is gained on any level by superficiality under the guise of "breadth." Survey, *not technical*, courses are the proper vehicle for such exploration, especially on the undergraduate level, where incompetence should not be tolerated.

One specialized course in writing techniques requires additional comment, namely, orchestration and arranging. The theory and practice of teaching orchestration was discussed in Chapter II, pages 35-36, but the planning of the course was not discussed. Orchestration occupies a unique place in the curriculum because of its professional value for instrumental teachers, conductors, composers, and arrangers. In the liberal arts college it quite properly is delayed until the final year; but in teacher-training institutions, especially on the graduate level where time is short, it often is necessary for it to be taken concurrently with other "theory" courses. This means that the background of individual students will vary widely, and consequently in such a situation the course must be organized to accommodate these individual differences.

This is done by setting up assignments at the student's own working level. Those of limited background work on easy transcriptions, but in terms of the approach outlined in Chapter II. By avoiding complicated scoring techniques the student at this level not only practices the techniques presented with aural association, but he also has opportunity to further his knowledge of the particular instruments being studied.

The intermediate student is expected to undertake scoring projects of greater difficulty than the beginner. Many students in this category devote much effort to the study of and writing in various styles of orchestration. Students are encouraged to select a composition, usually for piano, retaining the melodic line and harmonic structure, and on this base create appropriate orchestral material. In some cases as many as six or eight orchestral versions are made of one passage.

The advanced students are encouraged to write original composi-tions. Most students welcome this opportunity of combining compo-sition with orchestration, specially as it gives them the occasion to explore methods of scoring that they have either not tried before or else have tried unsuccessfully. All written work is tested immediately in class, as outlined in Chapter II.

This approach is an example of functional planning. It provides for individual differences of background and ability, implemented by flexible assignments which are evaluated by the group and the in-structor from a visible score and a "live" performance. Such organiza-tion of material and evaluation of results could very profitably be applied to other types of written skills, especially for large groups where attention to individual needs is often lacking.

2. READING

2. Reading is one of the most important means for the develop-ment of musical insight. As has been stated previously, it is primarily concerned with the ability to *think music*, that is, to read it silently. Vocal expression is only the objectification of this mental concept. Hence, ability to "sight sing" can hardly be regarded as the principal goal, but rather as a concomitant learning—resulting from the ability to think and to hear music abstractly. This understanding of the nature and purpose of reading is basic to all instruction in it. The im-mediate problem, of course, is to make notation meaningful, to trans-late symbol into sound. This ability develops from a broad and rich experience in rote singing, with emphasis, in the child's own terms, on the structural elements of the music. Early introduction of the score is desirable, but simply as a picture or symbol of the tonal pattern. In other words, reading grows from musical experience and should parallel, not anticipate, it. These considerations are essential in planning a music reading sequence. Needless to say, all material would be either folksongs or music drawn from literature.

(a) ELEMENTARY SCHOOL

Rote experience from which definite technical learnings and skills gradually develop, leading to the ability to read simple one- and two-part music. (See the Rochester Plan outlined in Chapter III, pages 49-51.)

(b) JUNIOR HIGH SCHOOL

Further development of reading skill, both vocal and instru-mental, based on musical experience. Singing in three parts.

(c) Senior High School

Four-part singing and extensive practice in instrumental reading, both for piano, and band and orchestral instruments.

(d) Liberal Arts College

First Year: thorough review of diatonic material from the beginning. Introduction of C clef on third line of staff, singing letter names of pitches, but not accidentals. Emphasis
on reading music silently. Drill singing chord progressions
in arpeggio form, from Roman numerals, using letter
names and accidentals. Study of major choral work for
solo and part-singing with words. (Preferably a recorded
work so that not only the portions studied but the entire
work be heard and discussed musically.) Singing of all
major and minor scales, using letters and accidentals.

Second year: continuation of the first year, using chromatic
material. Introduction of the C clef on the fourth line of
the staff. Singing letter names of pitches, but not accidentals. Silent reading and the singing of chromatic and modulatory chord progressions as described above. Major choral work employing chromaticism studied in class. Singing
of the chromatic scale in all major and minor keys, using
letters and accidentals.

Two books would be used for each year or semester: a
sightsinging manual without words for drill, and an important choral composition for singing with words. Several excellent manuals are available consisting entirely of
folksongs or melodies from music literature. The choral
work should be chosen in reference to the maturity of the
student and its relevancy to the harmonic material being
studied. For example, in the first year a good song collection might be used for the first semester, and Haydn's
Creation for the second. For the two semesters in the second year, Mozart's *Requiem*, Mendelssohn's *Elijah*, Brahms'
Requiem, or Bach's *B minor Mass* would all be appropriate. The easier solos could be assigned for individual work
and the simpler choruses sung at sight. In all cases, the expressive and structural aspects of the score should be discussed so that the experience be a truly musical one—not
merely a technical drill.

In connection with the learning of the C clef, it should be
noted that simple passages for viola or cello from orches-

tral scores used in dictation can be sung, thus integrating
different aspects of structural study.

Third Year: continuation of chromatic material of the second
year. Introduction of the C clef on the first line of the
staff, as above. More difficult modulations to all keys
through each chromatic chord, as above. Review of chromatic scales. Major choral works—at least one of the 20th
century. In the third year the only material used would be
choral works. For the first semester, Bach's *The Passion
According to St. Matthew* would furnish excellent material for study of the C clef on the first, third, and fourth
lines of the staff, as well as for an understanding of a
Baroque full score. The chorales are ideal for part-singing.
For the second semester, a modern work such as Kodály's
Missa Brevis is recommended for an acquaintance with
contemporary idioms.

Fourth Year: this year, when offered, should be devoted to an
historical survey of song literature and the further study
of contemporary choral works. At this level the stress
would be largely appreciative in the sense that there would
be no technical drills—the emphasis being entirely on the
historical, stylistic, and expressive characteristics of the
works studied.

(e) TEACHERS COLLEGE

The first and second years would be similar to (d) above, except that material for school use should be emphasized. These
courses would be designed for students majoring in music.
Other students would require specially planned courses in all
areas. The third and fourth years of (d) above would hardly
be suitable or practical in a teacher-training institution.

(f) PROFESSIONAL SCHOOL

Same as the first three years of (d) above for all students.
The fourth year mandatory for vocalists.

(g) GRADUATE LEVEL

At this level the ability to think music and to reproduce it
vocally should be sufficiently mastered for practical purposes.
Further work could well include an intensive study of choral
music of the Renaissance period through actual performance
and stylistic analysis. However, it should be stressed once more
that any undergraduate deficiency on this level should be met
without graduate credit.

3. LISTENING

3. Listening, as the only sensory response to music, permeates all avenues of learning at all levels. As William Schuman says, "The first requisite for a musician in any branch of the art is that he be a virtuoso listener, (but) an ability to hear the component parts of the language of music . . . does not *ipso facto* mean integrated understanding." (209). This is a clear statement of both the goal and the problem of listening. Although discussed in Chapter IV, pages 63-67, further clarification of the problem is needed before the content of specific courses in listening can be considered.

The problem lies in the relationship between general listening and specific "ear training." The former relies primarily upon language and the latter upon notation for the recording of what is heard. The existing dichotomy between them results from a misunderstanding of their respective functions and of their essential interrelationships. Here again, goals must be precisely defined in terms of the learner and of his status as amateur or professional. In general, however, it may be stated that functional listening is dependent upon a balance between vague generalizations and specific details. In other words, the aural focus must be sufficiently sharp to have real musical significance. This is the crux of the problem: what is the role of specific techniques in the development of general understandings?

This question is basic to all education, and the answer to it will be varied. Techniques are tools and should be so used—not as ends but as means; or, as Virgil Thomson remarks, "Technical routines, nevertheless, not talent or inspiration, are the basis of any transmissible skill." [19] Listening, because of its intangibility, especially needs the support of concrete and specific facts such as the distinction between chord qualities, registers, rhythms. and textures. These distinctions are best validated by writing. Dictation furnishes the most conclusive proof of precise hearing. Wisely used, it measures apprehension. It does not *necessarily* imply ability beyond the specific skill, but it usually does so, simply because it demonstrates a firm mental grasp of aural perception, which is the best basis for generalized understandings. Listening is mental, not physical, *and the difficulty of written dictation lies in this fact, not in the physical process of reproduction.* The objection that excellent musicians may lack this skill is irrelevant. As well say that fine pitch discrimination should not be cultivated because Robert Schumann lacked it, since one of the reasons for his dismissal as musical director at Düsseldorf was his inability to keep the orchestra in tune! As an index of aural perception, written dictation is an essential factor in any realistic approach to intelligent listening.

In planning courses in listening and "ear training" a clear distinction must be made between general and specific music study. On the elementary and secondary levels the emphasis undoubtedly should be general, yet the *opportunity* for specialization should be given as need arises, certainly in high school. Otherwise, latent talent will be sacrificed to musical mediocrity. Music is both a social and an individual art, and there is no reason to assume that these dual aspects are antagonistic or mutually exclusive. Furthermore, the *tempo* of class experiences and learnings on all levels should be adjusted to the mean, not to the extremes of ability within the group.

All these factors must be considered in planning courses to promote intelligent listening: clear goals and specific means for their achievement. The role of technique is involved with both. Naturally, all material used will be drawn from music literature with the purpose, not only of developing an integrated understanding of structure, but also of widening the student's musical horizon. The courses on various levels may be outlined thus:

(a) ELEMENTARY SCHOOL

> Orientation to listening through recognition of simple melodic patterns, sequences, and phrase lengths. Transfer to writing of original songs and possibly of familiar melodies. All listening exploratory and general, becoming more precise only for explanation of specific effects heard. Emphasis on oral responses, writing being used only incidentally.

(b) JUNIOR HIGH SCHOOL

> Introduction of harmonic feeling through the cadential tonic and dominant chords. Introduction of written dictation through familiar melodies. Oral recognition of I, IV, V, and V7 in the major mode, with experimentation in writing the melody, bass, and name of chord.

(c) SENIOR HIGH SCHOOL

> Aural analysis paralleling work in written harmony. Emphasize general effects rather than specific details of melody, harmony, and form. Use written dictation as a tool to gradually focus these general concepts. The material used should be familiar so that writing will be a transfer of previously recognized tonal effects.

(d) LIBERAL ARTS COLLEGE

First Year: written dictation paralleling diatonic material of written harmony. Recognition of simple one-, two-, and three-part forms. Directed listening to symphonic or chamber music works of the Classic period with miniature score, correlated with current harmonic vocabulary. Memorization of thematic material (melody only) of works studied.

Second Year: written dictation paralleling chromatic material of written harmony, including Bach chorales. Recognition of five-part song-form, song-form with trio, and simple rondos. Directed listening to symphonic or chamber music works of the Romantic period from miniature score, correlated with current harmonic vocabulary. Memorization of thematic material (melody only) of works studied.

In regard to material, passages for dictation should be presented *as a unit*, for the writing of the melody, bass, name of chord, and form, not as isolated drills for these elements. In other words, no separate drills should be given for rhythm, pitch, or any of these elements *alone* unless in exceptional cases. Furthermore, both records and the piano should be used for dictation, since the sound of the music varies with the medium. In directed listening, attention should be called to the general form of each movement, the organization of the score, and to harmonic progressions which are being studied currently.

Third Year: simple two-part dictation. Modal harmony. The 19th-century use of the twelve-tone scale. Continuation of directed listening, including works of the 20th century. Use of C clef.

Fourth Year: aural analysis (analytic dictation) of the principal musical forms recorded. These forms may be sketched by use of letters and various arbitrary symbols.[20]

(See Chapter IV, pages 73-75, for a discussion of two-part and analytic dictation. Work in the third year should include as much material as possible from the contrapuntal written work of that year. As in the liberal arts college courses outlined above, these listening courses would be open to non-music majors of adequate background.)

(e) TEACHERS COLLEGE

The first two years would correspond to those of (d) above,

but with emphasis on "corrective listening" for rehearsal, as described in Chapter IV, page 74. There should also be some use of the C clef for score reading. Should an additional year be offered, the most practical would be the analytic dictation suggested for the fourth year of (d) above. The material used for all courses probably would be more related to school use than that of (d), although breadth of view and cultural value must be taken into account in the selection of material for any school or level.

(f) PROFESSIONAL SCHOOL

Same as (d) above, with special orientation toward the student's performing medium, possibly through separate classes on the higher levels for singers, pianists, etc.

As regards specialization, a strong protest should be made against the prevalent practice of requiring less listening, including dictation, from certain types of students, particularly vocalists and orchestral players. Rational justification of such a practice is difficult, whatever practical considerations are involved. Aural discrimination and acuity are particularly necessary for non-keyboard performers. As regards time involved in mastery of a medium, certainly piano stands high, yet pianists are usually required to do more "theoretic" work than other students. It is difficult to conceive what *musical* and *educational* justifications exist for excusing singers and orchestral players from any "theoretic" study required of pianists, except keyboard harmony. As a consequence of this policy, our professional schools are turning out graduates in these areas whose musicianship is below the level of that required of the pianist. The conscientious singer and orchestral player justly resent such discrimination as a reflection upon their intelligence. Even more distressing is the artist-teacher who deplores the amount of time that his students are required to spend on the acquisition of musical insights in "theory" classes.

(g) GRADUATE LEVEL

Specialization in a particular period. Dictation of Bach chorales in open score, using soprano, alto, and tenor clefs. More difficult two-part dictation.

With adequate preparation, the graduate level offers limitless possibilities for aural exploration, e.g., exotic scales, contemporary idioms, or analysis of orchestral color, as well as large general problems of form, texture, and style.

4. PLAYING

4. Playing (keyboard application) may be one of the most valuable avenues of learning, both for the clarification of musical structure and for the solution of practical problems. All students should have some keyboard experience *from the beginning* of "theoretic" study. The problem of providing this experience for non-pianists has been discussed in Chapter V, pages 94-96, and hence the following suggestions apply *only to piano majors* or to students with adequate technical facility.

(a) ELEMENTARY SCHOOL

Work on this level should parallel other exploratory experiences in writing, singing, and listening. Activities might include finding or matching pitches on the piano (leading to an understanding of the octave groups), and the playing of simple melodies or melodic patterns *by ear*. Sequential melodies are helpful in all musical activities on this level. Melodic improvisation, either of short patterns or complete phrases, is useful in developing a sense of pitch and structural relationships. Instrumental experience can well begin with percussion instruments and then be transferred to the piano.

(b) JUNIOR HIGH SCHOOL

Continuation of exploratory keyboard experiences paralleling those in other areas. Develop ability to pick out major and minor scales—if only with one finger, as well as the I, IV, V, and V7 in major, using one hand. Encourage playing by ear.

(c) SENIOR HIGH SCHOOL

Harmonization of folksongs. Ability to play in close position all chords studied and simple cadential patterns. Encourage playing by ear, and improvisation.

(d) LIBERAL ARTS COLLEGE

First Year: keyboard application of all written techniques. Introduction of transposition, using folksong material or simple piano literature (e.g., portions of Schumann's or Tchaikovsky's compositions for children). Improvisation in the one-, two-, and three-part forms. Repertoire of themes to be played by ear in various keys. Each theme should illustrate the chord being currently studied.

Second Year: continuation of first year work in relation to written techniques. Transposition of song accompaniments giving general survey of song literature. Improvisation through the five-part song form with simple extensions. Enlarge thematic repertoire to be played by ear, illustrating current chord.

It should be noted that these activities *do not* include formalized chord drills except as specific needs arise. Such drill can be either prepared outside of class or done in class without preparation, but only to clarify the particular chord being presented. (See Chapter V, page 81.) Neither should playing from figured bass be a regular activity, although enough of it should be done for the student to understand its principles. When used, the soprano line should be given.

Third Year: intensive study of the chorale idiom, with more emphasis upon figured bass. Transposition of contrapuntal works to parallel written work (e.g., the Bach *Two-Part Inventions* and the *Well Tempered Clavier*). Introduce reading of the vocal score (first semester) and the string quartet score (second semester). Begin improvisation in the variation form.

Fourth Year: harmonization of difficult chromatic melodies in piano style, with stress on piano literature. Parallel transposition of song literature. Introduce reading of orchestral scores. Continue improvisation in variation form and experiment with simple rondos.

(e) TEACHERS COLLEGE

The first two years would correspond to those of (d) above with these differences: material used should be related to professional needs; improvisation should be geared to rhythmic activities of children; "ear repertoire" to consist of familiar songs, and finally the reading of vocal, string, and orchestral scores should be introduced, with emphasis depending upon the needs of the students. These four differences between the liberal arts and teachers college courses will, of course, reduce the quantity of material than can be covered in the latter. The courses should be oriented to practical professional problems, stressing insight into and use of the structural material of music. Hence it is particularly important that the courses in the teachers college recognize the differing needs of the general supervisor and of the vocal and instrumental teacher. This can be done best by providing *a common foundation for*

all, with differentiation in the second year. It is doubtful
whether the crowded curriculum will permit more than two
years of keyboard study. However, if more were possible,
further work should undoubtedly stress specialization in particular areas.

(f) PROFESSIONAL SCHOOL

Same as (d) above. Here the need for specialization is somewhat similar to that in teachers colleges, except that the work
may be technically more advanced. Less emphasis on figured
bass is required than in a liberal arts college, except in the case
of organists. The first two years of (d) are desirable for all
students with sufficient piano technique, otherwise two years
in the special classes for non-pianists described in Chapter
V, page 94.

(g) GRADUATE LEVEL

Advanced transposition and score reading. Study of contemporary chord forms and practices, (72), and their use in improvisation. Once more it should be emphasized that *some keyboard
application is essential for all students on all levels*. Failure to
recognize this fact contributes to the schism between "theory"
and practice. But even when recognized and applied, it functions imperfectly unless kept abreast of growth in other areas.
There is no logical justification for a "lag" in keyboard or
aural apprehension behind written skills, which should be adjusted to the learning capacity in these areas if necessary.

5. ANALYZING

5. Analyzing is the process of recognizing the relation of structural details to a unified whole. *It should be both aural and visual*,
and should permeate all musical activities, for without it music may
be only a succession of sensuous tonal perceptions devoid of coherence or design. Analysis can be either conscious or unconscious, or
a mixture of both. *It is primarily recognition of design*.

Analysis, as an integral part of musical experience, should never be
isolated or studied *per se*. It is an explanation of heard phenomena and
must be treated as a large unit of many factors, except when one of
these factors requires special clarification. For this reason separate
courses in harmonic analysis, contrapuntal analysis, or form are very
questionable indeed. The "teaching" of analysis is inseparable from the
teaching of any phase of musical structure. It is inconsistent to offer

a two-year course in harmony, followed by a course in "harmonic analysis." As well teach piano for two years and follow it by a course in phrasing, dynamics, or fingering! *Music is heard as a whole and must be studied as such*—it cannot be dismembered into meaningless fragments. To do so is to defeat musical understanding and growth at the outset.

Part of the responsibility for giving the student insight into the relationship between the materials of music and performance lies with the private teacher, who, however, rarely clarifies this relationship—if indeed he is aware of it. Too often, performing technique is the sole goal, and students are permitted to play concertos or sing arias without being aware of even the keys involved—to say nothing of harmonic and formal structure. Granted that even with adequate knowledge the private teacher cannot be expected to teach everything; but he should at least be assured, through inquiry, that the student has gained an understanding of musical structure elsewhere, and show him how it applies to performance. (188).

It is the primary responsibility of the "theory" teacher to supply this musical understanding which is gained chiefly through analysis. Analysis is the synthesis of all other learnings. Rightly viewed, it is the link between "theory" and practice. *In curriculum planning, this means that a conscious recognition of design or structure should be an integral part of all learnings from the beginning.* This is implicit in the following suggestions for organizing analysis for differing situations and levels.

(a) ELEMENTARY SCHOOL

Analysis on this level is concerned with tonal patterns, configurations, sequences, and cadential effects. The sense of melodic line and of "question" and "answer" phrases is important. A clear distinction is essential between a *figure* and a *phrase* if subsequent confusion is to be avoided. The terminology used should be informal, not technical. A concept of tonality and the difference in "feeling" of the various scale steps should be established. What makes a melody sound "right" or "wrong" as regards pitch, rhythm, and length? The child should understand, *in his own terms*, the structure of all music heard or performed.

(b) JUNIOR HIGH SCHOOL

Further clarification of structure by recognition of harmonic "color" and its cadential function. Analysis of simple school songs for use of primary triads in major, and small A-B-A designs, showing reasons for their effectiveness. Concept of necessity for *design in music* and its relation to performance. The functions of both repetition and variety in rhythm, melody, harmony, and form. Discussion of performance heard in the light of these concepts.

(c) Senior High School

Introduction of technical terminology and its application to previous learnings. Identification of structure of music used in student performances. Directed listening to recordings, introducing concepts of larger forms. Optional student notebook of unusual effects that require explanation. Constant exploration by both ear and eye.

Obviously, material used should be related primarily to the student's interests, but the widening of his musical horizon should also be considered. Much "classical" music has great appeal if carefully selected and presented as enjoyable music, rather than something to be revered but seldom liked for itself. For example, the *Scherzando* of Beethoven's Eighth Symphony, the *Finale* of Franck's *Symphonic Variations*, Ravel's *La Valse* or *Bolero*, Stravinsky's *Capriccio*, the second theme of Tchaikovsky's *Romeo and Juliet*, or the beginning of his B♭ minor Piano Concerto. Of course such material is unsuitable for detailed analysis on this level, but it is useful in widening horizons, stimulating interest, and emphasizing certain structural aspects.

(d) Liberal Arts College

First Year: visual analysis of short passages for chords, form, and non-harmonic tones. Aural analysis of small part-forms.

Second Year: visual analysis of piano compositions in the part-forms and song-form with trio, including recognition of chromatic chords being studied. The analysis should be a part of the written assignment. (Suggested material: any collection of representative 19th-century piano pieces.) Aural analysis of more difficult song-forms, including the five-part and group-forms, and song-form with trio.

Third Year: analysis of contrapuntal works paralleling written work. For example, a Palestrina Mass in the first semester, and Bach's *Well Tempered Clavier* (Book II) in the second. These works should be performed in class. (See Chapter II, counterpoint, pages 33-34.)

Fourth Year: analysis of the large variation, rondo, and sonata forms. On this level it is desirable to use the same material for both aural and visual analysis. One semester could be devoted to these forms as found in piano literature, and the other to examples in chamber or orchestral literature. Scores and records should be purchased, and an intensive analysis made of the material—aurally and visually. Both semesters should be correlated as far as possible with the written work of the fourth year.

All analysis should emphasize stylistic characteristics and cultural influences—particularly of the other arts. Though designed for music majors, these courses would be available to other students having sufficient background.

(e) TEACHERS COLLEGE

The first two years would correspond to those of (d) above, and the third year would be the same as the fourth year of (d), paralleling the written work in orchestration and arranging. As has been pointed out previously, material for analysis in a teachers college should be related as closely as possible to the material used in the field, with due regard, however, to breadth of musicianship.

(f) PROFESSIONAL SCHOOL

Same as (d) above, with special reference to professional needs and emphasis on relationship of structure to performance.

(g) GRADUATE LEVEL

Analysis of contemporary techniques. Study of the technical determinants of style. Intensive study of particular composer, idiom, or period.

6. CREATING

6. *Creating* through some medium is a basic human need. The fact that the child creates spontaneously gives a valuable clue for directed musical growth. The impulse for self-expression apparently is well-nigh universal. Such a strong impulse can be used effectively for learning. Many conceive creativity as a wild flower that withers with cultivation—yet this need not be true, for some of the greatest creators have been the most learned in their field. Geniuses are admittedly special cases, but for a normal child surely the *method* of education rather than education *per se* is largely responsible for any decline in creativity. In other words, it seems reasonable to assume that creative expression, properly guided, is one of the most

potent forces for functional education, especially in the arts. This being true, it must be recognized and utilized in planning the curriculum. The natural creativity of children suggests it as a primary motivation for musical learnings. Hence creative expression must be regarded as the cause, not the result, of insights. This means, of course, that creative expression will be an integral part of musical learning *from the first educative contacts with music*. The child learns music by creating it; he does not create because he has learned it. Learning can be achieved by creating at all levels. This is the basic premise of the following suggestions.

(a) ELEMENTARY SCHOOL

Imitation of melodic patterns and phrases (teacher sings "question" and student sings "answer"). Creation of group and individual songs or of melodies for toy instruments. Imitation of dance rhythms. "Play calls," etc.

The notation of children's music is often difficult, chiefly because of entirely free and unconventional rhythmic patterns. Unusual pitch patterns occur more rarely. However, the teacher is urged to notate the children's music whenever possible. Its notation has many practical advantages and in addition stimulates interest in the idea of writing music as a language.

(b) JUNIOR HIGH SCHOOL

Notation of original melodies and use of primary triads and dominant seventh chord for their harmonization, first in "block" form, later in simple accompaniment figures. Concept of musical design as shown in simple A-B-A form. Song writing either with or without accompaniment. Experimentation with dance rhythms. Melodies for instruments played by members of the group. Performance for group of all creative writing.

(c) SENIOR HIGH SCHOOL

Clarification of new harmonic and formal concepts. Experimentation writing for performing groups within the school. Introduce use of technical vocabulary with concept of cadence, phrase, period, etc. At this level it is particularly important that creative writing be free from the feeling of technical restraint, but on the other hand the relationship between technique and writing must be clear and vital.

(d) LIBERAL ARTS COLLEGE

First Year: setting of words for solo voice, and the writing of small song-forms.

Second Year: songs with accompaniments, and the writing of more elaborate song-forms for piano or instrumental combinations within the group.

Since the third and fourth years of written work are compositional in nature, creative activities will be absorbed by the regular written assignments. However, encouragement should be given to "free-lance" writing, especially as related to counterpoint in the third year or to orchestral writing in the fourth.

(e) TEACHERS COLLEGE

Same as (d) above adapted to professional needs.

(f) PROFESSIONAL SCHOOL

Same as (d) above.

(g) GRADUATE LEVEL

Composition in the larger forms; variation, rondo, and sonata-allegro for various instrumental combinations.

Worship of technique for itself can warp effective planning in any educational project, but perhaps it is most likely to happen in the professional school where technical facility is rightly prized and developed. Undue emphasis on technique results in two deficiencies in "theoretic" teaching: composition-majors often lack thorough basic training in the skills discussed in Chapters II-VII, because their marked creative ability presumably offsets these deficiencies. This philosophy produces symphonic composers who cannot harmonize a chorale, or conductors—of all people—who cannot pass ear tests! On the other hand, the artist-student suffers for the same reason, since he is often required to do little or no creative work or dictation because of his remarkable voice or exceptional virtuosity. These examples of imbalance simply mean that too often basic training in musicianship is in inverse ratio to talent. The underlying premise apparently is that the talented student requires a less well-rounded program than the average student, whereas the reverse would be the natural inference. Such practices have little to commend them, either musically or educationally, regardless of practical considerations.

One more phase of planning requires consideration—namely, the adjustment of regular programs to the requirements of the summer session. In the area of "theory," summer work has special values, but it also raises new problems, due to the telescoping of instruction and the short time for growth. Educationally, it is a compromise whose value is doubtful—except in special cases. In order to function successfully, a balance must be achieved between its virtues and its faults. The first requisite for this balance is that *the material covered shall not exceed that of one regular semester.* For example, a six-week session, meeting five times weekly, totals thirty hourly recitations, which is equivalent to a regular session of fifteen weeks having semi-weekly recitations. This is the maximum of work that can be adequately covered in a summer session.

The summer session meets four needs: (1) the repetition of courses failed during the year, (2) the completion of short one-term requirements, (3) the continuance of work for a degree by teachers-in-service, or by regular students wishing to accelerate their programs, and (4) the pursuit of special interests without reference to a degree. These needs are only partially met in many cases, due to the exigency of the situation.

As regards the above categories of summer school students, all may be admitted without special requirements, except those in (3) who wish to accelerate their regular program. These students should be carefully screened, admitting only those whose previous grades are good. Such program acceleration for weak students is fatal to real learning.

The basic criticism of the summer session is that it does not permit sufficient time for growth in skill subjects. This objection is particularly valid for "theoretic" study. Daily practice in class produces mushroom skills which are imperfectly assimilated and only partially retained. The ephemeral nature of such work is shown by the fact that weak students—especially if repeating a course—often show marked improvement which is not continued in the regular sessions. Daily work in any field produces permanent results only when continued over a considerable period of time. *Musical insights and skills require time for maturation.* Few teachers of applied music would expect a student to acquire and retain as much technique in six weeks as he would in six months, yet the "theory" student is supposed to do so in a summer session! Whatever its virtues, the summer session is not equivalent educationally to a regular session, and if a choice were to be made, *aside from practical considerations,* there would be no doubt as to which session would be chosen.

But since the problem of the summer session must be met, regardless of its value, certain basic differences in planning require comment. Daily recitations offer an excellent opportunity for the integration of all phases of "theoretic" study. If, however, the course is subdivided by subject, dictation and music reading should occur every day, and written and keyboard harmony on alternate days. This requires adjustment in planning the course. Even if the phases of "theory" are given as separate courses, the assignments must be reduced, due to the short time for preparation. In other words, summer session courses are more akin to the "laboratory" type of class than are those in the regular sessions.

In concluding our discussion of the planning of individual courses on all levels for various schools, it is desirable to stress once more that two of the basic principles underlying the organization of the curricula suggested above are, first, the use of music literature as primary source material; and second, the integration of all phases of learning into a single unified class giving complete, rather than fragmentary, musical experiences as a basis of learning. This integration can be partially secured by the use of the same material for the various phases of instruction, but it is done most functionally when all resources are applied to the solution of specific problems.

VII

The planning of assignments for all avenues of learning is one of the most crucial problems of the curriculum, since the assignments are the specific application of material presented in the class. If they are ineffective or inadequate the whole learning process is impotent. Hence, once the general pattern of any course has been determined, the problem is one of implementation by a series of assignments that will serve to unify and clarify the class discussions. This is an acid test of many course outlines: can its contents be translated into meaningful units of work? Too often excellent ideas for growth are sterile simply because of failure to project them into practical problems capable of solution by the student.

Any approach to the planning of assignments must be a musical one. Good teaching explains not "theory," but music. Consequently *assignments must be musical, not theoretic problems.* Ideally, each student should explain the structure of the music he is studying at the moment, and thus learn how music is organized and how to make its hearing and performance more meaningful. In class instruction obviously such a procedure is impractical. But if the student cannot learn entirely from his own repertoire, he at least can learn from music literature—not from textbook exercises that often have little relationship to the practice of composers. As Piston says, "In the

field of harmony we must first seek the answer to two questions—
what are the harmonic materials commonly used by composers, and
how have these materials been used?" [21] Hence we must turn to music
itself for the answers to both these questions.

The acceptance of music literature as the source of assignments
leads to the question of precisely how it is to be used. *First*, practical
fragments must be found. These should be as significant as possible,
preferably thematic material from well-known works. These fragments should focus clearly the problem being studied—to the ex-
clusion of unknown structural facts, although this is not essential if
the passage is a particularly pertinent one. *Second*, material chosen
should represent a good cross-section of music literature in all media
—piano, vocal, orchestral, chamber, organ, and choral music. It should
also be related to student interests, if any are predominant. *Third*, all
material used should be specifically identified. One of the causes for
limited knowledge of literature is the failure to identify precisely
what is heard. It is not enough to identify a work by its composer;
its name and opus number should also be known. Texts, in quoting
music, are particularly lax in this respect.

The purpose of the assignment, as suggested above, is to transfer
insights into skills. *Skills are insights in action*, and as such have an
important place in the learning process. Music literature can be used
for this purpose in several ways, but as regards problem solving, one
of its chief merits is its value as a norm; that is, it offers a ready
basis of comparison with the student's work. This is an important
point—not because a solution is always available, but because the student learns through comparison to think *with* the composer. A Grieg
melody or a Bach chorale harmonization offers many opportunities
for insight of the best type through comparison with the student's
own solution. Of course, this does not mean that the composer is
"right" and the student is "wrong," if the solutions differ: it simply
shows how composers solve their problems, and in so doing provides
a basis for real musical learning and growth.

The transfer of insights into skills requires time. Skills are an evidence of precise learnings. To learn is to assimilate. This can only be
done through strong desire. As Mursell [22] says, "Purpose is the true
cause of learning." Repetition is generally involved in the process but
it is not the primary cause. Repetition must be meaningful to promote
learning, and is best used, under guidance, in class for the clarification
of group problems rather than as assignments to be done outside of
class.

In determining assignments, the whole problem of drills and problem solving, as related to the development of desirable skills and in-

sights, must be briefly considered. No other area of education is more controversial, but from the welter of conflicting views let us try to arrive at some practical conclusions. Properly used, drill performs an essential function in mental growth. It originates in an experience whose meaning, though understood, requires clarification and expansion. It makes meanings explicit. To be functional, drill must have adequate preparation and a clear relationship to the generating experience. It should also be exploratory in nature and enlist the full cooperation of the learner. And finally, drill should result in a technical understanding adaptable to differing situations.

Problems are similar to drills as tools of learning, although much wider in scope. The problem, like the drill, must have intrinsic interest and be directly related to the student's experience. Too many problems are mere puzzles, having little or no connection with the musical life of the student. Again, precise understanding is the goal of problem solving, and every assignment must be so regarded. Skills contribute both to the solving of problems and to the resultant insights. They are the tools sharpened by drills. These three technical devices of learning—drills, problems, and skills—may all serve to clarify musical relationships and meanings. The purpose of assignments is to provide the student with materials that will promote learning through these means.

These ideas determine specific assignment planning, whose principal criteria may be summarized thus:

1. *Assignments should be meaningful*, since meaning rather than repetition causes learning. The material used should be directly related to and concentrated upon a specific problem. But clear focus is not enough. Problems or drills must be meaningful psychologically as well as technically. The learner must understand the problem, the requisite skill, and their relationship to his needs. Thus a problem has meaning in two senses—as regards both the subject matter and the student.

2. *Assignments should be challenging*, since desire for a solution is essential to learning through it. Problems, to be vital, must have intrinsic interest. This is the secret of the popularity of crossword puzzles: they are challenging, though of little practical value. It is the instructor's responsibility to construct problems which have both interest and value. Far too little thought is given to this aspect of planning. Herein lies one of the values of using literature rather than exercises for drills and problems. Wisely selected, music has an inherent appeal which promotes learning. Furthermore, problems should be somewhat exploratory in nature. They should provide opportunities for discovery—as Easter eggs are hidden for children to find.

These are not easy criteria to meet, but they are essential for learning.

3. *Assignments should be varied.* Nothing kills interest so rapidly as repetition, yet some repetitive drill is often necessary. The solution lies in assignments that have sufficient variety to make some repetition acceptable. Assignments for all avenues of learning should consist of a number of *different* things to do. The problem involved should be approached from all possible angles. This again demands resourcefulness and ingenuity on the part of the instructor but it is not an impossible task.

4. *Assignments should be flexible* to allow for individual needs and preferences. Several factors are involved in this concept—that of student interest and of self-direction. Both are essential conditions of functional drill and problem solving. Without the spark plugs of interest and initiative the engine of learning simply will not run at maximum efficiency. By giving choices or optional assignments the student is involved to a degree in the planning of procedures. Each assignment should provide for such cooperation. For example, if the problem is melody harmonization, give a choice from ten melodies; if a specific drill is to be applied in more than one key, let the student choose the other keys. Such flexibility has an additional advantage in fixing responsibility definitely on the student. Thus, if a drill were assigned in *all* keys, the student could justly claim proficiency in a key other than the one asked by the instructor, but the student, in selecting the keys himself, implies mastery in them. This does not mean that the student himself selects the particular key for recitation —but rather that he offers the instructor a choice of keys in which he is proficient. Rigid assignments, with no opportunity for individual choice by the student, are one of the earmarks of mechanized, routine teaching.

One other device for flexibility should be noted. It is sometimes desirable to set up maximum and minimum assignments with corresponding levels of achievement. Such a procedure might be justified if the class were a heterogeneous group, including, for example, both music and non-music majors or professional students and teachers. It is difficult to see its value for a homogeneous group, but if it were used for such a group, certainly B should be the top grade for a minimum of work and achievement.

5. *Assignments should be cumulative* in the sense, not of adding up separate units to form a unified whole, but of having a directional goal achieved through the continuous use of all skills developed by the solution of specific problems. This process is very different from the concentration upon isolated skills which the student is supposed to integrate in some mysterious manner. This means that every prob-

lem should contain both old and new elements; that acquired skills be used *continuously* and not, as is sometimes stated, be forgotten until needed in another situation. *All situations should require all skills, but in a natural not an artificial* context. Here again real music helps to solve the problem, for it presents all types of dexterities, but not in logical order as in textbooks. This is precisely why the skills, as presented in texts, are seldom functional outside of the textbook itself. There is no particular reason why they should transfer to real musical problems since they are artificial by nature. Lack of transfer from book to Bach has been demonstrated very clearly. The student, for example, sings "sight singing" exercises but cannot read a motet; or he can take familiar aural patterns by dictation but is lost in a simple Schumann piano piece. The reason being, of course, that real music is not organized in set patterns. If the student is conditioned to a formalized pattern and has a fixed reaction, the design of real music will escape him simply because it does not conform to his experience. Yet flexibility of reaction is surely one of the goals, not only of drill, but of education as a whole. A technical problem should always be approached as a problem to be analyzed and understood—not as a challenge to mechanical repetitive drill.

6. *Assignments should provide for reviews* in accordance with the accepted theory of "plateaus of learning." These pauses in the upward curve of learning provide for evaluation, self-criticism, and reorientation. A good type of review is to have the student himself find examples *in music* of all technical points discussed in class. This procedure not only promotes transfer but is an excellent measure of real understanding. Frequently it is disillusioning to the instructor. Points which are assumed to have been made crystal-clear to the group are found to have misfired completely. This "echo" from the class, supported by examples, is an excellent index of achievement. Furthermore, reviews are needed to consolidate learnings. The best integration in daily recitations will sometimes fail to relate all the various factors involved. This is because time is necessary to really establish functional relationships and insights. A *re-view* should be taken in its literal sense of appraising past progress. As in mountain climbing, the student pauses and takes stock of his position in relation to the past and the future.

7. *Assignments should be pointed toward definite achievement goals.* This concept involves the inevitable conflict between directional and fixed goals—between the relative importance of means and ends. Is the student to live or to learn? Such dichotomy of aims is unrealistic. The student learns in order to live more fully—both are essential. Naturally the best preparation for living is achieved by the best

means of learning. Definite achievement goals do not necessarily imply inflexibility of either procedure or of objective. Climbing a mountain involves both a goal and a pleasurable procedure. One does not wander aimlessly for the sake of the experience. The experience is *directed* toward an objective. The same reasoning applies to education. In the broadest sense experience is educational, but only when pointed toward a desired outcome *beyond the experience itself. Hence assignments must have an implicit goal achieved through functional skills.* This means that predetermined assignments are essential for good teaching; but it also means that these assignments must be adjusted to fit new and changing situations. Much ink has been spilled in discussing this point, but it seems clear that *planned experiences* are superior to random ones, and if so it follows that the transfer of these experiences into assignments must also be planned.

8. *Assignments should be related to the student's interests.* This notion is somewhat similar to (1) and (2) above but it has additional implications beyond those of being meaningful and challenging. Specifically, it refers to capitalizing upon the student's individual interests, and involves, to a degree, the differentiation of assignments. The interests of various types of performers differ and these differences should be recognized and provided for as far as possible. Practical difficulties are great in making different assignments for members of the same group, yet they can be partially overcome if *areas of interest* are recognized. Thus an assignment in harmonization might differ for singers and pianists. But such differentiation is only justified when based on a firm general foundation. It should not be applied on the elementary level where an extensive approach is indicated. The higher the level the more differentiation is desirable. Its application will depend ultimately upon the instructor and the local situation.

9. *Assignments should be designed in respect to the student's available time.* In planning assignments consideration must always be given to the amount of time required for their execution in relation to the time available. In general, one to two hours should be spent in preparation for each hour of recitation. This ratio appears reasonable in comparison with that of applied music, and, though students vary in their study habits, it may be assumed as a practical norm. When an excessive amount of time is spent on assignments, either the student's background, understanding, or work habits are faulty. On the other hand, since the acquisition of skills is involved, *regular daily practice is essential for growth in "theory" as it is in applied music.*

Some of the traditional difficulty of "theory" is undoubtedly due to the irregular attention devoted to it. Students might well have similar difficulty with applied music if their study periods for it were as spasmodic as is often the case for "theory." History may be "crammed" the night before class, but not harmony. Skills are assimilated gradually like food, and require daily nurture. Furthermore, the class period is too short to permit this assimilation, especially in partially physical skills such as reading, listening, or playing. For all these reasons, it is essential that the class period be supplemented by regular systematic work between recitations.

It is very doubtful whether real skill can be acquired in a "workshop" set-up devoid of outside preparation. The need for assignments is widely recognized, but the student often fails to realize the parallel between the practice of "theory" and the practice of applied music. He will state with pride that six hours were spent in preparation *the day before a recitation*, whereas an hour a day would have produced better results just as it would have in piano practice, for example. Hence, the temporal aspect of assignments must be clearly understood by both the instructor and the student if learning is to be promoted by their use.

10. *Assignments should be a natural continuation of class activities.* If the assignments are to transfer insights into skills, or skills into insights, they must project group learnings beyond the classroom. In other words, the student must feel, as he works on the assignment, that he is doing individually what he did in the classroom as part of the group, and that he has the power to do so from what he learned there. The atmosphere of the classroom should be projected to his study, and the group experience should be re-lived as he works.

This notion has several important implications. The first one is related to the timing mentioned above. The feeling of the group activity simply cannot be recaptured unless work on the assignment is begun soon after the class. Second, its recall will be more vivid and helpful *if the instructor has shown the student how to work*. For this reason, problems similar to those of the assignment should always be analyzed, understood, and solved in class so that the student, when working alone, will be on familiar ground and not waste hours in misdirected effort. This is what is meant by assignments being a natural continuation of class activities. The gap between group and individual work may also be narrowed by a few partially solved problems in the assignment. Any means which makes the student feel that his own work is a natural sequence, continuing classroom learnings, is desirable.

These then are some of the criteria for the planning of assignments. They should be applied individually to each assignment

planned. Certainly their application would radically alter many existing *schema*. Assignments implement class learnings and consequently
are a vital factor in planning. It should be stressed again that both
are most effective when integrated. A single unified class in musical
structure functioning through writing, reading, listening, playing, analyzing, and creating requires interrelated assignments in all these activities. This interrelationship can be secured by both the use of the
same material for different activities and by the application of all
activities to a single problem. An integrated course is outlined in
Appendix I, pages 227-238, with specimen assignments.

Before concluding our discussion of assignments several points of
procedure require comment. The first concerns self-determined assignments that allow the student to develop his own organization of
material toward precision. Since this procedure involves self-evaluation it will be discussed with other techniques of evaluation in Chapter
IX, pages 196-199. The second procedure is the practice of making
large over-all assignments at the beginning of the course to cover the
entire semester. Superficially this may appear to be a rather arbitrary,
mechanistic procedure, yet when examined it has much to recommend
it. For example, it clarifies objectives, saves class time, and most important. *it puts the responsibility for achievement upon the student.*
Thus, in a music reading class, if one of the desired goals was mastery
of the C clef, all the necessary material could be provided, necessary
methods outlined, and the student would then be responsible for
achievement within the allotted time.

There are two essential conditions for such a procedure: first, the
assigned work must be mechanical in the sense that it does not require constant criticism or guidance, and second, the student must
be of sufficient maturity to be given this responsibility. The latter
point is the crux of the matter. There are undoubtedly many desirable
skills that could be so acquired *from the beginning* by self-drill, but
can we develop the requisite interest and self-discipline in students
to execute this type of assignment? The method has been often used
for required course readings, but as yet it has not been applied to
skills. Here is a real challenge and an opportunity for experimentation. It should be applied from the lowest to the highest level. It has
some relationship to the self-determined assignments and evaluations
mentioned above. Properly motivated, it should promote the development of both self-discipline and self-evaluation—two essential elements of *real education* as distinguished from mechanical learnings.

The third procedure is concerned with student notebooks for
written assignments and class work. Criticism of written work has
been discussed in Chapter II, pages 37-38, but a word should be added

about the notebooks themselves. It is desirable that all written assignments be done in ink, preferably on loose-leaf paper so that the individual assignments can be criticized separately, then put together and turned in for a general evaluation at the end of the course. Careful and accurate notation also is important, both psychologically and professionally. Many students are amazingly ignorant of correct notation. Music should be written as accurately as a language—especially by professionals. Furthermore, class dictation material should also be kept in a notebook and submitted for evaluation at the end of the course, without, however, being copied in ink or corrected weekly. The requirement of a term notebook for both written harmony and dictation courses adds dignity and importance to the assignments and dictated material. The notebooks are also valuable for review purposes and thus serve to summarize and consolidate learnings. Students tend to reflect the instructor's attitude in regard to these matters, and hence it is his obligation to put a premium upon the presentation of written material and accuracy of notation.

VIII

In concluding our survey of planned curricula and assignments, it should again be stressed that the basic philosophy for both is the parity of ends and means. Educational planning is the selection and organization of meaningful experiences for satisfaction and mastery through insights and skills. The planning has a goal beyond the experience *per se*. It is primarily concerned with the growth of the learner through what is learned. Obviously educative experiences may be determined either by the individual, the group, or the teacher. None of these controls is adequate alone. In organized education a combination of group and teacher control is most fruitful. But since the experience of the teacher exceeds that of the group, both *the initial and ultimate responsibility rests with him*. Predetermined course outlines and assignments represent the application of his experience to specific situations, subject always to modification for new or changing conditions. The navigator sets a course with a definite goal in mind, but it is subject to a thousand variations. So the teacher must plan both his objectives and his procedures if he is to make port educationally. The course should be a pleasant voyage toward this goal. This is the basis of the above suggestions for definite outlines and assignments. They are intended to be meaningful experiences organized for personal growth and mastery, functioning, not as rigid requirements, but as aids in the individual planning of other teachers.

Young, inexperienced teachers need more guidance than those who have already wrestled with these problems. But all teachers need to constantly re-evaluate their aims and procedures. None need fear planning as a mechanistic device. Fatal formalism comes not from predetermination but from inflexibility. Students also should be trained to take an increasing share in planning and execution, but to expect the new group to determine competently for itself either goals or procedures is mere wishful thinking, and will result in a pooling of ignorance or aimless experimentation. And so we return to our initial premise that *organization is essential for successful teaching, with its corollary that the responsibility for such organization rests primarily upon the teacher.* Do not evade this responsibility by rationalization but face it squarely, and use planning as an instrument for the promotion of growth both in and through learning.

Chapter IX

EVALUATING

I

Evaluation is one of the agencies for the promotion of learning and as such it is an essential factor in teaching. Evaluation serves two purposes: first, it measures the result both of learning and of teaching, and thus establishes a set of values for the student and the teacher respectively. To do so, evaluation should be so organized that it helps the learner to develop criteria and skill in self-judgment. So conceived, evaluation is an integral part of the learning process and permeates all phases of it. Tests may be likened to the nodes of a vibrating string which produce the harmonics of the fundamental tone and are yet part of the total vibration. Tests are educational nodes that produce the overtones of learning while the fundamental process is in operation; and just as the overtones add quality and color to a tone, so focused evaluations give vitality and meaning to the total learning experience. It is sometimes said that the primary aim of evaluation is the development of the learner's ability for self-criticism and self-improvement, and, in the broadest sense, this is true, since ultimately the student is self-taught. But in the classroom the guidance of the instructor through evaluation is quite as important as that of the student, because the instructor, as the leader, needs this information as a basis for teaching procedures.

The second and more basic purpose of evaluation, however, is the training of the student to recall quickly, fully, and accurately essential knowledge or skill that he has acquired. The use of this ability reaches far beyond the transient needs of the classroom into practical life. The music teacher is often confronted by unexpected questions or use of skills that require an immediate response. The unexpected visit to the classroom of one of his superiors is certainly an evaluation or an examination. Throughout life we are constantly forced to muster all we can of our previous knowledge, and the habit of doing so can be cultivated by practice. How often when the occasion has passed do we ask ourselves, as a student does after an examination, why we did not remember some essential fact. It is a special art, not the same thing as a rich store of knowledge. Some men can recall rapidly, some require a certain time for reflection, and some can recall only in the solitude of their studies. More than to scholars or writers is the value to men of practical affairs of recalling rapidly the knowledge that they need. For this reason, both the student and the teacher-in-training requires the discipline of regular evaluations or examinations if he is to be adequately prepared for the examination of life.

II

Educators differ as widely on the desirable techniques of evaluation as they do on other phases of education. On one hand are minimum essentials objectively tested; on the other, on-going experiences whose variable outcomes are evaluated by the group in terms of satisfaction. The first viewpoint stresses *content*, the second emphasizes *method*. Both are inadequate since neither facts nor experience are educative *per se*. Evaluation measures growth, of both factual learning and discrimination and judgment. The techniques employed should be devised to achieve these results for the guidance of all concerned. The responsibility for setting up measures of achievement rests with the instructor as leader. He acts as guide through a country familiar to him but unknown to the group. A competent guide may offer a choice of routes, but he hardly asks to be shown the way! The notion that untrained group-judgment is superior to competent leadership is scarcely tenable.

Value is the keynote of evaluation. All means must be weighed in relation to it. Tests should summarize, clarify, and organize the learning-sequence for the student, and measure not only his progress but his needs in such a way that he will be aware of both. Such results can only be achieved by wise planning based upon wide experience. It is easy to construct hard problems, but hard to construct good ones. Problems should be challenging, but also satisfying, and should contain both familiar and new conditions. But the basic consideration is value: are the problems meaningful, are they accurate measures of desirable goals, do they clarify previous learnings? These and similar questions are essential in making evaluations.

One aspect of testing requires brief comment. At present both the words "test" and "examination" are suspect educationally. Their use is often avoided, sometimes rather awkwardly, because of current trends. Yet procedure for evaluation under these very names are regularly given in some of the most progressive schools. Today apparently an "examination" is sweeter by any other name. The popular word at the moment is "evaluation" which undoubtedly will be followed by others. Obviously, *the essential point is to improve procedures, not their titles.* We all have taken part in round-table discussions, clinics, and panels without being able to discover any real difference between them. "Review" and "refresher" courses are cases in point. The word "test" still is current coin, due to the objective and intelligence tests, but the word "examination" cannot be found in the indices of educational works, although in practice it remains the most widely used term for the systematic appraisal of learning. Hence, in the following discussion the word "examination" will be used in the sense of *a testing of knowledge or qualification, or the questions and answers made in such a test.*

Furthermore, few well prepared, normal students ever had reason to fear a fair examination. Rather it affords an opportunity for proving his worth. A good runner welcomes a race. Fear of examinations usually stems either from lack of preparation or lack of confidence in the instructor—unless due to special psychological causes. It is the teacher's obligation to dispel such fears and to give the student a confident attitude toward all types of evaluation. This can be done in many ways—but it is primarily dependent upon winning the student's confidence and cooperation. Naturally this attitude must have a factual basis: the teacher must have done his job well to justify it.

One outcome of the prevalent fear of examinations is the demand for their abolition. Nor does this demand come from students alone. It is said that the daily class work is a fairer and more adequate basis of evaluation. Furthermore, that judgments based upon examinations tend to be too fixed and absolute, and ignore many factors favorable to the student. Undoubtedly, there is truth in such statements, but the fact remains that in real life the individual is usually judged quite arbitrarily upon performance, not upon attitude. The employer or audience (in the case of a performing musician) is concerned with results rather than with efforts. In other words, outside of school *ability to produce is the chief criterion,* and if education is to teach adjustment to life it would seem desirable to set up similar standards in the school. In addition, daily work can hardly be used as the sole basis of evaluation for two reasons: first, because students tend to accept only favorable estimates of daily work, rejecting as unfair negative ones, and second, because in many cases some or all daily work is copied from better students.[23] Hence the most equitable appraisal of a term's work probably would be based both on an evaluation of daily work plus several carefully prepared tests.

III

Once the need of careful evaluation is recognized by both the teacher and student, the precise nature of the tests naturally arises. Here we leave the field of general educational theory and are confronted by definite and specific problems. What types of tests are suitable for technical courses in the structure of music? In general such tests attempt to measure achievement in terms of the past, present, and future of the student's professional life: in other words, tests at the beginning, middle and end of the course. Let us try to summarize the characteristics of each.

1. *Placement tests* are for guidance in program advisement. They are perhaps the most difficult of the three types to devise and administer. The reasons are obvious: the student's background is unknown, and the test must be so devised as to be comprehensive yet quickly and easily given. Furthermore, the student himself should have some choice of problems, based on his own background. For these reasons it is desirable that the test cover a wide range of clearly defined levels from which the student may choose. A placement test should include written and keyboard harmony and dictation. Music reading may be omitted since it is partially tested in the areas named, and also because a dictation rating is more indicative than a purely vocal reading test. To meet these requirements, a placement test might be organized in the various areas, thus:

  (a) *Rudiments*

    (1) The writing of several major and minor scales, using accidentals but no signatures.

    (2) The recognition of a few difficult signatures in both modes.

    (3) The writing and recognition of a few difficult intervals.

(4) The identification of meter and key for music printed without either time or key signature or bar lines.

(5) Several problems involving note values.

The test on rudiments should be quite difficult, demanding precise knowledge without benefit of alternate questions. This severity is justified because of the basic character of the knowledge involved. It should be short and to the point, but should demonstrate beyond doubt a knowledge of these fundamentals. No effective learning can result if this basic structure is weak. As in all placement tests, doubtful results cannot be accepted, especially on this level. Partial repetition for the student in a beginning course is preferable to leniency here.

(b) *Written harmony*

Here the student should be offered a choice of four melodies to harmonize for mixed voices, each one representing an average term of harmony—the first two diatonic and the second two modulatory and chromatic. A simple modulation could well be included in the concluding second and fourth term melodies. This type of examination apparently contradicts in a measure the philosophy set forth in preceding chapters, yet it must be recalled that a placement test is given to students whose backgrounds, though varied, are predominately conservative. Since four-part vocal writing is the typical medium used in the majority of harmony classes, it would be unfair to expect instrumental harmonizations. Furthermore, melodies only, *not figured bass*, should be given, since a student presumably can harmonize a vocal melody regardless of the text or system studied. Confronted by such an examination, the student is directed to choose the melody for harmonization that is, in his opinion, representative of his background and experience. In other words, he selects his own problem. Here again, leniency in evaluation is often harmful to the student. While justified in rare cases of wide background or obvious intelligence, the wise examiner will "low rate" rather than "over rate" a placement test. Psychologically it is always easier to promote a student who is placed in too low a class than to "demote" one who has been graded too high.

One other point regarding the organization of the written harmony test should be stressed: namely, that the problems to be solved should be musical ones presented in their totality. Thus, true-false questions or written answers are ineffective, inadequate, and unmusical as a means of evaluation. Hence, if proof of an insight into the nature and function of six-four chords is desired, the melody given for harmonization should provide opportunities for such insights—

but never a question as to the various uses of six-four chords, their doublings, or similar academic and non-musical procedures. Let the student show by music, not by words, that he understands music.

Finally, if a short, simple, and revealing test is desired, the student may be asked to harmonize the ascending and descending major or minor scale, using diatonic chords to validate one year's work, or chromatic chords for a second year of study. This simple problem will reveal more than pages of questions and answers.

(c) *Dictation*

This field offers peculiar and difficult problems. Many students have no background in this activity. Hence a dictation test may well begin with the writing of a familiar melody (e.g., *America* or *The Star Spangled Banner*) from memory, followed by any other melody recalled by the student. This procedure, which eliminates the problem of memorization, often gives an excellent idea of the student's musicianship and mastery of pitch and notation problems. Following the writing of known melodies, two passages may be dictated, the student writing in succession, after several hearings, the melody, bass, and name of the chord. These passages should represent approximately the level of achievement at the end of first- and second-year dictation classes. The student is directed to write as much of both passages as he can. These are only rough measures of achievement but, when interpreted by an experienced instructor, will nevertheless furnish adquate data for judgment. Such a test usually eliminates a large percentage of students before it is completed. If, however, some remain who have obviously passed the test, the instructor may either give them a further individual test or excuse them entirely from dictation —depending upon individual needs and objectives. It should be noted, however, that any good course is unique, and consequently students who pass placement tests successfully should normally be assigned to advanced classes rather than being excused entirely from "theoretic" study. It should also be noted that the above tests are not broken down into component parts, i.e., chords, melodies, rhythms, or intervals. This is because *music is a unified whole whose parts are meaningless when segregated;* and all evaluation—and teaching also, for that matter—should be geared *to the total impression,* never to the isolated elements, except in cases of special functional drills. If the student's background is insufficient for the recognition and notation of the complete whole, let him do what he can. What he omits will be as diagnostic as what he includes.

(d) *Music reading*

As suggested above, the other placement tests usually are sufficiently indicative of reading to obviate any real need for a specific test in this area, especially since it is the *mental* rather than the *vocal* ability that is essential. (See Chapter III.) However, if a vocal reading test is needed for special reasons it can easily be given. Test reading both with and without words. In reading without words, no special system or device is essential. In fact, for diagnostic purposes the use of a neutral syllable (*la* or *loo*) is much more revealing than dependence upon a specialized system.

(e) *Keyboard harmony*

Testing in this area must be done individually. Begin by asking the student to play by ear some familiar song—either with or without chords. Then give him a choice for harmonization of a simple folksong with accompaniment, or a chorale in close harmony. If time permits, a simple passage should be transposed at sight (*without playing it first as written*) and an opportunity should be given for improvisation if the student is sufficiently advanced. As in written harmony, the harmonization of an ascending and descending major or minor scale will often be sufficient for evaluation.

(f) *Counterpoint*

Placement tests are rarely necessary in this area since relatively few students have studied the subject. However, a thorough knowledge of written harmony is an essential prerequisite. If a test in strict counterpoint is needed, the descending scale again is an excellent *cantus firmus*. The ability to answer and counterpoint a modulatory fugue subject should indicate proficiency in free counterpoint.

(g) *Form*

As in the case of counterpoint, this area seldom requires a special test. A general idea of the student's knowledge of structure can be obtained from asking the student to identify the form of familiar songs or piano compositions.

The administration of placement tests is best handled in groups except in the case of keyboard harmony or music reading. When sufficient staff is available, three examinations should be held simultaneously in different rooms. The written harmony test can be given continuously, since no group action is necessary. A definite time should be allotted for the completion of the test—for example, an hour from the time the student begins. The instructor in charge should note carefully each student's progress so that time may be saved in case the outcome is obvious early in the test. The dictation test should be given to large groups at stated hours during the registration period, for example, twice or thrice daily. It is essential that the instructor in charge be experienced in giving dictation, otherwise

the results will be of little value. A third instructor should give the
keyboard test continuously, since it is given individually. The results
of these three tests should then be noted on the student's papers and
taken to a senior instructor who will give an over-all evaluation, and
record his decisions for guidance in making the student's program.
In this way large groups of students can be tested with a minimum of
time and effort. It is advisable that the written and dictation examinations be mimeographed to facilitate their administration.

The value of placement tests depends naturally on the tests themselves, their administration, and evaluation. In many respects they are
a necessary evil, but, under proper conditions, they can exceed their
primary diagnostic function, and have genuine educative value in the
sense that they can measure previous achievement for the student
as well as for the instructor. It is most important that they be given
in a manner to allay the natural fears of a new student in a strange
environment. But the best placement tests given under ideal conditions are tentative, and in many cases inconclusive, because no real
study has been made of this problem. Although applicable to all tests
to a certain degree, the placement test is particularly vulnerable educationally because of the lack of a common group background such
as exists in a class meeting together for even a short time. Consequently, the placement test requires very careful consideration as
regards organization, administration, and evaluation. Too frequently
it fails through deficiency in one of these aspects. As the basis for
initial guidance of the student it merits the most careful consideration. Many later difficulties both of teacher and student could be
avoided if it functioned successfully. In no case should any phase
of it be handled by inexperienced or incompetent instructors. *If it
is to perform its function it must be in competent hands.* It is one
of the primary requisites for effective teaching.

2. *Interim tests* are mileposts for the measurement of achievement
while learning is in progress. Their function differs from that of
placement tests in that they are essentially indicative rather than
diagnostic. They may be simply aspects of developing class experiences which are isolated for purposes of evaluation. Thus they possess neither the formality nor finality of either preliminary or terminal evaluations. Their quality depends upon the group and its
problems. In some cases a regular class assignment will serve for
evaluation; in others, emphasis is needed on special problems: again,
a general summary is required. The choice will depend upon the
sensitivity of the instructor to the needs of the group as expressed in
class discussions. Hence only general principles rather than specific

details can be discussed for this type of testing. These principles may be outlined for the various areas, thus:

(a) *Rudiments*

In accordance with the teaching of rudiments as discussed in Chapter II, any testing in this area should be done on a purely musical basis. Specifically, learnings and problems should be based on observations of actual music, not upon "theoretic" facts. Thus a test on notation might well consist of identification of symbols as found in familiar compositions rather than of the written repetition of learned definitions. The essential point is to measure insights not facts, and this can best be done by an examination of literature. Only in this way can the teaching of rudiments be vitalized. This new approach to rudiments is a challenge both as regards organization and evaluation.

(b) *Written harmony*

As previoulsy suggested, evaluation should be based upon the solution of real musical problems, not upon factual questions. The so-called true-false examination is of doubtful value in a course involving skills. Neither does the question-answer type of examination offer much opportunity for insights. A piano examination consists of playing the piano, and similarly a test of written harmony should consist of writing music. True, certain types of factual questions tend to promote insights, as for example, the naming of keys in which the C, F, and G chords occur, or the identification of familiar song-forms from memory; but these are exceptional cases, and generally speaking the focus should be on real musical problems. Also, in the light of the discussion earlier in the chapter on the disciplinary function of examinations, it is obvious that the so-called open-book examination is hardly adequate, since it fails in this respect. Its use is limited to special cases, e.g., evaluation of creative work where ready response is not involved. In general, alternative questions are desirable for psychological as well as for practical reasons, though naturally such questions must be of equal difficulty. Timing is also important. Many a good test fails because it is too long for the allotted time. Further, it is important that some of the problems require a new use of old skills, or a re-orientation of previous learnings. Herein lies one of the values in the use of music literature, for in it the application of general principles is infinitely varied, and the student must of necessity adjust himself to these changing conditions.

The number of tests given during a semester will naturally depend upon many factors, but, on the whole, evaluations should occur with sufficient frequency and informality to gage the progress of the group and to give it a sense of achievement. Monthly tests may be helpful if they are evaluations of the learning sequence at a particular time, but constant testing often retards rather than promotes learning. Certainly a test near the middle of the semester is desirable, but timed in relation to the learning sequence rather than to the calendar.

(c) *Dictation*

Work in this area is largely on a laboratory basis since it is a group activity. Nevertheless, need exists here, as elsewhere, for performance under controlled conditions, and hence the giving of fairly frequent tests during the course is desirable. Since psychological difficulties are probably greatest in dictation, care must be taken to set up procedures for evaluation that lessen rather than increase these difficulties. The tests should be short and relatively simple, giving ample opportunity for a variety of reactions and insights. Conversely, the tests must be comprehensive and present the material to be written *as a unified whole*, not as separate rhythmic, melodic, and harmonic problems. In other words, one or more carefully chosen passages from music literature should combine all these different aspects.

In addition to problems of notation, other elements such as recognition of chord color, form, or texture may well be included, as well as the writing of material from memory. All of these elements may be recognized from recorded music. Hence, a well constructed dictation test will include much more than the writing of pitches played on the piano by the instructor. As regards tests during the course, however, probably the material should be quite similar to that used daily in class. In fact, it is often best to use simply the class papers of a particular day for evaluation. Whichever procedure is followed, written dictation, by its very nature, requires frequent and competent testing. If the class is small, this can be done by close observation of the student's daily work, but in a large class fairly frequent written tests offer the best solution.

To summarize: a dictation test should include the writing of music already known or studied (e.g., folksong material or themes from instrumental or choral works being studied), the recognition of simple musical designs and textures, and the notation of the melody, bass, and name of chord in both choral and instrumental styles. All this material should be written after (*not during*) a few hearings whose number is announced in advance. The test should be replayed when the papers are returned to the students in order to correct and clarify previous impressions. Such evaluations during a course naturally are more accurate than those derived from a placement test.

(d) *Music reading*

In this area, evaluation during the course is best made from material assigned and prepared in advance. The purpose is to evaluate individual skills that are not apparent in group performance. Naturally, group rather than individual performance is typical of most recitations in music reading, and consequently it is desirable to evaluate the growth of individual skills rather frequently. Either the regular weekly assignment may be used for this purpose or the student may choose and prepare material used previously. The specific content of the examination will naturally vary, but it should include reading both with and without words, and some chord progressions (sung with letters and accidentals) that parallel work done in other areas.

(e) *Keyboard harmony*

Here again, as in music reading, evaluations are most easily made from hearing individually the weekly assignment, especially when the classroom is equipped with a number of pianos which make group recitation possible and frequent. In any case, the test should be informal but sufficiently comprehensive to give an adequate basis for evaluation.

(f) *Counterpoint*

The chief value of a midterm test in counterpoint is to determine both the facility of the student and his ability to write without the aid of the piano. Many students spend unnecessary time on written work, especially on counterpoint, and hence it is well to give frequent short problems *in class* to stimulate facility and independence. as well as a midterm test for general evaluation.

(g) *Form*

Design, as one of the integral factors of music, is related to all areas of study and hence should be isolated only in exceptional cases. Consequently, form plays a part in all areas—from rudiments to fugue. If the material for testing is drawn from literature its design can be recognized. Any melody sung, played, harmonized, or dictated should be so classified for practical, not academic, reasons; also, the form of familiar songs may be identified from memory. Hence, a separate evaluation of the student's sense of design is entirely unnecessary if he has been conscious of organizational principles in all areas of study. A test in any area will include some question on form.

There is a place, however small, for a specialized course in form, and procedures for its evaluation will be discussed in the next section on terminal tests, or (to use a forbidden word educationally) final examinations.

3. *Terminal tests* present one of the most difficult problems which the conscientious teacher must face and try to solve. As suggested above, educators differ widely on the value and type of a final estimate of the student's achievement. However, circumstances force the majority of teachers to make such an estimate, regardless of the pros and cons of educational theory, and it is on that basis that we shall proceed.

The sole function of the final examination is to guide the teacher, in contrast to the double purpose of interim tests discussed above. This difference means a stress on the measurement of facility, adaptability, and breadth of comprehension. There is little opportunity for learning, since in most cases the papers cannot be returned to the students. Yet a good final examination should summarize the content and meaning of the course for the student, as well as furnish the teacher with data for evaluation. On its completion the student should feel the satisfaction derived from a worthy task well done. This satisfaction, typical of the best type of student, is one measure of its validity.

Specific details of final examinations in various areas are shown by the examples given in Appendices I and II. In the light of the previous discussion of placement and interim tests, it is clear that final tests should include both specific skills and judgments. Probably the majority of the problems set should be new and not prepared in advance as for the interim tests: that is, harmonization, music reading, transposition, and improvisation should be done *at sight*. At this level there should definitely be a choice of problems which will allow for individual differences of interests and abilities.

In preparing for a final evaluation, one method of review is to ask each member of the class to construct a final examination for the course. These tests can be discussed in class and even exchanged and assigned for solution. Student-constructed tests are an excellent means of focusing values and procedures, and will aid in the classification of issues for all concerned.

4. *Two specialized types of examinations* require brief comment: analytic and postgraduate tests. The first refers to the analysis of form as discussed in Chapter VI. Evaluation of achievement in such a course should be both visual and aural. For example, the student is given

an inexpensive copy of a Beethoven piano sonata and asked to analyze one movement in detail and name the general form of the others—time permitting. The second half of the test consists of aural analysis of recorded music. Three playings of a record at ten-minute intervals are usually sufficient for a rather complete analysis: first for the over-all design, second for the details, and third for checking previous impressions. If thirty minutes are assigned for each half, a "look-listen" test of this type can be given within an hour. The completeness of the analysis will vary with individual ability. The period and composer of the recorded music should also be named by the student. As a matter of fact, recorded music is an excellent medium for any type of aural analysis—form, texture, period, or even precise thematic recognition. There are many interesting possibilities here that require exploration and development.

The second type of specialized examination—that on the post-graduate level—seldom fits into a general pattern, since it is usually either more intensive or extensive than undergraduate tests. On this level the emphasis tends to be on direct results with less attention to the learning process than on lower levels. This shift of emphasis may be simply traditionalism, or it may reflect the student's imminent entrance into real life where values are often more absolute than in the classroom.

As a condition of graduation, graduate departments in many fields give comprehensive examinations on all work done in the department. There are many excellent reasons for such a procedure: first, it serves as a summary of work done, and, conversely, prevents graduation by a mere accumulation of credits for a series of courses passed separately. Second, it is a selective process at a level where selectivity is essential for the production of leadership. Third, it tends to counteract over-specialization by emphasizing the general background. Fourth, and perhaps of most importance, it promotes a sense of individual responsibility for achievement—a factor too often neglected on all levels. Certainly a comprehensive examination in music education would aid in unifying and clarifying disparate insights and understandings gathered from many separate classes and areas.

A comprehensive examination obviously must include both extensive and intensive problems. To do so within reasonable time limits requires questions that test several areas simultaneously. For example, harmony, counterpoint, and orchestration can be combined in the harmonization of a chorale melody for mixed voices with an added descant, accompanied by a specified group of instruments. Understanding of the general aspects of music literature—style, form, texture, etc.—can be shown through analysis of recorded music. Precision in mental imagery and knowledge of repertoire can be combined in the writing from memory of one melodic theme from each of the various types of literature: choral, orchestral, vocal, and the like. Many such interesting combinations are possible when age level, maturity, and background of the student are expanding rather than limiting factors of the test.

IV

To summarize: theories of evaluation differ, but all aim at the appraisal of learning for the guidance of both the learner and the teacher. Stress may be laid on either direct results, on objectives, or on process. None is self-contained—all are interrelated. Evaluation of insights through skills is difficult, especially when dealing with an art possessing many overtones of learning. The examinations discussed above, though concerned with direct results, attempted also to face the problems of transferability and objectives, and to make the tests a part of the total learning sequence. The degree of group participation in the formulation of such tests depends largely upon the skill of the teacher in obtaining significant group decisions. There is little value in group participation in planning or evaluation *per se*, except possibly the satisfaction of the group in being considered. Educationally, group participation is of value only when it contributes to the learning, not to the self-esteem of the group. If, as is sometimes claimed, the untrained group is more competent to judge procedures than the trained leader, the situation is anomalous, to say the least. *Group action is important, but it is not the panacea for all educational problems.* Consequently, in the planning of tests the role of the group is by no means clear and its influence should probably be indirect.

Evaluation at three points of the learning sequence was discussed: entrance, interim, and terminal tests. The first was considered as diagnostic, the second as indicative, and the third as confirmatory of the learning process. *Their construction should be suited to their divergent purposes, but always in terms of musical and practical rather than of theoretic problems.* Finally, two specialized tests were discussed: the aural and visual recognition of musical design or form, and the graduate or postgraduate departmental comprehensive examination as an agency for the unification and clarification of diverse learnings and understandings. As previously stated, *the key to evalua-*

tion is value. Good evaluation is truly educative since it teaches both the learner and the instructor. Perhaps the essence of the evaluating process was best summarized by Goetschius when he said, "the purpose of examinations is to find out what the student knows, not what he does not know."

V

Aside from tests, two other important and interrelated aspects of evaluation require consideration, namely, the problems of grading and of self-evaluation by the student. Let us examine them with a view of suggesting possible solutions for each.

In organized education systematic records of achievement are essential. Hence a marking system is implicit in evaluation. Three general types of evaluation are current: the testing of factual knowledge based upon routine memory; an improvement in the construction of tests to include practical aspects, objectives, and some consideration of process; and finally the evaluation of the total learning process, including results. Obviously the last has superior values, but at present the second is most widely used, and often serves as a compromise between the two extremes. Consequently it will serve as a basis for our discussion.

The necessity for grades is sometimes deplored by both students and teachers, yet in real life such records are often kept. For example, large corporations make annual evaluations and written reports on all employees based upon their daily performance. The report is quite detailed, including a critical appraisal of specific personal attributes and abilities. It is prepared by the administrative officer under whom the individual works and its contents are confidential. In many respects it is similar to the folder on each student used to implement the third type of grading mentioned above. Undoubtedly, daily performance is a good measure of effective teaching, but, when tried, it has been found difficult of application simply because students question the validity of negative judgments based upon their daily work. Hence, to a degree the formal examination protects the student in the sense that it is more definite and easily evaluated than a long series of daily grades. Contrary to general opinion, examination grades rarely deviate widely from daily grades: both types of evaluation are usually consistent with the observed intelligence of the student. Rarely does a good student "fail" or a poor student excel—if the test has been well made. Daily observation of the student probably provides the best and most practical means of evaluation, so that the experienced teacher is seldom surprised or much enlightened by examination marks.

A basic requirement of grading is the participation of the student in it. A good teacher can rate students with fair accuracy after a few weeks of observation, provided he has the confidence and cooperation of the group. The degree and type of participation will vary in different situations. Teachers usually feel capable of making fair evaluations, and in the long run this confidence is justified. The actual errors made by experienced teachers are probably very much less than is often implied. The teaching of insights and skills undoubtedly is a valuable basis for the appraisal of the whole learning process. The teacher, wrestling with concrete problems of learning, has many unique and valuable contributions to make to the theory of teaching. Hence his judgment should receive serious consideration in the shaping of educational policy. Too often professional discussions of educational theory imply that the experienced teacher is hardly more than a novice as regards proper procedures, whereas the reverse is often true. Hence, the actual practice of wise teachers in respect to evaluation and grading is quite apt to be functional in the best sense of the word.

As suggested above, a definite system of marking based both on daily grades and examinations will probably secure more student acceptance than systems based entirely on either examinations or on daily performance. Definite grades, if required, are best given by the letters A, B, C, and so forth, with an optional use of plus and minus. In reality such general approximations are comparatively easy. Life is essentially competitive, notwithstanding educational theories. The experienced teacher has little difficulty in grouping a class in these categories. Granted the decisions are partially subjective—but so are all decisions not based on scientific findings. Much ink has been spilled in the attempt to discredit such a system of grading, but the fact remains that evaluations on much more elaborate data are also subjective and, regardless of the system used, the teacher must decide whether his students are good, average, or poor in relation to each other and to generally accepted standards of achievement. Educators can well consider the relatively simple standards of applied music in respect to grading. No amount of educational theory will justify poor performance.

However, one other important factor must be considered in making evaluations, namely, *the purpose of the student* which is basic to all learning. The goals of achievement naturally differ for amateurs and professionals in music, and the status of the student in this respect must be considered. The objectives for amateurs are naturally more flexible and less technical than for professionals, so that different outcomes may be expected. Much of the present confusion as regards standards is due to precisely this point. Too frequently professionals are treated as though their chief interests in music were cultural and recreational. This vital difference was discussed in the preceding chapter but it needs re-emphasis here, for it must be taken into account in any system of grading. *Music is a profession, and as such must be treated with the same technical integrity as medicine or engineering.*

The determination of a term mark should be based equally upon class work and test marks. In order to do so, all assignments, though evaluated as done, should be submitted at the end of the course for final evaluation. Furthermore, the final examination should be brief, fair, and offer as many choices as possible. In no case should it contain "trick questions" or impractical or unmusical problems. There seems to be no valid reason why the grade of A or even of 100% should not be a possible mark for such a test. In a shooting contest such a score is at least theoretically possible—and is often approached. The theory that the possibility of perfection indicates a poorly constructed test is a curious one. Whenever possible, the examination paper should be returned to the student, perhaps without a grade, and the various errors be discussed as well as the basis for the over-all rating. Precise mathematical values should not be assigned to various parts of the examination in an effort to objectify the grade or give added weight to certain problems. Such calculations are futile. The questions should be of relatively equal importance, or, if variable, can be adjusted without mathematical gymnastics. The whole process of grading is dependent upon intangibles whose values can only be approximated by experience and a strong sense of justice on the part of the teacher.

Undue leniency invalidates the whole process. A high grade for effort alone devaluates the grade won by superior ability. Students value and respect marks earned by achievement. Yet some teachers will give an entire group a high grade for attendance only, when no fixed grade should be given. The best type of student justly resents high grades received in this manner by inferior students.

Occasionally, re-examinations are justified, particularly in rare cases when the class work has been strong and the examination weak. In no case, however, should as high a grade be given for a re-examination as would have been given for the same quality of work done the first time. Obviously, specific re-examination problems should differ from those of the original examination.

Ultimately all evaluation is subjective in "theory" examinations. However, there are three means for reducing this subjective element, which may be summaried thus:

(a) *The identification of papers by number* rather than name was suggested in Chapter II, page 37, as an aid to objective grading. This device is most practical and useful in evaluating written tests of all types and is often used on the graduate level. The instructor's judgment is inevitably influenced by his knowledge of the student; and if this subjective factor can be reduced by use of numbers, the resulting evaluation will be much more objective and fair to the group as a whole.

(b) Another device for promoting objectivity is to have examinations involving performance, i.e., music reading and keyboard harmony, *conducted by a jury* that may or may not include the student's own instructor. Such a procedure is frequent in applied music examinations and contests, and certainly reduces to a minimum individual subjective judgments. It is strongly recommended as the best means of fair evaluation, and might even be extended by having teachers exchange examination papers for grading.

(c) A third device for improving judgments is *a meeting of the theory faculty* at the end of each semester for the purpose of exchanging grades, equalizing judgments, and eliminating students who have shown consistent weakness either in one or in several areas. "Borderline" cases are best decided by the faculty group rather than by the individual teacher. For example, a student receives C minus in one area and D or F in another from different instructors. Without a pooling of information, each instructor may incline toward leniency, but if all the facts are known the group can decide upon a consistent grade for both areas. Furthermore, the student who fails twice in any area, regardless of other factors, should be eliminated. This process of "weeding out" must be applied particularly to the lower levels, so that weak students are not permitted to reach the final year with any doubt as to their ability or competency. Without such group action, problem cases always occur during the graduate year, and when they do the innocent teacher rather than the weak student is usually "on the spot." Hence, for the protection of both the institution and the weak student, early *group decisions* should be made regarding his ability to successfully complete the course of study. The *average* grade of such a student is a poor approximation of his achievement, as in the case of grades of D and B averaging C. Only group action by the "theory" faculty can solve this problem adequately.

Grading, like many other problems, is often more difficult in anticipation than in reality. Though never an easy nor a pleasant task, it nevertheless can be met with confidence and equanimity if the instructor will approach it as objectively as possible and remember, in cases of doubt, to temper justice with mercy.

VI

Our final problem in evaluation is one related both to drill and to appraisal, namely, the best means for organizing and stimulating self-evaluation by the student. This vital area has seldom received the attention it merits. Admittedly, education is essentially a process of self-development, or, as Butler said, "Education begins with discipline and ends with self-discipline"; but as yet little self-discipline has been incorporated in the learning process.

Functional drill best originates with the learner, under guidance, to overcome a recognized difficulty. Self-evaluation by the student should be encouraged. A real understanding of this principle would improve learning and save class time that could be used for better purposes. Let us consider how the principle could be applied to both drill and evaluation.

Obviously, the best drill is the one suited to the student's own problems. Students are usually conscious of their needs but lack the ingenuity to contrive devices to meet them. Here the teacher can draw on his experience with similar situations and suggest remedial measures. Analysis is the first step and is certainly a major part of the problem. It is not easy to suggest devices for self-help—but it can be done. Here are a few suggestions:

1. *Written harmony*
   Harmonization of melodies to be compared with the composer's solution. (Bach chorales are one source—although somewhat difficult.) The teacher should be able to suggest a wealth of pertinent material to be used in this manner.

2. *Keyboard harmony*
   (a) The same procedure for melodies. Also playing by ear much familiar music, either melody alone or with harmonic background.
   (b) For transposition, the playing of music using the opposite key signature. For example, *Träumerei* in the key of F♯ rather than F major, or Mozart's familiar C major piano sonata in C♯ major. Bach's *Well Tempered Clavier* is excellent material, especially the preludes and fugues in remote keys. For example, play the C♯ major Prelude and Fugue, Book I, in

C major. Its complicated relationships will be amazingly clarified.

3. *Listening*

Familiar music, easily recalled, can be used for:

(a) Writing from memory, either melodies alone or with chords.

(b) Visualization of either the staff or keyboard.

(c) Recall of the "color" of specific chords or passages.

(d) Furthermore, the mental ear can be stimulated by the identification of various aspects of music heard anywhere. For example, determine the mode, meter, texture, relative consonance and dissonance, and rhythmic patterns. With practice, it is possible to recognize certain familiar chord progressions. Limitless possibilities for "ear training" can be found by these means.

(e) Play a melodic or harmonic phrase and write it from memory. This is much more difficult than would be supposed. The fact of having seen and performed the music aids in recalling it, but less than would be supposed. For non-pianists, this drill can also be done without performing the music.

(f) Memorize many new melodies. Write some and recall others.

(g) For pianists it is often helpful to try to recall either the treble or bass part of familiar music.

(h) For pianists, play a chorale while singing in succession the three lower voices.

4. *Music reading*

(a) Study all types of vocal and choral music by listening to recordings while reading the score. Repeat without recording.

(b) Make sequential drills out of difficult passages.

(c) Sing all major and minor scales up an octave beginning on the same pitch. (For example C, which would be 1 of C, 2 of B♭, 3 of A♭, etc.

(d) Sing all types of chords similarly from one pitch.

5. *Analysis*

(a) Study of forms by listening to records while reading the score. Repeat without recording.

These are only a few of many such devices which the student can use for self-drill.

One of the most interesting possibilities for self-study is the production of a series of graded records for the practice of dictation.[24] The material as projected would be divided into records of intervals, bass and soprano, major and minor triads, and seventh chords, so arranged that they could be used without the aid of an instructor.

While there are many problems to be solved in the execution of such a project, yet the idea is sound, and it is to be hoped that some material of this type will ultimately be available for the practice of dictation.

But there is another phase of self-drill or self-discipline that can be of great value. Reference has been made to the fact that too often present methods fail to develop individual initiative and responsibility. As a result much class time is wasted, particularly in music reading and keyboard harmony, in hearing individual recitations. This time can be saved and used for desirable group activities if the student is made responsible for the preparation of the assigned material. Most of it is of such a nature that the student himself can measure his own mastery. For example, in music reading could not all the reading material for the semester be assigned *in advance* (e.g., one hundred exercises) and the class time gained be spent in the study of a choral work through performance, analysis, and listening to its recording? Surely such a study is a more efficient and rewarding use of class time than hearing twenty students stumble through assigned melodies or drills! The same procedure can be applied to certain phases of keyboard harmony—transposition, chord formula or playing by ear— leaving time free for criticism of harmonization, improvisation, and many valuable group activities.

The teacher's role is hardly that of a policeman to check on the performance of assigned material! The success of the experiment depends upon the willingness of the student to assume responsibility for certain routine tasks. But surely self-discipline is one of the major objectives of education and one well worth striving for. The delegation of some responsibility should begin on the lowest level, so that when the graduate level is reached the student will have learned the meaning of self-discipline. Naturally the initial responsibility must be light. At the beginning it would probably be wise to perform *as a group* certain portions of the assigned material, but in no case should the experimental procedure be weakened by individual recitations. If properly presented, students will respond to the challenge, and welcome not only the relief from the boredom of other students' recitations, but the opportunity for real growth through the study of great music in the time released by this procedure.

The second aspect of self-discipline, namely, methods of self-evaluation, is more difficult to organize and foster. Undoubtedly the drill material suggested above would give some basis for self-evaluation by the student, but the whole process depends more upon proper orientation and motivation than upon specific devices. Realization of purpose is the core of learning, and it is the student who ultimately must formulate and realize his objectives if true learning is to occur. Again it is a problem of self-discipline, which, as suggested above, is promoted by the acceptance and discharge of responsibility. Self-evaluation originates in an active desire for improvement, and it can be carried on only through rigorous self-discipline.

For all these reasons, the relationship of the learner to evaluation is a crucial factor in the whole learning process. Indeed, if the thesis of these pages is correct, both the learner and the teacher play roles of equal importance in the drama of education: the learner because it is he who does the learning, and the teacher because he is responsible for the creation of an atmosphere favorable to learning. Having considered two of the teacher's activities—planning and evaluating— let us consider in the next chapter how he can be trained to meet his responsibilities.

Chapter X

TRAINING

THE training of the teacher is a basic problem in organized education, since it influences educational outcomes. The teacher is also a learner whose beliefs and actions are vitally related to what he learns. The present unrest has challenged both the goals and methods of teacher training, making a restatement and clarification of each necessary. The traditional notion that mastery of subject matter was the sole requirement for teaching was never adequate, although it is still widely accepted in practice, especially by liberal arts colleges and professional schools. To meet justified criticism of this criterion, various alternatives have been suggested whose underlying philosophies are indicated by their titles: social-needs, job analysis, persistent problems, developmental teaching, etc. Of these four, the developmental approach offers the most promise of positive improvement in current methods. However, it is unnecessary for our present purpose to discuss these philosophies specifically, since they are adequately treated in many educational works. Our immediate concern is with the preliminary training of the "theory" teacher. The more general problems of personal and musical fitness may be postponed for the present in order to consider the specific needs of this type of teacher and how they can be met.

I

Teachers are trained in three types of schools: the conservatory or professional school, the liberal arts college, and the teachers college. The programs of each must be evaluated in terms of professional needs. Those of the "theory" teacher differ from music teachers in general only in emphasis—all require a cultural background, a knowledge of pedagogy, and adequate professional training. The "theory" teacher obviously needs specialization in his own area, but there must be clear relationships between all these areas. The responsibility for establishing such relationships rests both with those in charge and with the trainees. This problem will be discussed in the next chapter. Here it is sufficient to observe that such relationships are essential to functional learning as related to teaching.

How do these three types of schools meet the problem of teacher training? In the conservatory and liberal arts college there is little if any emphasis on the training of teachers. In both schools the mastery of subject matter is too often accepted as the sole qualification for teaching. Few include any method courses in their curricula. Undoubtedly this lack is due to three reasons: first, their basic aim is not the preparation of teachers, although many of their graduates do teach; second, method courses are seldom given on the undergraduate level, and third, and perhaps most important, the focus is either on performance or scholarship. However, these reasons are hardly adequate for the lack of any training in teaching, considering the large number of their students who become teachers. Furthermore, methodology in both types of schools is seldom abreast of the best educational practice, and hence their graduates who become teachers tend to perpetuate traditional and outmoded teaching procedures. If they later take courses in pedagogy it is difficult for them to change their educational outlook and methods. But even when adequately taught, few are able to transfer their own class experience into a teaching situation without assistance. For all these reasons, neither conservatories nor liberal arts colleges, in general, offer adequate preparation for teaching. Fortunately there are notable exceptions in both groups—schools that are successfully meeting the challenge of teacher training—but on the whole, the challenge is not met, either on the undergraduate or graduate levels.

In general, teachers colleges are more successful, as such training is their major objective; yet they also, by their concentration on pedagogy, often fail in their objective. This is particularly true in music education in which the teacher must be a jack-of-all-trades.

Students of history or English, for example, have no performing skills to perfect in addition to factual knowledge and pedagogy. But the music student must wrestle with the applied as well as with the academic aspects of his art, and consequently lacks time for real specialization. The natural emphasis being on methodology, subject matter and performing skills suffer accordingly. Thus, in many respects the teachers college is as deficient as the conservatory or liberal arts college in the training of teachers, but for the opposite reason: namely, a crowded curriculum whose focus on methods retards the mastery of subject matter or specialized skills. Too often the jack-of-all-trades is master of none.

This failure to adequately prepare students for teaching creates a serious problem. Obviously, good teachers have been trained in all three types of schools, yet each one is open to criticism. The ideal solution for the prospective music educator would be to complete a liberal arts degree before any specialization, as in the case of medical or law students, but unfortunately the financial rewards of teaching preclude any such luxury. The only practical solution would seem to lie in a recognition of *the equality of methods, subject matter, and performing skills*, and consequently of a curriculum that would preserve a better balance between them. With this compromise in mind, let us consider in detail the training desirable for prospective "theory" teachers.

II

The training of the "theory" teacher may be divided into three general areas: musical, cultural, and educational. All are interrelated, yet preserve their independence in certain aspects. The salient points of each may be summarized thus:

1. *The musical qualifications* include both insights and skills in musical structures (harmony, counterpoint, form, and orchestration), a keen and trained ear, pianistic facility, a wide knowledge of music literature, and a clear historical perspective of music as related to style. Creative ability, though not essential, is an asset, both as an antidote for academicism and as a basis for the guidance of creative work. Mastery of this whole area of specialization is essential. Nothing will compensate for its lack, simply because the teacher must teach *both people and subject matter*. Otherwise, subject matter could be eliminated, and classes be devoted entirely to the joys of human service and better living! Surely one of the major objectives of education is the understanding of the present in terms of both the past and the

future, and such an understanding cannot be achieved without a knowledge of our cultural heritage—in other words, without a mastery of subject matter.

2. *The cultural qualifications* are of particular importance in preparing to teach music, since culture is the soil from which music grew and flowered. Languages, literature, the fine arts, and history—all are related to music. Hence the "theory" teacher, since he deals so largely with the cultural and intellectual phases of music, requires a rich background in this whole area. He must avoid, at all costs, the narrow professionalism that sometimes limits and warps the performing artist. Though much of this cultural background can be related to music, yet to make such a relationship the criterion of value weakens the entire program. "A man's reach should exceed his grasp." Too narrow or "functional" a view of education defeats its own purpose. In fact, it is doubtful whether complete integration of culture and musical studies would be desirable, for doing so would almost inevitably warp the total picture. In other words, life as a whole comes first, and the prospective "theory" teacher must fit music into its total configuration rather than try to fit life into music. Hence the teacher's training, while essentially professional, should also be truly liberal in order to provide for contact with many phases of life.

3. *Educational qualifications* are best met in the teachers college both because of its orientation and educational philosophy. Specialized method courses in the teaching of "theory" will be discussed later in detail. For the present, we are concerned only with general courses in the psychology and the principles of teaching. As in the cultural area, these courses are of two types: those related specifically to music and those couched in general terms. Both have value but it is well for the musician, as a specialist, to learn to think in terms of abstract ideas which, in reality, determine his actions. The value of such general courses is sometimes questioned, but, as pointed out above, the student should learn to see these relationships for himself. In fact, education may be defined in terms of this ability.

From this discussion it is clear that the training of the "theory" teacher should be functional in the general rather than specific sense. Hence, a well-rounded curriculum will maintain a parity between the musical, cultural, and educational areas. The maintenance of such parity entails considerable revision of existing curricula in the teachers college, but emphasis on any one area distorts values which are basic to breadth of vision.

III

Among the educational qualifications mentioned above, none is more important than courses in methods and materials for the teaching of musical structure. Such courses are rarely given, largely because "theory" too often is relegated to a secondary place in the curriculum. If the student is trained as a choral or instrumental "major," or even as a musicologist, it is assumed that he can also teach "theory" without specialized training in that field. As a result, many specialists in other areas are teaching a few classes in "theory" with little or no mastery of either its subject matter or its methodology. This is a deplorable situation, since effective teaching, even along traditional lines, is dependent upon competent instruction. Furthermore, this practice perpetuates the use of obsolete methods and materials, and in consequence the whole area sags under the weight of tradition and incompetency. Undoubtedly it is a major cause for the failure of "theory" to justify its means and ends. The crux of the whole matter lies in the value placed upon "theoretic" study. *The teaching of musicianship is the vital core of the curriculum*—the center from which all musical activities should radiate. If it were so regarded, the same teaching competence would be demanded in it as in other areas. This competence can only be attained through mastery of materials and specialized training in their presentation. Hence, any adequate teacher-training program should provide the opportunity for such study on both the graduate and undergraduate levels.

IV

For the implementation of this basic philosophy, the establishment of courses in methods and materials is obviously the first step in the transformation of "theory" into functional musicianship. Furthermore, such courses must be as broad and inclusive as possible. Undue concentration upon any particular system or "method" invalidates the whole process. All *musical* approaches to the subject should be considered, supplemented by examination of various texts and observation of a variety of types and levels of "theoretic" teaching. Using all this data, the student-teacher will be prepared to formulate his own philosophy, determine his methods, and select his own material. In other words, *the primary objective of such courses should be enlightenment, not indoctrination.* This is a radically different objective from the imposition of a predetermined philosophy with all its implications for teaching. It is our purpose now to consider the content and operation of courses devised to meet this need.

The specific purpose of method courses in the teaching of "theory" or musicianship is the formulation of a basic philosophy by the student, implemented by effective methods and meaningful materials. In other words, our primary questions of *why* and *how* must be answered for the prospective teacher in terms of desirable goals and the means of their achievement. To do so, we shall consider the organization and activities of these classes in respect to their philosophy, methods, and materials, on both the undergraduate and graduate levels, followed by suggested procedures for the evaluation of their outcomes.

1. *The philosophy* underlying the teaching of musicianship should be clearly formulated and understood at the outset. This is best done by guided group discussion supplemented by assigned readings. Clarity of purpose is the key that unlocks the door of successful teaching. Hence considerable time may well be spent in orientation along the lines outlined in Chapter I. In addition to the formulation of a basic philosophy, such discussion should establish the values and relationships of the six avenues of learning presented in Chapters II—VII inclusive.

2. *Methodology*, as the core of the course, naturally occupies considerable time and attention. Some of its many facets include:

(a) Demonstration lessons by the teacher furnish the basis for the establishment of procedures in the six avenues of learning. The approach here should be musical and practical rather than theoretic and pedagogical. Often the class period may be opened by the class memorizing and singing, by rote, songs from standard literature. A number of songs can be learned in this way during a semester. By having the class sing them first with neutral syllables, then with letters, followed by aural analysis, many valuable musical and pedagogical facts can be discovered. But the chief value of this practice is that, by group participation in a musical activity, it establishes the best conditions for discussion about music. The teaching of some specific theoretic point is then demonstrated, followed by class discussion. Usually it is best to treat each avenue of learning separately. Naturally only one or two demonstration lessons can be given in each area, but even a few will serve to establish principles and procedures. An actual classroom situation would serve the purpose better, and should be used for demonstration whenever possible.

In this connection it should be noted that the teacher of methods is most successful in that field when he also is practicing, in a class-room situation, what he preaches. The blight of "theory" can attack educational courses as well as music "theory" courses. Too often the method teacher's experience in the classroom is either limited or non-existent. The daily problem of actually teaching subject matter—especially those involving skills—has a salutary effect on educational theory. The practising surgeon is probably the best lecturer on surgery. True, many great teachers of applied music have not been performers; nevertheless, one would hesitate to say that non-performance, for any teacher, is an asset rather than a liability. In some cases, its lack is offset by past experience, but even so there is always danger that theoretic rather than realistic considerations will be emphasized. For this reason, the method teacher should, if possible, maintain contact with the classroom.

(b) Principles and methods of procedure in the six avenues of learning can be based on the demonstration lesson and subsequent group discussion. Young teachers require specific procedures for all areas which will later be individualized and molded by experience in the field. A bare theory of teaching is not enough—it must be clothed by definite ways and means. Hence, once the principles are established by example and discussion, they should be clearly formulated and then applied.

However, before discussing this application, it should be noted that a functional methods course will, of necessity, include some actual, though indirect, technical instruction. To teach a subject well, requires much more specific knowledge than to have passed a course in it—a fact which the methods teacher will soon discover. In order to apply the methods formulated, the student's own technical skills must be sharpened and made serviceable. This should be done indirectly as the need arises, but the necessity for it must be met to insure success in the next step.

(c) Teaching by members of the class should follow the formulation of procedures—in other words, students will in turn teach the group. This can be done by making a weekly assignment to all of a teaching outline for some specific point to be taught to the group the following week. Each student need not teach the entire lesson—but only enough to furnish a basis for evaluation by the instructor at the end of the period. Though this teaching situation is obviously artificial and difficult, yet much can be learned, especially by a comparison of different presentations of the same lesson. The transfer from theory to practice is surprisingly slow, and without this check it is absolutely impossible to determine how much transfer is being made. Term papers or similar devices simply are inadequate. As well discuss applied music techniques and then evaluate the students' facility in their use by a written report instead of by an actual performance! This lack of practical application is a serious weakness in many methods classes. The effectiveness of the solution suggested above is dependent upon the size of the class. Obviously it is impractical for very large classes—yet in groups of twenty or thirty there should be opportunity for each student to teach, for a few minutes, at least once during the semester. The lack, both of teacher demonstration and of student teaching, makes the large methods class purely theoretical in the worst sense. In such cases, the class probably should be subdivided into smaller "discussion" groups, possibly in charge of a graduate student, in which both activities could be carried on. Certainly, in courses dealing with the teaching of "theory," some provision should be made for these activities.

(d) Coaching weak students in other classes is another means of applying the methods formulated in class. This coaching can be done either individually or by forming "practice" or remedial classes for a number of weak students. Coaching of either type should only be done by competent student-teachers, preferably with some experience in the area, although occasionally intelligence and knowledge of the subject will compensate for lack of experience. This procedure is, in fact, a form of practice-teaching, and should have as much supervision as is practical. Both types of coaching have proven successful in practice.

(e) Methods may be clarified by assigning technical problems to be solved by the class as a whole, e.g., the setting of words to music, instrumental and vocal harmonizations, passages for analysis, or the finding of illustrative examples in music literature. This activity serves two purposes: first, it provides the teacher with material for the discussion of methods of evaluation and criticism, and second, it serves to review and to perfect the individual technical skills of the group. Let us consider some of the values of each.

In the first place, such assignments should be occasional and not preceded by any specific technical instruction, except that gained from the demonstration and student teaching for the group. Their primary purpose is to show procedures for evaluation. The teacher makes written comments on each paper, which is returned to the student and serves as a basis of class discussion. Individual technical learnings are concomitant. Nevertheless, this procedure does meet the need cited above of checking mastery of skills, and it gives both the teacher and student mutual insight in this respect. Such insight is essential for the teacher in estimating the present needs and potential possibilities of the student as a teacher. But, as stated above, it is merely a useful check, since students in a "theory" methods class should have mastered basic skills if they expect to teach them.

(f) One final facet of methodology requires comment, namely, the observation of as many different types and levels of "theoretic" instruction as possible. The scope and variety of this observation will naturally vary with the location of schools giving theory method courses. A large city offers many more opportunities for varied observation than does a small college town. Yet, within the framework of the environment, enough observation should be done by the student-teacher to give a cross-section of procedures on all levels. The student keeps a record of these observations, with critical comments, to be handed in for evaluation at the end of the semester. Observations of real teaching situations clarify and focus the philosophy and methodology discussed in class. Nothing can substitute for this comparison of theory and practice, and for this reason it is essential that organized observation be included in a well-rounded course in "theory" methods.

These, then, are the principal activities connected with the teaching of specific methods in the six avenues of learning. Let us consider next the materials to be discussed in a teacher-training class.

3. If educational philosophy must be channeled through methods, certainly methods, in turn, must be implemented by *materials*. There are a variety of materials to be evaluated in a "theory" methods class, including texts, use of musical literature, and various theories of musical structure. These three types of materials may be summarized thus:

(a) Textbooks are usually regarded as the main source of materials, although actually they are only one source. Here, as elsewhere, it is essential that the student-teacher be given as broad and comprehensive knowledge of the field as possible, yet there are so many textbooks that an evaluation of all of them is impossible. Furthermore, they vary greatly in value. The best solution is probably a selective bibliography of the best textbooks in all areas and on all levels from which a cross-section is selected for review. The student should review a number of these which he himself chooses on the basis of his interests and needs. His choice should be guided by the teacher's discussion and appraisal of the entire bibliography. The student will then select half a dozen or more which he will evaluate, in writing, on the basis of each book's unique features and utility for specific levels and situations. In order to cover as much material as possible, the teacher should specify that a certain number of these written reports be read in class—one by each student—assigning a definite date for each report. These reports furnish excellent material for group discussion and enable the group, as a whole, to get a much broader acquaintance with existing texts than could be obtained solely by individual reading. If desired, a student committee can be appointed to edit these class reports and to have them given to the group in mimeographed form at the end of the semester, thus providing valuable reference material.

(b) The use of musical literature as material falls into two categories: that of standard works suitable for classroom use, and that of passages for illustrative or teaching purposes. The first use is to supplement text material. As indicated in previous chapters, standard choral works should be used for music reading, and orchestral or chamber works for the recognition of large forms, style, texture, etc., as well as piano compositions for specific analysis of harmony or design. Suggestions for the selection and use of this material should be made in the methods class.

The second use—that of passages from literature for illustrative or teaching purposes—is one of the most important activities for the teacher both during pre-service and in-service training. It is the application of the basic philosophy set forth in Chapter I: namely, that the structure of music should be taught through music itself. Every teacher should compile a classified list of such material representative of each chord and form. In addition, a repertoire should be memorized from it to illustrate all points taught. This is one of the most valuable assets of the student-teacher: the ability to play *from memory* examples of any point which he is teaching. More will be said of this need in the next chapter, but definite work along this line must be begun and fostered in the methods class.

(c) It is important also that the student-teacher have a general conception of the various theories of harmony and of structure. Too often he is restricted by familiarity with only one system or theory. Four important theories—those of Riemann, Schenker, Hindemith, and Schillinger—were summarized briefly in Chapter VI, page 99. The atonal theory of Schoenberg is available chiefly in articles, since he himself has published nothing except his *Harmonielehre* (*Theory of Harmony*), a conservative treatise on traditional harmony, originally published in 1911. (71). Some discussion of all these theories belongs in a methods class—though possibly on the graduate level. Certainly the undergraduate student should at least be familiar with their principles.

Having outlined the philosophy, methods, and materials presented in the "theory" methods class on the undergraduate level, let us consider next how its outcomes may be evaluated.

V

The evaluation of work done by students in an undergraduate methods class is often difficult, especially in large groups. It can be based on the following criteria: term papers, weekly lesson plans, teaching in class, and the final examination. These factors require individual comment.

(a) *Term papers* include not only the book and magazine evaluations, and observations of teaching mentioned above, but also a one-semester outline for the teaching of "theory" in the six avenues of learning. Here the student should select the level in which he is interested or expects to work. Often this outline can be made to meet a practical situation which the student must face, especially for graduate students who are in service. The planning of a unified and integrated course is valuable in summarizing and focusing class learning.

In addition to general topics, the outline should include specific assignments for material for class use or drill. It can be set up on a weekly basis, in six parallel columns, representing the work to be done in writing, reading, listening, playing, analyzing, and creating. The student should be left entirely free in the choice of text and material, since the outline is not only to be of practical value to him, but is also to be indicative to the teacher of the extent of the student's learning and ability to organize material.

Somewhat related to this general outline for all students is the *special project* type of work either by individuals or groups. When the course is offered for a variable number of credits, maximum credit may be earned by some type of special project related directly to the student's needs or interests. It will consist primarily of special emphasis on some phase of "theoretic" instruction: extensive reading in or observation of a particular area, the compilation of extended material from literature for class use, study of a particular system, or a comparison of several systems, some historical or musicological phase related to "theory," or extensive analysis of musical material. For example, in the field of analysis a piano student copied, for the author, on the score a detailed analysis of the form of the Beethoven piano sonatas which the latter had recently made. While the project did not involve original research by the student, yet the transcription of the analysis of the music to his own copy was a valuable experience, as he attested. Of course, original analysis could be done on a smaller scale.

A group of students may also work out a special project which is summarized in a mimeographed report and given to the entire class. This procedure aids in the integration of learnings, but it requires tween the two types will depend, of course, upon student preferences more time and organization than individual projects. The choice be- and needs.

(b) *Weekly lesson plans* have been discussed above, but they should be included in the term paper requirements of the course and submitted for final evaluation at the end of the semester. They should consist of both topics and materials, with a specific outline of procedure.

(c) *Teaching in class* by members of the group should also be part of the final evaluation of outcomes. The number of individual presentations will vary with the size of the class, but, if possible, each student should teach before the group at least once in each semester. If the size of the class precludes individual presentations before the entire group, they should be made before a smaller "discussion" group, as outlined above.

(d) *The final examination* is most efficiently and effectively handled by a true-false or completion type of test. The essay type, written outside of class, is difficult to appraise, since it may be "ghost" written or merely be a compilation of the student's reading. A well-constructed objective test is always preferable to the subjective type, especially in a class concerned with educational philosophy which may become very theoretic and esoteric indeed. The very nature of a methods class demands specific, objective reactions under test conditions, rather than long, flowery essays about educational theory, in order to compensate for the essentially theoretic nature of the course. The learnings must be objectified and made concrete and definite, if any valid attempt is made to evaluate outcomes.

All these factors cited above—term papers, weekly lesson plans, student teaching before the group, and the final examination—must be considered in the teacher's final appraisal of the student's learning.

But even with these aids the teacher's ultimate judgment here, as elsewhere, will be essentially subjective in nature, for the human element always colors all judgments, except in purely objective tests for measurement of specific abilities.

VI

The "theory" methods class on the graduate level presents new problems of methods and materials. It is concerned, as in other areas, *with specialization,* and consequently should be preceded by some preliminary methods course as outlined above. In other words, it deals more with specific problems than with general philosophy.

Its organization varies with circumstances. It may be a one-semester course following a similar preliminary course, or it may occupy an entire year, which, of course, is preferable. It should be a highly selective, seminar type of course in contrast to the large, heterogeneous group-type typical of the undergraduate course. Hence, it should be limited to students who possess adequate technical skills and whose major interest is the teaching of musical structures. Its objective is the refinement of all procedures and skills dealt with in the preliminary class.

The activities of such a class are both group and individual. A minimum core of group activity is necessary to unify and focus learnings, but the class should also provide for individual projects. The proportion allotted to each will depend upon the time available and the credit given for the course. However, we shall consider the maximum of common group activity from which selection may be made according to circumstances.

(a) Probably the unique and essential group activity which distinguishes the graduate from the undergraduate level is the working of weekly assignments similar to those given in the typical "theory" class. These assignments should summarize the material covered in the first and second years of written harmony. The technical points involved should not be taught to the class, since writing skills are a prerequisite for the course. Their purpose is dual: primarily, they furnish a basis for developing skill in evaluation, but they also serve to focus and perfect individual skills. The procedure is as follows: the written work is exchanged, each student evaluating during the week another student's work. When this is done, the student-teacher, at the piano, plays and discusses in class the paper which he has criticized. This inevitably leads to group discussion as to the validity of the criticism and many valuable pedagogical and technical points emerge as a result. The assignments should include all types of harmonic problems as well as analysis, counterpoint, and creative work, in order that the student-teacher may have experience in criticizing and evaluating work in all these areas.

All these written assignments are submitted at the end of the course for evaluation as regards both the work done and the criticism made of it. At the end, each student constructs a final examination based on the material covered in the written assignments, exchanges it with another student, who works it out and then returns it to the maker for evaluation. In this way, concrete problems of practice are solved and evaluated by each member of the group. Such a procedure is a very fruitful and meaningful method both of teaching evaluation and of improving individual skills. It also serves as an excellent unifying core for a class which might easily disintegrate into a number of individual problems.

(b) Other group activities include an extension of undergraduate activities: namely, the preparation of course outlines, research for materials in musical literature, comparison of various "theoretic" systems etc. In most cases, however, the group assignments discussed above will be sufficient as a core activity and others may be treated as individual projects.

The graduate methods class offers the best opportunity to develop the coaching or "practice" class activities mentioned above. Here the background and maturity of the student can well be utilized both for the help of others and for his own growth as a teacher. Obviously we learn by doing, and hence the more experience the graduate student has in actual teaching, the better. Whenever possible, a program of practice teaching should be set up and supervised on this level. In no other way can the teacher of the group be assured that real competence in teaching is being fostered and promoted in the methods class.

A consideration of outcomes naturally leads to the question of evaluation of graduate work. Here, judgment is dependent upon the results of all the activities discussed above, and it becomes more complicated and subjective than on the lower level. Objective tests are of little value, and evaluation must be made in broad, general terms. However, in actual practice the difficulties involved are more theoretic than real. The small, selective group offers no real problems of judgment comparable to those of the large, mixed group. On this level, the teacher can confidently rely on his over-all estimate based upon observation of the student's native ability and his performance of assigned tasks, without the confirmation of any final examination.

VII

In conclusion, a number of basic factors relative to the training of "theory" teachers have emerged from the foregoing discussion. Neither mastery of subject matter nor "professionalized" subject matter are adequate as the sole basis for teaching. Adequate methods courses are needed *on both the undergraduate and graduate levels* in order to make clear the philosophy, methods, and materials requisite for successful teaching. Present curricula in professional schools, liberal arts and teachers colleges all fail, in varying degrees, to meet this need adequately, because of a lack of parity between musical, cultural, and educational training. A revision of curricula to secure such a balance is indicated, including, in the educational area, specific methods courses in the teaching of musical structure. The purpose, content, organization, and evaluation of such courses on the graduate and undergraduate level were considered in detail, with an emphasis upon the teaching of music rather than "theory."

In addition, it should be pointed out that an understanding of people and the ability to work with them is basic to all teaching and underlies any training program. This means much more than the content of conventional psychology or methods courses, although it is the basis of them. Successful social relations cannot be taught— except by example—although they permeate all good teaching. They originate in a genuine interest and concern for the welfare of others. In the truest sense, the expression "a selfish teacher" is a paradox.

It should also be noted that good methods will not, *ipso facto*, make a good teacher. Teachers are born, not made. Methods courses can cultivate and enrich natural ability, but they are no substitute for it. *A method is only as good as the teacher who uses it.* All discussion of methodology is conditioned by this fact. In the next, and final, chapter some of the characteristics, functions, and background of the *good* as well as the successful teacher will be discussed in an effort to focus and summarize the thesis of these pages.

CONCLUSION

Chapter XI

THE TEACHER AS MUSICIAN
AND EDUCATOR

Good teaching of musical structure rests upon the recognition of the teacher as both musician and educator. Their degree of parity is an index of functional teaching. Without equality of emphasis the teaching of "theory" degenerates into either sterile formalism or futile "appreciation." The major criticisms of current practices originate in the imbalance of these dual roles of the teacher. Musicians stress the former, educators the latter, and too often this results in technicians without educational perspective, or educators without musical competence. Rarely are both functions blended successfully. Though teacher training is directed toward their fusion, the ultimate responsibility rests upon the prospective teacher, and this problem is our immediate concern. After consideration of each aspect and its motivation, some general conclusions will be drawn regarding their combination. This fusion is the next step beyond the curricular training of the "theory" teacher as outlined in the preceding chapter. It is the flowering of his training in terms of general attitudes, goals, and responsibilities, whose clarification is the object of the following discussion.

I

Musicianship will be considered first since it is the unique requisite for music teachers. In this sense, neither pedagogy, psychology, social philosophy, nor personality can compensate entirely for its lack. Musicianship is the aggregate of individual aptitudes, insights, and skills in respect to music. It is based primarily upon two related elements: æsthetic and aural response to tone. Æsthetic responsiveness is an instinctive reaction of the total personality to the stimuli of the art. It is a complex process whose psychological basis need not be considered here. On the other hand, aural response through the *trained* ear usually is the result of conscious thought and effort, although innate tonal aptitude varies widely in individuals. In other words, of these two basic elements the first is largely instinctive and the other rational. From them result responses to music on three progressive levels: the sensuous, the intellectual, and the ethical. Musicianship is the leaven of "appreciation." It makes possible progression from the lowest to the highest level of response.

But there is another closely related element implicit in all responses to music, namely, *the love for music*. No genuine response, unless it be purely physical, is possible without it. Yet essential as it is, love for music should not be confused with talent for music. Enjoyment and aptitude are not synonymous. It is entirely possible to experience musical enjoyment without possessing musical ability. Both, however, are essential for good teaching of music.

There are a number of general activities that promote musicianship. Perhaps the foremost is a wide exploration of all areas of music literature, with an understanding of their æsthetic, stylistic, and structural characteristics. A broad survey can only be made by the constant hearing, performance, and study of music. The study of literature through hearing is most fruitful when reinforced by use of the score. Whenever possible, listen with the eye as well as with the ear. To do so requires a considerable music library which should be constantly and systematically enlarged. Miniature scores for chamber, orchestral, and even operatic works are readily available. Scores should be taken to solo or choral concerts, and also used in conjunction with recorded and radio performances. On the other hand, if music is heard without the score, at the first opportunity identify from the score any unusual effects noted, whether of melody, harmony, rhythm, form, or orchestration.

In this connection it must be emphasized again that this exploration of music literature covers *all media of expression*. Violinists should own the Beethoven piano sonatas, pianists should analyze Schubert's songs, orchestral players be familiar with Bach's *Well Tem-*

pered Clavier, and singers should be acquainted with the Brahms violin sonatas, etc. Too often the performer knows only a part of his own field—and practically nothing of others. If this is true of performers, it is even more desirable that "theory" teachers explore the entire range of literature, since their function is to explain its structure and organization. Yet there are those teaching "theory" whose knowledge and breadth of interest in literature, as represented by their personal library, is extremely narrow.

Directly related to this exploration of literature is the collecting and cataloging of significant examples for class use. This point has been mentioned before, when it was suggested that these examples be important thematic fragments suitable for various levels of instruction and drawn from all areas of musical literature. A cross-section of these examples should be memorized for teaching purposes.

Of equal importance is the building of a library of books dealing with all phases of music. Technical works on "theory" naturally take precedence, yet the list can be extended indefinitely as interests widen. For example, the relationship of music to the other arts is a wide and fascinating field. Professional journals and musical periodicals, especially of a scholarly nature, belong in this category.

Performance is also a vital activity for the "theory" teacher both for practical and musical reasons. In no other way can he come so close to the heart of music. Performance is an antidote for formalism. It tends to free one from petty "theoretical" notions that have no validity in sound—which is the ultimate test. For these reasons alone, aside from the pleasure of performance, the teacher should remain a "doer." As Emerson [25] says, "The man may teach by doing, and not otherwise. If he can communicate himself, he can teach, but not by words . . . Your propositions run out of one ear as they ran in at the other. We have yet to learn that the thing uttered in words is not therefore affirmed. It must affirm itself, or no form of logic can give it evidence."

Composition is another aspect of performance that merits more attention than it receives. The spark of creativity, however faint, should be kept alive by making needed arrangements or adaptations of music—if not by original creative work. This activity is so directly related to the function of the "theory" teacher that special effort should be made to pursue it in some form, however small. School music organizations offer unusual opportunities for performance to the teacher-composer or teacher-arranger. The important point is to be an active *professor* of music, in the true sense of the word, whether by pen or performance. *Make music as well as teach it.*

All these general music activities promote musicianship, but beyond them are many cultural interests that would enrich the teacher's life and thus benefit his teaching. The circle of culture is measured by the diameter of interests, and this diameter can never exceed the needs of the teacher, since through music he contacts all phases of cultural life. Acceptance of this notion would profoundly affect teaching. Too often the "theory" teacher's interests are circumscribed by a narrow professionalism that excludes the world of culture beyond music. The teacher-in-service sometimes becomes absorbed with his immediate and exacting tasks. The plea of lack of time for general cultural interests is hardly valid, since available time is always commensurate with real desire. This point will be further discussed in connection with the teacher as educator, but here it is sufficient to point out the necessity for a broad cultural background that exceeds the narrow range of music alone.

The teacher himself must be aware not only of this necessity but also of the relationship of other cultural fields to music. No one can establish these relationships for him artificially. They must grow from his own curiosity and interest in all phases of living.

Here, then, is a broad program for the promotion of musicianship through musical and general cultural activities. It should be clearly understood that all such activities, musical or otherwise, are the primary, though not the sole basis for the teaching of music. Without musicianship the "theory" teacher, however expert in the field of education, will inevitably fail to convey to his students an enthusiasm for and an understanding of music. Good teaching about music depends ultimately upon a love for it, supported by deep and comprehensive insights into its essential nature and the possession of the requisite skills for the expression of these insights.

Thus the "theory" teacher must be a musician in the general as well as the specific sense—and even more, he must be a truly cultured person capable of awakening all the latent possibilities of his students.

II

But if a primary requisite for the teaching of music—and especially its structure—is musicianship, a knowledge of educational philosophy, principles, and practices is hardly of less importance. Without these guiding ideas and techniques, much of his musicianship will evaporate as futilely as steam without an engine. Knowledge and insights must be channeled through effective educational procedures to achieve their maximum power. Knowledge is power—but only when used effectively. A thousand examples testify the failure of knowledge alone to produce desirable educational results, How often are we confronted with the paradox of the "successful" teacher who is a poor musician, or the excellent musician who is a poor educator! The term *music educator* is in itself significant, and describes perfectly the ideal mating of music and education. Yet frequently the ideal is obscured by undue emphasis upon one or the other. The balance between the two is delicate, but not impractical, provided the necessity for it is fully realized. Both professional and educational competence are essential for good teaching in any field—and "theory" is no exception.

It is often stated that teachers are born, not made, and this is essentially true; but teaching is also an art which, though difficult and requiring long practice, can be cultivated. Desire for human service through the transmission of knowledge can only be realized when the individual is temperamentally suited for teaching. Personality is assumed to be innate, yet even the personality can be adapted to teaching by attention to certain aspects of behavior that are controllable. Among them Ervin lists enthusiasm, appearance, attitude, patience, humor, sense of the dramatic, and leadership. (189). These are excellent criteria for good classroom behavior on the part of the teacher, and they all should be studied and applied. In this connection it is well to remember that there are no uninteresting subjects—there are only uninteresting teachers.

However, *to entertain is not to educate*. Education is more than pleasant or even meaningful experiences. It is the transmutation of educational experiences into the coin of practical life. The teacher must kindle in the student the enthusiasm through which learning occurs. Nor is mere information either educational or cultural unless such a transmutation has taken place. Just how or when it occurs is unknown. Undoubtedly it varies with individuals. But it can be promoted by the intelligent use of tested classroom procedures known as "methods," which must be fitted to the individuality of the teacher and the exigencies of the teaching situation—as clothes are to the person. Hence, methods are most useful to the young, inexperienced teacher who needs short cuts in the long road of experience. *Ultimately all methods are individual*, since they are ways of doing things, and paradoxically, the teacher only becomes a *good* teacher when he abandons them in the formal sense.

Good teaching promotes good learning, and means essentially good communication, though more often by personality and example than by precept. "If the teacher have any opinion which he wishes to conceal, his pupils will become as fully indoctrinated into that as into any which he publishes. Men feel and act the consequences of your doctrine without being able to show how they follow. Show us the arc of the curve, and a good mathematician will find out the whole figure. A man cannot bury his meanings so deep in his book but time and like minded men will find them." [26]

Poor teaching results in meaningless experiences that are educationally sterile. Principles and practices of education clarify and vitalize the organization and presentation of these experiences for the young teacher. But both are gradually individualized by experience until, like the butterfly, the teacher emerges from his chrysalis of training and becomes a teacher in his own right.

III

Yet musicianship and pedagogy, though important, are only external requisites of teaching that are conditioned by two basic inner drives, namely, the love of teaching and the love of learning. These subjective aspects require the same balance as do the objective ones discussed above. Let us consider each in turn and how their balance may be achieved.

1. *Love of teaching* is based primarily on an interest in people and a concern for their welfare. As Marcus Aurelius said long ago, "Men exist for the sake of one another. Teach them, then, or bear with them." For the real teacher, teaching is a passion, not an occupation. It is a continually new experience for both the teacher and the learner, to be anticipated with zest and recalled with satisfaction. The business of the teacher is not primarily to impart information, although the true teacher cannot help doing so. His function is to arouse in the minds of his students an unquenchable thirst for truth —and it may not necessarily be his "truth" at all. Facts are important; but ideas are more important, for while not every fact is an idea, every idea is a fact. In the vast field of knowledge all subjects have equal dignity. Sanscrit and vector analysis are as "important" as history, English composition, or harmony. The teacher's job is to stimulate a love for the subject taught. This can only be accomplished by the teacher's own love for it and by his eagerness to communicate it to others. He must be a prophet, even in an educational wilder-

ness: he must be a zealot, aflame with his cause. If subject matter is the blood of teaching, surely this enthusiasm is its circulation which gives life to the whole process. Obviously poor "circulation," in this sense, is the cause of much ineffective teaching. Teaching is a joy and a privilege as well as a challenge, and only those who fully realize this can teach effectively.

2. The other basic drive of the teacher—*love of learning*—is a broad extension of his love of music and interest in all cultural areas mentioned above. The true teacher loves learning *for its own sake*, as a sportsman loves a race or a sailor the sea. Love of learning is no ivory tower of retreat from reality into dead scholasticism. Rather it is a living and consuming interest in learning—an insatiable curiosity and desire *to know*. It is the spark that keeps the fire of knowledge burning. To educate, he must communicate; and to do so effectively he must love not only what he communicates, but learning *per se*. Otherwise he cannot kindle a similar spark in the student. This love of learning results in a multiplicity of interests which are the harmonics that enrich the fundamental tone of the teacher's personality. Without it he is "as sounding brass, or a tinkling cymbal."

Though education has been defined above in practical terms, the knowledge acquired through this love of learning cannot be appraised by any rule-of-thumb standard of utility. It is its own reward: the pleasure derived in its pursuit cannot be measured otherwise. In this practical world we must take time to be "impractical"; we must cultivate the "useless," as well as the useful. When James Russell Lowell said that "the glory of the university is that it teaches nothing useful," his paradox contained a profound truth. The purpose of education is not to turn out efficient money-making machines: its purpose is to promote learning, to produce interesting personalities and well-stocked minds. An entirely "practical" world would be intolerable. We live by our illusions—perhaps even our illusions of practicality. And so the teacher must transcend the limitations of purely utilitarian, vocational standards and be free to explore whatever his fancy dictates. He must enjoy both teaching and learning *for themselves*, as means of self-expression and self-development that give him one of the most lasting and complete satisfactions possible in so practical a world.

These two inner drives of the teacher—love of teaching and love of learning—require the same balance or integration as do the acquired aspects discussed above. The reason is obvious: stress on either weakens both. The born teacher who cares little about learning *per se* is often a "successful" but hardly a "good" teacher, since he fails to give his students all the rich cultural overtones. On the other hand, the scholar without a love of teaching often communicates his wisdom ineffectively, and thus also fails as a "good" teacher for precisely the opposite reason. The failure of each is similar to that noted above in regard to musicianship and pedagogy, but here the meaning is much broader and more general. It refers, not to the acquired insights and skills, but to deep psychological "drives" which demand satisfaction—the inner urge to teach and to learn. When these drives are complementary, good teaching results if implemented by real musicianship and sound pedagogy, *but not otherwise*. Insights and skills can be acquired, but these basic drives cannot be, and it is in this sense that a "good" teacher is born, not made. However, the realization of this fact is often helpful since it clarifies many obscure reasons for success or failure in teaching. If the reasons are understood, appropriate action can be taken. Their parity must be recognized and preserved at all costs. A teacher must have both something to teach and the skill to teach it; and even more, he must have an insatiable thirst for knowledge and for its communication to others.

IV

Hence, the phrase "the teacher as musician and educator" is full of meanings and implications. As a musician, he must possess æsthetic and tonal responsiveness, a love of music, and the requisite insights and skills to make clear its structure to others. These insights and skills can be developed through a variety of activities that were suggested. But above all, he must be a *growing musician*, interested and competent in all cultural phases of his art and related fields. His culture must be broad enough to transcend narrow professionalism, since he is concerned with an art that is related to many phases of life. As an educator, he must have a clear perception of the principles and practices of teaching, a good personality for teaching, and an understanding of and interest in people. He must use methods as flexible procedures to be adapted to circumstances and finally individualized through experience rather than as fixed ways of doing things. He too must be a *growing educator*, constantly alert for new devices of planning, teaching, and evaluating. Good teaching is dependent on a balance between musicianship and pedagogy—neither has precedence.

But in addition to these more or less acquired requisites are the basic inner drives to learn and to teach, which transform teaching from a science to an art. They are innate and must be as well integrated and balanced as the acquired requisites of musicianship and pedagogy, if the Scylla and Charybdis of scholasticism and educationalism are to be avoided. In a sense, these drives are the overtones of personality which add color and individuality to teaching. The "good" teacher is one who has, in fullest measure, the knowledge, skill, and desire for educative communication. Ultimately, good teaching is only good communication—with all its implications.

And so, by concluding our discussion of the teacher as musician and educator, we have completed the full circle of our inquiry into the teaching of musicianship, and answered, in part at least, our initial questions of *why* and *how* in respect to education. If the discussion at times has been general rather than specific, it is because the "theory" teacher differs in degree, but not in kind, from any teacher of music. The equation of teaching can only be solved in personal terms: the individual will always remain its most important factor. All communicable knowledge must be channeled through the teacher, and, like impersonal light passing through a prism, it emerges colored by his mind and personality. His genius consists in finding an opening into the student's mind through which these rays of knowledge may enter and illuminate it. *Illumination is the purpose of education*—not knowledge, skill, satisfaction, social adjustment, or earning a living—for illumination is enlightenment which, in the truest sense, solves all problems. This is the clue to good teaching, musical or otherwise. When applied to the structure of music it means that the student, *through the teacher*, sees clearly all its relationships and meanings and is able to express them through adequate techniques. The achievement of musical illumination for the student is the problem and the joy of the teacher. All means serve this end. When we see, we can discriminate; and so it is natural that Aristotle, quoting from Plato, should say, "True education is that we shall learn to form a right judgment about our pleasures and pains,"—and certainly, of all our pleasures, those derived from music are among the most keen and the most penetrating.

1. See Alexander H. Zimmerman, "Tonality of the Sonata-Allegro Form in Certain Representative Classical and Romantic Symphonies," Doctor of Philosophy thesis, Teachers College, Columbia University, 1950. [14]

2. The precise relationship of skills and insights is difficult to define. Undoubtedly many skills result from insights, but the reverse is also true. They may be regarded as the right and left hands of learning whose precedence depends upon circumstances. Often they occur simultaneously. [16]

3. The various uses of the C clef—especially for the alto and tenor voices on the third and fourth lines—should be taught very early through the examination of string and orchestral scores. [20]

4. Piston, *Harmony,* pp. 41-64. [27]

5. The contemporary composer, Harold Morris, has pointed out the curious fact that all great composers, with the exception of Wagner and Berlioz, played either the piano or organ. [30]

6. See Goetschius, *Elementary Counterpoint.* Toch, in *The Shaping Forces in Music,* argues that through the use of non-harmonic tones harmony becomes "arrested motion," thus implying its linear origin. However, in forming elementary concepts of texture, it seems best to differentiate the two techniques. [32]

7. There are a number of projectors available but not all are of suitable size. The one referred to is the Beseler, distributed by E. J. Barnes & Co., Inc., and Stanley Bowmar Co., New York. [38]

8. "Heard melodies are sweet but those unheard are sweeter." Mozart writes in one of his letters to his father that his chief pleasure in music was hearing his completed compositions mentally before their performance. Certainly this must have been the sole pleasure of the deaf Beethoven. [43]

9. Charles H. Miller, former Director of Music in Rochester, stated at the Eastern Music Supervisors Conference in Syracuse in 1931 that "the tradition of teaching by the use of syllables has done more harm to the cause of music than all other influences combined." (*The New York Times,* March 18, 1931) [46]

10. Perhaps the only justification for the dictation of the melody *alone* is that of unaccompanied melodies, such as the Sailor's Song which opens Act I of *Tristan,* the English horn melody at the beginning of Act III, or Siegfried's Horn Call in *The Ring.* [66]

11. Murphy, *Form in Music for the Listener,* pp. 179-195. [75]

12. Many such arrangements are available. See list in Murphy, *Form in Music for the Listener,* pp. 198-199. [95]

13. Katz, *Challenge to Musical Tradition,* pp. 355-358. [113]

14. The Manhattan School of Music, New York. [128]

15. See Creative Music Committee of the Music Educators National Conference, and the Scholastic Creative Music Awards offered by Scholastic Magazines, 7 East 12th Street, New York. One of the important by-products of such contests is the local prestige that results for the winning composer, his teacher, and his school. Local papers naturally feature the "success story" prominently, often with illustrations, e.g., the *Sunday Messenger,* Athens, Ohio, May 22, 1949: Young Athens Composers Win Awards in Scholastic Creative Music Contest. [131]

16. As in the college class, which was organized into groups by the instructor and left to learn by group discussion for the entire semester. [137]

17. Harold Bauer once remarked that *curiosity* was the one essential requisite for success in music, or in any field, for that matter. [140]

18. Both types of contrapuntal study should be supplemented by class performance of illustrative literature. [148]

19. *New York Herald Tribune,* March 19, 1950. [155]

20. Murphy, *Form in Music for the Listener,* pp. 179-195. [157]

21. Piston, *Harmony,* p. 2. [169]

22. Mursell, *Music in American Schools,* p. 50. [169]

23. In this connection it should be noted that students can be urged to *work together,* pooling their knowledge and skills. This is a desirable activity quite different from copying another student's work. [181]

24. K. L. Dustman, Southwest Missouri State Teachers College, Springfield, Mo. [197]

25. Essay on *Spiritual Laws.* [217]

26. Emerson, *Spiritual Laws.* [220]

Organization of

BASIC THEORY COURSE

Fundamentals of Music I (First Semester)

I. MATERIALS

1. Basic text for six avenues of learning:

   > Murphy and Stringham: *Creative Harmony and Musicianship* (New York: Prentice-Hall, 1950)

2. Supplementary material:

   (a) Reading, for singing with words and use of C clef—
   > Davison and Surette: *Home and Community Song Book*, Concord Series, No.2 (Boston: E. C. Schirmer, 1931)
   > McHose and Tibbs: *Sight-Singing Manual*, 2nd edition (New York: F. S. Crofts, 1947)

   (b) Listening, for analysis of general structure, pertinent harmonic details, orchestral score, and memorization of themes—
   > Mozart: *Eine kleine Nachtmusik*, K.525

Note: Of the supplementary material listed above, only the Mozart miniature score (for directed listening) and the *Home and Community Song Book* (for singing with words) need be purchased by the student. If the C clef is taught in the first semester, the *Sight-Singing Manual* will also be required.

II . OUTLINE FOR FUNDAMENTALS OF MUSIC I

Week	Writing	Analyzing	Reading
1	The I and V chords. Key and tonality. Melodic line.	The period, using I-V chords.	Simple melodies using words and neutral syllables. I-V-I in arpeggio form, singing letters.
2	The V_7 chord. Concord vs. discord. Piano accompaniment ($\frac{6}{8}$). Staff measurement.	(continued) Add V_7 chord.	(continued) I - V_7 - I arpeggios, singing letters.
3	The IV chord. Plagal cadence. Passing and neighboring tones.	(continued) Add IV chord, and passing and neighboring tones.	(continued) I - IV - V_7 - I arpeggios, singing letters.
4	The II_6 chord. The suspension. New accompaniment figures.	(continued) Add II_6 chord and suspension.	(continued) Add II_6 to chord arpeggios, singing letters.
5	The cadential I_4^6 chord.	(continued) Add cadential I_4^6 chord.	(continued) Add cadential I_4^6 to chord arpeggios, singing letters.
6	The I_6 chord.	(continued) Add I_6 chord.	(continued) Add I_6 to chord arpeggios, singing letters.
7	The VI chord. Intervals: perf. 5th, major and minor 3rds for chord quality. The deceptive cadence. The anticipation.	(continued) Add VI chord, deceptive cadence and anticipation.	(continued) Add VI to chord arpeggios, singing letters. Stress quality of chords studied.

(First Semester, 4 or 5 hours weekly)

Week	Listening	Playing	Creating
1	Simple melodic and chord phrases, using I-V. Writing of melodies from memory.	Harmonization and chord patterns (block form), using I-V. Playing melodies by ear.* Improvise melodies in period and repeated phrase form.	The period. Setting of words without accompaniment figure.
2	(continued) Add V7 chord.	(continued) Add V7 chord and accompaniment figure in $\frac{6}{8}$.	Add free instrumental melodies.
3	(continued) Add IV chord.	(continued) Add IV chord and waltz accompaniment figure.	(continued)
4	(continued) Add II6 chord and suspension.	(continued) Add II6 chord, suspension and new accompaniment figures.	(continued)
5	(continued) Add cadential I$^6_4$ chord.	(continued) Add cadential I$^6_4$ chord.	Setting of words in period form (cont.). Add instrumental melodies in small A–B–A form.
6	(continued) Add I6 chord.	(continued) Add I6 chord.	(continued)
7	(continued) Add VI chord, deceptive cadence, and anticipation. Stress quality of chords studied.	(continued) Use of deceptive cadence for period extension in harmonization and improvisation.	(continued) Period extended by evaded cadence.

*Playing by ear, first of melodies and then of familiar songs with chord background, should continue throughout course.

Week	Writing	Analyzing	Reading
8	The II and III chords. Chorale harmonization using close position.	(continued) Add II and III chords. Find example of small (phrase) A—B—A form.	(continued) Add II and III to chord arpeggios, singing letters.
9		← Midterm Review →	
10		← Midterm Examination →	
11	Modulation (C-G). Major scale pattern. Major and minor 2nds. 2-voice writing.	Modulation to dominant (C-G).	(continued) Chord arpeggios modulating to dom. (C-G), singing letters and accidentals.
12	The V_5^6 chord. Modulation (G-D). Major key signature.	Mod. (G-D). Add V_5^6 chord. Find example of A-B form.	(continued) Mod. (G-D) through V_5^6 chord, singing letters and accidentals.
13	The V_5^6 chord (cont.) Modulation (D-A). Major and minor 7ths. 3-voice writing (SSA). The appoggiatura.	Mod. (D-A). The appoggiatura. Find example of A — B form.	(continued) Mod. (D-A) through V_5^6 chord, singing letters and accidentals.
14	The V_3^4 chord. Modulation (A-E).	Mod. (A-E). Add V_3^4 chord.	(continued) Mod. (A-E) through V_3^4 chord, using letters and accidentals.
15	The VII6 chord. Modulation (F-C). Intervals: perf. 4th, aug. 4th, and dim. 5th.	Mod. (F-C). Add VII6 chord. Find example of A–B–A form.	(continued) Mod. (F-C) through VII6 chord, using letters and accidentals.

Week	Listening	Playing	Creating
8	(continued) Add II and III chords.	(continued) Add II and III chords. Harmonization of chorales and descending scale, using close harmony. Improvise extended period form.	Vocal and instrumental melodies in extended period and small A—B—A forms.
9		← Midterm Review →	
10		← Midterm Examination →	
11	Modulation to dom. (C-G). Simple 2-part dictation (2 measures only).*	Modulatory chord patterns (C - G). Improvise repeated period form.	2-voice writing (SA). 2-part vocal and instrumental rounds.
12	Mod. (G-D) through V_5^6 chord. Simple 2-part dictation (cont.).	(continued) Modulatory chord patterns (G-D), using V_5^6 chord. The A—B form.	The A—B form applied to vocal and instrumental writing.
13	Mod. (D-A) through V_5^6 chord. Simple 2-part dictation (cont.).	(continued) Modulatory chord pattern (D-A), using V_5^6 chord. Transposition. The A–B form (cont.).	3-voice vocal writing (SSA). 3-part vocal and instrumental rounds.
14	Mod. (A-E) through V_3^4 chord. Simple 2-part dictation (cont.).	(continued) Modulatory chord patterns (A-E), using V_3^4 chord. Improvisation and transposition (cont.).	(continued)
15	Mod. (F-C) through VII6 chord. Simple 2-part dictation (cont.).	(continued) Modulatory chord patterns (F-C), using VII6 chord. Improvise A—B—A form. Transposition (cont.).	(continued)

*The 2-part dictation should consist at first of short figures *played only once*, so that the two voices must be grasped simultaneously. Eventually entire phrases in two voices may be heard thus.

Week	Writing	Analyzing	Reading
16	The V_2^4 chord. Modulation (B♭-F). 3-voice writing (SAT).	Mod. (B♭-F). Add V_2^4 chord. Find example of A — B form.	(continued) Mod. (B♭-F) through V_2^4 chord, using letters and accidentals.
17	The V_2^4 chord (cont.). Modulation (E♭-B♭).	Mod. (E♭-B♭). Find example of A—B—A form.	(continued) Mod. (E♭-B♭) through V_2^4 chord, using letters and accidentals.
18	Implied modulation to the dominant (A♭-E♭). The échappée.	Implied modulation to dom. (A♭-E♭). The échappée. Find example of A—B or A—B—A form.	(continued) Implied mod. to dom. (A♭-E♭), singing letters and accidentals.
19	←	Review	→
20	←	Final Examination	→

Week	Listening	Playing	Creating
16	Mod. (B♭-F) through V_2^4 chord. Simple 2-part dictation (cont.).	(continued) Modulatory chord patterns (B♭-F), using V_2^4 chord. Improvise A—B form. Transposition (cont.).	3-voice vocal writing (SAT).
17	Mod. (E♭-B♭) through V_2^4 chord. Simple 2-part dictation (cont.).	(continued) Modulatory chord patterns (E♭-B♭), using V_2^4 chord. Improvise A—B—A form. Transposition (cont.).	(continued)
18	Implied modulation to dom. (A♭-E♭). Simple 2-part dictation (cont.).	(continued) Modulatory chord patterns to dom. without melodic accidental (A♭-E♭). Transposition (cont.). A—B or A—B—A form.	3-voice vocal writing (SAB).
19	←	Review	→
20	←	Final Examination	→

III. TYPICAL ASSIGNMENTS

FIRST WEEK (see outline above)

Writing:

        1a. Set stanza to music (melody only), *or*
        1b. Write original melody for your own instrument.
        2. List of familiar songs, indicating by number or syllable the first and last tone of each.
        3. Analyze passage for chords and form.

Playing:

        1. Harmonize folksongs, playing the chords in block form with the left hand.
        2. Play familiar melodies from memory.
        3. Improvise melodies in period or repeated-phrase form.

Reading:

        1. Sing folksongs with words and neutral syllables.
        2. Sing I-V-I chords in arpeggio form, using letters (uniform rhythm).

Listening:

        1. Write folksongs from memory.
        2. Keep notebook of class dictation.

EIGHTH WEEK (preceding review for midterm examination)

Writing:

        1a. Set stanza to music (accompaniment optional), *or*
        1b. Write instrumental melody in any of the forms studied.
        2. Harmonize chorale in close position.
        3. Analyze passage for chords, form, and non-harmonic tones.

Playing:

        1. Harmonize descending C major scale, and repeat, embellished by neighboring tones or suspensions.
        2. Harmonize chorale in close position—bass alone in left hand.
        3. Harmonize melody with piano accompaniment.
        4. Improvise extended period.
        5. Play from memory familiar song or assigned theme in both a sharp and a flat key.

Reading:

        1. Sing folksongs with words and neutral syllables.
        2. Sing I-III-IV-II-I$_4^6$-V7-I in arpeggio form, using letters (uniform rhythm).

Listening:
    1. Learn themes (melody only) of movement played in class.

EIGHTEENTH WEEK (preceding review for final examination)

Writing:
    1a. Using the given harmonization of an art song, arrange 16 measures for soprano, alto, and bass, *or*
    1b. Write an original composition or an arrangement for instrumental trio, *or*
    1c. Harmonize melody for soprano, alto, and bass.
    2. Harmonize melody with piano accompaniment.
    3. Analyze passage for chords, form, and non-harmonic tones.

Playing:
    1. Make an implied modulation to the dominant key from major, using the following or an original chord pattern:
    tonic: I-V$^6_5$-I-I$_6$, dom: I$^6_4$-V$_7$-I.
    Repeat in piano style, embellished by *échappées*.
    2. Harmonize melody with piano accompaniment.
    3. Improvise small 2- or 3-part form.
    4. Transpose passage up and down a major and minor second or third.
    5. Review memorized songs or themes.

Reading:
    1. Sing folksongs with words and neutral syllables.
    2. Sing modulation given in *Playing* (1) above, using letters and accidentals (uniform rhythm). Learn in both a sharp and a flat key.

Listening:
    1. Review memorized themes from movements played in class.

IV. FINAL EXAMINATION

A. *WRITING, ANALYZING & CREATING (2 hours)*

1. Write and resolve the inversions of the V$_7$ chord and the VII$_6$ chord, making the pitch E the lowest tone of each chord.
2. Name all the major keys in which the following chords occur:

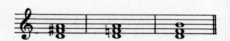

3. Name all the intervals in the following passages:

(a)　　　　　　　　　　　　　　　　　BACH, *W.T.C.*, I, Fugue 22

(b)　　　　　　　　　　　　　　　　　BACH, *W.T.C.*, I, Fugue 24

4. Work (*a*) or (*b*), and (*c*) or (*d*) of the following:
   (*a*) harmonize for SSA, SAT, or SAB

Allegro

   (*b*) harmonize for piano in close position:

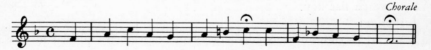

Chorale

   (*c*) harmonize for piano with melody in r.h. and accompaniment in l.h.:

Allegretto

   (*d*) set stanza to music for SSA, SAT, or SAB. (Accompaniment optional)

5. Answer either (*a*) or (*b*) below:
   (*a*) write a melody in A-B or A-B-A form
   (*b*) cite an example of the A-B and A-B-A forms

6. Write an example of each non-harmonic tone discussed in class.

   B. *LISTENING* (*2 hours*)

1. Answer either (*a*) or (*b*) below:
   (*a*) write from memory the melody of *America* in F major—
   the first half in $\frac{3}{2}$, and the second half in $\frac{3}{8}$.
   (*b*) write from memory a period of a melody that you recall.
   Identify melody, type of period, and cadences.

2. Write from memory one theme (melody only) from each movement of Mozart's *Eine kleine Nachtmusik*. Identify the theme and
   the form of the movement.

3. Write the melody, bass, and name of chord of the following dictated passage and identify the form:

4. Write the following phrase in 2 parts:

5. Analyze the form of a recorded composition. (Any simple A-B
   or A-B-A form, e.g., Mendelssohn's *Variations sérieuses*, theme
   only, or *Songs Without Words*, No. 48)

   C. *READING* (*2 hours*)

1. Sing the following chords in arpeggio form, using letters and

accidentals. (To be prepared in both a sharp and a flat major key chosen by the student):

$$I-V^6_5-I-V^4_3-I6-V^4_2-I6-VII6-I$$

2. Modulate to the dominant key, singing chords in arpeggio form, using numbers and letters. Enter new key through its I^6_4. (To be prepared in both a sharp and a flat major key chosen by the student)

Note: 1 and 2 above should be sung in major keys of four different letters.

3. Read a folksong at sight with neutral syllables (or letters for C clef).

4. Read at sight a folksong with words.

D. *PLAYING (2 hours)*

1. Harmonize the ascending and descending major scale. (To be prepared in both a sharp and a flat major key chosen by the student.)

2. Play and resolve the inversions of the V7 chord and the VII6 chord in close position from two bass tones. (To be prepared on tones chosen by student.)

3. Modulate from a major key to its dominant key. (To be prepared in major keys representing four different letters—two in sharp keys and two in flat keys.)

4. Harmonize a folksong at sight.

5. Transpose the following passage at sight (major or minor 2nd or 3rd, up and down):

Allegro   German Folksong

6. Improvise small A-B or A-B-A form on a given motive.

A P P E N D I X   I I

Organization of

FREE COUNTERPOINT COURSE

I. MATERIALS

1. Goetschius, Percy: *Applied Counterpoint* (New York: G. Schirmer, 1915)

2. Bach, J. S.: *Well Tempered Clavier*, Book II

3. *The 389 Chorales of Johann Sebastian Bach* (Princeton, N. J.: Association of American Choruses, 1944) *or*
   Anniversary Collection of Bach Chorales (Chicago: Hall & McCreary, 1935)

II. OUTLINE FOR FREE COUNTERPOINT COURSE

Week	Counterpoint	Chorale-harmonization	Analysis
1	Natural double counterpoint.	Melody in bass.	Bach, *W.T.C.*, II,* Prelude 24 for example of double cpt.
2	Artificial double cpt.	(continued)	Prelude 20 for example of double cpt.
3	2- and 3-voice canon.	(continued)	Prelude 8 for canonic imitation and double cpt.
4	Imitation at the 8th (2 voices).	(continued)	Prelude 10 to double bar for use of motive.
5	Imitation at the 5th (2 voices).	Melody in tenor.	Prelude 19 for use of motive.
6	Imitation at other intervals (2 voices).	(continued)	Prelude 6 for use of imitation.
7	Imitation by inversion, retrograde, augmentation and diminution (2 voices).	(continued)	Fugue 3 for use of motive.
8	Stretto imitation (2 or 3 voices).	(continued)	Fugue 2 for use of stretto.
9	←	Review	→
10	←	Midterm Exam.	→
11	Non-modulatory fugue subjects and answers (2 or 3 voices).	Melody in alto.	Classify all fugue subjects in *W.T.C.*, II, as real or tonal.

*In addition to material from Bach's *Well Tempered Clavier*, Book II, a chorale is assigned weekly for harmonic analysis and is sung and discussed by the class.

(One semester, 2 hours weekly)

Week	Counterpoint	Chorale-harmonization	Analysis
12	Modulatory fugue subjects and answers (2 or 3 voices).	(continued)	Find all modulatory fugue subjects in *W.T.C.*, II.
13	3-voice instrumental fugue in major. Non-modulatory subject. (a) Exposition.	(continued)	Exposition of fugues 1-5-11-15-17-21-23.
14	(b) Development of above.	(continued)	Fugue 9 for sections, cadences, and entrances of subject.
15	(c) Recapitulation of above.	Original chorale with melody in soprano.	Fugue 5 as above.
16	4-voice vocal fugue in minor (with words). Modulatory subject. (a) Exposition.	Original chorale melody of 15th week—melody in bass.	Fugue 22. Exposition in detail.
17	(b) Development of above.	Original chorale melody of 15th week—melody in tenor.	Fugue 22. Development in detail.
18	(c) Recapitulation of above.	Original chorale melody of 15th week—melody in alto.	Fugue 22. Recapitulation in detail.
19	←	Review	→
20	←	Final Exam.	→

III. TYPICAL ASSIGNMENTS

FIRST WEEK (see outline above)

Assignments

1. A number of examples of natural double counterpoint (at the octave) on assigned and original motives. (Goetschius, pp. 132-136)
2. Harmonization of chorale with melody in bass. (Goetschius, pp. 188-193)
3. Analysis of *Well Tempered Clavier*, Book II, Prelude 24, for examples of double counterpoint at the 8th.
4. Harmonic and stylistic analysis of Bach chorale.

Class Activities

1. Examine following examples of double counterpoint at the octave:
   Bach: *Two-Part Inventions*, No. 6 and No. 9
   Mozart: *Piano Sonata in F major*, K.533, first movement
   Beethoven: *Piano Sonata in F major*, Op. 10, No. 2, *Finale*
   (For additional examples, see Goetschius, p. 136)
2. Demonstration of method used for writing assignments 1 and 2.
3. Discussion of chorale harmonic idioms.
4. Sing, in four voices, chorale discussed.

EIGHTH WEEK (preceding review for midterm examination)

Assignments

1. A number of examples of *stretto* (above and below) at various intervals on both assigned and original motives. (Goetschius, Ex. 10, p. 93)
2. Harmonization of chorale with melody in tenor. (Goetschius, pp. 188-193)
3. Analysis of *Well Tempered Clavier*, Book II, Fugue 2, for *stretto*.
4. Harmonic and stylistic analysis of Bach chorale.

Class Activities

1. Examine *Well Tempered Clavier*, Book II, for examples of *stretto*, especially Fugue 1.
2. Demonstration of method used for writing assignments 1 and 2.

3. Sing, in four voices, the chorale assigned for analysis.
4. Play *Well Tempered Clavier*, Book II, Fugue 1, on multiple pianos and phonograph, noting *stretti*.

EIGHTEENTH WEEK (preceding review for final examination)

Assignments

1. Write the recapitulation (third division) of the 4-voice vocal fugue (with words) begun in the 16th week.
2. Harmonization of original chorale melody (15th week) with melody in alto.
3. Analysis in detail of *Well Tempered Clavier*, Book II, Fugue 22, recapitulation.
4. Harmonic and stylistic analysis of Bach chorale.

Class Activities

1. Sing, in four voices, the chorale assigned for analysis.
2. Play *Well Tempered Clavier*, Fugue 22, recapitulation, on multiple pianos and phonograph.

Note: Beginning with the study of the fugue in the 11th week, many recorded examples of fugues found in literature should be played and discussed in class, for example:

Bach: *B minor Mass*, and the organ fugues
Beethoven: Fugues in piano sonatas and string quartets
Bloch: *Concerto Grosso (Finale)*
Franck: *Prelude, Chorale, and Fugue*
Handel: *Messiah* (Amen Chorus)
Haydn: *The Creation* (Final Chorus)
Mendelssohn: *Elijah* (Overture and Final Chorus)
Mozart: *Requiem* (Kyrie)
Mozart: *String Quartet in G major*, K.387 *(Finale)*
Smetana: *Bartered Bride Overture* (principal theme)

There are also many contemporary works, e.g., William Schuman's *American Festival Overture*, that contain fugal passages. All the resources of literature should be used to show the fugue as a living expressive medium rather than as a dry academic exercise. Only pertinent details of these works should be noted. Thus performance in class should be primarily for musical rather than for technical reasons.

IV. FINAL EXAMINATION

(2 hours)

1. Write the exposition of a 3-voice fugue, using either of the following subjects:

(a) **Moderato**

Announce subject in soprano

(b) **Andante**

Announce subject in soprano

2. Analyze a short fugue in detail, e.g., Bach *Fughetta* in D minor (G. Schirmer Library, Vol. 15). (Write analysis on mimeographed copy)

3. Harmonize the following chorale for mixed voices, placing the melody in the voice indicated:

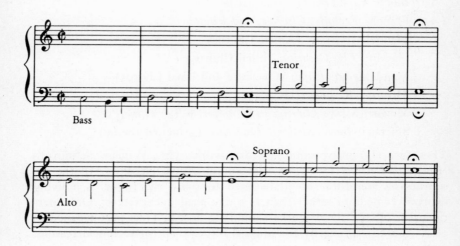

A P P E N D I X   I I I

COLLEGE HARMONY SURVEY

I. Selected Items from 1947 Harmony Survey

(Professor Frank W. Hill, Iowa State Teachers College)

This survey was based upon replies received from 70 institutions of higher learning, in response to a questionnaire concerning the operation of harmony courses in those institutions. A few of the pertinent facts drawn from the survey are given below with comments.

Of the responding colleges, 63 offer a course in ear training and dictation, 37 of them giving it as a separate course. Of the remainder, 4 do not offer such a course, while 3 did not respond.

As regards ten designated items included in first-year and second-year harmony, 63 colleges responded with the following results:

	NUMBER OF COLLEGES	
	1st YEAR	2nd YEAR
1. triads	62	25
2. dominant seventh chords	57	30
3. secondary seventh chords	34	42
4. diminished seventh chords	34	44
5. modulation to related keys	46	45
6. modulation to remote keys	5	59
7. chromatically altered chords	5	55
8. suspensions, anticipations, etc.	27	50
9. passing tones	45	44
10. harmonic analysis	38	55

[*Note*: The distribution of items included in a two-year course indicates that non-harmonic tones, harmonic analysis, and even secondary sevenths are often delayed until the second year in many institutions. The question arises as to how the presentation of dominant seventh chords (item 2) could be postponed so long in 30 colleges. H.A.M.]

245

In response to the query regarding original work required in outside assignments, 47 colleges answered *yes;* 14, *some;* 9, *no.*

In regard to correction of papers, 32 colleges indicate correction in class; 63, correction by the instructor outside of class; 13 indicate correction by assistants.

Of 69 colleges responding, 66 indicate that they think more basic theoretical work should be offered in high schools. However, 11 of those 66 qualify their statements, indicating dissatisfaction with the work now being done in high schools.

An interesting tabulation was made of the classroom texts used. The following list includes all books used in more than one college:

Frequency	*Author*	*Pub. Date*
19	Piston	1941
15	Wedge	1930–1931
11	Hindemith	1943
8	Bach chorales } not harmony texts	
8	McHose and Tibbs } not harmony texts	
7	Heacox	1920–1932
6	Goetschius	1892–1915
6	McHose	1947
6	Chadwick	1902
5	Foote and Spalding	1905
3	Alchin (rev. Jones)	1917–1930
3	Emery	1890
3	Smith and Krone	1937
3	Tweedy	1928
2	Andersen	1923

[*Note*: The frequent use of old texts is most significant, i.e., Goetschius, Chadwick, Emery, and Foote and Spalding, which were used in 20 colleges as against texts, published since 1930, in 54 colleges—a ratio of almost 3 to 1. Even more significant is the use of Emery (1890) in as many schools as Smith and Krone (1937). In fact, the use of the older books outnumbered that of Alchin (1917-1930).

A similar consideration of antiquated material is shown in the *Music Education Source Book* (1947) whose bibliography of theory texts, page 232, lists fourteen books whose average age is 25 years, the oldest being the venerable Bussler (1891). The only "modern" work cited is Cowell's *New Musical Resources* (1930). This book is not a theory text but a series of essays on experimental tone combinations, rhythms, and chord formations.

Both the Hill Survey and the *Music Education Source Book* show clearly that neither our colleges nor our educational groups are fully aware of recent developments in the teaching of "theory." How many colleges or high school English departments are using texts over 25 years old? Considering this shocking lag in "theory" texts used, the current criticism of both procedures and results is hardly surprising. H.A.M.]

COLLEGES RESPONDING TO HARMONY SURVEY (1947)

Alabama College
Albion College
Amherst College
Bluffton College
Boston University
Bradley University
Brevard College
Central College
Cincinnati College of Music
Coe College
College of Emporia
College of the Pacific
College of St. Catherine
Colorado College
Colorado State College of Education
Cornell College
Drake College of Fine Arts
Eastman School of Music
Emmanuel Missionary College
Florida State College for Women
Grinnell College
H. Sophie Newcomb College
Hamline University
Heidelberg College
Hendrix College
Howard University
Hunter College
Indiana Central College
Indiana University
Iowa State Teachers College
Keuka College
Lindenwood College for Women
Macalester College
McKendree College
McPherson College
Monmouth College

Municipal University of Wichita
Nazareth College (Michigan)
New Mexico College of Agriculture
    and Mechanic Arts
Northwestern University
Oberlin College
Ohio State University
Ohio Wesleyan University
Pomona College
Queens College (North Carolina)
Simpson College
Taylor University
Temple University
University of Arizona
University of Arkansas
University of California
University of Illinois
University of Kansas
University of Michigan
University of Missouri
University of North Dakota
University of Pennsylvania
University of Redlands
University of Tulsa
University of Wyoming
Vassar College
Washburn Municipal University of Topeka
Webster College
Wells College
West Virginia University
West Virginia Wesleyan College
Western Reserve University
Westminster College (Pennsylvania)
Wittenberg College
Woman's College of the University of
    North Carolina

II. A Comparison of the 1939 and 1947 Surveys

(Professor Frank W. Hill, Iowa State Teachers College)

This comparative study is based on returns from 87 colleges in 1939 and 70 colleges in 1947. Of the 70 colleges included in the 1947 survey, 57 are also included in the 1949 survey.

Any generalizations growing out of this study are made on the assumption that the colleges included in the two original surveys are representative institutions.

1. The prevailing practice is for harmony classes to meet three times weekly.

2. In 1939 the average enrollment in harmony was 40 students; in 1947 the average enrollment was 69.

3. There has been virtually no change in the average size of classes in harmony: 1939—16 students; 1947—17 students.

4. A wide variety of texts are used: 26 different authors are referred to in each of the two surveys. Piston and Hindemith have made the greatest gain in frequency of usage.

5. Of the 70 responding colleges, 76 percent indicate that the text used is at least reasonably satisfactory.

6. Approximately 85 percent of the responding colleges in each of the two surveys indicate that they are using supplementary instructional materials.

7. Approximately 15 percent indicate that they do not include keyboard harmony in the harmony course. There is practically no difference in the percentage of colleges not using keyboard harmony.

8. Both studies indicate that in almost all colleges (98 percent) final examinations are administered at the close of the course in harmony. In 80 percent of these colleges the administration of final examinations is looked upon with approval.

9. There seems to be considerable inconsistency as to what phase of harmony presents the greatest difficulty. Of the eight phases listed most frequently in the first survey, four (voice leading, modulations, chromatic alterations, inversions) are found among the first twelve in the second survey. The one phase (choice of chords) listed most frequently in the first survey is located in the 28th place in the second survey. The phases (minor mode, ornamental harmony, figured basses) listed 3rd, 4th, and 8th, respectively, in the first survey, are not found among the 32 listed in the second survey.

10. In 1939, 28 percent of the colleges indicated that they offer a course in modern harmony. In the 1947 survey this percentage had increased to 51 percent. Of the colleges offering work in modern harmony, 70 percent indicated that they were offering it as a separate course; 10 colleges indicated that modern harmony is required of those who are majoring in composition.

SELECTIVE BIBLIOGRAPHY

I. TEXTBOOKS

ELEMENTARY SCHOOL*

1. Diller, Angela: *First Theory Book* (New York: G. Schirmer, 1921)
2. Harris and Sims: *Learning to Listen* (New York: G. Schirmer, 1929)
3. Pitts—Glenn—Watters: *Our Singing World Series* (Boston: Ginn & Co., 1949 [The Kindergarten and First Grade Books, and the Accompaniment Books for Grades II—VI contain directions for teachers.]

HIGH SCHOOL*

(a) *rudiments*

4. Cookson and others: *Creative-Analytical Theory of Music* (Chicago: H. T. FitzSimons, 1948)
5. Diller, Angela: *First Theory Book* (New York: G. Schirmer, 1941)
6. Jones and Bailey: *Exploring Music* (Boston: C. C. Birchard, 1941)

(b) *written harmony*

7. Alchin, Carolyn: *Applied Harmony*, Parts I-II, rev. by V. Jones (Los Angeles: L. R. Jones, 1934)
8. Heacox, Arthur E.: *Harmony for Eye, Ear and Keyboard* (Oliver Ditson, 1932; Theodore Presser, Philadelphia, distributors)
9. McConathy and others: *An Approach to Harmony* (New York: Silver Burdett, 1930)

* On the elementary and secondary school levels there are available a number of student workbooks whose utility can be determined only by individual needs.

10. Murphy and Stringham: *Creative Harmony and Musicianship* (New York: Prentice-Hall, 1950)
11. Smith—Krone—Schaffer: *Fundamentals of Musicianship*, Books I-II, abridged edition (New York: M. Witmark, 1937)

(c) *keyboard harmony*

12. Diller, Angela: *Keyboard Music Study*, Books I-IV (New York: G. Schirmer, 1936-1949)
13. Lowry, Margaret: *Keyboard Approach to Harmony* (Philadelphia: Theodore Presser, 1949)
14. Murphy and Stringham: *Creative Harmony and Musicianship* (New York: Prentice-Hall, 1950)

(d) *dictation*

15. Murphy and Stringham: *Creative Harmony and Musicianship* (New York: Prentice-Hall, 1950)
16. White, Bernice: *Melodic Dictation* (New York: American Book Co., 1935)
17. White and Jones: *Harmonic Dictation* (New York: American Book Co., 1932)

(e) *music reading*

18. Hall, Minna F.: *Music Reading*, Book I (Boston: C. W. Homeyer, 1942)
19. Murphy and Stringham: *Creative Harmony and Musicianship* (New York: Prentice-Hall, 1950)
20. *The Folk Song Sight Singing Series*, Books I-X (London: Oxford University Press, 1933)

COLLEGE AND PROFESSIONAL SCHOOL

(a) *rudiments*

21. Bauman, Alvin: *Elementary Musicianship* (New York: Prentice-Hall, 1947)
22. Cookson and others: *Creative-Analytical Theory of Music* (Chicago: H. T. FitzSimons, 1948)
23. Jones and Bailey: *Exploring Music* (Boston: C. C. Birchard, 1941)
24. Hindemith, Paul: *Elementary Training for Musicians* (New York: Associated Music Publishers, 1946)

25. Smith—Krone—Schaffer: *Fundamentals of Musicianship*, Books I-II, unabridged edition (New York: M. Witmark, 1937)
26. Wedge, George A.: *Ear-Training and Sight-Singing* (New York: G. Schirmer, 1921)

(b) *written harmony*

27. Alchin, Carolyn: *Applied Harmony*, Parts I-II, rev. by V. Jones (Los Angeles: L. R. Jones, 1934)
28. Hindemith, Paul: *Traditional Harmony* (New York: Associated Music Publishers, 1943)
29. McHose, Allan: *The Contrapuntal Harmonic Technique of the 18th Century* (New York: F. S. Crofts, 1947)
30. Mitchell, William J.: *Elementary Harmony* (New York: Prentice-Hall, 1947)
31. Murphy and Stringham: *Creative Harmony and Musicianship* (New York: Prentice-Hall, 1950)
32. Piston, Walter: *Harmony* (New York: W. W. Norton, 1941)
33. Wedge, George A.: *Applied Harmony*, Books I-II (New York: G. Schirmer, 1930-1931)

(c) *counterpoint*

34. Bridge, J. Frederick: *Counterpoint* (Oliver Ditson, 1878; Theodore Presser, Philadelphia, distributors)
35. Goetschius, Percy: *Applied Counterpoint* (New York: G. Schirmer, 1915)
36. Jeppesen, Knud: *Counterpoint*, trans. by Glen Haydon (New York: Prentice-Hall, 1939)
37. Kanitz, Ernst: *A Counterpoint Manual* (Boston: C. C. Birchard, 1947)
38. Kitson, C. H.: *The Art of Counterpoint* (London: Oxford University Press, 1944)
39. ——: *Counterpoint for Beginners* (London: Oxford University Press, 1927)
40. Lytle, Victor: *The Theory and Practice of Strict Counterpoint* (Oliver Ditson, 1940; Theodore Presser, Philadelphia, distributors)
41. Piston, Walter: *Counterpoint* (New York: W. W. Norton, 1947)
42. Porter, Quincy: *A Study of 16th Century Counterpoint* (Boston: Loomis & Co., 1948)

43. Soderlund, Gustave F.: *Direct Approach to Counterpoint in the 16th Century Style* (New York: F. S. Crofts, 1947)

(d) *form and composition*

44. Doty, E. W.: *The Analysis of Form in Music* (New York: F. S. Crofts, 1947)
45. Goetschius, Percy: *The Homophonic Forms of Musical Composition* (New York: G. Schirmer, 1915)
46. ——: *The Larger Forms of Musical Composition* (New York: G. Schirmer, 1915)
47. ——: *Lessons in Music Form* (Oliver Ditson, 1904; Theodore Presser, Philadelphia, distributors)
48. Schoenberg, Arnold: *Models for Beginners in Composition* (New York: G. Schirmer, 1947)

(e) *keyboard harmony*

49. Lowry, Margaret: *Keyboard Approach to Harmony* (Philadelphia: Theodore Presser, 1949)
50. McHose and White: *Keyboard and Dictation Manual* (New York: Appleton-Century-Crofts, 1948)
51. Murphy and Stringham: *Creative Harmony and Musicianship* (New York: Prentice-Hall, 1950)

(f) *dictation*

52. McHose, Allan: *Teachers Dictation Manual* (New York: Appleton-Century-Crofts, 1948)
53. McHose and White: *Keyboard and Dictation Manual* (New York: Appleton-Century-Crofts, 1948)
54. Murphy and Stringham: *Creative Harmony and Musicianship* (New York: Prentice-Hall, 1950)
55. White, Bernice: *Melodic Dictation* (New York: American Book Co., 1935)
56. White and Jones: *Harmonic Dictation* (New York: American Book Co., 1932)

(g) *music reading*

57. Hall, Minna F.: *Music Reading*, Book I (Boston: C. W. Homeyer, 1942)

58. Lenom, Clément: *Rhythm by Solfeggio* (New York: Coleman-Ross, 1946)

59. McHose, Allan: *Sight Singing Manual* (New York: F. S. Crofts, 1944)

60. Murphy and Stringham: *Creative Harmony and Musicianship* (New York: Prentice-Hall, 1950)

61. *The Folk Song Sight Singing Series*, Books I-X (London: Oxford University Press, 1933)

II. TECHNICAL BOOKS

(a) *harmony*

62. Gannett, Kent: *Bach's Harmonic Progressions* (Oliver Ditson, 1942; Theodore Presser, Philadelphia, distributors)

63. Hindemith, Paul: *The Craft of Musical Composition*, Book I (New York: Associated Music Publishers, 1946)

64. Hull, A. Eaglefield: *Modern Harmony* (London: Augener, 1914[?])

65. Katz, Adele T.: *Challenge to Musical Tradition* (New York: Alfred A. Knopf, 1945)

66. McKay, George F.: *The Technique of Modern Harmony* (1944; Gamble Hinged Music Co., Chicago, selling agents)

67. Miller, Horace A.: *New Harmonic Devices* (Oliver Ditson, 1930; Theodore Presser, Philadelphia, distributors)

68. Piston, Walter: *Principles of Harmonic Analysis* (Boston: E. C. Schirmer, 1933)

69. Richardson, A. Madley: *The Medieval Modes* (New York: H. W. Gray, 1933)

70. Schillinger, Joseph: *The Schillinger System of Musical Composition* (New York: Carl Fischer, 1946)

71. Schoenberg, Arnold: *Theory of Harmony*, trans. by R. D. W. Adams (New York: Philosophical Library, 1948)

72. Slonimsky, Nicolas: *Thesaurus of Scales and Melodic Patterns* (New York: Coleman-Ross, 1947)

73. Toch, Ernst: *The Shaping Forces in Music* (New York: Criterion Music Corp., 1948)

(b) *form*

74. Bairstow, Edward: *The Evolution of Musical Form* (London: Oxford University Press, 1942)

75. Eschman, Karl: *Changing Forms in Modern Music* (Boston: E. C. Schirmer, 1945)
76. Hadow, W. H.: *The Sonata Form* (London: Novello, 1930)
77. Morris, R. O.: *The Structure of Music* (London: Oxford University Press, 1935)
78. Murphy, Howard A.: *Form in Music for the Listener* (Camden, N. J.: RCA Victor, 1945)
79. Nelson, Robert U.: *The Technique of Variation* (Berkeley: University of California Press, 1948)
80. Pauer, Ernst: *Musical Forms* (Oliver Ditson, 1878; Theodore Presser, Philadelphia, distributors)

(c) *arranging*

81. Andersen, Olaf: *Practical Orchestration* (Boston: C. C. Birchard, 1929)
82. Davison, Archibald T.: *The Technique of Choral Composition* (Cambridge: Harvard University Press, 1945)
83. Gardner, Maurice: *The Orchestrator's Handbook* (Great Neck, N. Y.: Staff Music Publishing Co., 1948)
84. Jacob, Gordon: *Orchestral Technique* (London: Oxford University Press, 1931)
85. Wilson, Harry Robert: *Choral Arranging* (New York: Robbins Music Corp., 1949)

(d) *improvisation and transposition*

86. Lagourgue, Charles: *Complete Treatise on Transposition* (Chicago: H. C. L. Publishing Co., 1925)
87. Richardson, A. Madeley: *Extempore Playing* (New York: G. Schirmer, 1922)
88. Schlieder, Frederick: *Lyric Composition Through Improvisation* (Boston: C. C. Birchard, 1927)
89. Slonimsky, Nicolas: *Thesaurus of Scales and Melodic Patterns* (New York: Coleman-Ross, 1947)
90. Whitmer, T. Carl: *The Art of Improvisation* (New York: M. Witmark, 1934)

(e) *counterpoint*

91. Fux, Johann J.: *Steps to Parnassus*, trans. by Alfred Mann (New York: W. W. Norton, 1943)
92. Haydon, Glen: *The Evolution of the Six-Four Chord* (Berkeley: University of California Press, 1933)

93. Jeppesen, Knud: *Palestrina's Style and the Dissonance*, trans. by Glen Haydon (London: Oxford University Press, 1927)
94. Merritt, Arthur Tillman: *16th-Century Polyphony* (Cambridge: Harvard University Press, 1945)
95. Morris, R. O.: *The Contrapuntal Technique in the 16th Century* (London: Oxford University Press, 1922)

III. NON-TECHNICAL BOOKS

96. Abbott, Lawrence: *The Listener's Book on Harmony* (Philadelphia: Theodore Presser, 1941)
97. Finney, Ross Lee: *The Game of Harmony* (New York: Harcourt, Brace, 1947)
98. Goetschius, Percy: *The Structure of Music* (Philadelphia: Theodore Presser, 1934)
99. Slonimsky, Nicolas: *The Road to Music* (New York: Dodd, Mead, 1947)
100. West, Alvaretta: *Signposts to Music*, student's workbook (New York: Carl Fischer, 1935)

IV. GENERAL REFERENCES

A. Books

101. Barbour and Freeman: *How to Teach Children to Know Music* (New York: Smith and Durrell, 1942)
102. Barnett, David: *Living with Music* (New York: George W. Stewart, 1944)
103. Barzun, Jacques: *Teacher in America* (Boston: Little, Brown, 1945)
104. Brooks and Brown: *Music Education in the Elementary School* (New York: American Book Co., 1946)
105. Brown, Calvin S.: *Music and Literature* (Athens: University of Georgia Press, 1948)
106. Budge, Helen: *A Study of Chord Frequencies* (New York: Bureau of Publications, Teachers College, Columbia University, 1943)
107. Burns, Samuel: *Harmonic Skills Used by Selected High School Choral Leaders* (New York: Bureau of Publications, Teachers College, Columbia University, 1945)
108. Dykema and Gehrkens: *The Teaching and Administration of High School Music* (Boston: C. C. Birchard, 1941)
109. Flagg, Marion: *Musical Learning* (Boston: C. C. Birchard, 1949)

110. Fox and Hopkins: *Creative School Music* (New York: Silver Burdett, 1936)
111. Gehrkens, Karl W.: *Music Notation and Terminology*, rev. ed. (Chicago: Laidlaw Bros., 1930)
112. Hopkins, L. Thomas: *Interaction: the Democratic Process* (Boston: D. C. Heath, 1941)
113. James, William: *Talks to Teachers* (New York: Henry Holt, 1939)
114. Jones, Vincent: *Music Education in the College* (Boston: C. C. Birchard, 1949)
115. Leonhard, Charles: "A Study of the Teaching of Transposition at the Piano by the Use of the Seven Clefs," Doctor of Education Report (New York: Teachers College, Columbia University, 1949 [Typewritten]
116. Mursell, James L.: *Developmental Teaching* (New York: Mc-Graw-Hill, 1949)
117. ———: *Education for Musical Growth* (New York: Ginn & Co., 1948)
118. ———: *Educational Psychology* (New York: W. W. Norton, 1939)
119. ———: *Human Values in Music Education* (New York: Silver Burdett, 1934)
120. ———: *Music in American Schools* (New York: Silver Burdett, 1943)
121. ———: *The Psychology of Music* (New York: W. W. Norton, 1937)
122. ———: *Successful Teaching* (New York: McGraw-Hill, 1946)
123. Pitts, Lilla Belle: *The Music Curriculum in a Changing World* (New York: Silver Burdett, 1944)
124. Sachs, Curt: *The Commonwealth of Art* (New York: W. W. Norton, 1946)
125. Schoenberg, Arnold: *Style and Idea* (New York: Philosophical Library, 1950)
126. Sheehy, Emma D.: *There's Music in Children* (New York: Henry Holt, 1946)
127. Silvey, Clel: *A Study of Personal Reactions to the Solmization Method of Teaching Music Reading* (Nashville: George Peabody College for Teachers, 1937)
128. Walthall, Marjorie: "Teaching of Music Theory: A New Approach Through an Extended Study of Style," Doctor of Education Report (New York: Teachers College, Columbia University, 1949) [Typewritten]

129. Wilson, Harry Robert: *Music in the High School* (New York: Silver Burdett, 1941)

Tests

130. Madison, Thurber: *Interval Discrimination as a Measure of Musical Aptitude* (New York: *Archives of Psychology*, No. 268, 1942)
131. Ortmann, Otto: *Problems in the Elements of Ear Dictation* (Baltimore: Peabody Conservatory of Music, 1934)
132. Wood, Carl Paige: *Ear Tests in Harmony* (New York: American Book Co., 1930)

B. ARTICLES SINCE 1940
EDUCATIONAL MUSIC MAGAZINE

133. 1940 (Jan.-Feb.) Thomas: *Music When There Are Ears to Hear*
134. 1940 (Mar.-Apr.) Carr: *Musicianship vs. Sight Reading*
135. —— Fain: *Toward Better Sight Reading*
136. —— Halfvarson: *Experiments in Ear Training for Vocal Groups*
137. 1940 (Sept.-Oct.) Shuck: *Waning Syllables*
138. 1940 (Nov.-Dec.) De Lasaux: *High School Pupils Give Recital of Original Music*
139. 1941 (Jan.-Feb.) Beeler: *Training for Sight Reading*
140. 1941 (Mar.-Apr.) Cain: *Choral Composing and Arranging*
141. 1943 (Mar.-Apr.) Dvorak: *Training of the Teacher of Music*
142. 1943 (Nov.-Dec.) McAdow: *Transposition in the High School Bandroom*
143. 1944 (Jan.-Feb.) Elledge: *Creative Music*
144. —— Melcher: *Integrated Harmony Teaching*
145. 1944 (Mar.-Apr.) Neil: *Music Reading*
146. 1944 (Sept.-Oct.) Hiteman: *Let's Postpone Music Reading!*
147. 1944 (Nov.-Dec.) Bulber: *Music Reading Thoughts*
148. 1945 (Jan.-Feb.) Gregory: *Why Study Theory?*
149. 1946 (Jan.-Feb.) Bullis: *Considerations in Teaching Theory*
150. 1946 (Mar.-Apr.) Bullis: *More Considerations in the Teaching of Theory*
151. 1949 (Jan.-Feb.) Squire: *Enjoying Music Through Rhythm*
152. 1949 (Nov.-Dec.) Adam: *Functional Harmony*

THE ETUDE

153. 1942 (Apr.) Mursell: *Practical Ear Training*

154. 1942 (May) Mursell: *Acquiring Skill in the Reading of Music*

JOURNAL OF THE AMERICAN
MUSICOLOGICAL SOCIETY

155. 1948 (Spring) Gutman, book review: *The Commonwealth of Art* (Sachs)
156. 1948 (Fall) Kerman, book review: *Direct Approach to Counterpoint in 16th Century Style* (Soderlund)
157. 1949 (Fall) Ratner: *Harmonic Aspects of Classic Form*

MODERN MUSIC

158. 1934 (May-June) Schoenberg: *Problems of Harmony*
159. 1937 (Nov.-Dec.) Sessions: *Hindemith on Theory*
160. 1938 (May-June) Schuman: *Unconventional Case History*
161. —— Sessions: *The Function of Theory*
162. 1940 (Mar.-Apr.) Krenek: *Teaching Composition*
163. 1944 (Jan.-Feb.) Citkowitz: *And Now, Basic Harmony*
164. 1946 (Fall) Schoenberg: *On the Appreciation of Music*

MUSIC EDUCATORS JOURNAL

165. 1939 (Dec.) Murphy: *Harmony Through Music*
166. 1940 (Feb.) Gaston: *Motor-Visual Imagery in Tonal Thinking*
167. 1940 (Oct.-Nov.) Jones: *Applying Harmony*
168. 1941 (Feb.) Kallander: *Ear Training and Musical Understanding.*
169. 1941 (Sept.-Oct.) Gordon: *Major Objectives in Teaching Theoretical Music*
170. 1942 (May-June) Masters: *The Creative Project Used to Teach Musical Skills*
171. 1943 (May-June) Bohn: *Importance of Rhythm*
172. —— Davids: *Say It With Music*
173. 1943 (Nov.-Dec.) Nelsen: *Song Writing in a Junior College*
174. 1944 (May) Dixon: *Solving Rhythmic Problems*
175. 1944 (Nov.-Dec.) Mason: *Song Making by the Non-Singers*
176. —— Morgan: *Movable Do, Fixed Do, Syllables, No Syllables*
177. 1945 (Apr.) Bailey: *High-School Theory Course*
178. —— Harley and Roggensack: *Teaching Fundamentals to Fifty*
179. 1946 (Apr.) Otey: *Basing Theory on Living Music*
180. 1947 (Jan.) Seeger: *Music Education and Musicology*
181. 1947 (Feb.-Mar.) Spencer: *Ear Training in Music Education*
182. 1947 (Nov.-Dec.) Mursell: *Growth Gradient in Music*
183. 1948 (Feb.-Mar.) Romaine: *The Teaching of Theory*

184. 1948 (Sept.-Oct.) Dykema: *Some Fundamental Questions About Music Reading*
185. 1949 (Jan.) Flagg: *The Written Language of Music*
186. —— Murphy, book review: *Thesaurus of Scales and Melodic Patterns* (Slonimsky)
187. 1949 (Feb.-Mar.) Van Bodegraven: *Music Reading*
188. 1949 (Sept.-Oct.) McElheran: *The Use of Theory in Rehearsals*
189. 1949 (Nov.-Dec.) Ervin: *How Is Your Teaching Personality?*
190. 1950 (Jan.) Hanley: *Music Theory for College Freshmen*
191. —— Hunkins: *Music Is Our Language*

THE MUSIC [PUBLISHERS] JOURNAL

192. 1944 (July-Aug.) Freed: *An Experiment in College Music Education*
193. 1946 (Sept.-Oct.) Murphy: *The Listening Ear*
194. 1947 (Sept.-Oct.) Mills: *Teaching Music Reading*
195. 1948 (Sept.-Oct.) Kaho: *Ear Training by Sight*
196. 1949 (Mar.-Apr.) Grover: *An Evaluation of Present Methods of Teaching Theory*
197. —— Leonhard: *On the Teaching of Theory*
198. —— Van Vactor: *Function of Theory*
199. 1949 (Sept.-Oct.) McHose: *Harmonic Foundation of String Intonation*
200. 1949 (Nov.-Dec.) Freed: *A Composer's Credo*
201. —— Jacobi: *Some Ideas About Music*
202. —— Piston: *What a Young Composer . . .*

MUSICAL COURIER

203. 1946 (Jan.15) Jonas: *Is Theory Teaching in a Blind Alley?*

THE MUSICAL QUARTERLY

204. 1943 (Oct.) Brunswick: *Tonality and Perspective*
205. 1944 (Jan.) Hindemith: *Methods of Music Theory*
206. 1946 (July) Slonimsky, book review: *The Schillinger System of Musical Composition* (Schillinger)
207. 1946 (Oct.) Mursell: *Psychology and the Problem of the Scale*
208. 1947 (Oct.) Greene, book review: *The Commonwealth of Art* (Sachs)
209. 1948 (Apr.) Schuman: *On the Teaching of the Literature and Materials of Music*
210. 1949 (Apr.) Ferand, book review: *The Technique of Variation* (Nelson)

211. 1949 (Oct.) Editorial I on the College Music Department (Lang)
212. 1950 (Jan.) Editorial II on the College Music Department (Lang)

MUSICOLOGY

213. Vol. I, No. 1, Porter: *The Education of the American Composer*
214. Vol. I, No. 2, Gehrkens: *The Rise and Development of Music Education in the Public Schools*
215. —— Mitchell: *Heinrich Schenker's Approach to Detail*
216. —— Schillinger: *Variations of Music by Means of Geometric Progressions*
217. Vol. I, No. 4, Blanker: *A New Method of Education for the Composer Based on a New Psychology of the Arts*

NATIONAL SOCIETY FOR THE STUDY OF EDUCATION, 35th YEAR BOOK (Part II, Music Education)

218. Chap. VIII, *Ear Training* (Russell V. Morgan)
219. Chap. X, *Listening* (Lillian Baldwin)
220. Chap. XI, *Reading Music* (James L. Mursell)
221. Chap. XII, *Music Theory* (Louis Woodson Curtis)
222. Chap. XIII, *Creative Activities* (Will Earhart)
223. Chap. XX, *The Selection and Training of Teachers* (John W. Beattie)

NOTES [Music Library Association]

224. 1945 (June) Burkat, book review: *Technique of Choral Composition* (Davison)
225. 1945 (Sept.) Haydon, book review: *Listening to Music Creatively* (Stringham)
226. —— Keyes, book review: *How to Read a Score* (Jacob)
227. —— Seeger, book review: *The Schillinger System of Musical Composition* (Schillinger)
228. 1945 (Dec.) Reichenbach, book review: *Challenge to Musical Tradition* (Katz)
229. 1946 (June) Barbour, book review: *The Schillinger System of Musical Composition* (Schillinger)
230. 1946 (Dec.) Finney, book review: *Elementary Training for Musicians* (Hindemith)
231. 1947 (Mar.) Cowell, book review: *Thesaurus of Scales and Melodic Patterns* (Slonimsky)
232. —— Seeger, book review: *The Schillinger System of Musical Composition* (Schillinger)

233. —— Spivacke, book review: *The Commonwealth of Art* (Sachs)

234. 1947 (June) Palmer, book review: *Counterpoint* (Piston)

235. 1948 (March) Noss, book review: *Elementary Musicianship* (Bauman)

236. 1948 (June) Bales, book review: *Score Reading; a Series of Graded Excerpts* (Bernstein)

237. —— Lockwood, book review: *The Orchestrator's Handbook* (Gardner)

238. —— Newman, book review: *The Technique of Variation* (Nelson)

239. 1948 (Sept.) Gelrud, book review: *Marks and Remarks; Musical Examinations and Their Problems* (Fielden)

240. —— Noss, book review: *Theory of Harmony* (Schoenberg)

241. 1948 (Dec.) Fox: *Modern Counterpoint: a Phenomenological Approach*

242. 1949 (Mar.) Bush, book review: *Harmonic Writing in the Tonal Idiom of the Classic and Romantic Periods* (Woodruff)

243. 1949 (June) Cohn, book review: *Treatise on Instrumentation* (Berlioz-Strauss, trans. by Th. Front)

244. —— Cunningham, book review: *Recordings for the Elementary School* (Leavitt and Freeman)

245. —— Yasser, book review: *The Mathematical Basis of the Arts* (Schillinger)

246. 1949 (Sept.) Henderson, book review: *Musical Learning* (Flagg)

247. —— Wellesz, book review: *The Origin of the Eight Modes of Music* (Werner)

248. 1949 (Dec.) Hill, book review: *Theory of Hearing* (Wever)

249. —— Keith, book review: *Keyboard Dictation Manual* (McHose and White)

PROCEEDINGS OF THE MUSIC TEACHERS NATIONAL ASSOCIATION

250. 1940 (Series 35) Elkus: *The Teaching of Counterpoint from a Contemporary Point of View*

251. —— Murphy: *A Method of Bridging the Gap between Theory and Music*

252. —— Newman: *Controlled Experiment in the Comparative Evaluation of High School Theory Methods*

253. 1941 (Series 36) Merritt: *The Teaching of Counterpoint in the Liberal Arts College*

254. —— Woodruff: *Plan for a Comprehensive Theory Course*

255. 1944 (Series 38) Elwell: *Exploration of Contemporary Harmonic and Contrapuntal Techniques*
256. ——Krenek: *Traditional and New Techniques in Teaching Theory*
257. —— McHose: *The Pedagogy of Contemporary Harmonic and Contrapuntal Procedures*
258. 1945 (Series 39) Inch: *Contrapuntal Devices in Contemporary Music*
259. —— McKay: *Harmonic Evolution*
260. —— Read: *Teaching Contemporary Compositional Techniques*
261. 1946 (Series 40) Beswick: *The Dominant Seventh Chord in the Works of William Byrd*
262. —— Murphy: *Composition Clinic*
263. —— Wylie: *Rhythm in Contemporary Music*
264. 1947 (Series 41) Finney: *The Composer and General Education*

YEARBOOK OF THE MUSIC EDUCATORS NATIONAL CONFERENCE

265. 1944 (MENC Committee Reports) Mursell and Bergethon: *Music Theory and Culture in the College Curriculum*

MUSIC EDUCATION SOURCE BOOK (MENC, 1947)

266. McKay: *Music Theory, Composing and Arranging*

INDEX

INDEX

Ability to sing, failure of, 44
Academic counterpoint, 31-33
Accidentals, 22, 48, 49
  in modulation, 49
  in transposition, 83, 92, 93
Ach du lieber Augustin, 68
Achievement goals of assignments, 172, 173
Activities, group, in graduate methods class, 212, 213
Activities to promote musicianship, 216-218
Advanced level
  keyboard study, 90, 91
  written dictation, 72, 73
  see also College level; Graduate level; Postgraduate level
Alteration, chromatic, 100, 101
America, 107, 108, 111, 183
Analysis, 25, 98-116, 149, 161, 162
  aural, 112, 114-116, 123, 156-158, 163, 164, 190
  contrapuntal, 107-109
  drills for self-evaluation, 197
  formal, 69, 70, 109-112, 115, 116, 162-164, 197
  harmonic, 98-107, 114
  melodic, 64, 162
  planning on all levels:
    elementary school, 162
    junior high school, 162, 163
    senior high school, 163
    liberal arts college, 163, 164
    teachers college, 164
    professional school, 164
    graduate level, 164
  stylistic, 112, 154, 164
  summary, 116
  visual, 113-115, 163, 164
Analytic dictation, 73, 75, 76, 116, 157
Analytic reports, 76
Analytic tests, 189, 190
"Appreciation," 18, 75, 78
Areas of interest, 173
Areas of learning, 13, 17-19, 52, 79, 119, 140, 144, 147, 149, 205, 206
  see also Analysis; Creative writing; Listening; Playing; Reading; Writing

Arnold, Charles D., 6
Arpeggios sung in chord drill, 56, 153
Arranging, 35-37, 124, 164
  theory and practice, 35-37
  planning, 151, 152
Artificial scales, 150
Assignments, planning of, 168-177
  criteria, 170-175
  points of procedure, 175, 176
Assignments in graduate methods class, 212, 213
Assignments of problems in methods and materials courses, 207, 208
Atonality, 45, 209, 212, 213
Augmentation, 108
Augmented chords, 104, 105
Augmented sixth chord, 104
Aural analysis, 112, 114-116, 123, 156-158, 163, 164, 190
Aural experience, 25
Aurelius, Marcus, 220
Availability of time in assignments, 173, 174
Avenues of learning, *see* Areas of learning

Bach, Johann Sebastian, 14, 31, 36, 90, 143, 172
  B minor Mass, 109, 153
  chorales, 15, 34, 41, 72, 90, 154, 158, 169, 196
  First Lessons in Bach (Carroll), 74
  fugues, 108
  St. Matthew Passion, 58, 154
  Two-part inventions, 74, 95, 160
  Well Tempered Clavier, 30, 34, 114, 160, 163, 196, 197, 216, 217
Background, requirement for creative expression, 118, 132
Barnby, Joseph
  Sweet and Low, 105
Baroque period, 31, 41, 148, 154
Bartók, Béla
  Mikrokosmos, 74
Basic drives for teaching, 220-222
Basic drives of the teacher, 220-223
Basic learning sequence of written dictation, 71

CHILDHOOD
MALIGNANCY

CHILDHOOD MALIGNANCY

The Psychosocial Care
of the Child and His Family

By

DAVID W. ADAMS, M.S.W.

Director of Social Work Services
Co-ordinator of the Psychosocial Program
Psychosocial Consultant and Clinical Social Worker
Pediatric Hematology and Oncology Clinic
McMaster University Medical Centre
Assistant Clinical Professor
McMaster University Department of Psychiatry

Foreword by

Alvin Zipursky, M.D., F.R.C.P. (C)

Professor of Pediatrics
McMaster University Department of Pediatrics
Director of the Pediatric Hematology and Oncology Clinic
McMaster University Medical Centre

CHARLES C THOMAS • PUBLISHER
Springfield • Illinois • U.S.A.

Published and Distributed Throughout the World by
CHARLES C THOMAS • PUBLISHER
Bannerstone House
301-327 East Lawrence Avenue, Springfield, Illinois, U.S.A.

With THOMAS BOOKS *careful attention is given to all details of
manufacturing and design. It is the Publisher's desire to present books that
are satisfactory as to their physical qualities and artistic possibilities and
appropriate for their particular use.* THOMAS BOOKS *will be true to those
laws of quality that assure a good name and good will.*

Printed in the United States of America
V-R-1

Library of Congress Cataloging in Publication Data
Adams, David Walter, 1942-
    Childhood malignancy.

    Includes index.
    1. Medical social work--United States. 2. Tumors
in children. 3. Terminal care. 4. Terminally ill
children--Family relationships. I. Title.
HV687.5.U5A33   362.7'8'196994   79-11954
ISBN 0-398-03928-3

FOREWORD

WHEN I was asked to write the Foreword to this book I was honored and also pleased since it caused me to reexamine our experience with malignant diseases in childhood. That field has evolved rapidly so that with each passing month there have been new advances or nuances of treatment which must be brought to our patients.

Hope and aggressive treatment have replaced resignation and gloom. Yet in these families, the risk and fear of death persists, suffering occurs and still there are those who die.

The medical school at McMaster University is new, and it was a goal of its founders that this school should bring together the highest standards of medical care with a complete humane approach to patients and their families. These were our goals also when we established the Pediatric Hematology and Oncology Program.

It was at this point that Dave Adams and I met and began our work. We did not know the entire path ahead; however, we did recognize that the needs of these children and their families extended beyond the specific drug, radiation or surgical treatment of their disease. In planning our approach we believed that it would not be sufficient simply to provide a response when a crisis occurred. Rather, we felt that our patients and their families should relate to all members of our team and thereby come to know them. In this way they and their problems would not be strange to us and we would be in a better position to bring to them our knowledge and experience when necessary.

In this book Dave Adams describes his approach to these families and how they gently become part of the team. This has given him, as a social worker, an opportunity to analyze the response of patients and their families to disease and to their roles in its continuing care. In this context and setting Mr.

Adams reviews for the reader his approach to specific problems and his interpretation of the relevant work of others. His is the mature wisdom of one who observes and speaks from a position of experience and responsibility for the care of these patients.

He reminds us also that knowledge and experience in the psychosocial management of these patients is not the prerogative or sole responsibility of one person such as the social worker. In his book he describes the role of the nurse as she provides on-going care and contact, of the play therapist who observes the child and family in a relaxed nonthreatening atmosphere and of the physicians responsible for medical therapy. The key to successful management is individual responsibility within a team setting.

The child with a malignant disease deserves the best of medical care. Dave Adams' approach to the psychosocial care of these children and their families has added a dimension that is appreciated by the parents and all of us working with them. In this book we are led carefully and skillfully through many of the problems these families face. This surely must be of benefit to all of us responsible for the care of children with malignant disease.

Alvin Zipursky, M.D.

PREFACE

THE primary goal of this book is to provide a major learning resource for staff and students in medicine, nursing, social work, psychology and other health-related disciplines who work with children with malignant diseases and their families. The main text is formulated from the experiences of my colleagues and I in our work in the Pediatric Hematology-Oncology Clinic at McMaster University Medical Centre in Hamilton, Ontario, Canada.

In principle, this text underlines the need for health-care professionals to be aware of and responsive to the concerns and adaptational problems generated within families and within the child as a response to illness. It is devoted to the underlying theme that professionals, regardless of discipline, must work in unison to develop roles and relationships which breed understanding, caring, helpfulness and mutual respect for each other as well as for the child and family. The mutuality of respect within a close working relationship among team members can facilitate provision of the strength, resourcefulness and maturity required to provide effective, comprehensive care in this difficult psychosocial area.

Throughout the text is the recognition that stressful life experiences should be dealt with realistically and honestly. Intervention and staging of integrated medical and psychosocial care should be carried out carefully and tailored to meet the individual needs of each child and family. Health care in childhood malignancy must also be based on the current picture and must embody premises which bury the myths of the past. These myths include the belief that only physicians can be of value in the provision of care in this area, that death in leukemia and most other types of cancer is inevitable, that all children and families can cope with adaptation on their own and that children do not ask about their illness because they do not want to know about it.

This text does not imply that the learning experiences, research and past debates reflected in the literature should be ignored or discredited. Rather, the reader is encouraged to review those works and studies by the pioneers such as Friedman, Easson and Hamovitch, which can serve as building blocks for current and future study and practice in psychosocial care. Wherever possible the works of other authors have been integrated with my own views and experiences in the development of this text.

The Challenge of Today

Today, physicians, nurses, social workers and other practitioners are faced with a situation which differs considerably from the 1950s. Now some children with leukemia and cancer have the potential to live a complete and normal life. Statistics suggest that cures can be achieved in many types of childhood cancer. However, the underlying threat of relapse or return of the disease, creates an imperfect balance. For example, in the 1950s the child with leukemia faced a prognosis of death within weeks or months. Today it appears that 50 percent of children with acute lymphoblastic leukemia live a minimum of four years or longer with a number achieving what could be designated as a cure.

In light of this change new challenges have been precipitated for health care providers. Ironically, the professional finds that he or she is on ground which is less secure than in the past. Despite the fact that the situation is more hopeful, the emotional components are greater. The physician and his associates as they become more hopeful, more successful and more optimistic about cure are also prone to marked emotional setbacks generated by relapse, death or failure of the patient to respond to available drugs. Working in this area is difficult. The challenge, both medically and behaviorally is great. This text suggests that a multidisciplinary team approach can provide additional support to health professionals. It also emphasizes that on the basis of experience families and children benefit from the type of personalized, humanized, caring approach which can be offered by people who genuinely work together.

Recent works have also stressed the need for health care workers to seek out new and better ways to provide service to cancer patients. Home care, ambulatory care and an alliance between the hospital and community care givers are all present concerns. So also is the need to seek out ways to help the long-term survivor cope with the meaning of cure.

The Structure of the Text

This is a comprehensive reference book. The opening chapter begins with a review of the literature and takes note of the changes which have taken place in the psychological and social care of families since the 1950s. Chapter 1 closes with my description of leukemia as an example of an illness cycle. This description is based on carefully documented comments from parents and children and is included to help the reader understand the impact of this life-threatening disease on the child and his family. In Chapter 2 I describe the multidisciplinary team and our experiences in working together at McMaster. Chapter 3 focuses on the family and the changes which take place within the family unit when a child's life is threatened by cancer. In the ensuing chapter, I examine the major factors affecting how parents cope with the stress of their child's illness and describe specific patterns of parental responses. I also describe the nature of helpful intervention as I see it and include a review of the type of information required for a psychosocial assessment of the family. In continuing, I move on to discuss the impact of the disease upon the child. Chapter 5 is devoted to a discussion of the implications of the hospitalization and ambulatory care experiences, the problems faced by the adolescent and the ways hospital staff can help the child cope with the illness experience. The closing section of Chapter 5 focuses upon the long-term survivor and approaches which may help this child live a life which approximates that of his peers.

Unfortunately, even in these times of optimism and success in treatment, some children die from malignant diseases. With this in mind I discuss in Chapter 6 the child's understanding of death at various ages and examine the impact of terminal illness on the child and his family. In closing, I draw heavily on my clinical experience in discussing the subject of bereavement following the death of the child and our need to ensure that follow-up care is provided for the survivors.

An Annotated Bibliography has been prepared which provides a concise catalogue of abstracts of current papers and books which reflects not only the trend in psychosocial care of the child and family but highlights major learning areas associated with the provision of care. The arrangement of chapters is designed so that the annotated materials closely parallel the works in the main chapters. The Annotated Bibliography is available from me at the cost of printing and handling in care of the Department of Social Work Services, Office 4V36, McMaster University Medical Centre, 1200 Main Street West, Hamilton, Ontario, Canada L8S 4J9.

D.W.A.

ACKNOWLEDGMENTS

THE preparation of this work represents not only a consolidation of many learning experiences, but also the development of close and lasting working relationships with my colleagues in the Pediatric Hematology-Oncology Clinic at McMaster University Medical Centre. I am grateful to Dr. Alvin Zipursky for the major role he played in shaping the nature of psychosocial care provided in pediatric hematology and for his continued support of my work. I am equally indebted to Dr. Mohan Pai, to Ellie Deveau, B.Sc.N., and to Marie Dafoe, M.H.Sc., for their continued editorial assistance and encouragement. I thank my secretaries, Peggy McAlpine and Maureen Wright for their endurance in the typing and correction of this manuscript. Other persons who have been of major assistance include Barbara Love, B.Sc.N., Mary Wallis, M.H. Sc., Shirley Krochuk, Reg. N., Ahuva Soifer, M.S.W., Joan Epstein, Cert. S.W., and Dr. A. B. MacMillan, Former Chairman of the McMaster University Department of Pediatrics. The following members of the Pediatric Psychosocial core group are also due special acknowledgement: Dr. Ken Finkel, Pediatrician, Dr. Ivan Carter, Child Psychiatrist, Margaret Enright, M.S.W., Carol Anne Vair, B.Sc.N. and Ruth Snider, Director of the Child Life Program. Special recognition must go to Ruth and her staff for their contributions in the area of the child in hospital. Others who have helped greatly are Mrs. M. Dart from Chaplaincy Services, Connie Dunnett from Volunteer Services and my wife, M. Anne Adams, B.Sc.N.

Recognition for administrative and personal support are due to Dr. J. M. Cleghorn, Chairman of the McMaster University Department of Psychiatry, and to Mr. R. C. Walker, Executive Vice-President of Chedoke-McMaster Hospital.

The contributions of the many staff, students and residents who have helped with this manuscript over the years must be gratefully acknowledged. By the same token there are many writers who have stimulated my continuing interest in this work and many have willingly provided papers to assist me. A special thanks goes to Claire Mulholland from Glasgow, Scotland, for the opportunity to use her poetry within the text.

D.W.A.

CONTENTS

CHILDHOOD
MALIGNANCY

CHAPTER 1

AN OVERVIEW OF THE PSYCHOSOCIAL CARE OF CHILDREN AND FAMILIES

The Impact of Cancer on the Child and His Family

THERE is nothing more upsetting to a family than the threat to the life of a child. For many parents the child symbolizes their hopes for the future and is felt to be an extension of their own lives. Even in families who neglect their children there is often an underlying need to protect the child and see him grow up to achieve greater status and wealth than his parents. For siblings, despite the conflicts encountered in growing up together, there is frequently a special bond between them and their brother or sister fostered by facing the same life experiences. When a child is ill with cancer the whole family suffers; when death is imminent each family member agonizes over the impending loss; when death occurs each family member must grieve, and the whole family must reorganize itself to find a new equilibrium. When a child survives an ordeal with a malignancy he and his family have been changed by the experience. If his cancer was treated easily, then the changes may be minor. If he has suffered through two years or more of chemotherapy complete with the vomiting, hair loss and worry, or has faced the bone marrow aspirations, lumbar punctures and the three or more years of uncertainty that accompanies leukemia, he and his family have usually changed a great deal. At present we have reached a turning point in the care of the child. We have every reason to hope that more than half of newly diagnosed children will grow up and live normal lives. We hope that more and more children will be unscathed by their experience with the disease. We must realize, however, that right now we need to face the realities of living with and, when necessary, dying from cancer. Some children and families suffer and some children die.

3

As we seek to understand the changes that have taken place in the psychological and social components of care of the child with cancer and his family, it must be recognized that such changes have evolved gradually in keeping with the advances of medical treatment. These changes are reflected in the literature. This chapter is devoted to reviewing the development of psychosocial knowledge and care as found in the literature from the 1950s to the present, and to the provision of an example of what happens to children and families when they live with leukemia as carefully documented from my clinical experience. The latter should be useful as a point of reference in understanding the main body of this text.

The Literature on the Medical Aspects of Cancer

Before beginning my review of psychosocial care and the literature from the 1950s I would like to point out that recent articles are available that provide medical information about malignant diseases of childhood and their treatment. A review of these papers may be helpful for some readers who are unfamiliar with these diseases or wish to have current information about them. Leukemia, the major focus of much of the literature on psychosocial care is described in detail by Nesbit and Kersey (1976). Their description includes a review of diagnostic procedures, appropriate chemotherapy and the use of bone marrow transplantations. Laboratory information related to leukemia is reviewed by Karni (1976). Haghbin and her associates (1974) discuss in detail one of many major treatment protocols currently in use. Knudson (1976) discusses the etiology of childhood cancer and provides some basic information about tumors as well as leukemias. Hughes (1976) discusses chemotherapeutic agents in treating malignancy along with their side effects and the problems created by infections. Jaffe (1976) provides an extensive review of the problems of drug toxicity.

Psychosocial Care in the 1950s

In the 1950s most types of malignant tumors and leukemias

were fatal. Life spans of children with leukemia were usually no longer than six months and many children died within three months of the onset of the disease. Families were faced with the finality of the cancer from the point of diagnosis and mourning in anticipation of the child's death began immediately. The literature from this period reflected a concern for the parents and a need to understand in greater depth the dimensions of their ordeal. Although concern for the child was mentioned and one study actually focussed on the child, the concentration on the parents probably occurred because it was easier to talk to the parents and provide emotional support to them. The child died rapidly and sometimes in a great deal of pain, thus making it difficult for the hospital staff to approach him, not only because he was very ill, but because his death was hard for them to face. Bozeman and her colleagues (1955) studied twenty mothers in order to determine how they adapted to the threatened loss of their children due to acute leukemia. She found that mothers initially denied the illness and interpreted the diagnosis in terms of physical injury to themselves. Many mothers felt guilty and personally responsible for their child's illness. Acceptance of the illness and its consequences was mostly intellectual, the mother-grandmother relationship was lacking in emotional support and nurses and mothers were often in conflict. Richmond and Waisman (1955), in studying 48 leukemic children, found that children were isolated, passive and depressed but were not openly concerned about death. They also found that parents needed to participate in the physical care of their child. In 1956, Cobb reported on her study of twenty parents six months after their child's death from leukemia. She found that parents were grateful for the time spent with their child as long as the illness and suffering were controlled. She noted that parental hopes accelerated during remission and that if a marriage was sound, the illness drew the parents together. Cobb also found that some siblings changed their behavior and exhibited such problems as loss of appetite and increasing concern about illness. Solnit and Green (1959) stressed the importance of providing information to parents gradually and of not predicting the length of the illness. They also recognized that parents would often feel relieved when a child died, that the physician might be the target for anger and resentment and that siblings were affected by grief. Greene and Miller (1958), in a controversial paper, reported on a study of 33 children with leukemia under the age of twenty, most of whom were males. They suggested that the mother's emotional state, the quality of the relationship between the mother and child, the separation or loss of a significant person and disruption of the stability in the child's life situation were major contributors to precipitating the disease.

The 1960s

This decade was marked by an expansion in the number, quality and scope of research studies and clinical papers. Greater attention was given to the recognition of family units and the need to examine in detail the relationship between the parents and the sick child, between the child and his siblings and between the family and the emotional support systems surrounding it. Because children were living longer and there was a desire to build upon the beginning knowledge of the 1950s, clinicians and researchers began to pay attention to the needs of the child. They recognized that children were intelligent and perceptive and had a right to at least ask questions about their illness.

During this period there was also a change in the number and sophistication of the disciplines caring for and studying the child and his family. Nurses, social workers and psychologists became more actively involved and added to the expansion of interest to areas beyond the basic medical care. At the same time, pediatric oncologists began to examine more closely their role in the care of the child and his family, including how their approaches influenced the adaptation of the child and family members to the disease process.

At the beginning of the 1960s the care of the dying child came in for further scrutiny when Natterson and Knudson (1960) found that behavioral changes occurred in relation to separation from their mothers, traumatic procedures and deaths of other children. They found that fears of separation, mutilation and death in their patients were age related. This realization that children at various ages responded differently to hospitalization, to medical procedures and to the experience of dying provided the groundwork for later studies and facilitated the changes in the nursing and medical care of these children which inevitably followed.

Friedman and his associates (1963) reported on their study which included twenty seven children with neoplastic diseases and forty six of their parents. They found that the parents had often suspected the illness and frequently blamed themselves for not identifying symptoms sooner. They also found that parents sought much information about the nature of the illness and details of test results such as blood counts. As the child became sicker and distanced himself from the parents they tended to feel guilty. Discipline, overprotection and overindulgence were other problems which occurred frequently. Relatives, friends and grandparents were often liabilities, and the greatest help came from other parents who were facing or had faced the same situation. Friedman and his colleagues also found that grief work increased in terminal phases and that after death parents felt guilty about wishing that the child would die and end the ordeal.

In 1964, Hamovitch described his study of eighty two children with leukemia and their families. These children died during a three year period. He learned that diminished capabilities for coping in these families occurred when the medical diagnosis offered little hope of survival. This was especially true in the case of inoperable sarcomas. Other situations that reduced the parents ability to cope occurred when either parent had been married before, when families already had problems with daily living and when the child was over the age of ten. Hamovitch also found that families who were involved in the care of their child in hospital coped most effectively, provided they were able to continue family life outside of the hospital. Vernick and Karon (1965), in studying children ages nine to twenty on a leukemia ward, found that death on the ward could not be hidden, that concealing the diagnosis did not stop a child from worrying and that children needed to share in plans for their treatment. A later paper by Vernick and Lunceford (1967) reflects the need to discuss ward events and the child's illness both individually and in groups. The work of Vernick and his colleagues seriously challenged the beliefs of many physicians who advocated that the diagnosis could be hidden from adolescents and children in order to protect them from knowing about the seriousness of their disease and their prognosis. Despite Vernick's findings, the controversy over how much the child should know continued on.

Other writers such as Toch (1964) and later Lascari (1969) provide their views on clinical management of families and children. Toch advocates a straightforward approach, maintenance of normalcy in areas of disciplining children, constancy in medical care and the provision of care at home where possible.

Toch believes in answering children's questions, in spending time with them and in not providing heroic measures when the disease is no longer responding to therapy. Lascari pinpoints the need for the physician to understand his own feelings and to set forward a gradual plan of care which prepares the family for a time when drugs will no longer work and the child may die.

1970 to 1974

In the first part of this decade more sophisticated research techniques were employed to study in greater detail whether or not the child with cancer had changed because of what he had heard or perceived about his illness and prognosis. Studies again revealed that children with cancer could not be shielded from knowing about the life-threatening nature of their disease. At the same time increased recognition was being given to the fact that parents of children with cancer could benefit other parents in the same situation through discussion of their mutual knowledge and concerns. During this period as well, the impact and the dimensions of the stress of the illness experience on families was again documented. New knowledge was added about the nature of family responses at various stages of the disease process and in respect to the various types of problems families developed because of their child's illness.

Hoffman and Futterman (1971) reported on a unique program which used the waiting room as a place to help parents deal with anticipatory mourning. The purpose of the program was to help parents master their feelings and to work together with the sick child and his siblings. Additional attention was also given to the child to help him cope with his illness and the treatment experience. In their observations of the children Hoffman and Futterman found that their findings paralleled those of Richmond and Waisman (1955) in that the children were isolated, passive, dependent, depressed and showed no overt concern about death.

Waechter (1971) also enhanced knowledge about leukemic children. She studied children ages six to ten and found that children with leukemia were more preoccupied with fantasies about death, had less feeling of control in their lives and felt more lonely and isolated than children with chronic diseases or those who were well. Share (1972) emphasizes the importance of communication in alleviating family stresses and anxieties when the child is dying. She draws heavily on the literature in contrasting the benefits of communicating openly with the child as opposed to taking a protective approach. Spinetta and his associates (Spinetta, Rigler and Karon 1973; Spinetta, 1974; Spinetta, Rigler and Karon 1974), in doll play experiences, found that as leukemic children became increasingly ill and hospitalization increased they placed more distance between themselves and their parents as well as medical personnel. They found that children with malignant diseases were concerned about the seriousness of their illness and the possibility of being separated from their family. These children were also afraid of intrusions into their body and worried that something serious would happen to them. A repeat of the study in an ambulatory setting yielded similar findings.

Easson (1972) draws attention to the necessity for physicians to recognize the intensity of their influence on the family. Easson ties the post-death reaction of families closely to the physician's own understanding of the role he has played in the total process and how well he has been able to personally accept the death of the child.

In another paper from this period McCollum and Schwartz (1972) present a conceptual framework for understanding the process of anticipatory mourning in families of children with leukemia. They discuss affect, defensive processes such as denial and issues which arise within families during the disease. Two additional papers from this year reflected a change in the provision of health care in childhood malignancy. Heffron, Bommelaere and Masters (1973) and Knapp and Hanson (1973) describe group discussion programs for parents of leukemic children. In their paper, Heffron, Bommelaere and Masters endorse the group as a means for catharsis, for the giving and receiving of emotional support and for increasing parents' knowledge of their own feelings. Parents learn to live with the uncertainty of the illness. They also learn how to deal with discipline problems and how to use the group to solve their own problems. Knapp and Hanson observed that parents could only participate after they had adjusted to the initial shock of the illness. They found fathers denied longer than mothers and that they did not want to discuss the possibility of death. Throughout their description of the group experiences they match the parents' responses to the stages of adaptation to life-threatening illness as initially described by Kübler-Ross (1969). These stages include denial, anger, bargaining, depression and acceptance.

In 1973, the *Medical World News* reported on Kaplan's study of the adjustment of the families of fifty children who were interviewed prior to the child's death and thirty-nine families reinterviewed after the death. Kaplan and his associates found that in the thirty-nine families,

> . . . eighteen had divorced or separated after the child became ill, and marital problems became exacerbated for eleven others. In fourteen families the surviving children had difficulty, and four of them were placed outside of the home. Preoccupation with the surviving children's health was noted in twelve families. Unresolved grief, reflected in such behavior as going to the cemetery daily, preoccupation with the deceased child in conversation, complete avoidance of the subject, or "shrine building" was admitted by twenty seven parents. Drinking problems surfaced in fourteen families, eight parents sought psychotherapy for the first time, and six had psychosomatic complaints such as ulcers. Problems at work were encountered by fourteen parents, and six children

had serious difficulties in school

Unfortunately, even in their own report Kaplan and his associates (1976) do not clarify what type of intervention, if any, the families in their study received. What is apparent is that the severity of the impact of the disease is extreme and that psychosocial care in childhood malignancy should be a major concern for health professionals in each and every clinical setting.

1975 On

In the past few years there has been evidence of major advances in learning and thinking. Detailed examination of family communication patterns has revealed how children benefit from open communication about their illness. Instructional books have been provided to help the parents cope with their child's illness and to help the child learn to live with one major type of cancer. Recognition has been given to the fact that care can be given to the child with cancer in his own home and that greater attention should be paid to developing comprehensive home-care programs. However, the most challenging and thought-provoking impetus comes from the realization that when children survive we must change the pattern of medical care from a focus which anticipates death to one which enables the child who is free of disease to live a long and normal life.

Speaking as a clinician, Tannenbaum (1975) summed up the situation for the child with malignancy as follows, "people with cancer and those who are close to them are isolated in a form of cultural limbo, a special ghetto." She adds, "children with cancer become acutely ill frequently. They become bald and bloated from the side effects of their medications." In addition, she emphasizes the fact that the fear of anticipated relapse is continual and that the child with cancer is a problem because "he may never become (an adult) and that upsets us." What Tannenbaum is saying is that these families and these children need to be helped to live today complete with the lack of warrantees on life. They must be helped to live together in the face of societal problems where many families are already plagued with a multitude of difficulties.

In 1975 and 1976 some new dimensions were added to the care of the child. Martinson (1976) describes a home-care program for families of children with leukemia. Although this is a program for children who are usually terminally ill and facing death, it reflects progress in the concern for the care of the children and the families. Martinson emphasizes the confidence and satisfaction that families can feel as they participate in the care of their terminally ill children. Kulenkamp (1976), the mother of a child who died, reinforces the benefits which accrue from the program. She attributes the peacefulness of her son's death to the fact that he was allowed to die at home. Anglim (1976) in the same collection of papers, stresses the value of care which is provided after death. She describes how families need to reconstruct events in order to realize their own strengths. In another chapter, Martinson and her colleagues stress the fact that hospitals have not geared themselves to follow-up care after death. In cases where a home-care program is suitable, its benefits, both economically and interpersonally, are greater than those of the hospital.

A contribution of a different nature to care was made by McCollum (1975) in her book for parents entitled *Coping With Prolonged Health Impairment in Your Child*. McCollum draws heavily on experiences with childhood malignancy in setting forward a simple, readable and comprehensive book which deals with issues such as who is to blame for the child's illness, how to understand the behavior of a sib when he is upset, what kind of problems grandparents encounter when they are faced with a grandchild who has a life-threatening illness and why treatments affect young children so severely. McCollum also deals with death, with anxieties created by hospitalization and with the value of play.

During this time period Spinetta and his colleagues (1977) again contributed to our knowledge of the child by studying family communication patterns. They found that when families were open and allowed the child to talk about his illness he was most able to cope with both the positive and the negative aspects of his life. In the open family system, the child is able to express negative feelings in an accepting environment and tends to want his family closer. Consequently, in doll play and in actual life he will place less distance between himself and family members and between himself and medical personnel. Goggin, Lansky and Hassanein (1976) continue our learning. They found that younger girls with cancer experienced less anxiety than younger boys. Older boys were more realistic than older girls. Strong emotional stimulation tended to be more disruptive than in normal children, and the children with cancer were more prone to unrealistic thinking.

Up to this point, the literature has reflected an increasing enhancement of our knowledge about the child and his family. It is only recently, however, that the long-range implications of the impact of medical progress on the child with malignancy has surfaced as an area of concern. In a unique study, Holmes and Holmes (1975) found that 134 of 655 children with cancer who were diagnosed under the age of 15 survived longer than 10 years. Of these, 124 were still alive at the time of this study and had survived between 10 and 27 years. Holmes and Holmes were concerned about the impact of the disease on the quality of the survivor's life and explored the medical, educational, employment and marital adjustment of the 124 survivors. Ninety persons reported that cancer had not affected their lives; twelve noted a marked change in life-style and only nine had experienced serious problems. The latter suffered from severe mental and physical impairment due to treatment for cranial tumors. Surprisingly, thirteen persons stated that their illness had made a positive change in their lives. Medically, only two patients were known to have had active cancer at the time of the study, and only eighteen of the survivors had marked mental or physical post-treatment disabilities. Educationally, there was little variance in achievement between the survivors and the general populace. Eighty-five persons achieved high school graduation at the same average age as that of the general populace. In the area of employment, only fourteen had failed to reach the same level as their parents. The remainder were employed in a diversity of occupations approximating the variety of jobs found in the general populace. Maritally, sixty of the participants were married or had been married, and eight had been divorced. Forty-one patients over the age of twenty, with an average age of twenty four, stated that cancer or resulting disability prevented their considering marriage. One quarter of those who were married had children. In closing, Holmes and Holmes conclude that the participants in their study had made an excellent adjustment. They suggest that if persons with childhood cancer can survive ten years they have a 90 percent chance of survival and that aggressive and even mutilating treatment regimens can be justified in cancer treatment.

Despite the optimism of Holmes and Holmes and the evidence they present, their study has many weaknesses and does not provide us with a complete picture of the consequences of aggressive treatment protocols. For instance, some of their patients were diagnosed and treated more than two decades ago when chemotherapy was limited. In addition, the categorization of tumors in their study is very general, and there is no staging related to the severity of the various types of cancer. This means that the majority of those persons who survived may have had tumors which were easily removed and were cured with very little treatment beyond the initial surgery. It must also be noted that the study takes place in Kansas. Because Kansas is a state characterized by a high proportion of rural areas, small towns and a low degree of out-of-state mobility, Kansas can hardly be viewed as representing all states. Because of the characteristics of the state it is quite possible that participants in the study received more emotional support from family members and the community than they would if they had resided in an urban setting. It is also most unfortunate that there were no data available related to the socioeconomic status of the participants and the existence of social stresses during the time of treatment. Today, if this study were attempted in an urban setting, the findings would probably be much different. Higher mobility, higher incidence of urban family breakdown and the lack of family and community supports provided in many rural settings often make persons in large cities prone to severe responses when the stress of childhood illness is added to daily life. Today as well, current treatment protocols for some diseases, such as osteogenic sarcoma and certain types of leukemia, lymphomas and cranial tumors subject the child to severe side effects and sometimes, lasting disabilities. It can be said then that, at this point, we know very little of the impact of aggressive treatment protocols on the long-term survivor from an urban setting who has undergone months, or years, of intense treatment in his childhood. The work of Holmes and Holmes should be kept in mind when we consider long-term survival, but the caution of others should be considered as well.

In looking ahead at both the medical and psychosocial care of children with cancer, Dr. J. van Eys (1976) cites the need for physicians to realize that, "now that we are talking about continuous, unmaintained remissions, we have to consider what our definition of cure should be." When considering the child himself, van Eys adds

> ... Unless after such years of therapy the child has developed and grown commensurate with his expectations, and unless the physical cost of therapy is kept to a minimum, a truly cured child has not resulted. In addition, it must be remembered that a child has no independent existence in society. Therefore the impact of life-threatening illness on the family stability must be continually acknowledged and family pathology must be dealt with as much as the pathology in the child itself.

As a further point, van Eys emphasizes "that there is no childhood cancer that is a priori hopeless; even leukemia may not be invariably fatal. Therefore to approach each child with cancer as a child who will die is committing psychological euthanasia."

It is only fitting then that we continue to grapple with ethical issues related to aggressive treatment regimens and that we individualize psychosocial as well as medical care of children and families. We must continue to maximize the use of ambulatory and home care in order to help each child and family live as normal a life as possible. Amy Louise Timmons (1976), an 11 year old with leukemia, wrote a paper before she died. In it she states that people with leukemia suffer because they want to stay alive, that their chances for living are greater and that instead of feeling sorry for them, "just say to yourself, look how much medicine has accomplished." She adds, "you must treat them (leukemia patients) as people with feelings, not as pitied objects. Is it really so awful?" With this approach in mind,

Baker, Roland and Gilchrist (1976) have prepared a comprehensive educational book for the child with leukemia entitled "You and Leukemia: A Day at a Time," which describes the disease, diagnostic procedures and the treatment process in simple terms.

The literature reviewed thus far provides us with an understanding of what has transpired in psychosocial care in the past quarter century and highlights major areas of concern for the child, his family and hospital staff who must care for them. It is helpful, however, to provide a more specific orientation to the needs and responses of the child and his family as a framework for understanding what can happen during the course of a malignant disease. In the following section, I have documented in detail the actual responses of children and families at various stages in childhood leukemia. It is hoped that the reader will review this framework in detail before proceeding to other chapters.

Childhood Leukemia: An Example of an Illness Cycle

This illness cycle includes responses at diagnosis, during remission, at relapse, prior to death, after death and during long-term survival.

At the time of diagnosis families are overwhelmed by the diagnostic label and their perception of its meaning. During remission life returns to "normal" and families try to forget the fact that their child may die. Relapses bring back the anxiety generated by the diagnosis and the threat to their child's life. Family responses at the time of death and after death are also included as are the responses of families whose child is a long-term survivor.

As previously mentioned, an increasing number of children are achieving a new landmark of remaining disease free and healthy for a period of three years while on chemotherapy. Current chemotherapy programs are completed after a three-year period following the initial diagnosis as long as the child does not relapse. Of those children who achieve this goal a large percentage will probably be cured.

CHILDHOOD LEUKEMIA: AN EXAMPLE OF AN ILLNESS CYCLE
AT DIAGNOSIS

Response Factors are Dependent Upon:

1. Past experience with death or crisis or potentially fatal illness.
2. Common behavioral response to stress and crisis, e.g. parental drinking, crying; child becomes irritable or mute.
3. Relationship between parents.
4. Relationship between parents and child.
5. Relationships between siblings.
6. Relationships in the total family system.
7. Support systems — the responses of relatives or friends.
8. The behavior dictated by the family's culture and religion.
9. Amplification of problems already existing in family, e.g. financial.

Family Responses

1. Shock — we were stunned.
2. The doctor must be wrong.
3. Not us, not our child.
4. Leukemia means death.
5. Why should God punish us?

Child Responses

1. Irritable, sick.
2. Isolated.
3. Suspicious, fearful of procedures, white coats.
4. Regression.

Note: Older child and adolescent needs to know what is happening. Younger child will benefit from reduced separation from mother.

WHEN NEARING REMISSION

Observations Concerning Families

1. This is a time to read and to think.
2. Initial stress response continues or subsides due to child's physical improvement.

Family Responses

1. Why our child?
2. Could we have caught it earlier?
3. Who should we tell about it?
4. Will he survive, really?

Child Responses

1. Fear of radiation, procedures, and possible loss of hair.
2. Fear of weekly injections tempered by rapport with team

Observations Concerning Families

3. There are many discussions with relatives, health-care team and friends.
4. There may be reshaping of closeness in the total family.
5. Siblings may regress, seek attention, feel loss of parental affection, wonder why parents are upset. Parents consider how much to tell other children.
6. Parents often have difficulty disciplining the sick child. They may defer disciplining the other siblings because of the demand for additional attention by the sick child.

Family Responses

5. He won't grow up!
6. Can I survive?
7. Radiation may hurt my child.
8. Those drugs have made him ill and fat.
9. He's going to lose his hair.
10. I can't bear to see her lose her hair.
11. Should we put him through all this only to lose him?
12. Even the word cancer upsets me, so do these people I see at the cancer clinic.
13. How can we convince our relatives that this treatment is the right thing?
14. I must trust these doctors. They don't even know what causes leukemia.
15. Could we have prevented this?

Child Responses

and parents emotional support.
3. May be worried, confused because family has changed, e.g. may get what he/she wants and can do as he/she pleases.
4. May act out, test parents.
5. May become uncooperative in regard to treatment regimen.

Note: The child may not verbalize feelings and may require play as a medium for expression and working through of feelings, especially in regard to procedures and bodily changes.

FAMILY STRESS: LEUKEMIA – AN EXAMPLE OF AN ILLNESS CYCLE

AT THE TIME OF REMISSION

Observations Concerning Families

1. Child appears well again.
2. Need to blot out anxieties.
3. Need to grasp possibility of child living normal life, perhaps growing up.
4. May try to show child the world.

Family Responses

1. How can he/she be ill? He looks so well.
2. How long can it last? Maybe forever?
3. Let's do everything we can to live normally.
4. Let's put our fears in the back of our minds.

Child Responses

1. Return to normal activity pattern, e.g. play, school.

Note: The response of the child and family here will depend upon the severity of the treatment protocol. In aggressive regimens the behavior discussed in relation to relapse will probably continue

Observations Concerning Families	Family Responses	Child Responses
		due to the stress of frequent clinical visits, injections and procedures.

AT THE TIME OF RELAPSE

Observations Concerning Families

1. Shock, surprise — wish to deny.
2. Return of intense anxieties.
3. Return of initial stress response.
4. Reconsideration, a search for truth and at least temporary lowering of hope.
5. Probably doing better with discipline.
6. Clinic visits bring back unhappy memories and return to more difficult and painful procedures and injections.

Family Responses

1. Oh God No! It's just not so!
2. How long?
3. What's left?
4. Is there anything else we can do? Can we take him to the United States, or anywhere?
5. What about the drugs you used before?
6. Can we hope he may live?
7. How we hate to see our child suffer. Those procedures make him cry and scream! If it were only me!
8. What do we tell our child now?

Child Responses

1. I don't feel well.
2. I hate those needles, they make me sick.
3. Why are my parents so upset? Why does mommy cry?
4. Those procedures hurt; I don't want to come.
5. I can't go to school; I hurt; I'm sad.
6. I don't want to play or see my friends.
7. That doctor says he's my friend but he hurts me and pokes me.
8. Those pills make me look funny.

THE SECOND RELAPSE

Observations Concerning Families

1. Return of intense feelings — may deny — may develop similar pattern to initial response.

Family Responses

1. This is it. It's a matter of time.
2. How long? When will it end? How much will he suffer?

Child Responses

1. Return to needles, procedures that hurt.
2. Reflection of parents' emotions,

Observations Concerning Families

2. Time is crucial. Time is running out. There is a need for a final search. A need to do everything possible.
3. Anticipatory mourning usually intensifies.

Family Responses

3. Where are the new drugs? Why doesn't research help us with a miracle?
4. He's so sick and so irritable.
5. Should we plan a funeral while we can still cope?
6. Why should our child lose out?
7. Why can't doctors do more? Should we write to Russia?

Child Responses

e.g. sadness, anxiety.
3. May be hospitalized — may regress, withdraw.
4. Older child may verbalize fear of impending death. Younger child may express feelings via play. All children may express themselves through artwork.

DEATH

Observations Concerning Families

Positive adjustment equals —

1. Honesty and expression of feelings.
2. Preparation for death. Right to be angry, sad, to attempt to deny and reach resignation.
3. Ability to communicate with each other.
4. Parents who are close and close to their children. The child is not abandoned.
5. Use of family, neighbors, health team for support as needed.
6. Taking death as reality, mourning, supporting each member of the family and returning to living.

Negative adjustment equals —

1. Emotional or physical abandonment of child by one or both parents.
2. Denial of the impending death.

Family Responses

1. How do we explain death to our three and one-half-year-old?
2. Have we told our child enough? What is he thinking?
3. I hope he won't suffer any more; he's so sick.
4. I'm going to lose my child. He won't grow up.
5. How can I face a funeral? Will I survive?
6. Can I be with him? Will they call us?
7. I wish he would die and stop disrupting our lives. Oh God, I can't think that way!
8. Death: Thank goodness it's over. I couldn't take it any longer.
9. How will I manage without him?

Child Responses

1. Irritable.
2. Physically unwell.
3. Change in appearance, activity level.
4. May be demanding, hostile.
5. Hard to discipline.
6. Hard for parents and staff to understand.
7. May play off parents.
8. May suffer, become comatose.
9. May become very sad or very anxious.
10. Older child may verbally express dashing of hopes and ask questions about death.
11. Needs comfort, closeness of parents and fears separation from them.

Observations Concerning Families
3. Inappropriate emotions, e.g. continued hilarity.
4. Constant vigil, parent unwilling to leave child's room to eat or bathe.

Family Responses

Child Responses
12. May distance himself from everyone including close family members.

AFTER DEATH

Observations Concerning Families
Response will depend on:
1. Preparation and working through feelings.
2. Supports available in family from relatives, friends, neighbors.
3. Age, culture, religion, presence of additional social, emotional problems.

Family Responses
Parents may want follow-up for purposes of:
1. Emotional support — I'm glad I can still talk to you (the team).
2. Clarification about the cause of death — We hope what you learn from our child's death will help other children.
3. Review as to whether or not they did the right thing — We feel he died without pain. You felt that way too, didn't you doctor?
4. Helping siblings with loss of brother or sister. His four-year-old brother talks to him as if he is still alive. Is that okay?

LONG-TERM SURVIVAL
(No relapses after three years of treatment)

Observations re Family
Positive adjustment occurs when:
1. The child carries out all of the activities expected of a child his or her age.
2. Parents can think positively about the child and his or her activities

Family Responses
1. We live each day to the fullest.
2. We thank God for our child's life.
3. We appreciate each other more and are closer.

Child Responses
1. I'll still get needles next year for me.
2. Clinic visits will never end
3. I'm going to be alright.

Note: Learning in this area will

Observations re Family	*Family Responses*	*Child Responses*
without overprotecting or imposing restrictions. 3. Parents, the child and other family members gradually reinvest emotionally in the child's future.		continue. We will work toward helping families grant their child the freedom to experience what other children experience and do what other disease-free children do as part of a normal life experience.

REFERENCES

Nesbitt, M. and Kersey, J.: "Acute Leukemia of Childhood." *Home Care for the Dying Child: Professional and Family Perspectives.* Edited by Ida M. Martinson, Appleton-Century-Crofts, New York, 1976.

Karni, K.R.: "The View from the Laboratory." *Home Care for the Dying Child: Professional and Family Perspectives,* Ida M. Martinson (Ed.), Martinson, Appleton-Century-Crofts, New York, 1976.

Haghbin, M., Tan, C.C., Clarkson, B.D., Mike, V., Burchenal, J. and Murphy, M.L.: "Intensive Chemotherapy in Children With Acute Lymphoblastic Leukemia (L2 Protocol)." *Cancer,* 33:6, 1491-1498, 1974.

Knudson, A.G.: "Genetics and Etiology of Childhood Cancer." *Pediatr Res.,* 10:513-517, 1976.

Hughes, W.T.: "Early Side Effects in Treatment of Childhood Cancer." *Pediatr Clin N Am,* 23:1, 225-232, 1976.

Jaffe, N.: "Late Side Effects of Treatment: Skeletal, Genetic, Central Nervous System and Oncogenic." *Pediatr Clin N Am,* 23:1, 233-244, 1976.

Bozeman, M.F., Orbach, C.E. and Sutherland, A.M.: "Psychological Impact of Cancer and Its Treatment, 111, The Adaptation of Mothers to the Threatened Loss of Their Children Through Leukemia: Part 1." *Cancer,* 8:1-19, 1955.

Richmond, J.G. and Waisman, H.A.: "Psychological Aspects of Management of Children With Malignant Diseases." *Am J Dis Child,* 89:42-47, 1955.

Cobb, B.: "Psychological Impact of Long Illness and Death of a Child on the Family Circle." *J Pediatr,* 49:746-751, 1956.

Solnit, A.J. and Green, M.: "Psychological Considerations in the Management of Deaths on Pediatric Hospital Services; 1. The Doctor and the Child's Family." *Pediatr* 24:106-112, 1959.

Greene, W.A. and Miller, G.: "Psychological Factors and Reticuloendothelial Disease. IV. Observations on a Group of Children and Adolescents with Leukemia: An Interpretation of Disease Development in Terms of the Mother-Child Unit." *Psychosom Med,* 20:2, 124-144, 1958.

Natterson, J.M. and Knudson, A.G.: "Observations Concerning Fear of Death in Fatally Ill Children and Their Mothers." *Psychosom Med,* 22:6, 456-465, 1960.

Friedman, S.B., Chodoff, P., Mason, J.W. and Hamburg, D.A.: "Behavioural Observations on Parents Anticipating the Death of a Child." *Pediatr,* 32:4, 610-625, 1963.

Hamovitch, M.B.: *The Parent and the Fatally Ill Child,* City of Hope Medical Center, Duarte, California, 1964.

Vernick, J. and Karon, M.: "Who's Afraid of Death on a Leukemia Ward?" *Am J Dis Child,* 109:393-397, 1965.

Vernick, J. and Lunceford, J.L.: "Milieu Design for Adolescents with

Leukemia." *Am J Nurs*, 67:3, 559-561, 1967.

Toch, R.: "Management of the Child With a Fatal Disease." *Clin Pediatr* 3:7, 418-427, 1964.

Lascari, A.D.: "The Family and the Dying Child: A Compassionate Approach." *Med Times*, 97:5, 207-215, 1969.

Hoffman, I. and Futterman, E.H.: "Coping With Waiting: Psychiatric Intervention and Study in the Waiting Room of a Pediatric Oncology Clinic." *Comp Psychiatry* 12:1, 67-81, 1971.

Waechter, E.H.: "Children's Awareness of Fatal Illness." *Am J Nurs*, 71:1168-1172 1971.

Share, L.: "Family Communication in the Crisis of a Child's Fatal Illness: A Literature Review and Analysis." *Omega*, 3:3, 187-201, 1972.

Spinetta, J.J., Rigler, D. and Karon, M.: "Anxiety in the Dying Child." *Pediatr* 52:6, 841-845, 1973.

Spinetta, J.J.: "The Dying Child's Awareness of Death: A Review." *Psychol Bull* 81:4, 256-260, 1974.

Spinetta, J.J., Rigler, D. and Karon, M.: "Personal Space as a Measure of a Dying Child's Sense of Isolation." *J Cons and Clin Psychol*, 42:6, 751-756, 1974.

Easson, W.M.: "The Family of the Dying Child." *Pediatr Clin N Am*, 19:4, 1157-1165, 1972.

McCollum, A.T. and Schwartz, A.H.: "Social Work and the Mourning Parent." *Soc Wk* 17:1, 25-36, 1972.

Heffron, W.A., Bommelaere, K. and Masters, R.: "Group Discussions With Parents of Leukemic Children." *Pediatr*, 52:6, 831-840, 1973.

Knapp, V.S. and Hanson, H.: "Helping the Parents of Children with Leukemia." *Soc Wk* 18:4, 70-75, 1973.

Kübler-Ross, E.: *On Death and Dying*, Macmillan Publishing Co. Ltd., New York, 1969.

Kaplan, D.M., Grobstein, R. and Smith, A.: "Predicting the Impact of Severe Illness in Families." *Health and Soc Wk*, 1:3, 72-82, 1976.
Also see *Med World News*, April 6, 1973, p. 23

Tannenbaum, D.T.: "The Future is Now: Helping Families to Live with Children Who May Die." Paper presented at the Annual Conference American Orthopsychiatric Association, Washington, D.C., March 21-24, 1975.

Martinson, I.M. and Jorgens, C.L.: "Report of a Parent Support Group." in *Home Care for the Dying Child*. Ida M. Martinson (ed.), Appleton-Century-Crofts, New York, 1976.

Kulenkamp, E.: "Eric: A Mother's Recollection." in *Home Care for the Dying Child*. Ida M. Martinson (ed.), Appleton-Century-Crofts, New York, 1976.

Anglim, M.A.: "Reintegration of the Family After the Death of a Child." in *Home Care for the Dying Child*, Ida M. Martinson (ed.), Appleton-Century-Crofts, New York, 1976.

McCollum, A.T.: *Coping With Prolonged Health Impairment in Your Child.*

Little, Brown and Company (inc.), Boston, Mass., 1975.

Spinetta, J.J.: "Communication Patterns in Families of Children with Life Threatening Illness." Paper presented at a postgraduate symposium, "The Child and Death," University of Rochester, Rochester, N.Y., September 15, 1977.

Goggin, E.L., Lansky, S.B. and Hassanein, K.: "Psychological Reactions of Children with Malignancies." *J Am Acad Child Psychiatry,* 15:2, 315-325, 1976.

Holmes, H.A. and Holmes, F.F.: "After Ten Years, What are the Handicaps and Life Styles of Children Treated for Cancer." *Clin Pediatr,* 14:9, 819-823, 1975.

Van Eys, J.: "Supportive Care for the Child with Cancer." *Pediatr Clin N Am* 23:1, 215-224, 1976.
    Also see Van Eys, J.: *The Truly Cured Child: The New Challenge in Pediatric Cancer Care.* University Park Press, Baltimore, Md., 1977.

Timmons, A.L.: "Leukemia: Is It So Awful?" *J Pediatr,* 88:1, 147-148, 1976.

Baker, L.S., Roland, C.G. and Gilchrist, G.S.: *You and Leukemia: A Day at a Time.* Mayo Comprehensive Cancer Center, Rochester, Minn., 1976.

CHAPTER 2

PROVIDING CARE:
THE MULTIDISCIPLINARY TEAM

Introduction

IN 1961, when I first began working in a general hospital as a student, encounters with several children with tumors and a young adult with leukemia led to my realization that there was no coordinated approach to the care of the child and his family. Children remained in the hospital for long periods of time. They were sent off to another part of the hospital for radiation and apart from the time they spent in unstructured play under the supervision of a volunteer in the sun room, their closest relationships were with nurses who were often overworked and had little time to spend with them. In some instances where parents lived close by, they were allowed to visit in the afternoon and evening. When they lived in rural areas, visiting was often infrequent. The physician saw the child briefly on rounds and discussed the treatment and prognosis with the parents. Knowledge of the impact of the disease on the child and his family was seldom shared and discussion with the child of his impending death happened only occasionally. At times the hospital priest or minister was in contact with the family, but the social worker or psychiatrist were seldom part of the pediatric program.

I experienced the implications of this disjointed approach to care firsthand when Gerry, aged 23, was admitted to an adult ward with acute mylogenous leukemia. Gerry had become pale and weak and following admission he deteriorated quickly. He soon developed petechiae, extreme pallor, pain in his limbs and nasal bleeding. He became depressed, angry and very irritable. He cried out and wept, withdrawing both from his wife and the staff. His wife was overcome with sorrow and had difficulty understanding her husband's outbursts. The ward staff had difficulty understanding as well, and only a few staff were willing to care for him. Gerry died within five weeks in an experience that was filled with sadness, anger and pain. Little was known by the staff of what had happened to Gerry's wife, except perhaps by the physician. If he did know about the outcome and follow-up care of the young widow, no information was ever shared.

Nearly a decade later, the opportunity arose for me to become involved with the care of cancer patients again. This time I was given a different role and the chance to help develop an effective approach to the care of the child and his family by working together with staff from other disciplines. This chapter reviews our experiences.

Providing an Approach to Care

The provision of care for the child and his family is a complex undertaking from both the medical and psychosocial perspectives. Just as the hematologist or oncologist relies upon the radiologist, radiotherapist, virologist, nurses and other disciplines to help him attend to the medical concerns, so too does he rely on the nurses, social worker, child life worker, psychiatrist, clergy and others to help him attend to the psychosocial needs of the child and his family. In effect, there should be no real dichotomy in care. The interrelationship of medical and psychosocial needs must be recognized and met as efficiently as possible in an approach which truly provides total patient care. Consequently, at McMaster University Medical Centre we have evolved a multidisciplinary approach which unites disciplines in the provision of this care. We have a core team consisting of pediatric hematologists*, nurses, a social worker and a child life worker. This team expands with the addition of residents, fellows and students to form an extended team.

The Beginning of Teamwork from a Psychosocial Perspective: The McMaster Experience

Seven years ago when I first discussed the move of the pedi-

---

*The pediatric hematologist in our clinic is not only a specialist in the diagnosis and treatment of blood diseases but is also an oncologist who diagnoses and treats cancerous diseases.

atric hematology and oncology clinic* from another teaching hospital to this new health sciences teaching facility, the clinic consisted of a small group of pediatric hematologists, residents and a clinic secretary. Interaction was mainly with other medical disciplines, and the clinic was of necessity a medical operation with extremely limited involvement with the psychological or social concerns of the patient and his family. At our new facility interaction between the registered nurse, the clinic director, a staff hematologist and myself led to the development of a small pilot clinic and the holding of multidisciplinary case discussions which included a large number of faculty from various medical disciplines. In my role as clinical social worker I made joint presentations with the nurse which focused upon the adjustment of families to the illness experience. We noted their ongoing problems, described how they used the support systems around them and brought forward questions that the family had raised about the care of their child. Our approach was well received because we often introduced new data about the family or confirmed the physician's suspicion that they were having difficulty coping with the stress created by the illness. At times, some of our suggestions and concerns could be incorporated to modify approaches to the care of the child and his family. Presentations by the radiologist, pediatric radiotherapist and others were of value to the total group in planning patient care and aided in expanding medical knowledge.

Up until the total clinic moved to the Medical Centre in April 1973, my involvement and participation by the ambulatory or out-patient nursing staff remained peripheral. Our contributions consisted mainly of offering opinions or information at rounds and providing consultation as requested. The move to McMaster led to the employment of two nurses with baccalaureate education and later as the clinic expanded other personnel were added. These included a child life worker, an occupational therapist and a psychiatric consultant. The com-

*The pediatric hematology and oncology clinic encompasses both the care of children with blood diseases and those with oncologic disorders such as leukemia and solid tumors.

monality of interest with other ambulatory clinics facilitated the employment of receptionists who were sensitive to the needs of children. The growth of the total hospital made available other service personnel such as the nutritionist, chaplain and physiotherapist. These professionals were of value to the clinic team even though initially most did not have a special interest or training in the care of children.

The Ambulatory Core Team

Since 1973 the ambulatory core team has remained almost constant and the nurses, social worker, physicians and child life workers have shared a learning experience that is focused on the assimilation of knowledge psychosocially, interpersonally and medically. The core team has struggled with the development of its own commitment to an honest, realistic and shared approach to the provision of total care for the patient and his family. Through careful planning and assigning of specific supervisory responsibilities, the core team has positively adapted to the addition of residents and fellows and views these participants as valued members of the extended team. In addition, the core team has incorporated students from medicine, nursing, social work and other disciplines for varying periods of time and considers them to be important contributors to the extended team. Staff physicians and residents from medical disciplines such as radiotherapy, radiology, virology and microbiology have also been included as major participants in developing approaches to patient care. In working with the inpatient unit, the core team has grappled with its relationship with nurses, residents and staff pediatricians in respect to the roles and responsibilities of all participants in care. Internally, the team has solved conflicts in disciplinary roles and responsibilities, short-term changes in leadership and interpersonal differences between individuals in the same or different disciplines.

In our experience, we have learned that team work is a dynamic undertaking with an ever present need to readapt to new situations. Kane (1975), in summarizing her review of interdisciplinary studies suggests that attempts to integrate disciplines often lead to a high risk of poor communication and lack of clarity in purpose as well as role definition. Conflicts related to status seeking behavior are also pronounced. Rosini (1974) delineated for discussion three major areas of interdisciplinary functioning. These were as follows: work function and roles; decision making and leadership; and stereotyping of disciplines. In analyzing our team, these three areas will be examined in detail.

Functions and Roles

Within the core team we have been able to clarify mutual expectations about roles and functions by working together and discussing our differences. Increased knowledge, the growth of ambulatory and in-patient care and the availability of other disciplines with additional skills have changed the role of the physician, nurse and social worker. Personal trust, competence in practice and willingness to share in the best interests of the patient and family have facilitated a close working relationship. This relationship encompasses the extended team and helps the total group survive the crises generated by occasional communication gaps and constant demands brought about by the challenges of providing patient care. Changes from traditional roles and structures have led to the following role allocations for the various disciplines.

The Pediatric Hematologist

The participating pediatric hematologists are responsible for the overall care of the child. In addition to traditional medical roles, the hematologists have increased their sensitivity to child and family behavior and play a key role in the identification of child, parent-child and family problems at the point of diagnosis. The hematologist as the physician in charge is constantly aware of the care given by residents and fellows. He is often directly involved with the child and his family. He provides clarification about the direction of medical treatment and delineates how parents can help the team to care for their child.

The hematologist also provides emotional support for the families at times of relapse, impending death and death itself. The honesty, openness and availability of the hematologist as a source of support and direction to the resident staff and as a major resource to other staff is a necessary factor in making teamwork a reality.

Honesty and openness with the child and his family is also a positive attribute which sets the tone for all care within the pediatric hematology-oncology clinic. This approach as practiced by the hematologist lends credence to the involvement of other team members and aids in making the acquisition of psychosocial knowledge and skills an expectation for residents, fellows and students.

In the traditional sense, the hematologist is the leader in education, research and patient care.

The Registered Nurse

In our pediatric hematology-oncology clinic the nurse has developed a role which expands beyond the traditional role expectations for the hospital nurse. Our two nurses divide the patient load on a random basis so that each has one-half of the children and families. In a traditional way the nurse organizes patient flow, completes requisitions and assists the residents with examinations and procedures such as bone marrow aspirations. A major change in the role of the nurse hinges upon her ability to perform with expertise in the psychosocial area, often in close cooperation with the social worker and the child life worker. The ambulatory clinic nurse is usually involved in the formulation of the basic psychosocial assessment when the child is diagnosed on the in-patient unit. She establishes rapport with the child and family and evaluates along with the staff physician, resident and other team members, the type of psychosocial care the family requires. If in doubt, she precipitates further assessment by the social worker or may request that she, the social worker and the child life worker deal jointly with identified child and family problems. In continuing her relationship with the family the nurse becomes the pivotal point for the management of care. She works closely with the

resident, keeps up to date with medical treatments and psychosocial care and is accessible to families for questions related to
either area. When hospitalization is necessary, the nurse will
communicate her concerns about the child and his family to
nurses who work on the ward. She becomes a person that the
child and his family can rely on to provide continuity in patient care through time. The nurse can be their advocate and a
major source of emotional support. When required, she may be
the liaison person between the team and home care or public
health nursing services. If a child dies, she will usually be
involved in his care at the time of death and in the post-death
follow-up support for family members. As an educator she
assists residents and students with learning basic psychosocial
and medical skills. She is also responsible for the field practice
experiences of nursing students and helps facilitate the learning
of all students who participate in the clinic.

In our team the nurse is a graduate with additional preparation. She is a skilled practitioner with considerable psychosocial knowledge gained from within the team, from clinical
teaching programs and past nursing or life experience. She is
very much a part of the team and her effectiveness in practice
hinges on her ability to work with other team members.

The Social Worker

Just as the nurse has undergone considerable training so also
has the social worker. Enhancement of clinical assessment and
treatment skills, continued learning through working with
clinic patients and their families, and increased knowledge of
medical and chemotherapeutic care and experience with dying
children and family bereavement have all been necessary to
help the social worker practice effectively.

These experiences have also facilitated the expansion of my
role as a social worker. Smith (1973) indicated that the social
worker could function in a medical setting because of his
knowledge of human personality, his knowledge of sociolog-
ical factors and attitudes toward illness and death and his
ability to combine both in forming relationships with parents.
Schrager (1974) suggested that social workers were valued for

their instrumental skills. In practice these factors may all be of value as far as they go. In our clinic, I carry out traditional roles in managing relationships with community services and helping multiproblem families cope with daily living, but I also serve as a counselor to parents, families, adolescent patients and sometimes to children as well. As a caseworker, my job is to help families solve problems related to personal adjustment, marital conflict, child discipline and adaptation to illness and bereavement, as many social workers do in medical settings. However, I also assume an additional responsibility as the major psychosocial resource. Within the range of my capabilities, I assess and treat situations where families experience extreme difficulty in adaptation to illness, relapse, death and bereavement. I also serve as the major advisor in respect to team management of problems in the area of family relationships. I always function as part of the team, and I usually precipitate the relatively rare involvement of the consulting psychiatrist. As a team member, I play a role in monitoring team functioning and in facilitating the identification and discussion of interpersonal differences within the team. As an educator, I assume individual and shared responsibility for practice experiences in psychosocial care for students working for degrees in social work, health science and medicine.

Within the clinic my role provides me with the opportunity to help residents learn how to work effectively with families. In addition, I have the opportunity to participate in seminars and clinical rounds along with other team members, and inevitably I come into contact with nursing, child life and other students who seek knowledge in the psychosocial area.

Like the nurse, I am a person with commitment to the team and program. I am a senior M.S.W. with a faculty appointment in psychiatry.

The Child Life Worker

A valuable addition to our core team came about with the advent of the child life worker. The child life worker is a graduate of an approved program in child studies. She also receives an extensive in-service training program to orientate her to the hospital, to the impact of specific types of illnesses on children and to the ways which the roles of various disciplines compliment each other. The child life worker must be capable of working with both children and adults and demonstrate a sensitivity to the needs of children and adolescents in both the in-patient and ambulatory settings. She must be creative, mature and capable of helping parents and staff understand and interact with children. Her emphasis on the "quality of life" of the child in in-patient and ambulatory care in combination with the "normative" view of child behavior has added a much needed component to patient care. There is no situation more stressful to the child than being physically ill, being subjected to painful procedures and being hospitalized with a life-threatening disease. Our team needed to understand children, to communicate with them effectively and to facilitate care in the least traumatic way possible. Although pediatricians, nurses, social workers and other disciplines had theoretical knowledge and experience in working with children, the gentle nature of the child life worker's approach, the time she set aside solely for the child and her focus on the use of therapeutic play experiences as a tool for assessment and treatment, made her contribution to the care of the child superior to that of other disciplines. As a facilitator of treatment, the child life worker could assist the child in coping with anxiety and releasing anger prior to and after procedures. She could contribute to diagnosing behavioral problems and intervene with the child, his parent or parents and the team to alleviate or end such difficulties.

Today in our clinic, the child life worker works very closely with the nurses, residents and social worker. She works easily with the nurses and social worker in helping families to understand and to facilitate the care of the child. She provides residents and other team members with valuable information about the impact of treatment and in many situations she serves as the child's advocate.

If the child life worker requires greater skills than she possesses she consults with the supervising play therapist. On occasion the skills of the child psychiatrist are also required.

In practice, I have found that the child life worker has encouraged all of us to relate more closely to children. The level of knowledge of all our team members has increased, and our concern for the child is very much a part of daily clinic activities.

When the child is hospitalized, our child life worker or when appropriate her counterpart on the pediatric ward, works with the child to make the stay in hospital as normal an experience as possible. Continuity of her involvement from the clinic to the ward is often valuable in reducing the trauma of hospitalization and sometimes reduces the recovery time required. Once again, the child life worker is an advocate for the child because she helps make his needs and concerns known to staff on the ward.

Beyond the Core Team: The Extended Team

In our setting, the core team discusses and deals with issues related to the continuity of the team through time. Core team members play a major role in determining education and service priorities, in maintaining the structure of the clinic and in bringing into focus concerns about the team's relationships with the hospital administration, hospital departments and community services.

In order to provide clinical service in a teaching hospital the core team must expand or extend and add the residents, students and staff from other disciplines which help provide a comprehensive approach to patient care. When we consider the formulation of our extended team we must give recognition to two disciplines which frequently play important roles in the assessment and treatment of the child. The occupational and physiotherapist have gained increasing importance because the growth in the number of children with physical disabilities has coincided with the growth of the clinic. The occupational therapist has contributed greatly to the team's ability to assess how much the child's physical state will allow him to carry out activities of daily living such as dressing, maintaining hygiene and going to school. She has also added her skills in the assessment of fine motor abilities of the hands and the movement of the upper extremities. The physiotherapist has contributed to the assessment and treatment of physical problems, particularly in relation to changes created by brain and bone surgery. The observations of these health professionals and their intervention has been a positive addition to psychosocial care as well.

As we look beyond the clinic, constant communication with representatives of other disciplines who support treatment are also valuable. For example, the observations of the radiotherapist and the technical staff from radiology and laboratory services can add useful information about the child's ability to cope with diagnostic and treatment procedures. Contact with these disciplines can also lead to the surfacing of important information about family difficulties. However, maintenance of ongoing communication with all but a small number of these services is extremely difficult. In daily practice, the effectiveness of the extended team is greatly influenced by fellows, residents and the child and his family. These roles are examined in the sections that follow.

The Resident

When he comes to our clinic the resident brings with him his past experience, anxieties about new learning required for practice in our clinic and a cultural background which is often at variance with the patient populace. As in most clinical settings, he has little time to adjust and almost immediately the resident becomes a key person in the delivery of clinical care. When possible, he serves for a minimum period of six months and is expected to become knowledgeable about the medical and psychosocial needs of the majority of patients who visit the clinic. He is a front-line person who is available after regular hours and must learn to deal not only with the medical complexities of care but also with anxious parents, children who act out, children who are dying, bereaved families and many other patient care problems with major psychosocial implications. The resident must work closely with the fellow and with the staff hematologist and must also develop a relationship with other team members who can help him learn sufficient psychosocial skills so that he can cope with the problems presented by our patients and their families. As a member of the extended team, the resident influences the system, philosophy and priorities of care as well as the development and implementation of treatment protocols. Although he must initially conform to the norms of the team, he most definitely influences the team's approach.

The resident contributes to the education of other team members and to the learning of medical and nursing students in particular. He can function effectively as a preceptor for medical students on a short-term basis and facilitate their learning about the medical and hematological concerns in patient care.

The Fellow

As a physician who has completed his residency but is pursuing further study in the specialties of pediatric hematology and oncology, the fellow is available for a minimum of one year. Like the resident, he is faced with a situation which forces him to undergo a marked personal adjustment in his working relationships, in learning new protocols and medical information, and in developing his role in the psychosocial area. He is viewed as more of an authority than the residents and has greater influence in areas related to service, education and research. Often, however, his background has not forced him to become closely involved in the psychosocial care of his patients. Also, his background has not forced him to deal with his personal feelings about death and bereavement and other situational crises which require him to respond as a person.

In the process of integrating with the core team, the fellow can pose a challenge to the norms of the group. He can command authority and challenge leadership because of his past achievements. At the same time, he can be a valuable asset in bringing new ideas and suggestions which influence and improve the team's approaches to clinical care and education. He can contribute much to the education of the residents and students and usually carries an important role in research as well.

The Unique Role of the Child and His Family

Our extended team includes the patient and his family. Clinical practice demands that plans for ongoing care be formulated with the child, the child and his parents, the nuclear family and at times the extended family. The concerns and opinions of patients and families have a bearing on the formulation and implementation of treatment protocols, the service delivery system, the conduct of staff and students, the philosophy of patient care and community attitudes towards hospital and clinic.

Although families attending the clinic may not be party to all aspects of patient care planning and professional knowledge about treatment protocols, they most certainly wield considerable influence. The child and his family are often the most valuable educators of staff and students. As they are going through the treatment experience, they can interpret their observations and perceptions to team members and can usually evaluate explicitly the quality of care being given.

Maintaining the Extended Team

At all times the integration of the extended team is a major concern. As the team grows it increases the potential for communication problems and the need for sub-units or sub-teams becomes greater. This is particularly true when various groupings of team members must work together to treat a given child or a number of children. Just as leadership must be defined in the overall team, so must leadership and accountabilities be established in sub-groupings. The addition of other physicians to the core group can either facilitate the effectiveness of sub-groupings or create conflict and confusion. The integration of additional students from various disciplines can create uncertainty unless the integration of the students is carefully planned and the supervision is delineated specifically. The development of allied approaches to treatment and service delivery within the extended team requires frequent structured opportunities for sharing. In our situation it has been essential to plan specific times for conferences about patients so that opportunities are provided to discuss medical and psychosocial care. In addition, time is provided for educational sessions where current clinical developments can be shared. Most important, however, is the fact that any member of the core team or extended team can request a "tea party." This event is usually held every month and is a time for discussing concerns, for problem solving and for planning. Most discussion focuses on problems related to communication difficulties between team members, issues about clinic management and patient services, suggestions about how to improve relationships with external consultants or in-patient units, plans for student assignments and needs for staff or supplies. Obviously, this meeting is the place for dealing with major issues. Many of the minor day-to-day problems, if dealt with openly, can be resolved outside of the "tea party," through discussion between the various team members or groups of team members.

Relating to the In-Patient Unit

The development of a positive working relationship between our ambulatory team and the in-patient pediatric unit has required considerable time and attention. Many problems have arisen around the roles of staff and residents. For example, the assignment of new residents has made it necessary for the medical staff to periodically clarify responsibility for various aspects of patient treatment. In respect to psychosocial care, problems have occasionally arisen between the pediatric resident and the ambulatory team due to differences in the perception of patient and family behavior and needs. In a similar manner problems have also arisen with nursing staff. There has been a need to clarify the nature of the roles of ambulatory staff and how these integrate with the involvement of nurses on the ward. A continuing dialogue between the ambulatory team and in-patient nursing staff has resulted in the narrowing of the number of in-patient nurses assigned to working with our patients. In most instances it is the ambulatory nurses who update the in-patient nursing staff advising them about the current needs of the child and the family during the child's hospitalization. Discussion has resulted in a willingness to recognize that both the daily observations and contributions to care by the ward staff and the long-term knowledge of the child and his family contributed by the ambulatory nurses and other team members, can be combined to facilitate the best care possible. Movement of ward nurses into nursing positions in ambulatory care has also increased the amount of understanding between nursing staff in both areas.

As in other centers, our greatest difficulties in communication are created when a child is terminally ill. Other writers have pointed out that physicians are uncomfortable with death. They associate dying patients with failure and disappointment and tend to cope with death through avoidance of patient contact. They also state that physicians sometimes cannot cope with their anger when parents become resentful and at other times they suffer because they over-identify with the person who is dying (Tietz and Powars, 1975). Nurses and doctors have also been reported to have neglected dying patients and to have failed to share their prognosis with them (Schulz and Aderman, 1976). It is not just doctors and nurses who have problems facing death. All hospital staff are prone to feelings of sadness, anger and anxiety. We have found that during terminal care we must bring those involved with the dying child and his family together and make certain that patient care plans are clear and suitable to everyone.

When the child dies, we have found that in the ambulatory team we have a diversity of methods which members use to cope with the death experience. Some persons cry openly, some withdraw to work out their own feelings and some want to talk about what has happened. Because of this diversity, we do not usually hold a post-death session where feelings are shared openly. Instead, because of our close working relationship and concern for each other, persons will usually seek out other persons who want to discuss the death, or members of the core team will intentionally spend additional time with residents, staff and students who are upset. In relating to staff and residents from the in-patient area, we have used a similar approach. Since the ambulatory and in-patient areas are in close proximity and since the ambulatory staff tend to remain in contact with the dying child, the staff from both areas can often discuss what has transpired. It is often very necessary for in-patient nurses and residents to know that they have cared for the dying child and his family well. So far we have steered away from other than the occasional post-death conferences which involve a large number of staff. Recently, a senior pediatrician with considerable psychosocial interest and experience and a senior social worker from the in-patient unit have implemented discussions with the in-patient staff to enhance the staff's psychosocial and medical knowledge of various illnesses. These discussions have included the opportunity for participants to discuss their feelings. Because of needs that have been articulated by the residents and nursing staff, members of our team will probably devote more time to discussing feelings about specific losses with those who work on the pediatric ward.

In a teaching hospital the high turnover rate of residents and students on the in-patient unit necessitates a continued dialogue about their needs in working with children with cancer. Because of the emotional strain of facing seriously ill and dying children with cancer and other medical diseases, the nursing staff most certainly need ongoing support and the opportunity for discussion as well. Our ambulatory team is in a key position to meet these needs.

Factors Influencing Teamwork

Decision Making and Leadership

In her monograph on interdisciplinary teamwork, Kane (1975) refers to two other works which contribute to our knowledge of leadership. Brieland (1973) found that the ideal size of a team is five to six members. Berelson and Steiner (1964) found that as teams expanded, the demands on the leader increased and their tolerance of direction from the leader increased as well. In addition, the active members of the teams tended to become more dominant and the more passive members withdrew from participation. In general, they found that the larger the group, the more anonymous action of individuals became, the longer it took to reach decisions, the more sub-groups formed and the more formal the rules and procedures of the group became. Democratic leadership tended to generate satisfaction in individual team members, greater team productivity and a tendency for the team to function effectively even when the leader was absent. Berelson and Steiner suggest that when team members share equally they tend to adopt similar values and norms and develop an affinity for one another. These findings are all applicable to our team and the changes that have developed due to growth.

The core team is very much a place of shared decisions, for closeness and for mutual respect. As described earlier, as the team expands to its extended state, the need increases for greater direction, use of the leader's final authority in making major decisions, formulation of working sub-groups and development of more formal rules to govern activities such as the implementation of treatment protocols.

Leadership is important at all times. Inevitably when disciplines come together there is a question of accountability, power and control. In our team, because the patient is an integral part of the clinic and has been referred due to hematology or oncology problems, the basic and continuing accountability for the treatment of the patient rests with the physician in charge of the clinic. In our setting the physician is recognized and respected as the team leader. Leadership, however, often means availability for consultation to all team members or for monitoring the overall patient care given by the team, or the giving of a final last word. Often the necessity for the leader to take direct command is remote if the other components of our team are functioning effectively. For instance, in clinical practice the individual team member can, by competence and performance, demonstrate leadership in dealing with problems of individual patients while recognizing that it is important to communicate with the team leader and other team members. The democratic nature of guidance by the team leader is growth producing and ensures accountability. Staff are encouraged to use their own initiative and are free to share their values and beliefs with other team members. Such leadership also enhances the opportunity for the incorporation of feedback from the patient and his family so that patient care practices can be changed to make the team more responsive to their needs.

The Stereotyping of Disciplines

Kane (1975) states that team members are first individuals, later professionals and much later members of interprofessional teams. Horowitz (1970) states that individual attributes of team members may be as important as professional affiliations. Bernard and Ishyama (1960) suggest that the personality of the staff member, the formal demands of the position and individual striving for authority must be balanced.

Berelson and Steiner (1964) in their research, found that the more disciplines share on equal terms the more they share norms and values. Garland, Kolodny and Jones (1965), in discussing the small group, describe how the group engages in an equality struggle ending in closeness and a feeling of belonging. When this state is reached the group is then able to appreciate the unique contribution of each team member.

All of the findings described above are relevant to our experiences. As a small group, the core team has struggled with personality differences between members and with the establishment of territorial rights and privileges of some participants. Through the experience of solving problems of patients, establishing a service delivery system of the clinic and determining service and educational priorities, our core team has moved more closely together. Membership in the core group has led to feelings of equality between individual participants and reduced the need to strive for authority. This feeling of equality has led to a balance between personalities and the formal demands of positions. This balance carries over to work within the extended team as well. In the extended team the core group shapes the pattern of expected behavior and through time ensures the viability of authority, roles and relationships that are acceptable to them. In the larger forum the leader is not only the formal power and decision maker, but he is also the instrument of the core group. He ensures that norms and values acceptable to the core team are adopted and continued in practice.

Stereotyping of disciplines in the traditional procedure oriented approach to nursing, the instrumental roles of social work and the omnipotent role for medicine is not currently an issue. Stereotyping will only become an issue if the value of the core team and the nature of small group behavior therein is radically modified through changes in leadership or membership within the group, or by external influences emanating from within the extended team. The fortunate part of our experience has been the opportunity to evolve the multidisciplinary team without many of the trappings of established structures, disciplinary traditions and preestablished expectations.

Is Multidisciplinary Teamwork Worth the Effort?

The previous sections reflect the complexity involved in maintaining a multidisciplinary team. The process continually requires the attention, cooperation and ongoing collaboration of all participants. The evaluation of the success or failure of teamwork can only be measured by the patients and families who receive care and by those who participate as team members. We have found that the children and families are usually in favor of our team approach. They are most content when they are allowed to be cared for by a small number of team members. They are less confused and feel more confident when they have established a rapport with those who care for them. In a university teaching center this narrowing down of numbers becomes a major challenge, especially when residents and students need to know a variety of patients in order to meet their own learning needs. We have found that the core team is of major value and that the constancy of the nurse, the staff physician, the social worker and the child life worker is of great value in ensuring continuity of care and in reducing the child's and the family's anxiety about meeting new residents. We have also learned that at critical periods where children are starting a new series of injections or are critically ill or dying, it helps to keep the same resident involved in the child's care. When we have introduced students to the child and his family we have had the greatest success when the student remains in contact on a longitudinal basis over a number of months. By so doing he becomes close enough to the child and the family to be accepted by them. When we have maintained as much constancy as possible in the provision of care, families have often been very appreciative.

When we examine how we as members of the core team have altered or progressed as a result of our participation in the team, we find that there is an overwhelming increase in our respect for the abilities of other disciplines and in our recognition of the complexity involved in providing both medical and psychosocial care to our clinic patients. Perhaps the greatest recognition of the benefits of the team process was provided by the team director when he analyzed his own thoughts and feelings and found that because of his involvement with the team he had the following experiences:

1. He appreciated that there is greater demand for involvement with the family than he would otherwise have recognized;
2. he admired the dedication and professionalism of each participant;
3. he felt the need for continued upgrading of his own unique contribution in the study of disease; and
4. he appreciated the problems of inserting "learners" into a smooth-working core group.

From my personal viewpoint I would add that I have found the team experience has provided me with a great deal of emotional support, has increased my knowledge about children and about medical care and has been a major stimulus in encouraging me to write this book.

When I have had the opportunity to discuss our approach with the residents and students who have worked as part of our extended team, they have frequently given recognition to the benefits that collaboration with other disciplines has provided. This has been particularly true when we have had the opportunity to work together with children and their families when the medical and psychosocial aspects of care have been extremely challenging. Residents and students have also appreciated the nature of information and the difference in viewpoints which other disciplines have contributed to case discussions. By the same token they have benefited from presentations that staff members, students and residents have given during seminars, tumor conferences and rounds. On the negative side some members of our extended team have expressed their concern that there were too many people with authority in given cases, that because of the numbers of staff, communication between team members was difficult and that the nature of our program placed extremely heavy learning demands upon them in both the medical and the psychosocial areas. When I contrast the benefits of our team approach with my experiences in the early 1960s I find that there is no real comparison. Despite the hard work that genuine teamwork requires, the benefits accruing to the child, the family and team members far outweigh the deficits of the individualistic and isolated approach provided by disciplines who refuse to share their knowledge and responsibility. The following section brings together some of the major components which I believe are necessary to make a team work properly.

The Components of an Effective Team

I believe that the development of an effective team requires the establishment of a relationship in which team members have these characteristics:

(a) They are dedicated to making the approach pay dividends for the patient and for them personally;

(b) they are willing to communicate openly and challenge each other constructively;

(c) they are willing to respect the contribution of each discipline and each team member; and

(d) they are willing to learn from each other, whether it is the physician or nurse who learns about behavioral or social difficulties from the social worker or the social worker who learns about the medical components of an illness from a physician or nurse;

(e) able to work side by side with each other on a given problem, which may necessitate the blurring of roles but which means that the team members collaborate in solving the problem and implementing a plan of care for the patient and his family.

REFERENCES

Kane, R.A.: *Interprofessional Teamwork.* Syracuse University School of Social Work, Syracuse, N.Y. 1975, Manpower Monograph Number Eight.

Rosini, L.A., Howell, M.C., Todres, I.D., and Dorman, J.: "Group Meetings in a Pediatric Intensive Care Unit." *Pediatr* 53:3, 371-374, 1974.

Smith, C.R.: "Social Workers in the Hospital: Misplaced Intruders or Essential Experts." *Br Med J* 3:443-446, 1973.

Schrager, J.: Social Work Departments in University Hospitals. University of Syracuse School of Social Work, Syracuse, N.Y., 1974, Manpower Monograph Number Six.

Tietz, W. and Powars, D.: "The Pediatrician and the Dying Child." *Clin Pediatr* 14:6, 585-591, 1975.

Schulz, R. and Aderman, D.: "How the Medical Staff Copes with Dying Patients: A Critical Review." *Omega* 7:1, 1·1-21, 1976.

Brieland, D., Briggs, T. and Leuenberger, P.: *The Team Model of Social Work Practice.* University of Syracuse School of Social Work, Syracuse, N.Y., 1973, Manpower Monograph Number Five.

Berelson, B. and Steiner, G.A.: Human Behavior: An Inventory of *Scientific Findings.* Harcourt, Brace and World, New York, 1964.

Horowitz, J.T.: "Interprofessional Teamwork." *The Soc Worker.* 38:1, 5-10, 1970.

Bernard, S., and Ishyama, T.: "Authority Conflicts in the Structure of Psychiatric Teams." *Soc Work* 5:77-83, 1960.

Garland, J., Kolodny, R. and Jones, H.A.: "A Model for the Stages of Development in Social Work Groups." *Explorations in Social Group Work.* Edited by S. Bernstein. University of Boston School of Social Work, Boston, 1965.

CHAPTER 3

UNDERSTANDING FAMILY RESPONSES: ANTICIPATORY MOURNING AND ANTICIPATORY GRIEF AS A CONCEPTUAL FRAMEWORK

ALTHOUGH some families are able to cope extremely well with the stress of life-threatening illness in their child, there are none who would suggest that the illness has not had an impact on their emotions or their style of living. In fact, most families experience very similar reactions, and these follow the sequence of the illness. Consequently, a conceptual framework which enables clear descriptions of the components is required in order to understand these reactions. Crisis theory and the description of a life-threatening illness as a situational crisis is one possibility. Barrell (1974) refers to a crisis as "an emotionally significant event, a stressful occurrence, a threat, a disaster, a decisive moment or a turning point." In reality, the diagnosis of childhood leukemia or another malignant disease generates not just one crisis but a series of crises. As a result, this limits the value of crisis theory. I believe that the concepts of anticipatory mourning and anticipatory grief provide a more pervasive and extensive framework. Rather than dealing with isolated events or crises, these concepts reflect the constancy of stress which afflicts both the child and his family. I have chosen to use these concepts in this chapter and to interchange them at random. This random interchange is in keeping with Webster's definition of grief as "intense emotional suffering caused by loss, disaster, misfortune; acute sorrow; deep sadness." Grieving then is the experiencing of such feelings. Webster also defines the word mourn as the expression of sorrow or lamenting or grieving for someone who has died. Anticipatory grieving and anticipatory mourning mean that these feelings of suffering are experienced in advance of the loss or death. Together, these concepts provide a useful framework for understanding families with children who have malignant diseases.

Aldrich (1974) defines anticipatory grief as any grief which happens before a loss. He states that it is usually "experienced (or denied) simultaneously by both the patient and his family." He says that anticipatory grief usually has an end point and that the intensity of the grief reaction should increase as the anticipated loss becomes closer. When the grief process is prolonged, however, Aldrich suggests that much of the grief work has been carried out in advance so that the symptoms of grief may actually decrease at the time of loss.

Aldrich (1974) points out the role that defense mechanisms, such as denial, play in the anticipatory experience, and he emphasizes the difficulties families face when they cope with natural feelings of ambivalance when the family member is still very much alive and vulnerable. In illustrating these difficulties he refers to the work of Richmond and Waisman (1955) and their study of families of leukemic children. They delineate the need for the physician to maintain responsibility for medical treatment in order to help the parent.

> We believe that the feelings of guilt which every parent has to some extent are too great to permit the intensification which may occur when the parent is placed in a position of making a decision which may or may not alter the course of the disease.

Fulton and Fulton (1971) in their review of the literature on anticipatory grief cite the works of Binger and his colleagues (1969), Natterson and Knudson (1960) and Lindemann (1944) as major contributors to knowledge in this area. Binger and his associates and Natterson and Knudson provided observations and descriptions of parents of leukemic children as well as the children themselves. They describe the intensity of the reactions, and Binger and his colleagues found that one-half of the parents in this study required psychiatric intervention. Fulton and Fulton emphasize how anticipatory grief can protect and enhance living while at the same time they say that it can "undermine fragile existence and rupture our tenuous social bonds." Lindemann is known for his study of the survivors and

relatives of the Coconut Grove fire. Many of his findings related to acute and maladaptive grief can be applied in our
understanding of anticipatory grief.

McCollum and Schwartz (1972) have delineated a schema for
understanding anticipatory mourning. They divide their con-
ceptualization into the following components: defensive process, affective states, issues presented and adaptive behavior. In
the next two sections I will draw heavily on their work and use
the first two and the last component as headings for discussion.

Defense Mechanisms

McCollum and Schwartz (1972) suggest that denial, repression, isolation of affect and avoidance are all defense mechanisms which are utilized by parents of children with
life-threatening illnesses. They state that denial is the replacement of reality by a "wish fulfilling fantasy" and that this is
very common in the prediagnostic period, at diagnosis and
when facing a negative prognosis. I believe that the wish to
deny is present in every parent and that short-term denial is
often necessary to enable the parent or parents to sort out their
feelings and to come to grips with the reality of the situation.
Denial is often a major stimulus for our need to repeat medical
information to parents and to maintain the reality of the disease process as part of the discussion at the point when a child
faces relapse.

Repression occurs when information is blotted out or not
assimilated. Repression often occurs at the beginning of the
illness or at times when parents cannot handle the information
given. In my experience this reaction is often seen at the time of
diagnosis when parents are overwhelmed by the label placed on
the illness, by the conjuring up of facts and fantasies which
shape their understanding and by the anxiety which this combination generates. I have frequently observed the use of repression during the stress of relapse, during hospitalization due to
infection and when families are afflicted with additional
burdens, such as financial problems or the illness of another
family member.

Isolation of affect is experienced as an absence of feeling that helps the parent intellectualize prior to accepting crucial information and the emotions such communication generates. It is usually a transient feeling. I have often seen this phenomena in parents who appear to accept an event such as a relapse with a straightforward approach or in parents who feel that they must stay strong in order to cope with a dying child. In both instances there is usually a delayed reaction characterized by intense anger. Isolation of affect differs from denial in that the parent is not creating a fantasy but is holding back feeling during a time when he or she is fully conscious of the facts.

McCollum and Schwartz (1972) describe *avoidance* as the "conscious suppression of thought and associated emotions (I don't let myself think about it)" which provides areas of functioning devoid of feelings of mourning. A part-time job for a mother, a father's full-time work or a tennis match are some examples of how families can use this defense mechanism. As Knapp and Hanson (1973) noted, fathers often avoid talking about death and tend to be more remote. I have found that fathers are usually much more capable than mothers in finding these "islands of functioning that are relatively free from mourning." Mothers usually have to face the continued stress of their child's illness because the sick child and other family members provide no other alternative. Sometimes her intense need to protect her child or overwhelming feelings of guilt regarding illness inhibit her ability to find other alternatives.

Affective Responses

Another area in the schema provided by McCollum and Schwartz (1972) focusses upon affective responses. They discuss sorrow, anger, guilt and anxiety. They suggest that in most instances families will experience *sorrow* following diagnosis. I have also found that this is frequently true in the later stages of an illness, especially if the child has suffered greatly, and parents are sad because they must see their child face misery. I believe that an understanding of Elizabeth Kübler-Ross' (1969) stages in the process of dying, i.e. denial, anger, bargaining, depression and acceptance, is helpful in facilitating an understanding of sorrow. Sorrow is often associated with the natural depression which brings with it the reality of pain and eventually death.

Anger is frequently present at the time of diagnosis. Parents often become angry with God, with a partner or with the hospital and clinic staff. In discussing anger in her book for parents, McCollum (1975) focusses upon irritability in the total family, critical feelings toward doctors and nurses and bitterness toward God. She suggests that throughout the course of the illness there may be periods when parents and children become extremely angry. I have seen this anger surface in frustration with clinic visits, with waiting, with having to be cared for by a new resident, with starting a new medication or with having another treatment. Anger toward God, the physician or sometimes the child may be sublimated to something or someone more acceptable, such as a neighbor, relatives, schools or the hospital. Anger may also be misdirected toward the child or partner or another family member or directed inwardly, manifesting itself as guilt. I have found it is important to label the anger and to discuss its purpose with the parent or parents. If we leave anger unresolved or allow anger to be misdirected, then it can aggravate existing communication problems in families or it can impede the maintenance of satisfactory relationships between the family and the clinic team.

Guilt, according to McCollum and Schwartz (1972) arises because

> Nurturance and protection of one's child are central to parenthood. Thus when the child is jeopardized, most parents undergo a transient but agonizing process of self-examination and self-reproach.

McCollum (1975) also suggests that parents often suffer guilt due to the uncertainty about why the disease occurred. She relates this guilt to the need to blame each other for inheritance of the illness and neglect or delay in seeking treatment. In order to help families work through guilt feelings McCollum and Schwartz (1972) emphasize the importance of understanding prior feelings about the child, about the child's symptoms and about the child's behavior during the illness. They stress the need to help family members express their feelings. I must also emphasize the value of such expression. For example, when one mother in our clinic was faced with caring for an immobilized child she could not believe that she could actually wish that her child's life would end. Another mother felt the same way when the terminal stages of her son's illness were protracted. When we talked to each mother about their feelings the discussion provided them with an understanding of their responses and facilitated a release of emotions. It was important for them to realize that they were not strange or bad because they were preoccupied with such "horrible" thoughts. The child's behavior in each of these situations had aggravated both the parent and the hospital staff as well. The child had the need to express his anger and sadness and directed his anger at those closest to him. In other situations, where parents have sought faith healers or decided to seek consultation from another treatment center, it has been important for us to help them understand their feelings and where necessary to help them in their quest to do everything they could for their child. Our efforts have helped parents release or alleviate a building up of emotions, thus preventing intense guilt feelings after the child has died. Sometimes simply the discussion of the search has sufficed. If, however, the pressure for the search for a cure comes from outside of the family, the parents may need an intermediary from our clinic team to explain the child's illness and treatment to grandparents, aunts, uncles or others. We have found this to be most necessary when apparent cures or treatments are described by the news media as being a major research discovery.

Anxiety is a crucial component in the emotional response of the child and the family. In both leukemia and solid tumors, anxiety is present even if the child achieves what could be termed a cure. I have observed that such anxiety most certainly lingers on beyond the cessation of the initial chemotherapy program. Anxiety is often present before diagnosis and always at diagnosis. McCollum and Schwartz (1972) suggest that anxiety can also be generated when parents feel "intense emotion," when they use defense mechanisms like repression or isolation of affect and when separation occurs through death. The latter can stimulate the parents' own fear of survival. There is no doubt in my mind that the pervasiveness of anxiety is felt by the whole family. The child is greatly influenced by his parents' response. For instance, the feelings of helplessness that parents feel prior to or during treatment are often communicated to the child. The subsequent increase in the child's anxiety then makes the procedure more difficult, thus amplifying the natural fear which the child inevitably experiences depending upon his age. This reaction is particularly visible in children ages six to nine. These children are already prone to experiencing mutilation anxiety when faced with injection, bone marrows and lumbar punctures.

Anxiety affects family life. For example, I frequently see that the fear of recurrence of the illness and the fear of infections severely affect a family's life-style. Such anxieties lead parents to overprotect their children and to narrow the circle of family activities. Anxiety also stretches outside the nuclear family to friends and relatives. McCollum (1975) points out that "grandparents may become so upset, even distraught that there is a reversal of roles" with the child's parents. These grandparents require comforting themselves rather than providing their own children with comfort, compassion and much-needed assistance. In my experience, parental fatigue associated with peak periods of activity, such as when a child is hospitalized, when a child receives daily courses of radiation or chemotherapy or when a child is severely ill or dying, is very much related to intense anxiety about the life-threatening nature of the illness and the prognosis for the child.

Adaptational Responses

In their schema McCollum and Schwartz (1972) delineate four adaptational responses. These include "information seeking, invoking emotional support, compartmentalization and rehearsal of death."

Information Seeking

In the parents' search for information McCollum and Schwartz suggest that three types of information are sought. These include information about the illness, information about their child and "the search for meaning." In the latter, parents look for an explanation which may blend fact and fantasy. Examples would be the parents who conclude that because Uncle Joe died of leukemia it must "run in the family," or the parents who believe a trip to the zoo caused the malignancy. I would suggest as well that sudden increased attention to religion may also be a symbol of a parental search for meaning. In my experience the search for information about the illness can create problems if parents or children read outdated books or believe a sensationalistic newspaper account of a treatment program. Discussion of any such findings with an appropriate medical resource becomes crucial. Similarly, I have found that the search for information about the status of the child can become an obsession. Parents and sometimes the child become preoccupied with blood counts, often without fully knowing the meaning of the information. I believe that information seeking is a natural, healthy process, which when guided appropriately can be of great help to parents and children in coming to grips with the illness, with the treatment process and with their own feelings.

Invoking Emotional Support

Invoking emotional support through friends, relatives, clergy, clinic staff and at times other parents can, according to McCollum and Schwartz (1972), "reduce feelings of loneliness, temporarily satisfy heightened dependency needs and afford some gratification experiences." Schiff (1977), speaking as a bereaved parent, stresses the value of sharing experiences with those who have already been through it. Families who are suffering through the same ordeal can share a common identity and experience the same emotions in response to the same stimuli. In our setting, this sharing often happens spontaneously as parents meet in the waiting area or as children, especially older children, share common play experiences. In other settings this sharing may be available through parent groups (Pollitt, 1976).

The support offered by staff can often be extensive as well, especially when parents are devoid of close relatives and community supports. I have found that when families rely on professional resources it is very apparent that they select those who can relate to them openly and honestly. Families, and especially children, seek out warmth and sincerity and are usually very aware of certain professionals who must use the white coat, professional label or identity symbol such as the clergyman's collar, as a means of insulating them from responding as a caring person.

Ideally, we would all like to believe that family members can receive emotional support from within the nuclear or extended family. However, the disruption in family relationships generated by the threat to stability which the illness creates can often lead family members to find new ways of obtaining support. Some of these uncommon methods can generate a great deal of stress for both the child and his family. For instance, at our setting John, an eight year old, knew he had leukemia and knew about all of the implications of his illness. After undergoing induction, radiation and placement on maintenance chemotherapy, he began to act out. He hit other children, defied his parents and misbehaved at school. In a family session he told us very clearly that he was fed up with the inability of his parents to discipline him and that his behavior helped him to release his anger and in return receive some type of disciplinary response. John had a need for emotional support and security which would have been provided by treating him as a normal child. His behavior was his attempt to receive normal discipline and to regain the security he felt before his parents became afraid to enforce even simple rules and boundaries. I have found other examples of maladaptive methods of seeking emotional support in situations where parents seek extramarital relationships or a family member develops symptoms which enable him or her to receive a great deal of medical attention. On occasion fathers, in particular, will seek gratification from material objects such as a new car or truck or boat, which symbolize emotional security, provide diversion and artificially replace some of their needs for human support. This gratification can be beneficial or detrimental depending on the living situation and the internal relationships within the family.

Partialization or Compartmentalization

Partialization or compartmentalization is an elaborate way of saying that families learn to take one day at a time. I strongly believe that this approach helps families obtain the most they can from life, especially when there is considerable uncertainty about their child's prognosis. Parents faced with the threat that their child might not grow up and become the doctor, lawyer or truck driver that they had anticipated, sometimes need help to restructure their thinking and temper their long-range outlook. Many families have told me how they have reordered their priorities, set short-term goals and radically revised not only their philosophy about life but also their values. They have also described how the approach of the treatment team helped them achieve this change. Solnit and Green (1959) stressed the importance of feeding information gradually to families so that they have time to cope with one piece of information before being faced with another. I have found this to be most important when families are faced with the diagnosis, with a relapse which comes "out of the blue," or when the child's physical condition is deteriorating and the physician is beginning to run out of effective anticancer drugs. This gradual provision of information, coupled with our team's conscious effort to help the family maintain a realistic perspective, and the uncertainty of the exact course of medical treatment due to side effects, infections and other problems, aids the partialization process.

Rehearsing Death

The rehearsal of death is a preparatory period in which parents fantasize or work through their anxieties about parting with their child. This can be explained as moving through the stage of depression in an effort to reach acceptance (Kübler-Ross, 1969). At this point of depression, significant emotional and general behavioral adjustments occur in response to the anticipated loss. The burden of the illness and the meaning of death can become the basis. In my experience it has been a common occurrence for parents to either singly or jointly plan burials, concern themselves about donations to cancer funds, plan for vacations after their child's death and dream or day-dream of funerals, burials or previous deaths. Older children and relatives may be advised of the impending death, and the child himself may be prepared by a parent or parents. I have also observed the presence of deep sorrow and anger toward the child or the physician as part of this process. Sometimes parents are under such great stress that they have withdrawn themselves from the child or cease to show affection for him. Occasionally, the intensity of feeling can be so profound that a parent or parents may feel relieved as though the child had already died. In other situations parents have prepared themselves for their child's death by reviewing or sorting through the good times, the bad times and a variety of landmarks which the family has faced with the child. In one situation, a father brought a series of photographs to the clinic which pictured his daughter at various points in her life. These included a series of happy pictures as well as pictures from the period just prior to her diagnosis. Other pictures that followed from the point of diagnosis revealed the telltale signs of his daughter's demise. By showing me the pictures the father was able to talk about his feelings for his child. He told me how very sad he was with the current situation and how he knew he was going to lose his daughter. The overlays of tearfulness and depression, coupled with his inability to maintain his usual life-style, were symptoms of the emotional costs of his preparation for the impending loss.

The rehearsal period prior to death is extremely important and requires the special attention of the clinic and hospital staff. The constructive working through of feelings can help families cope with the actual death with greater closeness and comfort than if they are still grappling with the intensity of depression mixed with spasms of anger and guilt. I believe that when families have at least begun to intellectually accept death and can talk about death in a supportive and comforting way, then the sick child can benefit from the preparation. I also believe that the older the child is the more he has a need to work through his own feelings about his impending death. When the child is excluded, he may feel abandoned, unwanted and confused by the behavioral change in those close to him. Often, he wonders what he has done to hurt them. Sometimes a bond of religious belief assists the child and the family by adding additional comfort, reassurance and an explanation of what awaits the child.

Adaptation Versus Maladaptation

Toch (1974) lists behaviors that are manifested by "grief-stricken and frustrated" parents. In my opinion it is often difficulties in family relationships, lack of support systems, emotional burdens and other problems which have given rise to the continued appearance of many of the behaviors Toch lists.

In his list, Toch includes protracted denial of the diagnosis or prognosis, searching for cures from other centers, manipulating differences of opinion between the physicians in respect to prognosis, overprotecting the child and overemphasizing concerns such as rest and diet. In addition, he cites refusing to tell the child about the nature of his problem or prognosis, searching for publicity, assigning guilt to others or to themselves, concentrating on blood counts, acting as if the child were dead and becoming overly concerned about minor details as problems. Toch sees these responses as unhealthy and suggests that they should be viewed as signals for the provision of more intensive emotional support.

It is hard to argue with Toch's suggestion that these behaviors must be identified and understood as early as possible by attending staff. It is also difficult to disagree with the fact that additional emotional support may be in order. However, unlike Toch, who seems to suggest that the behaviors he lists are all unhealthy in terms of both attitudes and activities, I think that the manifestations of such behaviors and attitudes may be absolutely necessary. Parents may use these behaviors as a natural means of obtaining sufficient time to face a threatening situation realistically. Anticipatory mourning complete with outward manifestations of grief, grief fantasy and at times morbid or unrealistic thoughts, behaviors and attitudes helps the family prepare for painful events and can facilitate a positive adjustment to death in parents or family members. In my opinion it is the protraction of the behaviors Toch cites that are pathological. The dilemma that arises for the health-care team is the question of when and how to intervene. The establishment of openness in communication and willingness to talk about uncomfortable areas at the time of diagnosis becomes of crucial importance in caring for the child and his family during the course of the illness.

If an illness progresses beyond the first relapse to later stages, then the intensity of feelings will often increase. Families will tend to have more difficulty coping with intense anxiety and release less acceptable feelings, such as anger and guilt. The health-care team's ability to understand the reasons for the family's use of the behaviors Toch cites and to facilitate discussion of why these behaviors occur will have major implications for all aspects of treatment. Comerford (1974), a parent who experienced the loss of her child, provides a set of guidelines for physicians who deal with parents experiencing anticipatory grief. Comerford stresses the need for physicians to be honest and straightforward about the illness and the possible prognosis. She suggests that families should receive a positive orientation to the treatment process and to the hospital. She advocates the need for physicians to explain what the impact of the disease will be on the child, the parents and the siblings. She proposes that physicians consider providing a list of questions that the child might ask. Comerford also emphasizes the need for the physician to be warm, sensitive and willing to discuss his or her uncertainty about the illness and the treatment with the parent. She stresses the need for doctors to recognize that parents sometimes panic; that occasionally they cannot stand to see their child receive painful treatment any longer; that mothers are often sensitive to even the most minute change in their child's condition; and that parents must be advised about what medical treatment is possible when the child is approaching death. By the same token, parents are often fearful that their child will die in agony.

Comerford's suggestions merit careful attention. It is one problem to understand what happens to a family and quite another to intervene in a manner which will minimize the anticipatory mourning response. In the following chapter I examine how our team provides psychosocial care to families.

REFERENCES

Barrell, L.M.: "Crisis Intervention." *Nsg Clin N Am* 9:1, 6, 1974.

Guralnick, D.B. (ed.): *Webster's New World Dictionary,* Nelson, Foster and Scott, Toronto, 1970.

Aldrich, C.K.: "Some Dynamics of Anticipatory Grief." *Anticipatory Grief*: Edited by B. Schoenberg, A.C. Carr, D. Peretz, A.H. Kutscher and I.K. Goldberg. Columbia University Press, New York, 1974.

Richmond, J.B. and Waisman, H.A.: "Psychologic Aspects of Management of Children with Malignant Diseases." *Am J Dis Child* 89:42, 42-47, 1955.

Fulton, R. and Fulton J.: "A Psychosocial Aspect of Terminal Care: Anticipatory Grief." *Omega* 2:91-100, 1972.

Binger, C.M., Albin, A.R., Feuerstein, R.C., Kushner, J.H., Zoger, S., and Mikkelsen, C.: "Childhood Leukemia: Emotional Impact on Patient and Family." *N Engl J Med* 280: Feb. 414-418, 1969.

Natterson, J.M. and Knudson, A.G.: "Observations Concerning Fear of Death in Fatally Ill Children and Their Mothers." *Psychosom Med* 22:6, 456-465, 1960.

Lindemann, E.: "Symptomatology and Management of Acute Grief." *Amer J Psychiat* 101: Sept., 1944. Also in *Crisis Intervention: Selected Readings.* Edited by Howard J. Parad. Family Service Association of America, New York, 1965.

McCollum, A.T., and Schwartz, A.H.: "Social Work and the Mourning Parent." *Soc Work* 17:1, 25-36, 1972.

Knapp, V.S. and Hanson, H.: "Helping the Parents of Children with Leukemia." *Soc Work* 18:4, 70-75, 1973.

Kübler-Ross, E.: *On Death and Dying,* Macmillan Publishing Co. Ltd., New York, 1969.

McCollum, A.T.: *Coping with Prolonged Health Impairment in Your Child,* Little, Brown and Company (inc.), Boston, Mass., 1975.

Schiff, H.S.: *The Bereaved Parent.* Crown Publishers Inc., New York, 1977.

Pollitt, E.: "The Family Leukemia Association." *Essence: Issues in the Study of Aging, Death and Dying.* 1:2, 107-115, 1976.

Solnit, A.J. and Greene, M.: "Psychological Considerations in the Management of Deaths on Pediatric Hospital Services; 1. The Doctor and the Child's Family." *Pediatr* 24:106-112, 1959.

Toch, R.: "Management of Parental Anticipatory Grief." in *Anticipatory Grief.* B. Schoenberg et al. (eds.), Columbia University Press, New York, 1974.

Comerford, B.: "Parental Anticipatory Grief and Guidelines for Caregivers." in *Anticipatory Grief.* B. Schoenberg et al. (eds.) 1974.

CHAPTER 4

THE PSYCHOSOCIAL CARE
OF FAMILIES

Our Approach to Families

A T our clinic when we meet the child with a malignant disease and his family at the point of diagnosis, we know that we will often be in close contact with them for months or even years. We recognize that such families are at risk. They are prone to fragmentation, and individual family members can easily develop severe and lasting emotional difficulties. Existing problems can be amplified and new ones created due to the continued stress of living with the knowledge that cancer can recur or spread and may result in death. We realize that if we are going to be required to help many of these families cope with the illness experience then we must know them and understand how the hospital and disease is affecting them. We must not only be knowledgeable about who is in the family and how they interact with each other, but we must be aware of how the total family relates to its environment and is influenced by it. Consequently, our approach is directed toward obtaining basic psychosocial data about the family and providing whatever counselling is deemed to be appropriate. At the very least, we strive to establish rapport with the child and his family and develop a relationship which will continue as long as the child attends the clinic. By so doing we have the opportunity to use our understanding of the child and his family to help them deal with medical and psychosocial problems as they arise, as part of clinic routine.

In this chapter I will describe the components of the psychosocial assessment, patterns of parental adaptation, influences on parental coping and the nature of helpful intervention as I see it.

The Purpose of a Psychosocial Family Assessment

At the time of diagnosis we have found that our priority is to establish rapport with the parents, the child and other family members and to observe closely what happens when the parents initially receive the news about their child's illness. This beginning relationship facilitates the provision of information to the total family about the nature of the illness and the beginning stages of treatment. After the parents and other family members have begun to recover from the initial shock of the diagnosis we can begin to assess family relationships in detail. This assessment encompasses the study of the total family as a system and as a series of internal sub-systems which include parental, parent/child and sibling relationships. (Munson, 1977). At the same time we can also determine the nature and extent of the total family's relationships with other systems, such as the extended family, work, school, church and neighborhood.

This initial psychosocial assessment enables us to determine the kind of help the family requires and how we can best provide it.

Obtaining the Initial Psychosocial Assessment

We have learned that initial psychosocial data can be collected by the nurse, the resident or the physician provided they have sufficient experience to obtain accurate information, are able to interpret it correctly, and are sensitive enough to know when to involve more highly skilled psychosocial resource persons. For inexperienced staff it is imperative that supervision by appropriate team members is included as part of the process.

At our center the initial psychosocial assessment is routinely carried out by the nurse in consultation or in combination with myself, the resident and the pediatric hematologist. Usually a summary discussion of the observations and impressions of the total team helps ensure that a comprehensive overview has been obtained. This also serves to validate initial findings and delineate areas requiring further exploration. When marked family difficulties or adjustment problems are identified, I usually become involved very early in the assessment process in my role as the clinic social worker.

Some Factors Affecting Approaches to the Family

In my experience I have learned that maintaining a concern for the total family is often difficult and that there are a number of factors which influence our ability to complete psychosocial assessments. For instance, when families reside in another community, the nature of family life may inhibit contact with the total family. This problem often occurs where there is a large age spread between the sick child and his siblings. Older children may be employed or in school, thus making them inaccessible at times when the mother and child or both parents must travel to the hospital clinic. By the same token, regardless of where the family resides, the father may be legitimately unable to leave work, and the mother must take the child to the clinic. In other situations the illness of one partner or the unwillingness of one parent to participate in the child's care are factors which can make an accurate assessment of family functioning difficult or impossible.

I believe that each family and each situation must be assessed carefully and that we must be flexible enough in our approach to adapt to these inhibiting factors. When we find that it is impossible or inappropriate to assess the total nuclear family, then we should involve the child and his parents as the most relevant family members. In other situations our approach to the family may become complicated due to the possibility that the child may die (Share, 1972). The parents and sometimes we, as hospital staff, have the need to protect the child. As a consequence, it becomes difficult for us to state that discussions will take place only if the parents and the child or the total nuclear family is present. When this occurs then we must begin by initially working with the parents. Similarly, when the sick child and his siblings are very young we must again concentrate our attention on the parents. In some families, when only the mother and child are available, we may have to settle for incomplete data and make a decision as to how essential it is to demand that both parents or the total family be interviewed in the clinic. On a number of occasions we have interviewed a family in the evening or waited until a parent has changed shifts or has vacation time in order to complete a comprehensive assessment of the family. In other instances, where the father has been totally inaccessible, we have proceeded to help the child adapt through play activities and have provided emotional support to the mother until we have had the opportunity to meet with the father some months later. In severe situations when there is a pressing need to engage an unwilling father, we have found that it is legitimate for the physician or another team member to contact the resistant parent directly and insist upon a conjoint or family session.

The Components of a Psychosocial Family Assessment

In evaluating the family we must include the observations of all team members and incorporate any relevant current or historical data provided by the family physician, public health nurses or others who may know the family well.

We have found that the assessment should contain an understanding of the following:

1. The family's communication pattern, particularly between the parents, including the amount, quality and openness of communication.
2. The quality of the emotional relationship between the parents, between the parents and children and, if possible, between the children themselves.
3. The emotional and intellectual makeup of each family member.
4. The roles of family members.
5. The family leadership style and patterns, including decision-making.
6. The parental response and response of the child and members of the nuclear family to the diagnosis.
7. The fears and the current emotional state of the parent and the child.
8. The child's knowledge of his illness.
9. The dependence, interdependence and individual freedom of each family member.

10. The socialization pattern of members in interactions out-side of the nuclear family.
11. The cultural, religious and socioeconomic disposition of the family.
12. The employment and employment relationships of parent or parents.
13. The positive and negative aspects of the support systems surrounding the families, particularly in relation to emotional support provided by friends, relatives and neighbors.
14. Past experience in the marriage with illness or death, or experiences of each individual partner in dealing with the same prior to marriage.
15. The methods used to resolve conflicts or overcome crises.
16. Current problems the family itself identifies, e.g. emotional, social, financial and other medical problems.
17. Past problems related to the above and the means the family used to resolve them.
18. The disciplinary patterns commonly used.
19. Other items of importance identified by family members.

Parental Response Patterns

When we approach the family at or near the point of diagnosis, we find that the parents and sometimes the total family are in a state of shock. The diagnosis deals an initial blow which generates a feeling of numbness and disbelief, complete with anger, sadness and guilt. I am convinced that the pattern of response between the parents at this time is the key to under-standing the type of relationship which exists between the partners, including their means of communication and ways of caring for each other. This pattern is also reflective of the nature of family communications as the parents set the tone for all aspects of interaction between family members. I have also found that the total parental response pattern provides specific information about what type of problems we can expect to face later on in the illness if the child should relapse or become terminally ill or die. There are several response patterns which are commonly observed. In the ensuing sections I will describe these patterns and their implications for the care of the child and his family.

Type 1: Open Communication — Open Emotional Response

In this response pattern communication about the illness, personal feelings, caring for other family members and short-term family management is straightforward and completely open. There is no attempt made to mask either verbal or non-verbal communication. Emotional responses are focussed upon mutual support and caring for each other, being together to receive information, sharing tears and sorrow, sharing responsibility in caring for the total family and acceptance of each other's need to release anger and feel guilty or sad.

In my experience this response pattern is usually associated with well-integrated, well-balanced families with a clear definition of roles, relationships, leadership and power distribution. Such a response frequently signifies that the parents and in turn the family will adapt to stress well with minimal input from the health team.

Type 2: Open Communication — Disrupted Emotional Response

This response is usually observed when the parental communication pattern is superficial and focuses on instrumental or task oriented discussions characterized by an absence or inconsistency in feeling tone. The parents may independently or jointly ask questions about the illness, plan for care of the family and verbalize concerns but cannot share either their distress or their concern for each other. One partner may deny the reality and continue as if all is normal, or he or she may withdraw or draw up rules which protect himself or herself from having to deal with the emotions of his or her partner or family. For example, the father may only visit when other friends or relatives are present. He may encourage his wife to stay with the sick child or take him to the clinic alone, or he may suggest that other family members who are old enough to understand the illness should not be told.

I have found that when this type of emotional withdrawal or defensiveness occurs, further difficulties are predictable. If, for instance, the couple and the family are left on their own throughout the illness without any intervention to bring the parents and the family closer together, there is a great possibility that the same pattern will return at other times of upset, such as at relapse, during terminal illness and following death. This pattern may also signify an eroding of the marital relationship or the presence of other family problems. A common example is the presence of an external power base such as a grandparent who dominates family life. The impact of a crisis on this type of marital relationship pattern will often amplify existing problems and generate new ones. This makes it necessary to at least build in or strengthen the emotional support systems around each partner and the family. It is also desirable that a concerted effort be made to help the parents work to improve their relationship.

Type 3: Disrupted Communication — Open Emotional Response

This response is the most difficult to assess because of the subtleties involved in recognizing and understanding both the nature and the quality of nonverbal communication and the expression of caring emotions. The marital partners may be able to support each other emotionally by being together in facing the child's illness, caring for the sick child and other family members and sharing their sadness. They may hold hands and comfort each other and their children physically but may not be able to talk about the illness or ask questions of the physician in the presence of each other. The partners may in fact appear to protect one another.

When we are confronted with this response we usually have to spend additional time with the couple to discern exactly why they cannot communicate. Sensitive nursing staff on the pediatric ward may be alarmed by the parents' inability to talk about their child's illness and his treatment. They may believe that the family is falling apart, particularly if the couple does not demonstrate positive feelings for each other within the ward setting but do so in private. It must be determined if this type of response has been caused by the illness or is the couple's usual response to any stressful event.

When I encounter parents who respond this way I proceed with caution. The importance of the communication system must be carefully assessed. If the communication pattern is disrupted only temporarily and if the emotional response pattern is consistently supportive, then time and acceptance of the illness as a part of day-to-day life will probably alleviate the disruption. On the other hand, if the family responds this way to every crisis or important problem in their lives, it may well be that closer scrutiny will denote a mutually supportive emotional relationship between the parents which is built upon a base laden with anxiety. For instance, experience may show that one partner who is extremely anxious will increase the other partner's anxiety so that both worry to the point of losing all objectivity. Signs of this type of anxiety may occur when one parent faints or is prone to outbursts of anger or tears. In addition, these parents frequently transfer their anxiety to the child. A good example of this is seen when anxious parents are present during their child's treatment. The child becomes upset and resists. Once the parents are removed from the room the child becomes cooperative. Through time this couple and this family will require considerable emotional support. This may create the necessity for periodic sessions which will help them understand the illness, their adjustment and their underlying anxieties.

Type 4: Disrupted Communication — Disrupted Emotional Response

There are many variations of this response pattern. Consequently it is necessary to understand whether disruptions in family relationships are the result of the current crisis or are related to long-standing difficulties. Often family life is disorganized or completely chaotic due to the existence of a multitude of problems, such as the emotional instability of one or both parents; marital conflict related to infidelity or incompatability; and underlying financial, employment, sexual, medical or social problems. I have often found that alcoholism is frequently present and that sometimes the disruption in the parental relationship pattern has been so long standing and so

progressive that the added strain of the child's illness divides
the family. When this has happened I have found that I can
sometimes help negotiate an amicable separation which can
reduce the anger, frustration and guilt which has resulted from
open conflict. If this is possible then emotional support can be
given independently by one or both parents to the sick child
and his siblings and each parent can reinvest in separate lives.
On occasion I have seen the crisis of the illness help parents
improve their relationship and the family's functioning, but
such a change is seldom permanent. It is more common to
encounter the mutliproblem family which often remains intact
intermittently, consumes a vast amount of emotional support
and barely manages to survive financially and nutritionally.
Many of these families live in poorer districts and occupy low
quality housing complete with an unhealthy physical environment. They may also have standards of cleanliness which are
below those which would enable their child to remain free of
infection. These families need support and understanding. The
classic work of Minuchin and his associates (1967) illustrates
the need to understand the cultural, social and other variables
present in many multi-problem families. I have found that it is
often difficult for nurses, medical staff and other health professionals not only to understand but to accept the life-style of
these families. Assistance from the hospital staff can become an
experience in total frustration if it is not recognized that goals
for social and emotional care will have to fit the needs of the
family. Therefore, psychosocial input may simply be directed
toward providing either parent with a chance to talk about his
or her problems. Assistance may also be provided by "going to
bat" with the welfare department in order to make certain that
the family will obtain sufficient funds to maintain an acceptable level of nutrition for the sick child. The focus of care is
usually on helping the family remain intact and on helping
them make minor but necessary modifications in their life-style
in areas such as cleanliness and nutrition. Sometimes the parents will make a positive shift in their relationship and in their
efforts to solve instrumental problems. If positive changes
begin to occur I believe that the family warrants help to
change, but it must be recognized that they may never wish to

adopt the same value system as team members. I should add that with these families we have found it necessary to provide additional emotional support to the child and help him work through his problems in coping with his illness.

Patterns of Parental Adaptation to Stress of Childhood Malignancy at or Immediately Following Diagnosis

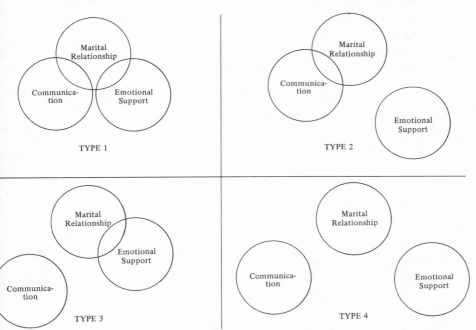

Additional Factors Which Influence Family Adaptation

The Nature of the Illness

Hamovitch (1964) suggests that "family coping adequacy" is significantly affected by the child's diagnosis. For example he found that the diagnosis of inoperable sarcoma generated anxiety and family problems that were so severe that the hospital staff could do little to help the family. The family was most seriously affected by the lack of or short duration of remissions, prolonged pain and the lack of hope associated with the poor prognosis. Today, despite improvements in treatment techniques that include the wider use of radiotherapy and chemotherapy, some tumors fail to respond, and some leukemias are so aggressive that the child dies within weeks or months. In addition to the factors mentioned by Hamovitch the family must face other sequelae of their child's illness such as his hair loss, body distortion and lengthy or frequent hospitalizations. When the child's prognosis is poor, families become anxious, often use massive or prolonged denial and lose hope. When this happens they usually require help to face the reality of the situation and prepare for the child's death. They need the opportunity to deny, to be depressed and to negotiate or bargain in a clinic and hospital environment which gently maintains the reality of the illness (Kübler-Ross, 1969). In many instances I have found that counselling of families can be beneficial in helping them live in a manner which enables them to make their remaining time with the dying child as memorable and happy as possible.

Past Experience with Crises, Death and Illness

When their child's life is threatened by cancer many parents and sometimes total families respond to the stress in ways which have been learned through past encounters with crises. Parents have frequently gained experience prior to marriage in their families of origin or have faced major stresses in their life together. Examples of past experience may include dealing with such diverse life stresses as the loss of a parent, the failure of a business, difficulties during pregnancy, spontaneous abortion or the ending of a previous marital relationship. Response patterns that have been learned through such experiences usually surface at or close to the time when the parents assimilate the reality of the diagnosis. Needless to say, many young families lack the experience necessary to deal effectively with the stress of the diagnosis. They have never seen people with severe illnesses or been confronted with a death in their immediate family. Many have never attended a funeral, visited a nursing home or been exposed to any severe emotional or social problem. Reassurance and understanding provided by hospital staff who are of similar or greater maturity may be very helpful in assisting families in their efforts to adapt. Of equal importance, however, is the necessity to learn how helpful and supportive relatives are to the parents. Couples who have accumulated considerable experience in dealing with crises may have developed sufficient strength to help them cope with this severely stressful problem with minimal disruption to family life.

Support Systems

Whenever families are faced with major problems in their lives they usually need to turn to persons outside of the nuclear family for emotional support and understanding. As I discussed in Chapter 3, relatives can be a major source of such support, but their mere existence does not mean that the family can rely upon them to help. Sometimes grandparents in particular are serious liabilities, especially if they interfere with medical treatment, abandon hope for their grandchild when it is inappropriate to do so or force the parents to travel hundreds of miles to seek additional consultation or treatment. When relatives and friends can be relied upon and parents wish it, their involvement in the care of the sick child and his siblings can be invaluable. For example, grandparents who can face the stress of the illness can be a stabilizing influence because their maturity and wisdom are reassuring to the parents, to the sick child and to his siblings.

Unfortunately in these days of high mobility, we often find that couples are removed from the extended family and have not yet established themselves as part of any community system. When we have encountered young families in these circumstances, we have sometimes found that they are well adjusted and by relying heavily on each other have managed to face the threat to their child's life with minimal disruption. Even when this has been the case, we have learned that during radiation treatments, during relapse, in terminal phases of their child's illness and after death, these families frequently need and benefit greatly from the objectivity and emotional support that our staff can provide.

The Age of the Child

In his study Hamovitch (1964) found that the family's adaptation to their child's illness was most uneventful when the child was in the age range of five to nine years. Children over ten and their families had many problems adjusting to the threat to the child's life. When the child was under the age of five years separation anxiety tended to be upsetting and created many problems for the mother and the sick child. Our findings are very similar. Beyond the age of ten years, teens and preteens face many conflicts related to body image, identity and dependency (Erikson, 1965). When the child is faced with a threat to his life these conflicts become amplified. In the child under the age of five, hospitalization and the resulting separation anxiety can be very disruptive. I will discuss the impact of the illness experience, hospitalization and the threat of death on children at various ages in later chapters.

Parental Participation

When Hamovitch and his colleagues (1964) designed their study, they wanted to determine how valuable it would be to have parents participate in the care of their sick child while he was in hospital. With this in mind they encouraged parents to help care for their child from early morning until the child's bedtime. They were free to assist in the bathing, feeding, clothing and temperature taking of their child and were allowed to witness medical procedures, to play with the child and to carry on with their child as normally as they wished or as the child's medical condition permitted. Hamovitch found that when moderation was maintained in parental participation both the parent and the child benefitted.

Today at our setting, we are faced with a different situation. Much of the care given to the child with a malignant disease is provided in the ambulatory or outpatient setting. Nevertheless, hospitalization is an important if not crucial part of the child's care because when he is hospitalized the child is usually very ill.

At our center, in-patient care is facilitated by open visiting privileges for parents, siblings and relatives in small numbers, with an option that either the mother or father or both may remain overnight in the child's room. In addition, parents are encouraged to help care for their child during hospitalization. In a similar manner to Hamovitch, but strictly from observation rather than stringent study, we have found that families that can participate with moderation do benefit most. Difficulties with the open visiting system usually arise when families are experiencing problems in adapting to the life-threatening nature of the illness or are having interpersonal conflicts. Major difficulties occur when:

(a) parents attempt to take over nursing care completely and impinge upon the ability of the nurses to carry out appropriate procedures.

(b) one parent, usually the mother, remains overnight in the hospital with her child for days on end. Often, she refuses to go home or refuses to leave the child even to go for walks. She dedicates herself so totally to the care of the child that her other children and her husband are completely neglected.

We have found that when the latter occurs, we need the help of a ward nurse who is capable of maintaining control over the medical and nursing care of the child and has established a positive working relationship with the mother. If the mother trusts the nurse, the nurse's persistence may be enough to help the mother gain sufficient objectivity to periodically leave the child in her care. If the mother can be encouraged to leave her child even for short intervals, the parent usually benefits as she learns that both she and the child can cope with the separation experience. It must be recognized, however, that working with the parent requires a great deal of sensitivity. It is very easy for the mother to feel rejected by the staff, because they may convey to her that they resent her participation in her child's care. On the other hand, when a mother has participated a great deal in the care of her child, her leaving can be interpreted by staff as making more work for them and, consequently, when she returns they may inadvertently make her feel guilty.

Other Factors: The Single Parent Family

Hamovitch (1964) notes that parents with a history of prior marriages and those who are single parents have great difficulty in adaptation to the stress of a child's illness and to his death. He advocates reaching out to such families and hopes that social workers in particular might help to prevent severe adaptational difficulties or alleviate problems. In a review of 55 families of children with malignancies I found that the prior marriage factor emerges as a lesser concern than the single parent family. Single parents often lack emotional supports, have socioeconomic problems and appear to have great difficulties coping. In some situations the parent depends on the sick child or a sibling for emotional support. The impact of sharing responsibility for the total family and the sharing in parental anxiety about the illness can be very stressful for the sick child, especially if he must fulfill the role of surrogate partner (Glasser and Navarre, 1967). When single parents lack the closeness which the positive relationship with a partner can bring, they often feel overwhelmed by the illness experience and require the opportunity to discuss their feelings about their child's illness, the impact of the illness of their child and the impact of the total experience on themselves. I have found that single parents often shy away from sharing everything with grandparents because grandparents tend to want to turn back the clock and treat their son or daughter as a dependent child. When they do this they add to the stress of the single parent and his or her need to manage his or her own life. When the child's illness becomes worse, the treatment program intensifies or death becomes imminent, the single parent's need to rely upon another person intensifies. When this need cannot be met by a friend or the family, I have often found that I can be of value simply by establishing a relationship with the single parent early in the child's illness and providing the parent with a chance to use me as a counsellor. If the child's physical condition deteriorates, the existing relationship and trust which we have already established is a source of emotional support to the parent. In instances when parents are divorced or separated and both partners are concerned about the child and must face the illness experience independently, the nurse and I have worked together in counselling the parents.

Influences on Parental Coping

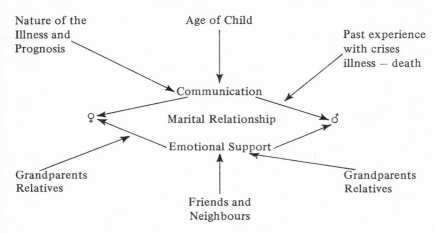

The Nature of Helpful Intervention

In the preceding sections I have described the importance of parental responses, the major factors which influence how the family copes with their child's malignancy and the components of our initial psychosocial assessment. In addition I have mentioned that we are willing to counsel the family in order to help them deal effectively with the stress of the illness experience. With this in mind I will discuss in detail my approach to assessment and counselling. Several roles and two major concepts show how the interviewer as an assessor and counsellor can help parents, and where feasible, the total family. In their description of therapeutic strategies, Glick and Kessler (1974) discuss the facilitating role that the therapist plays in enabling family members to communicate thoughts and feelings, the mobilizing role he uses to change rigid roles and unstable alliances and the modelling role he utilizes to educate families and destroy myths. In his work, Wynne (1971) describes the concepts of directive limit setting and self-awareness as they apply to any type of therapeutic intervention with families.

The Facilitating Role

When assessing families it is important to be aware of both the visible and the underlying communication patterns including all aspects, verbal and nonverbal communications. These communications include indirect or inferred messages and signs expressed in body language, facial expressions, seating arrangements, etc.

At the outset the assessor can be a facilitator of communication simply by setting the tone of the interview and making the couple or the family feel as much at ease as possible. I am convinced that the following are necessary in order to facilitate this.

(a) The parents or family should be met by someone who they perceive as being warm, concerned about them and willing to listen.

(b) They must recognize that they are meeting a person who has been in the same interview situation before and who in effect has some past experience and prior knowledge of families in this situation.

(c) They should be met with openness and honesty so that they can feel that it is alright to share in confidence their shortcomings, their strengths and their problems with someone who is not going to act as a judge but will be helpful and supportive. They should be helped to understand that the agenda is not to enhance their medical knowledge but to review how they are coping with this crisis in their lives.

In the initial interview I often point out that families help our team in our learning and that in turn if they have uncertainties or difficulties I or other team members may be able to help them. I also make it clear that the team works together and that psychosocial as well as medical knowledge is shared by all team members. If earlier encounters have turned up specific questions, impressions or problems, I point out early in the session that the team is aware of them. In reverse, if we perceive that the family is coping well, I make certain that I tell them so.

I believe that in the assessment interview a helpful approach should include the following:

(a) a labelling of differences in communication between family members as perceived by the interviewer;

(b) request for clarification by the other partner or other family members when communication seems inconsistent with previous information, is hidden, given as an aside or seems to be missed and needs to be understood by other family members. For example, when a father was viewed by the ward staff and by the mother as denying the seriousness of their child's malignancy and consequently left his wife to cope with the child and the relatives, the couple was seen conjointly for a more in-depth and detailed psychosocial assessment. In the interview the father stated that he was concerned about the child and that he was aware of the facets of the illness. The mother passed this over and was quick to move on to something else. I requested clarification of what the father understood about his child's illness and how he felt about it. It was of crucial importance that the mother listen to her husband's realistic perceptions about the illness and recognize the role his feelings were playing in his inability to help her and their child. As a consequence of this clarification, the interview moved from a superficial discussion into the couple's feelings about the child, about each other and about how difficult it was for both of them to face the reality of the illness;

(c) drawing out of the past experience by moving the family's focus back to past crises and discovering both the positive and negative learning that they had gained from the previous situation. The ability of the interviewer to help the family recall strengths and positive learning is finely balanced with helping the family to talk about painful experiences. These may have created or helped precipitate relationship difficulties that are currently affecting the family's ability to face the crisis of the child's illness. It must be recognized that if we uncover the source of major conflicts we must be prepared to go beyond an initial assessment and provide further sessions directed toward problem solution;

(d) introduction of new learning by assisting the family to

Childhood Malignancy

recognize what they are doing. This can be accomplished through feedback from the interviewer about how he is assessing the family interaction, structure and adaptation. For example, in the previous family situation it may have been appropriate for me to state that the father had deep concerns about his daughter and that it was worthwhile for the couple to talk about them. This summation of the dialogue would have enabled the parents to realize that sharing their feelings with each other can be of benefit to them;

(e) assurance that they are not extraordinary or strange because they are angry or feel guilty, but to help the family understand that it is common for life-threatening illnesses to precipitate strong emotional response. By providing this reassurance the interviewer facilitates the expression of feelings and enables the family member to show his or her feelings openly. Such expression often leads to the realization that support and understanding is present because others feel the same way. In addition, discussion and release of feeling is often comforting;

(f) systematization in the review of problems which enables the participants in the interview to identify specific problems and where appropriate to begin to use the positive aspects of their relationship to solve problems. For instance, a couple who is both uncertain and has been unable to discuss their 10-year-old son's illness and prognosis may be able to

  (1) compare how closely their viewpoints coincide,
  (2) realize that they need more complete information,
  (3) make a specific point of obtaining the information and discussing the matter with the resident or physician,
  (4) make a joint decision, supported by the physician, on how to approach their child in the most constructive manner.

The Mobilizing Role

I believe that as a mobilizer the interviewer can, through his objectivity and a direct or indirect approach, help the family capitalize on its already developed abilities or move toward a new balance in role functioning. For example, the couple or family may identify a need to approach a demanding grandparent who is adding to the stress already present in a family which is trying to cope with taking their child to daily radiation treatments. The dominance of the grandparent and his physical and emotional proximity to the family have made confrontation very difficult. The identification of why the parents have been unable to approach the grandparent, the identification of family leadership and style and the review of positive past experiences in which the couple or family have pulled together to cope with external stress may be sufficient to mobilize the parents to deal with the grandparent. In some instances, a more directive interviewer may lend to the discussion the stimulating force and support which will generate positive problem solving. For example, if the couple have reached a situation in which family leadership is suppressed or totally lacking, one or both partners may be forcefully encouraged to approach the grandparent as a means of alleviating the stress. I must emphasize, however, that such changes rarely take place via one assessment interview and that mobilizing requires time and patience. It is usually necessary to work through a process of setting and attaining achievable goals as mutually agreed upon by the interviewer and the family participants. For many families with a few minor problems, one to three sessions plus informal follow-up discussions with team members can facilitate positive change. In others, continued and timely sessions, especially at times of a crisis such as a relapse, can help the family gradually learn to work together.

The Modelling Role

When opportunities arise for continued interaction with the family beyond the initial assessment interview, the interviewer as a family counsellor or therapist can serve as what Glick and Kessler (1974) call: "A model for identification," or an educator in the realities of life. The family which is faced with childhood cancer is often in need of reality based input from an experienced, objective observer. The interviewer's openness, honesty and willingness to tackle delicate interactional problems in a simple, straightforward manner is a source of strength, particularly if the families do not have the life experience available from positive coping experiences created by past crises. I believe that the interviewer can use himself as a flexible role model which may shift the family's view of a problem. For instance, when dealing with autonomy or lack of it in a couple's relationship, the counsellor may temporarily shift the balance by lending his support to the partner who requires more freedom. A typical example in my experience involved the mother of a child with leukemia who had two other young children and had no chance of working outside the home or going out for any type of recreation due to her husband's unwillingness to have her work or to use a babysitter. In this situation I became a permissive role model who supported the wife's need in order to mobilize a shift in her husband's rigid position.

Another modelling role described by Glick and Kessler (1974) is that of "reality tester." The interviewer is an external and objective source of information about the world outside of the family and operates apart from the turmoil created by the child's disease. For instance when parents are angry with God because their child is ill, the interviewer can provide reference material which enables the family members to realize that their emotional response is appropriate, understandable and accepted. Similarly, when parents have difficulty accepting the reality of the illness and say that they feel they are living in a dream world and that they hope they will wake up free of the burden of their child's illness, the interviewer can help them remain in touch with reality.

As I mentioned earlier when discussing the nature of the illness, it is not just in the psychosocial assessment or additional counselling sessions when this reality testing component is required. Reality testing must become part of the role of the two or three key people whom the family will prefer to use as models for reality testing. In our setting this may involve a nurse, a staff physician, a resident, the social worker or the child life worker. Their role as reality testers is based on their long-term relationship with the family and the family's willingness to trust these team members when the family needs to continually test out reality in times of major stress.

The final component described by Glick and Kessler (1974) involves the role of "demythologizer or philosopher of family life." This role is closely tied to mobilization and to the understanding and erosion of false beliefs which family members may support mutually or independently. I have found that the recognition of the importance of myths can be a key factor in understanding family functioning and adaptation to stress. For example, the family who may believe that everything must be shared openly with all nuclear family members may have created an environment which abounds with mutual support, understanding and open communication so that the family is strong enough to deal with any crisis of its own. The interviewer will not try to change this belief and will recognize its importance because the family has built their relationships upon it. However, another family may have the same belief and feel that when they share openly they can cope with any type of stress. When they are faced with the crisis of childhood malignancy the parents may overload the children with distorted information, unnecessary speculation and intense anxiety. This may inhibit constructive adaptation to illness and negatively affect medical treatment. The interviewer, by identifying the problem and providing sufficient time for discussion, may help the parents change their pattern so that they can sort out relevant information and the feelings which are associated with it before passing the information on to other family members.

Limit Setting

Limit setting is a technique used by interviewers to direct and control part of an interview (Wynne, 1971). By setting limits, the interviewer can narrow the focus of the interview sufficiently enough to enable the family to explore a specific problem in great detail or to work it through to solution without being sidetracked by irrelevant issues. I have found that to set limits often requires the interviewer to be frank and straightforward and consequently it is of benefit to have established a solid rapport with the family prior to using this technique to any great extent. For instance, when one couple was faced with the relapse of their son's leukemia they began quarreling. They tended to bring into their arguments their problems with in-laws, the husband's past difficulties with employment, the wife's inability to keep the house clean and an array of past conflicts and unresolved feelings. By narrowing the focus and limiting the amount of diversion to past conflicts we were able to concentrate on the real problem. Both parents were terrified of their son's illness and felt that if he relapsed he would most certainly die. Neither partner could reach out and support the other emotionally and instead they used previously established patterns of conflict to bring out their frustration. Once the parents were able to share their anxieties we could then begin working on the emotional deficits in their relationship.

The Use Of Self

As interviewers, counsellors and therapists we must always be aware of how we use ourselves and how others perceive us. I cannot think of any situation where the use of ourselves is of more importance than in dealing with families facing childhood malignancy. In this emotionally laden area each of us is prone to feelings which parallel the mixture and staging of responses to life-threatening illnesses which Kübler-Ross (1969) has delineated. Overtly or unconsciously we dread the diagnosis of another case, feel depressed at times of relapse, are angry when treatments fail and want to bargain by doing our best in hopes that a child may recover. For example, recently a child relapsed and a staff member had to comfort an upset parent. Even though the staff member had been helpful and supportive she felt that she had failed to assist the parent. In fact, she was feeling like other team members, because the others felt they had failed to help the child. In another situation I was angry for three days before realizing that I felt helpless that two little children were going to die and nothing could be done to prevent their deaths.

Our susceptibility to emotional responses and our ability to recognize and understand our feelings is of great importance since they can readily be transmitted to the parents and child. We must also learn to work through our feelings and by so doing control them. This is particularly true when we face a death and must in turn face the inevitability of our own death. Frequently, young students and staff members work through their feelings on the job and require help to do so. Sometimes when any of us are faced with personal burdens, we may respond more intensely to work situations than we realize, and the objectivity and support offered by another team member can be very helpful.

For those of us who are continually involved in psychosocial assessments and intervention, our ability to understand and to use ourselves to benefit the child and his family requires that we be knowledgeable about our own views on family life and factors that pertain to it. We must be aware of our values and prejudices and the ways we respond to stress, to various types of personalities, to problem families and to a host of other factors which will influence our behavior in clinical practice. Our confidence in approaching emotionally laden issues in childhood cancer can be increased by feedback from families and colleagues. In addition we also need a solid grounding in psychological and social theories, including family dynamics, and we must be willing to change approaches in keeping with new information and individual situations.

Group Approaches and the Buddy System:
Additional Help for Families

As discussed briefly in Chapter 1, the value of group approaches and the benefits experienced by parents have been described in detail by others [Heffron, Bommelaere and Masters (1973); Knapp and Hanson (1973); Martinson and Jorgens (1976) and Pollitt (1976)]. As Pollitt (1976) points out, only half or less of the total number of parents or families will participate in parent or family group programs. When the group is structured by professionals for the purpose of learning, personal growth and mutual support for the participants, the issue of selectivity and the need for a substantial patient volume becomes extremely important.

At McMaster the patient volume is small in comparison to a center such as the Hospital for Sick Children in Toronto. Consequently, we have not used a group discussion approach, and to date no spontaneous banding together of parents to form an association has taken place.

However, due to the informality of our play room, the involvement of the child life worker and the proximity of the waiting room, parents often use the opportunity to get to know other parents and become knowledgeable as well as concerned about other children who are attending the clinic. In addition we have, on a number of occasions, intentionally facilitated or seen by happenstance the effective pairing of mothers and to a lesser extent the pairing of couples and total families. This pairing usually commences when each sick child is facing a similar problem or a similar phase of treatment. Often this relationship persists throughout the years and support continues whether or not the child lives or dies. Even when parents are very upset about their child's illness other parents can be very helpful. The interaction can be a positive learning experience on both sides.

Children also establish contact with one another and compare notes, particularly as they reach age ten. Periodically, informal get-togethers for the preteens and teens have been held by the nurses and have been resoundingly successful in enabling the children to share their concerns and achievements. At Christmas, a gathering for all children on the pediatrics ward and inclusion of children from the pediatric hematology clinic, along with siblings and parents, enables children to play and parents to talk in an environment where staff members are the entertainers and are available to meet informally with the family. Seeing the staff as people with a sense of humor has helped us develop even closer relationships with families.

REFERENCES

Munson, S.W.: "Family Structure: The Family's General Adaptation to the Crisis and Loss." Paper presented at a postgraduate symposium "The Child and Death," University of Rochester, Rochester, N.Y. September

16, 1977.

Share, L.: "Family Communication in the Crises of a Child's Fatal Illness: A Literature Review and Analyses." *Omega*, 3:3, 187-201, 1972.

Minuchin, S., Montalvo, B., Guerney, B.G., and Schumer, F.: *Families of the Slums*, Basic Books, New York, 1967.

Hamovitch, M.B.: *The Parent and the Fatally Ill Child.* City of Hope Medical Center, Duarte, California, 1964.

Kübler-Ross, E.: *On Death and Dying.* Macmillan Publishing Co. Ltd., New York, 1969.

Erikson, E.H.: *Childhood and Society.* Penguin Books Ltd., Harmondsworth, Middlesex, England, 1965.

Glasser, P.H. and Navarre, E.: "Structural Problems of the One-Parent Family" *Behavioral Science for Social Workers.* Edited by Edwin J. Thomas, The Free Press, New York, 1967.

Glick, I.D. and Kessler, D.R.: *Marital and Family Therapy.* Grune and Stratton, New York, 1974.

Wynne, L.C.: "Some Guidelines for Exploratory Conjoint Therapy." *Changing Families: A Family Therapy Reader.* Edited by Jay Haley, Grune and Stratton, New York, 1971.

Heffron, W.A., Bommelaere, K. and Masters, R.: "Group Discussions with Parents of Leukemia Children." *J Pediatr,* 52:831-840, 1973.

Knapp, V.S. and Hanson, H.: "Helping the Parents of Children with Leukemia," *Soc Work,* 18:4, 70-75, 1973.

Martinson, I.M. and Jorgens, C.L.: "Report of a Parent Support Group." *Home Care for the Dying Child,* I.M. Martinson (ed.), Appleton-Century-Crofts, New York, 1976.

Pollitt, E.: "The Family Leukemia Association." Essence — *Issues in the Study of Ageing.* 1:2, 107-116, 1976.

CHAPTER 5

CARE OF THE CHILD: HOSPITALIZATION, CLINIC VISITS AND LONG-TERM SURVIVAL

IN our work with the sick child we must recognize that we are providing care that influences his total life. His experiences in coping with his illness involve his personal well-being; his life within his family; and his social experiences at school, with his friends and in the community at large. For the child with cancer the pediatric ward and the ambulatory clinic have a pervasive and sometimes lasting influence on his life. As caregivers we are faced with the major responsibility for what happens in the hospital. Each hospitalization and each ambulatory visit can affect the child's ability to cope with his illness, enhance or detract from the necessary trust required to enable staff to treat him and shape his perception of what his illness will mean to him in the future. This chapter examines the impact of hospitalization and ambulatory care on the child. A special section is provided on the care of the adolescent patient and in closing the discussion turns to the issue of long-term survival. Ways of helping the child to cope with his problems through such means as therapeutic play are also discussed.

HOSPITALIZATION

Over the years the major focus of care for the child with a malignant disease has shifted from the pediatric ward to the ambulatory or out-patient clinic. At McMaster University Medical Center the major focus of our teaching hospital is to treat patients on an ambulatory basis so that hospitalization is kept to a bare minimum. Consequently, the ambulatory clinic assumes prominence as the child receives the majority of his care as an out-patient. Nevertheless, the hospital ward and the hospitalization experience are both prominent because of their association with critical periods in the child's experience in coping with the disease. Hospitalization is necessary at the time of diagnosis and even though the child's stay may be brief, the actual admission to the hospital and the child's encounter with painful procedures may be his first such experience. Hospitalization also assumes importance if the child develops a major infection, such as septicemia or pneumonia, and is sometimes required if the child relapses. We have frequently observed that if the child becomes seriously ill due to metastasis or a florid relapse of leukemia which does not respond to chemotherapy, then he may require several short admissions prior to returning to hospital for terminal care. Even with the use of short stay units and home care as measures to prevent hospitalization, the hospital ward is the place where the child goes when he is extremely ill.

The threat to the child's well-being when he is faced with severe emotional strains in his illness can bring forward a number of behavioral responses that warrant careful examination. These responses often occur at times when he is facing severe stress both within the hospital and while he is being treated as an out-patient. In the following section I discuss these responses. Although much of the literature relates to the pediatric ward a great deal of knowledge gained from the hospitalization experience can be applied to ambulatory care as well.

Some Possible Consequences of Hospitalization

Hospitalization is one of the most anxiety-provoking experiences of childhood (Dimock, 1959). The child is placed in a setting which is alien to him and which often disrupts his life unexpectedly. Plank (1971) points out:

When a child is hospitalized, the hospital has to take on tasks beyond its healing function, tasks which must be accomplished so the rhythm of life and growth can go on. The child's normal way of living involves relating to other children, to grown-ups, to play and learning. It has to be fitted in to a day filled with diagnostic and treatment procedures. The task is complicated by the threat of the illness itself, of operations and the possible nearness of death.

Consequently, when we consider that children with malignancies may be subjected to repeated hospitalization, it is important to understand some of the responses that may be precipitated by the experience. Sherman (1976) in discussing her daughter's ordeal with leukemia, summarizes her young child's response to hospitalization as follows:

> The child may cry often and cling to parents; eat or sleep poorly; struggle against treatment and resist taking medicine; evidence great fearfulness whenever treatment is in the offing; respond with anger even to the friendliest of approaches. He may also ignore the parents; undergo treatment procedures with unusual stoicism; remain silent and withdrawn in the face of all efforts to engage him in conversation or play.

There is no doubt that the preparation of the child before hospitalization, parental involvement and making one person responsible for the child's care have helped curb the severity of the reactions cited by Sherman (Langford, 1961; Oremland and Oremland, 1973). However, the fact remains that hospitalization is anxiety provoking and forces the child to use various types of behavior as defense or coping mechanisms. Some of the types of anxiety are described in the following paragraphs.

Separation anxiety has been described as being most intense in children under the age of five (Bowlby, 1960; Dimock, 1959; Heinicke, 1965; Plank, 1971). Langford (1961) emphasizes how this natural phenomena can be intensified by policies which limit parental visiting, restrict the possessions a child may bring to hospital and by the lack of preparation by the parents and the hospital staff in regard to the child's hospitalization experience. Heinicke (1971) stresses the importance of the length of separation for the child, especially the child under the age of three. He points out that separations that exceed two weeks may take up to five months to resolve. Jessner, Blom and Waldfogel (1952), in their study of tonsillectomy patients, clearly identified this type of anxiety to be present in a larger number of their subjects who were under the age of five. In our setting, we frequently find that young children will cling to the parents initially and will often refuse to go to the playroom or participate in any ward activities. Our experience has demonstrated that this type of anxiety can be alleviated or at least reduced when parents are involved in their child's care and when they are totally honest with the child about the anticipated return of his mother if she cannot stay with him all day and night. Children who have repeated hospitalizations may adapt more easily because of familiarity with the staff and the setting, but adaptation can often be offset by the nature of the treatment received. Problems can be amplified by necessary isolation due to infections, by repeated procedures and by the inability of parents to return at anticipated times. At our setting, involvement of parents in the care of the child is facilitated and encouraged wherever feasible. Enabling parents to remain overnight has been a very important component in our efforts to prevent, alleviate or resolve separation anxiety.

Communicated anxiety is a problem most commonly arising from the uncertainty of parents and sometimes from the uneasiness of relatives and staff (Langford, 1961). Parental anxieties are a natural occurrence when a child is ill or faces surgery. However, when the anxiety is excessive and the parents fret about the care the child is receiving to the point where the child's anxiety increases, then the intensity of his symptoms may also be increased. In addition, he responds so fearfully to procedures that he may subject himself to unnecessary physical trauma. We have often seen this type of anxiety in young couples who have their first encounter with the hospitalization of their child. In children with malignant disorders this type of anxiety may be anticipated immediately following diagnosis or when parents think that their child may soon die.

For example, Tommy, age eight, experienced a recurrence of his tumor. This recurrence jeopardized his life. Ordinarily when attending the clinic, Tommy would go into the playroom and paint pictures while his mother sat in the waiting area and talked with other parents. After his disease returned his mother began hovering about just outside of the ward play room. Occasionally she would make negative comments about her child's artwork and thus convey to Tommy her insecurity about his ability to manage on his own. Her anxious behavior persisted after Tommy was discharged from hospital and returned for clinic visits. As time went on, Tommy became more uncertain about himself and more anxious when faced with the repeated injections which were necessary to treat his illness. I believe that management of this type of response can be facilitated early in the hospitalization experience through involvement of the social worker, nurse, child life worker or other staff who are willing to counsel the parents and help them deal with their anxiety.

Mutilation anxiety is a common response of children from ages six to nine and beyond. The child with cancer perceives the physical symptoms of his illness as a threat to his bodily integrity or to his life (Nagy 1948, Waechter 1971, Spinetta, Rigler and Karon 1973). This type of anxiety can also be generated by the child's view of the illness as a form of punishment for having aggressive thoughts toward adults or having committed wrongful acts (Blom 1958, Langford 1961). Langford (1961) stresses how parents sometimes reinforce this anxiety by threatening to punish the child by sending him to the hospital or by viewing the illness as a means that God uses to punish the family for its sins. The latter is particularly true in the case of families who must face malignant disease as a threat to their child's life. Jessner and his associates (1952) found that in the age range of five to seven years, the fear of tonsillectomy operations and the fear of needles increased markedly. From ages seven to ten the fear of the operation remained high, but the fear of needles gave way to anxiety about narcosis and the threatened loss of control created by anesthesia.

An example of mutilation anxiety is found in the case of Paul. Paul, age nine, had undergone surgery for osteogenic sarcoma of a lower limb. Several days later, he suffered a severe hemorrhage. Paul's wound required debriding, and Paul and his mother were visibly shaken by the experience. When given a chance to talk about his feelings Paul said in earnest that he believed that "the doctors would keep chopping away" at his leg until it was all gone.

The three types of anxiety just described generate responses within the child that are directed toward maintaining his psychological equilibrium. These responses are called defense or coping mechanisms (Hofmann, Becker, and Gabriel, 1976). Some of the major coping mechanisms used as a result of hospitalization and the illness experience are examined in the following section.

Defense Mechanisms

Regression is defined as a reversion to an earlier stage of behavior. Kenny (1975) stresses how the hospitalization experience curbs a child's need to release energy, to build upon positive experiences and to find stimulating activity. Oremland and Oremland (1973) emphasize that the deprivation of the child's ability to control his autonomy and the resulting regression is more threatening to the child than to the adult because it signifies a loss of recently acquired and very important achievements. Langford (1961) suggests that regression is necessary as a means of retreating from an anxiety-provoking situation in order to allow the child to regroup his strength and to cope with the anxiety. Hofmann and her associates (1976) in discussing the adolescent patient, point out that the teenager passes over responsibility for care to his parents and to others. The tendency for parents to overindulge in the care of the adolescent can lead to enjoyment of the increased attention. This response is common when the adolescent is immobilized. In the care of the younger child there is no doubt that this situation may also occur. We have found that once the child has experienced the benefits accrued from regressing it becomes increasingly difficult to regain his previous autonomy. The child with cancer who is kept in hospital for long periods and faces a rigorous treatment regimen often becomes more demanding or withdrawn. Both types of responses are often expected from a child who is younger. Our play therapist suggests that in her experience the most common form of regression is the use of baby talk. Even Paul, the nine year old with osteogenic sarcoma, reverted to baby talk as one means of coping with his intense anxiety. Measures must be introduced through play, discussion, artwork and other media to make the situation less threatening and minimize the child's need to regress. For the adolescent patient the same principle applies.

Rebellion and other aggressive acts are means a child may use to cope with anxiety. Langford (1961) states that underlying panic may precipitate a sudden aggressive act, or the child may respond by bothering staff with provocative actions. This type of behavior helps reduce the intensity of the anxiety for the child but makes management of his care in the hospital extremely difficult. Hofmann and her associates (1976) point out the seriousness of this type of acting-out behavior in the adolescent and emphasize that it is a maladaptive form of displacement or redirection of feeling to a tangible situation. They suggest that aggressive activity is stimulated by an unrealistic or irrational desire to escape from the situation. At times rebellion can also be provoked by the necessity to seek reassurance of the adolescent's worth when reassurance is not forthcoming. In a child under the age of seven, the response must be viewed in the light of the child's tendency to react more primitively to the stress. For example, we have often seen children reach the limit of their tolerance of treatment and lash out spontaneously. By the same token we have seen children bother staff through defiant behavior in order to gain much needed attention, even though they did not appear to understand the dynamics of their actions. Langford (1961) suggests that some children will become more aggressive towards parents or staff as a means of consciously or unconsciously ridding themselves of feelings of responsibility for the illness. I think that it must be recognized that such aggressive acts need not be maladaptive, particularly in the child with malignant disease who has faced repeated injections, bone marrows and tests. The child has a need to respond spontaneously and to express both his anxiety and his anger. For instance, Patsy was a well-mannered, well-behaved and passive seven-year-old who always cooperated with the doctors and nurses in our clinic. Following the relapse of her leukemia, she was subjected to many injections and several painful procedures. In doll play she had remained passive and frequently gave the dolls intravenous injections. One day she became angry and resistant to treatment. After a difficult session in which her resistance had forced the physician to attempt the injection several times, she returned to the playroom. Upon her return she tore out the injection equipment that she had previously left in the arms of two dolls. She then proceeded to jab the dolls full of holes as she screamed and screamed.

After about 15 minutes she ceased screaming and cried for more than an hour. Initially, Patsy's parents and the staff were shocked that Patsy had reached the end of her tolerance. She needed to rebel and to release the frustration that had slowly been building up inside of her. Her release helped her face future injections with less resistance and periods of intense doll play seemed to help her manage her feelings more easily. Patsy's experience highlights the need for staff and parents to understand the underlying causes of a child's response and provide measures to ensure that aggression can be released constructively. The means for such release will vary with the child and with the type of play or diversionary activity made available. As children grow older it becomes obvious that the provision of physical activity is a primary way of helping the child cope with aggression. Unfortunately, many hospital settings lack the recreational space, equipment and programs to make such activity possible. Our ability to connect our patients with the university facilities makes us very fortunate indeed.

Withdrawal with resulting silence and at times passive compliance, can be a natural process. I believe that anyone facing an intolerable situation may want to quietly remove themselves. At times, however, passive compliance to hospitalization can be mistaken for positive adjustment, particularly by busy nursing staff. Children who use this means of coping often behave differently in hospital than they behave at home or in school. They tend to have difficulty expressing anger, and they internalize anxiety (Langford, 1961). Differentiation between the need for rest and solitude and withdrawal behavior can be difficult, particularly when the child is facing a severe illness, an intense treatment regimen, or when he is recovering from major surgery. In older children and adolescents in particular, temporary withdrawal can be understood as a reasonable means of retreating from stress. (Hofmann, Becker, and Gabriel, 1976). However, when the withdrawal is prolonged the need for measures to encourage resumption of normal social interaction becomes very necessary. In our experience, we have found that older children and adolescents often need time away from the intense pattern of ward activities and the lack of privacy that this pattern creates. Children who are feeling physically ill also need to withdraw and to be left alone to sleep, to rest quietly or to feel sad for a few hours or even for a couple of days. When children do withdraw, staff tend to become anxious and feel very uncomfortable when they have to care for a child who is not "happy." Sometimes this creates a problem when the residents and ward staff quickly label the child as being depressed and without further exploration request a psychiatric consultation. As one teenager with leukemia stated, when she felt physically ill her spirits lowered, she became depressed and felt very sad. She wanted to be left alone, sometimes for several days, without her parents and the staff constantly dropping in to force her to talk. When she felt better physically she was the reverse and wanted to be with people and to help younger children on the ward. She had no desire to be away from her parents or the staff. When she was able to tell the staff how she felt it made her care easier for them and made life less difficult for her.

Denial is a common response to stress at all ages. The child is no exception. Children want to be home, to remain at school and to see their friends. When faced with hospitalization some children will fantasize about being well, while others will attempt to convince staff that they are capable of returning home (Langford, 1961). Occasionally, children will become extremely brave and will ignore and endure symptoms of their illness in order to avoid remaining in hospital. Adolescents tend to make much greater use of denial. This is discussed in more detail later on when we deal with malignant disease and the subject of death. However, it is important to note that denial can be valuable, especially when the implications of hospitalization or disease allow the adolescent to hope that he may eventually be well. Denial in this situation provides buoyancy so that the adolescent can gain further strength to cope with the sequelae of his disease and the treatment process (Oremland and Oremland, 1973; Hofmann, Becker, and Gabriel, 1976).

Displacement is another very common coping mechanism. In hospital, we have found that children may displace their anxiety on to some other part of their body or to some other place or item that is more removed emotionally and, consequently, more easily managed. The child may become intensely worried about his dog, his school work or his bicycle, or as Langford (1961) suggests, he may be concerned about a mole or a toe nail which is completely unrelated to the nature of his illness. Oremland and Oremland (1973) and Hofmann and her associates (1976) suggest that the adolescent displaces his anxiety by becoming preoccupied with hospital food or the problems of other patients. In our experience we have found that children who face a long-term illness with repeated hospitalizations, frequently use this mechanism and that the intensity of the anxiety which is displaced unto another object usually parallels closely their anxiety about their physical well-being or their prognosis. Sometimes alleviation of the external anxiety through measures such as reassurance by the parents that they will look after the child's dog, can provide a calming effect on the child. Hospital staff must recognize the necessity of providing the opportunity and the time for the child to work through his anxiety as it relates to both the hospitalization and the illness.

Patrick, age four and one half, provides an excellent example of displacement. Patrick had suffered several relapses in his struggle with leukemia. In the last few weeks of his life, he asked a number of questions about death and became obsessed with the need to know whether or not he would live to see his birthday. His birthday became a daily topic in his discussion with his mother, and he incorporated his birthday into many aspects of his play activities. When his family was convinced by friends and relatives to hold a birthday party several months early, Patrick became upset, responded with anger and expressed a desire to leave. His attempts to displace his anxiety in this instance had been countered by the reality that he would not live to see his birthday. This resulted in confusion and the resurfacing of his underlying anxiety.

Needless to say, there are many other mechanisms that are used by children and by teenagers to cope with hospitalization. At every age these reactions may include panic attacks, obsessions about damage to parts of the body, hypochondriasis, compensation and projection of the blame for their illness or treatment unto others. Adolescents and older children may add to this the tendency to intellectualize in order to avoid discussing the reality of their illness.

The Importance of Depression

Depression is not specifically a defense mechanism. Instead, depression is a symptom, a syndrome or a diagnostic reaction. Depression has been described as the emotional response to the loss of something valued (Cameron, 1963). This loss can be deprivation of regular social relationships, changes in social status, changes in living situations or changes in health. All of these are relevant to the hospitalized child. As a reaction to the hospitalization experience we have often seen depression appearing as a situational response which is controlled by the nature and extent of the hospitalization and the illness experience. In this context, depression may be a symptom which is only part of the clinical picture and is related mainly to the lowering of mood. This lowering of mood may be a perfectly natural response, especially when it is based on the reality of having lost something which the child values as part of his daily life. In a more extensive manner, depression is often found as a syndrome created by a life-threatening illness or by a reaction to extended hospitalization and treatment experiences (Kübler-Ross, 1969). This type of response is characterized by sadness, reduced activity and usually retardation of the individual's normal behavior. Some of the other signs which are commonly seen include insomnia, anorexia, constipation and extended withdrawal (Cameron, 1963; Lidz, 1968). Langford (1961) sees depression as the result of the child's feeling inwardly sad and viewing the illness as being his fault. In effect, this is a type of mourning where a child internalizes both love and hate, resulting in feelings of loss of self-esteem, guilt and reproaches against himself.

Most often, carefully structured hospital activity programs and continued involvement of the mother and, where possible, both parents prevent depression from being severe. I must stress that in many situations depressive reactions are legitimate, particularly if they can be attributed directly to hospitalization and illness. For instance, teenage girls tend to respond to prolonged life-threatening illnesses with depressive syndromes. Hospitalization may aggravate this response. For the ward staff one of the most difficult situations in recognizing and understanding the child's behavior occurs when it is necessary to assess the nature and extent of depression. Sometimes, as a result of the illness or chemotherapy, depression may be a common pattern anticipated in children with malignant disorders. At other times, depression may simply be a normal, fleeting response and reflect a time when the individual child or adolescent needs to withdraw to sort out his thoughts or to engage in some much-needed self-pity for a day or two. Involvement of parents in the care can be a great asset in assessing the nature and extent of the mood change in the hospitalized child or adolescent.

In all aspects of child behavior related to hospitalization, it is essential that the child have the opportunity to express feelings of anger and anxiety (Sherman, 1976). Such expression needs to be free of the fear of punishment (Stacey, 1970; Harvey and Hales-Tooke, 1972). In Sherman's experience, when her daughter was hospitalized due to leukemia, she stresses how she welcomed her daughter's occasional outbursts because they reflected the child's need to react to the hospital experience. The child is not only vulnerable but at such times is open to receiving love, comfort and reassurance. As will be discussed later, play can be a major asset in helping the child release and discuss such feelings (Harvey and Hales-Tooke, 1972; Petrillo and Sanger, 1972; Klinzing and Klinzing, 1977).

Following hospitalization, children are often left with intense feelings. Dimock (1959) sees regression, anxiety, hostility and night terrors as being the major sequelae to hospitalization. Kenny (1975) stresses the need to deal with these conflicting and disrupting feelings by providing firm support and external controls. When care continues beyond the hospital and the child returns to the ambulatory clinic, staff can be a major support to the parents in their efforts to help the child readapt to the external environment. If necessary, the child can also receive specialized attention at this time.

The Pediatric Ward

The Environment

In principle, I endorse Van Eys's (1977) suggestion that the ward should be "a therapeutic community" which enables the child to respond freely to both positive and negative aspects of his care where his right to be happy, sad or angry is accepted as natural and normal. Warmth, concern and understanding of the staff and their continued willingness to individualize the care of each child are essential ingredients for maintaining such an environment. Inherent in such a setting as well is the recognition that the child is a person with rights that must be respected. I believe that these rights include having the family nearby whenever family members are needed. Mothers and fathers should be allowed to stay with their child; brothers and sisters should be able to visit; and when possible, children should be allowed to go out with their parents for walks on the grounds, for lunch or for weekend visits home. Other rights include the opportunity to continue schooling, the right to be left alone to rest or sleep, the right to have procedures explained and the right to companionship from staff or volunteers when relatives are not nearby and readily available.

The Physical Setting

The pediatric ward should be a place where the child feels welcome. Warm colors, supervised play areas and room for the child to explore and socialize are essential. Ideally, the ward should contain a quiet room where older children can escape to study or to think. A place is also needed where parents can go in order to give themselves and their child an often much-needed rest from each other. In our setting, the availability of a view to the world outside of the hospital, the proximity of the ward to the out-patient pediatric clinics and the accessibility to recreational areas where children can play Ping-Pong™ or billiards are valued assets.

Ambulatory Care

The Setting

In the early stages of malignant disease, after what amounts to a short stay in hospital, the child returns home and then comes back to the ambulatory or out-patient clinic. The child and his parent or parents will spend much time in clinic attendance. Waiting to see the physician, waiting for test results, undergoing special procedures and examination by consulting physicians mean that many hours will be spent in the out-patient area.

Hoffman and Futterman (1971) have underlined the importance of capitalizing on the chance to make the waiting area a place for interpersonal interaction. I believe that it is essential that the physical setting lends itself to socialization and diversion. Comfortable surroundings and a well-supervised play area which is accessible to both children and adults are crucial. Children need the chance to play with other children, to color, to draw, to paint and to work with hospital equipment, e.g. syringes and rubber tubing. Their parents need to feel free to talk to other parents, to relax and to participate in play with their child if they wish. A billiard or Ping-Pong table for the older child can be placed where children congregate or where a parent and child can pass the time while awaiting a difficult procedure or a regular clinic visit.

In our setting, the receptionist who welcomes the child and the family is a major asset. Children and families can readily identify with her as someone who cares about them and helps them with problems such as making appointments and finding their way to other parts of the hospital. The child life worker too is a familiar person in the play area whom parents and children soon learn to talk to and to trust.

The Child's Perspective

Naturally, responses to hospitalization will be governed by a child's age, his past experience, the intensity of his illness and treatment, the nature of the setting and the response of his parents. Parents, particularly mothers, are natural objects for feelings of rejection by the child and may receive the brunt of the child's anger. The parent may also feel a loss of control and may respond with feelings of guilt. When children are suffering from a malignant disease, hospitalization may intensify the interpersonal difficulties which already exist between the child and his family.

From the child's point of view, hospitalization may make him feel like he lives on wheels as people move him back and forth between places such as nuclear medicine, radiology and the operating room. Maybe he will be in the Intensive Care Unit where other people do not talk much and machines make funny and frightening noises. Back on the ward, he may be isolated physically because he has or is prone to developing infections. He may feel isolated and lonely because his mother cannot stay or his parents do not visit or he misses his dog. On the other hand, he may feel that his room is inundated with people who ask him silly questions, poke him and prod him, whisper at the end of his bed, keep shoving a thermometer in his mouth, keep jamming a blood pressure cuff on his arm or force him to allow them to puncture him with needles. Nurses may wake him up at night, get him up early and tell him to eat food which is not appealing to him.

The child has little choice but to comply. The child with a malignant disease or any other life-threatening or chronic disorder is especially vulnerable, because he must often face an illness that makes him feel miserable, that exposes him to a great deal of medical attention and forces him to be hospitalized more frequently and for longer periods than a child who experiences a single hospitalization for a relatively minor problem.

When he comes to the ambulatory clinic initially, the child has often just been released from the hospital and is anxious about returning. He feels uncertain and for several visits may be so fearful that he refuses to go into the playroom and stays close to his mother instead. After a few visits he soon learns that when he is summoned from the waiting area or the playroom he must pass through the doors to the clinical area and enter a different world. He knows that the examination room is the doctor's domain and is the place where he must take off his clothes, be weighed, examined and possibly treated. If he is simply examined he usually adapts positively to the experience and cooperates fully because he knows that he will not be harmed. On the other hand, if he is faced with repeated injections, fairly frequent lumbar punctures, bone marrow aspirations or a combination of these painful procedures, he may anticipate the pain and worry about coming to the clinic. On the nights before clinic visits he may not sleep, or he may suffer from night terrors that are more intense and longer lasting than he has ever experienced before. When he comes to the hospital he dreads the suffering which he must inevitably face and may try to hide in the playroom, negotiate with the physician, fight off the needles or cry out as loud as he can.

The Feelings and Needs of the Child: Bodily Concerns

McCollum (1975) points out:

> Early childhood is the period of intense interest in bodily characteristics and concerns about physical powers and limitations. It is a time of growing awareness of male or female identity. The totality of the child's ideas, both realistic and imaginary, and his attitudes and emotions about his physical self comprise his body image.

Nagy (1948), Morrisey (1963) and other researchers have described the intense mutilation anxiety felt by children ages six to nine.

The diagnosis of malignant disease means that the child becomes the victim of more needles, procedures and treatments than he could ever have imagined. He is faced with changes in his body image and with changes in how his body is treated by others. He is often subjected to frequent prodding, to needles which take his blood or inject a medicine, to painful bone marrow aspirations and spinal taps. Prednisone pills may make him bloated, and other pills or needles may make him vomit. If he receives radiation, he may have blue or green lines drawn on his skin, he may have to be fitted for a face mask and he will have to spend time alone lying beneath an ominous looking machine. If he receives cranial radiation, he will probably lose his hair. He will also receive a tatoo as a permanent reminder of the experience.

The discomfort and anxiety generated by these procedures is considerable, let alone the additional fears generated by the natural developmental phenomena of castration or mutilation anxiety. McCollum (1975) suggests that young children use their imaginations to assimilate what is really happening to them. The child believes that the parts which receive the most attention are the parts which are the most important. In addition, the child may develop negative feelings about his body "as a source of discomfort rather than pleasure or excitement." When McCollum explains the impact of this anxiety on treatment she states that because the child may think of the skin as a wrapping, he may believe that a puncturing of the skin may lead to an outpouring of his insides.

I have observed this anxiety on a number of occasions. For instance, Joanne aged seven, a child with leukemia, had a severe infection in her thumb. Her parents could not understand the intensity of her worries, and indeed these were much greater than we would anticipate. After a few minutes of discussion, Joanne revealed that her concern was that this infection might make it necessary to cut off her thumb. It took considerable reassurance to help her understand that her thumb would heal properly.

At any age a child tends to be upset by bodily changes which provoke anxiety in those around him. This is especially true in children with leukemia when they experience a severe nosebleed or have extensive bruising or see increasing numbers of petechiae. They soon learn that their bodies are the major focus of attention for their parents and their doctors. Consequently, they concentrate their attention on their body as a governing factor in their lives.

As mentioned earlier, anger is another response to injections and procedures. Anger is often combined with anxiety. For instance, Matthew, aged four, a child with leukemia, was faced with an intense treatment program which involved frequent clinic visits. During this time, he came in with a toy hammer which he swung back and forth menacingly as he glared at staff in the clinic. He took the hammer into the examining room and kept it beside him at all times. When the child life worker saw this she loaned Matthew other tools from the playroom, and he began taking the box of tools into the examining room. On subsequent visits, he would act out his feelings in his play and stated that he would "fix the doctors and nurses." In play, he would cut off their arms, their legs and their heads. As he worked out his feelings he became less angry and received his injections with much less resistance. Matthew exemplifies in his very concrete thinking, the intensity of the need that all children feel when they are subjected to painful experiences. As a child grows older he moves into a thought pattern that Piaget (1955) calls the intellectual stage of concrete operations where he relates his experience to an organized whole and moves away from egocentrism (where the world shares the characteristics of the self) and animism (the ascribing of life to inanimate objects). As his thought process changes, the child after age seven or eight develops a more rational fear of the pain of procedures and will usually resort to verbal or written means of expressing his anger, sometimes with a series of expletives which shock his parents and the staff as well.

Other responses of the child related to his treatment and its impact are illustrated by the findings of several researchers.

Goggin and her colleagues (1976) point out that in children with malignancy, strong emotional stimulation is more disruptive than in normal children and children tend to be more prone to unrealistic thinking. In addition, they also suggest that young boys are more anxious than young girls but that the situation reverses as children grow older. In studying children with life-threatening illnesses in the age range of six to nine years, Waechter (1972) found that the general anxiety level of such children was twice as high as that of normal children even though only one-eighth of the study group knew their probable diagnosis. In his research, Spinetta (1977) found that children with leukemia exhibited much more awareness of their illness and anxiety about bodily intrusion than normal children or children with chronic diseases.

Recent work by Dafoe (1977) also reflects this anxiety. As part of her Masters studies in our clinic, Dafoe developed a pilot study on the impact of hair loss. She utilized the Piers-Harris Children's Self Concept Scale to study eleven children between the ages of seven and fifteen who were suffering from malignant diseases at various stages of progression. She found that 82 percent of the children said they were sick a lot, none indicated that they were leaders in games or sports and 64 percent said that they would rather work alone than with a group. These findings contrasted greatly with a comparison group of seven children with their limbs in casts. None of the comparison group said that they were sick a lot, 57 percent said they were leaders and none wanted to work on their own.

With this information in mind it becomes increasingly important that we pay careful attention not to minimize the trauma faced when children attend oncology clinics. Explanation of procedures, familiarity of personnel, closeness of parents and openness of communication all reduce the natural anxiety which children must inevitably experience. Although staff may find explanations of procedures time consuming, the cooperation achieved makes the process more efficient. In addition, greater trust is built into the relationship between the child and the staff.

Hair Loss: An Example of Bodily Concern

Children who undergo cranial radiation or are subjected to extensive chemotherapy often lose their hair and remain totally or partially bald for many months. Anderson (1976) in her study found that in the Netherlands the major concern was to maintain the child's body image and quality of life. In Great Britain the significance of hair loss was viewed to be important to individual patients. In the United States there was a greater tendency to pay attention to the process of the disease and to chemotherapy, than to focus on the child's loss of hair. Anderson implies that the response of children seems closely linked to the attitude of his parents. She indicates that if hair loss is not linked to parental love and parents show patience and understanding, children will accept this bodily change in a matter-of-fact manner.

In our experience, it was also apparent that peer acceptance seemed to be a factor worthy of recognition, as peers are often a major source of antagonism for the child who has lost his hair. In order to explore the impact of hair loss in more detail, Dafoe, (1977) in her study, added a hair-questionnaire to the Piers-

Harris Self-Concept Scale and asked the child to draw three pictures reflecting how he saw himself in the past, the present and the future. Dafoe found that although she could not draw many specific conclusions she could say that: (1) the child's self-concept does change negatively after the initial hair loss and any subsequent hair loss; (2) there is no difference in the mean self-concept score between males and females; (3) there is a positive correlation between the self-concept score and the time span since diagnosis; (4) children who have not relapsed tend to have a higher self-concept score than those who have; and (5) there is a positive correlation between the child's self-concept and the number of siblings in the nuclear family. Dafoe suggests that the children's drawings of themselves reflect an alteration in body image but that this was not readily apparent in the results of the self-concept scale. When she applied the hair-loss questionnaire to nine of the eleven children she found that most were well informed about the reasons for their baldness.

In her other findings, Dafoe learned that about half of the children had been helped by the teacher in their efforts to maintain their school work and to explain the illness to other children. She also found that the support of families was extremely important. When asked about head apparel only four children wore nothing on their heads in public while three wore wigs and the remainder wore hats or similar apparel. One child initially went to school bald but began to wear a wig because her mother wanted her to. She was the only child to wear a wig in the presence of her family. When asked about their needs the children stressed the importance of reassuring the child that his hair would grow back and that radiation will not hurt.

The Child's Concerns About His Illness and His Relationship With Others

After the diagnosis of childhood malignancy the child is prone to being treated differently than before. He feels the change in his parents, his relatives and others like his teacher or the family doctor. He also feels more insecure in the presence of his friends and classmates and has an even greater need than before to be accepted by his peers and to regain his status in the community, at school, on his baseball team or wherever he has been known socially. As a person whose life has changed markedly, the child needs to be able to do his own type of mourning for his loss of status and requires time to help him accept permanent changes in his parents' behavior or his style of living. He has a right to feel angry when he is restricted or subjected to procedures. He has a right to be depressed because he feels rotten or deprived or rejected. Unfortunately, he may also be made to feel guilty because he believes himself to be responsible for cancelling the family's vacation or keeping his parents at home at night. Sometimes he may feel guilty because he believes his illness to be a form of punishment for his misbehavior.

Bluebond-Langner (1974) delineates six stages of awareness through which children pass in learning about their cancer and what is happening to them. In sequence these stages relate to knowledge about: (1) the seriousness of the illness; (2) drug names and side effects; (3) treatment procedures and their purpose; (4) relapse and remission cycle without knowledge of death; and (5) the same cycle including the prognosis of death. In the sixth stage the child internalizes the implications of the prognosis. In the early stages of illness most children learn about the seriousness of their illness quickly. However, learning about the exact diagnosis and its implications depends on the child, the parents and the child's contacts. For the health professional, what is most important is that we recognize that the child from age six on either learns quickly that he can strive harder to keep pace with his peers or he can use his illness and the advantages it offers to control his parents, his friends and his social life. When parents are open, supportive and willing to explain the illness to teachers, who in turn help the child explain it to classmates, the child often responds with amazing strength and maturity greater than his years.

When the social environment in his peer group at school or in the neighborhood inevitably leads to discrimination and resulting emotional trauma, parental support and family life can provide a haven of acceptance. Laura, age seven, had strong parental support. At the beginning of her bout with leukemia she had left school and undergone radiation. When she was about to return, her mother discussed Laura's condition with the teacher, who in turn advised the other pupils. Since Laura had lost her hair she was fitted with a new wig which her parents expected her to wear. After one day at school, Laura returned home to say that no one had teased her and she would not wear the wig. Later, after her death, the teacher recounted how after having missed her morning classes due to attendance at our clinic, Laura would come back to school and demand to know what she had missed. She refused to go outside and play even at recess until all she had missed was explained and completed. Similar situations have occurred with a number of children. Many have excelled in school despite long absences or begged to have a teacher come to their home so that they could keep up with their work. In many cases academic prowess appears to be the major means of compensating for the child's loss of prestige in athletic events when illness has interfered with their ability to participate.

When parents have difficulty disciplining their children, when relatives deluge the child with gifts and when the stability in the life of the child disappears, the confusion and insecurity generated by the loss of boundaries forces the child to act out or manipulate. For instance, after Tammy, age three, developed acute lymphoblastic leukemia her mother became extremely anxious. She continually called the physician and persisted in taking Tammy's temperature frequently. As a result, Tammy quickly learned to use her illness to avoid taking pills and going to clinic. She also used her illness to avoid punishment and to generally do as she pleased. Fortunately, when her mother sought counselling from the pediatric hematology team and realized what was happening, she was able to reverse the situation and Tammy became less manipulative.

Helping the Child on the Ward and in the Ambulatory Clinic

The Importance of Supervised Play Activities

Children must have the opportunity to express their feelings not just before or during treatments but after painful procedures as well. Children especially need this opportunity during the long hours when parents cannot be with them on the ward or during out-patient visits when they might otherwise return home full of trepidation about the next visit. The media of play is an important component in facilitating expression of feeling in children. In our clinic, the child life worker has enabled us to become more aware of the importance of child behavior during treatment and to more fully appreciate how nonverbal expression can help a child release feelings. Such expression helps our team understand what is bothering the child and how we might help reduce anxiety by modifying our approach with him and his family. Verbal expression during play or a picture of the family drawn by the child can also be of great assistance to the social worker and to other team members in assessing the family. Children are usually honest, and their verbal or artistic descriptions often verify or clarify clinical impressions.

For instance, in one situation where there were communication difficulties within the family and other areas of conflict between the parents, it was difficult to know how seven-year-old Carol perceived the family situation and how she felt about the family's problems. It was not possible to do a total family interview and despite the trust which Carol had established with the child life and nursing staff, she would not discuss her feelings. When the child life worker asked her if she would like to draw a picture of her family she proceeded to reflect on paper exactly the same problems her parents had described. In addition, she illustrated her feeling of remoteness from one parent and one sibling. When asked about the meaning of her picture she was then able to discuss her feelings.

In another situation, six-year-old Mavis liked to draw pictures of her house, with the trees around and the sun. Over the course of a few months, she had allowed two of these pictures to remain with the child life worker. Following her relapse after almost three years of therapy, Mavis became quieter and visibly sad. She would not talk about her feelings. Shortly before her death, she drew the same picture, but the colors were drab and the sky was painted black. Although she would not talk about her picture, she had expressed how she felt on paper.

The school teacher on the pediatric ward has been a major facilitator in helping children describe their feelings through their art work. She has also helped the child life staff in their work by encouraging children to write stories and poetry about their feelings related to illness, to hospitals, to their families and to other subjects which bring them joy, relief or sadness. Children who are old enough to write can often describe their concerns very candidly and sometimes rid themselves of a great deal of hostility and anxiety in the process. By the same measure, through play, the child can tell you a great deal about his understanding of his illness, the problems it creates for him and areas in which he needs help to deal with what has happened or is happening to him. Prior to leaving hospital, play can help reduce the anxiety, hostility and regression which Dimock (1959) discusses as being the sequelae of hospitalization. In addition, if such reactions do occur and are severe enough to make the parents concerned, then play can be utilized on an ambulatory basis to help the child work through these intense feelings.

Bone marrows, transfusions and multiple injections, although no less frightening and painful, can become easier if a trained person can facilitate the child's comfort in reenacting the procedures via play. Acceptance of the hospital and of certain types of illness can be facilitated as well. Putting together the child's creativity, imagination and spontaneity with concrete experiences through supervised play helps disperse the anxiety and the anger which his illness and the treatment regimen can create. For example, Judy a seven-year-old with aplastic anemia, by playing with red liquid and transfusion equipment, was able to talk about her feelings more openly and express through her art work her overwhelming preoccupation with blood and her illness.

In a more humorous example, Larry, age five, had been undergoing chemotherapy injections for one year following the removal of a malignant tumor. He came back each week and accepted the treatment with an appropriate release of tears, a modicum of resistance and much silence. One day, prior to clinic, he had the opportunity to play with a basin of water, a syringe and some medical dolls. He took the syringe, filled it with water and sprayed it in the face of the doctor doll and the nurse doll. When asked what he was doing, he was silent. The child life worker asked if he was giving them a needle, at which point he said, "No! I'm peeing all over them!" Larry's expression of feeling exemplifies the need to provide the time, the opportunity, the medium and the understanding necessary to help the child. The child life worker and play therapist can be instrumental in facilitating this understanding and their resourcefulness and knowledge are an asset both in implementing and interpreting play experiences.

Talking With the Child

Paying attention to the words, thoughts and feelings of the child should be a part of each clinic visit and hospitalization. As adults, and particularly as hospital staff and students, we are frequently inept in our approaches to children. Often, when a child has been admitted or is facing an anxiety provoking clinic visit, we avoid talking with the child, thereby reflecting our own inability or desire to listen to him. Time after time, we make comments like "Oh, what a pretty dress you have," or "My, haven't you grown," or "I'll bet that you are glad to miss school on a nice day like this." Such comments are often insensitive and meaningless to the child. He may need diversion from his anxiety, but such comments will do little to facilitate such diversion. The child may benefit from a chance to discuss his feelings or talk about something he enjoys when he feels free to talk and when someone is really listening and really interested in what he has to say. Although we are busy people, talking with the child should not just be the task of the child life worker, but should be an enjoyable experience in which each pediatric staff member and student can share. If we are concerned about the expenditure of time, we should remember that a child has much to contribute to our understanding of how he perceives his illness, how he feels about himself and his family and how he feels about those of us who are treating him. If a child cannot directly discuss such feelings sometimes he will discuss them indirectly. For example, one boy described a school project in which he had discussed his illness with his class. In another situation, eleven-year-old Ronald was having great difficulty accepting his treatments and time was provided for him to come in after school to meet with the play therapist. He was a child who had suffered a great deal during hospitalization from the consequences of the surgical removal of an extensive tumor. During hospitalization and during his brief attendance at the ambulatory clinic he had remained quiet and had not talked about his feelings. When upset he simply became angry and rebelled. Because of his interest in animals the play therapist arranged a tour of the animal laboratory where the chief technician showed him how animals developed tumors and were treated for cancer. When the ensuing discussion centered around the animals and their tumors he was able for the first time to pour out his own feelings, complete with the anger and sadness that he had previously kept hidden from others.

The Familiar Face

The child with a malignant disorder is often a high volume consumer of health care. He relies on the physician, the nurse and other health practitioners to care for him and frequently to comfort him. Just as his parents like to single out a resident or staff physician as a person on whom they can rely heavily and entrust with the care of their child, so also does the child select a small number of persons whom he can trust. Despite the pain and the disruptions which arise from clinic visits and hospital experiences, the child often grows fond of the resident, the nurses and other staff who treat him. When he does need to release his anger, he will often lash out at the staff that he knows care most about him. He recognizes that they will accept his feelings without recrimination. In my experience, one resident was outstanding in his ability to care for children, to love them and to have them love him as well. His success resulted from his genuine concern for them and his willingness to sit down on the floor to talk with them and play. Despite his heavy workload he never made the child feel that he did not have his undivided attention and concern.

When he is hospitalized for the first time in a university

teaching hospital, the newly diagnosed child is faced with the same deluge of personnel who confuse and often upset his parents. He is often subjected to a series of medical consultants and a variety of nurses, interns, residents and other staff. Consequently, it becomes necessary for the ward staff and the attending physician to allow selected staff to spend more time with him. When the child moves to the ambulatory setting it is essential that he is able to recognize the physicians and the nurse who will be responsible for his care. In our setting, we strive to have not only the pediatric hematologist and resident or residents meet the child, but we also have the clinic nurse who will follow the child and his family spend time on the ward with the child and his parents. The consistency in care this arrangement provides lowers the anxiety of both the child and his parents and alleviates the stress which is generated by a change in personnel. In a reverse situation, if the child is hospitalized for a severe infection or for relapse of his disease, the staff from our ambulatory team go into the pediatric ward and continue their interest and involvement with the child and his family. When the child is seriously ill, he will respond best to the physicians, nurses and other staff with whom he is most familiar and with whom he feels safest. The involvement of the ambulatory team in his care will help facilitate continuity. To complement this approach, the head nurse on the pediatric ward tries to assign a primary nurse or nurses who can become familiar with the child and work closely with the ambulatory staff. The relationship with the in-patient nurse or nurses can be an essential support to both the child and his family, especially when it is recognized that the child may be hospitalized frequently over a period of several years. At our Center, children, of their own volition, often come back to the ward to see the ward clerk, the nurses, the school teacher, the child life worker and the social worker, as well as the medical staff. Children frequently bring in pictures, poems, riddles and little handicrafts to the people they care about and who care about them in both the ambulatory and in-patient area. One little boy, when hospitalized, spent five hours very carefully writing a letter to a doctor he had grown to love. Another made paper hats for all the members of the clinic team.

Beyond the ward and the clinic we frequently forget that in the laboratory and in the radiotherapy clinic the same principle applies. Children grow to like specific technicians and in radiotherapy, in particular, they spend considerable time with the radiotherapist and with technicians who help them through what can be a very frightening experience.

When we become engrossed in a busy clinic, we forget to recognize the importance of the long-term community professionals in the child's life. These are people who have known the child and the family for long periods, often since the child's birth. The contribution of the family physician and the minister, priest or rabbi who has the time to visit the child and the family at times of crisis should be recognized. It is easy to forget to include these valuable persons in helping to care for the child.

THE ADOLESCENT WITH MALIGNANCY

Although many of the behavioral responses discussed previously are applicable to the adolescent patient, the adolescent requires special recognition and consideration. Children entering adolescence begin to think like adults and struggle to establish their identity. They face major changes in body image as they grow rapidly and develop secondary sexual characteristics. They struggle for peer acceptance and try to separate themselves from the values of their parents. Erikson (1965) points out that adolescents are preoccupied with how others view them. He also states that

> In their search for continuity and sameness, adolescents have to refight many of the battles of earlier years, even though to do so adolescents must artificially appoint perfectly well meaning adversaries; and they are ever ready to install lasting idols and ideals as guardians of a final identity.

When discussing adolescents with bone cancer, Kagan (1976) emphasizes how the anxiety and conflict of the adolescent makes the diagnosis of a potentially fatal illness more overwhelming for him than for persons in any other age group. For this reason, she and Karon (1973) both stress the importance of denial as a defense mechanism for the adolescent with a malignant disease as a means for shutting out the prognosis. They also support an honest and straightforward approach for discussion of the disease itself as a means of helping the adolescent temper his need to deny.

Other adolescent reactions have been presented by writers such as Kikuchi (1972). She describes the case of a fifteen-year-old adolescent with leukemia and cites how the girl relapsed three times in an eight-year bout with the disease. The girl experienced hair loss three times and quadraparesis. She was angry with the physician who told her the diagnosis, felt that she was in a dream world and when hospitalized wanted desperately to be back home. She was intensely anxious about dying and was very sensitive to the bodily changes caused by her illness.

In their review of 182 adolescents with malignancy, Moore, Holton and Marten (1969) delineated four problem areas experienced by their patients. These included changes in self-concept, changes in body image, difficulties in interpersonal relationships and interference with plans for the future. Loss of self-esteem, loss of hair or limb, conflicts with friends or family and issues related to education, work, marriage and death were the major problems encountered. Plumb and Holland, (1974) in their experience with adolescents with cancer, stress that all of the emotional responses and behaviors of the adolescent patient and those close to him revolve around the specific symptom as a focal point. They found this to be true irregardless of whether the symptom was created as a result of their treatment or was due to the brutality of the disease itself. They point out that at the time of the diagnosis the adolescent may feel mildly bewildered or confused or may be in a state of terror, depending on his physical state. They suggest that as the adolescent patient enters remission he moves from the point where he fears death to a time when he begins feeling different from his peers. He loses his status and may be the center of jokes or unkind remarks. In addition, he may also feel that he is restricted or "entrapped" at the time of relapse. He may also become angry with his parents and with those treating him and be very depressed if he learns of the loss of other patients he has known.

I believe that throughout the illness, the response of parents must be monitored and understood. Relationship gaps, which are necessary and natural between the adolescent and his parents, are often widened, and health practitioners may support the gulf by dealing with adolescents and parents as two complete and separate entities. In reality the adolescent needs the support and comfort which parents offer and parents in turn need help in understanding him. Parents also experience the hopes and fears that inevitably accompany the diagnosis, remission and relapse of their son's or daughter's illness. In practice, their closeness and the knowledge that they have accumulated about their child's behavior through time can be invaluable in facilitating approaches that will help the adolescent deal with this very difficult life experience.

Ambulatory Care for the Adolescent

I am convinced that just as children require constancy in health care personnel, so also does the adolescent. He needs to be able to relate to and to trust a small number of honest people. He also requires time for diversion and time for privacy when faced with ambulatory visits which require him to undergo procedures or to have painful injections that cause nausea and vomiting.

In practical terms, the greatest difficulty for the adolescent who comes for ambulatory treatments is the facing of these painful procedures and injections. They generate intense anxiety in both boys and girls. Drugs like cyclophosphamide produce a metallic taste and subsequent vomiting which for some adolescents lasts for up to three days. The nausea and vomiting assumes major importance and the preoccupation with the clinic visits, the drug and the side effects lead some adolescents to condition themselves to vomit in anticipation. No doubt the intensity of the anxiety not only leads to earlier but also more prolonged vomiting. Vincristine, a drug which at present is often alternated with cyclophosphamide and received every other week, is less apt to cause gastrointestinal symptoms. However, after a few weeks or months the patient may be seen to experience vomiting before or following the vincristine as well. In fact, we have observed that not only have patients become agitated by clinic visits, but they become so intolerant of the smell of the hospital that entry into the hospital precipitates nausea and vomiting which will be more intense on weeks when cyclophosphamide is given but is also present on weeks when the milder vincristine is injected.

To date, attempts to combat such vomiting by antiemetic agents have only been minimally successful. Parental support, as well as discussions with the adolescent and his parent or parents in the company of the social worker, nurse and physician, has sometimes been helpful in encouraging the patient to keep receiving the injections. In one situation, Bill, age 14, had suffered many disruptions in his life due to osteogenic sarcoma. His surgery had made it impossible for him to continue his athletic activities and his frequent visits to the hospital for injections and the days of nausea which followed disrupted his schoolwork and his leadership role in school activities. Bill received excellent support from his parents and he gradually became capable of returning to some of his athletic interests. As he did so, he also recognized that he only had a few months of injections remaining. In order to cope, he requested that he be allowed to go to an area remote from the clinic to await his injection and receive it immediately upon being called over to the out-patient area. When he used this routine in combination with his renewed vitality and interest in life, Bill managed to accept the balance of his treatment with minimal vomiting.

In another instance, Carol, age 17, a patient with Ewing's sarcoma, had problems that increased and progressed during her treatment program. She wanted to rebel and continually threatened not to return. Her mother kept encouraging her until she neared the end of her treatments when Carol rebelled and refused to continue. Since only one month remained her decision was only mildly disputed.

Rose, age 17, received little support from her parents and on her own she could not tolerate the intensity of the ordeal of receiving weekly injections. After one year of a two-year treatment program, she became so overwhelmed by her aversion to the hospital and her injections that she totally refused to continue her treatment program. In the face of these experiences and the difficulties we have encountered we are currently looking toward behavior modification techniques as an approach to try to help the adolescent patient deal with this type of treatment regimen. We have also found that younger children exhibit similar responses but the intensity of the reaction is usually greater in the adolescent patient.

Adolescents with cancer face temporary disfigurement from steroids and sometimes permanent disfigurement from radiation, surgery and metastasis. Sometimes chemotherapy may threaten the adolescent girl with sterility at a crucial time when she is beginning to contemplate life as a sexual being and a potential bearer of children. I believe that helping the adolescent cope with bodily changes requires sensitivity, understanding and the willingness of parents and staff to provide emotional support and reassurance. As Joe, one of our fifteen-year-old patients with leukemia, pointed out, "Talk to them (adolescent patients), show them that you care, that's what is most important." When asked how he knew that someone cared he said, "You can feel it somehow."

Susan, a seventeen-year-old with cancer who became very thin as a result of her disease, expressed how hard it was for her to fit in at school. She stated that she felt different from other girls even though on the surface she maintained most of her school activity and drove herself to live as normal a life as possible. She stressed the importance of the support of her family to her, but at times she felt isolated even from them, especially when she relapsed and her family had problems facing the fact that she was going to die.

In caring for the adolescent I think that it is crucial not to assume that he knows all about his illness. We must find out directly how much he knows so that we can sensitively tell him as much as he wants to know at any given point in time. Although denial is used frequently, there are times when denial can be mistaken for ignorance about the medical facts and prognosis related to the illness itself. It is necessary to explore the adolescent's feelings and provide emotional support so that the isolation, denial and displacement of his feelings can be minimized (Kagan, 1976). As Karon (1973) points out, staff should never hide behind the fact that since the adolescent does not ask questions they can safely assume he does not want to know.

Hospitalization and the Adolescent

Many of the needs of the adolescent which are visible in ambulatory care reemerge when he is hospitalized. His need for constancy in care, for honesty about his illness, his prognosis and his treatment regimen and for acceptance by his parents remains the same. In hospital, however, his need for socialization with others the same age and for contact with his peers increases. He wants to feel he belongs and that he can continue to participate in group activities and share group experiences as much, and as often as his physical condition permits. If he is not mobile, an effort should be made to move him into an area where he can converse with other teens and where he can participate in social activities, see out the window, use the telephone or do schoolwork. He also requires intellectual challenges and the chance to give to others. Diversionary activities such as preparation of a poster or completion of a model may be of great value to an adolescent patient, especially at a time when he has severe doubts about himself and about what his illness is doing to him. Helping younger children on the ward to play, to eat or to organize a party are examples of how a teenager can feel he is useful.

Fatigue, normal needs for reflection and the pace set forth by continued tests and treatments dictate the need for privacy, rest and sleep. It is imperative that the nursing staff in particular recognize that they may have to protect the adolescent patients' rights by enforcing visiting rules, realizing that examinations, treatments and waiting periods in hospital are tiring and that a suitable time for sleep at night is mandatory. Malignant disorders compounded by infection make the adolescent more easily fatigued, more traumatized than most other patients and more in need of the attention and protection of the staff.

Just as the adolescent with cancer needs privacy and rest, so also does he need to move around. One patient complained that the intravenous did not hurt him, but it really slowed him down when he had to adjust it at every doorway. Another complained that hospitalization hampered her physical fitness program. Most adolescents want to be mobile. Kagan (1976) discusses how adolescents after major surgery or amputation often have unrealistic expectations about mobility. There is a need for staff to help the teenager realize this. In our experience we have found that mobility is a major stimulus for increasing the adolescent's desire to return home and, consequently, the desire to be mobile can be used to the patient's advantage. It becomes important for staff to allow the adolescent to go shopping for birthday or Christmas presents or to return home on weekends if his physical condition permits such outings.

Hospitalization generates anxiety and often anger and sadness for all adolescents, not just the adolescent with cancer. For example, several teenage boys with varied illnesses were on the ward for several days together. They began to be destructive by damaging the billiard table, breaking Ping-Pong bats and setting fire to Ping-Pong balls. Their behavior led to a confrontation in which they finally revealed that they were having difficulty relating to several mentally retarded children on the ward. When the child life staff included the boys in the activities of the mentally retarded children, they became very willing to help care for them and the destructive behavior of the boys ceased. In another situation, fifteen-year-old Joe, the patient I mentioned earlier, became very irritable and visibly sad. When questioned, he related how upsetting it was for him to leave his brothers and sisters and how angry he was that his leukemia was stopping him from helping his father on the farm.

The adolescent facing a life-threatening illness at diagnosis, at relapse or at terminal stages often needs the time to talk with an objective, caring adult, apart from his parents. Naturally he will choose the person whom he trusts. Because of availability, this may be a child life worker who relates with him on the ward or the nurse who provides him with his physical care and generates a trusting relationship. Sometimes staff members may readily fill the role of a surrogate mother or sister, or for girls, the nurse or child life worker may be an identity figure. In other situations, the physician whom he views as controlling his care may be the most important person with whom he will share his feelings. Similarly the objectivity of the social worker or chaplain may be of value. The feelings of trust which can be established between the adolescent and medical and nursing staff are essential in the maintenance of humanistic and personal health care. During lengthy hospitalizations, painful procedures, physical pain from illness and in situations where there is loss of control of bodily functions, this trust and understanding lessens the emotional stress. Communication with people who care can also help increase the tolerance of pain and work through the anxiety and anger related to traumatic events. This type of positive relationship will also help ensure that the necessity for rest and privacy can be communicated by the patient to the staff. Embarrassment over mishaps such as nocturnal emissions or incontinence will be minimized because of the genuine acceptance and understanding provided by the staff.

In summing up, I believe that in attempting to meet the needs of adolescents, including those with malignant disease, hospital ward care should include:

(a) Humanistic, personalized care complete with honest, open communication and time to talk about problems.
(b) Time for privacy and rest.
(c) Flexible visiting which meets both the needs of the patient and of the staff.
(d) Activities and opportunities for adolescents to meet, play and work in groups.
(e) As much mobility as possible while minimizing withdrawal and isolation.
(f) Opportunities for intellectual stimulation and achievement.
(g) Rules that can be negotiated concerning cleanliness, neatness, bedtime and noise. By mutual agreement these rules should be binding.
(h) Means of maintaining contact with the outside world through provision of telephones, opportunities to go out for walks, chances to go home overnight or for the weekend, etc.
(i) Respect for the uniqueness and individuality of each adolescent.

NORMAL LIVING AND LONG-TERM SURVIVAL

Throughout this chapter I have reflected a continuing concern for the child and the adolescent in the face of the stressful experiences which accompany malignant diseases. It is important, however, that we recognize that there are bright spots in the child's life and that during remission when a child is feeling well he will resume most, if not all, of the activities he undertook prior to the onset of his disease. When he feels well and those around him allow it, he can appear to be physically, emotionally and socially the same as any healthy, disease-free child. If he is fortunate enough to have no permanent physical impairment and remains in remission permanently, then he becomes a long-term survivor, a child who can carry on life the same as the next person. In Chapter 1, when deficits of a study of ten-year survivors by Holmes and Holmes (1975) were cited, the need to pay careful attention to the long-term survivor was stressed, and the balance of this chapter is directed toward meeting this need.

Today a small number of children with leukemia and a greater number of children with malignancies such as Hodgkins' disease (stages 1 and 2) are already long-term survivors. As chemotherapy improves, increasing numbers of children with malignancies will be cured (Sutow and Sullivan, 1976). Consequently, there is a need to take up the challenge of Van Eys (1976) and recognize that we need to do everything possible to enable a child who is cured to live a normal life.

Cure: A Dilemma for Everyone

The possibility of cure creates a major dilemma for the child and his family. Van Eys (1977) states that complete removal of the cancer from the child's life denies a major part of the child's reality. By the same token, to center the child's life on the cancer denies the child life in the normal world. This dilemma is reflected in our approach to patient care. Despite the fact that the child may be cured, the medical profession cannot risk the cessation of follow-up examinations. Cancer patients are required to return to cancer treatment centers for years, perhaps for the rest of their lives, to be subjected to diagnostic tests and medical examinations. On the positive side, this follow-up process is an insurance measure which can result in early identification of a recurrence of the cancer. In addition, the follow-up care contributes to medical knowledge. On the negative side, the message is clear that cures are only possible or probable. Cures are never guaranteed. The family and the child cannot take for granted the expectation of health and long-term survival that most families anticipate when children are deemed to be healthy.

Changing our Approach to Care

The uncertainty described previously and the major impact of the illness on the child and the family inevitably affects the approach of the pediatric hematologist or oncologist and the health-care team. These physicians and their associates from other disciplines are highly specialized in their patient-care practices. The nature of care that they provide necessitates a disease and problem-oriented approach to all aspects of patient care. Consequently, the development of an orientation to care that provides sufficient security and freedom for the child to parallel activities of his healthy peers is extremely difficult. This task requires the integration of a health-oriented model which has been, out of necessity, alien to the care of the pediatric cancer patient. In practice, this integration requires ongoing evaluation and reevaluation of care similar to the process required in administering chemotherapy. Chemotherapy protocols must be continually reevaluated. This reevaluation takes into account the patient's medical condition and facilitates the addition of agents that enhance the efficiency of treatment. In the psychosocial area, achievement of change in the attitudes and approaches of members of the clinic team can only be obtained when disciplines can honestly and openly strive to place the needs of the child first. They must reevaluate their approach frequently and share their hopes and their doubts about the child's illness with each other and with families as well. Belief in the benefits gained from medical progress must be integrated into the daily practice of the clinic. Because clinic staff are working with such a variety of patients at various stages of illness and because some patients inevitably die, this integration is in itself a major challenge.

In our experience at McMaster we have learned that the process of changing our approach is gradual and very much related to the knowledge developed in our close working relationship with the child and his family. Observations and feedback from the child and family members reflect the fact that we have a great deal to learn about the lasting impact of the illness on the child and to a lesser extent on his family. We have recognized, however, that the nature of the relationship that we have established with the child and his family has had a positive and marked effect on the family's ability to adapt to long-term survival. It appears that the child has benefitted from this relationship as well because families are helped to approach their lives realistically. They are also helped to work through their feelings and are encouraged to openly and honestly support each other.

Helping the Child and His Family Toward Normal Living

In a number of cases, children with solid tumors live essentially normal lives after completion of chemotherapy and radiotherapy. Physical activity, school attendance, socialization and regular family life are not altered radically. The threat to life, however, remains, and the intensity of family concern will vary in keeping with the perceived threat of the illness as governed by factors such as past experience, family functioning, the emotional status of family members and the assimilation of pertinent medical information.

In acute lymphoblastic leukemia of childhood, remissions are lengthening and, therefore, increasing numbers of children can live nearly normal lives after the initial diagnosis and the onslaught of diagnostic procedures, induction therapy and radiation. Clinic visits become less frequent and if the child is maintained on an oral medication the side effects may well be tolerable. Thus, the strain of the uncertainty of the illness, although present, becomes less acute and the intensity of concern reduces but never disappears. The risk of infection, the need to limit physical activity to varying degrees and the necessity to comply with medical treatment are also subtle reminders that the illness could return. If parents during remission, and particularly during the first remission, can resume family life similar to the period before diagnosis with as complete a range of activity as possible, then I believe that the child seems to suffer little both psychologically and socially. As Timmons (1976) states leukemia is not so bad when most activities done prior to the illness may be continued during the disease process. In addition, children tend to be oriented to the present and can often leave past difficulties with treatment experiences behind and return quickly to their regular activities at home and at school. This is especially true when treatment experiences have been mostly positive, medication has been given orally and hospitalization has been infrequent.

As the chances of survival improve, life at school, in the playground and at home can be a happy, fulfilling experience. The issue of death and the need for terminal care becomes more remote. The need to tell the child that he might die becomes less acute. The situation does not mean, however, that he is completely free of anxiety about his illness or that he does not perceive the threat to his life. In fact, children are very perceptive. They experience the changes in the family and they feel the changes in their parents and in their older siblings. They may not interpret their parents' feelings exactly, but they know things are not right. Sherman (1976), speaking as a parent, points out that the child with leukemia has experienced both painful procedures and hospitalization. She suggests that his self-concept has been "severely damaged and will not immediately be repaired in remission." Despite our personal optimism, parents say that the label leukemia and often the label cancer means "death sentence." Children will feel what their parents believe. It becomes very important not to frighten children with overwhelming information but to encourage parents to talk with their children, to answer questions and to be as positive as possible about the prognosis, in accordance with their own beliefs, feelings and actual knowledge. Children can mature and grow by facing life experiences and should be given the chance to do so.

When the child is a long-term survivor it is crucial that the physician utilize the opportunity provided by the cessation of treatment to reinforce his belief that the child will live a long and healthy life, if in fact he believes that this will be the case.

I believe that as long as they feel well physically and emotionally, children can get the most out of their lives, no matter how long they live. Children often have an amazing ability to achieve much more than adults believe is possible, especially if they are given the chance to release their anxiety about their illness and their prognosis. Needless to say, parents have to avoid smothering and over-protecting their child (Kulenkamp, 1976). They must also pace family life to a day-by-day fulfillment. Where possible, medical care should be given at home and be as nontoxic but as effective as possible. When a child has the opportunity for healthy survival beyond the initial treatment protocol, then the minimization of medical care, the ability of the family to reduce tension related to the illness and the gradual reintegration of long-term goals in the life of the family and child are all necessary to help make life as normal as possible.

REFERENCES

Dimock, H.: *The Child in Hospital*, MacMillan Co., Toronto, 1959.

Plank, E.: *Working with Children in Hospital*. Case Western Reserve University, Cleveland, 1962.

Sherman, M.: *The Leukemic Child*. U.S. Department of Health, Education and Welfare, Washington, 1976.

Langford, W.: "The Child in the Pediatric Hospital — Adaptation to Illness and Hospitalization." *Am J Orthopsychiatry*, 31:667-684, 1961.

Oremland, E.K. and Oremland, J.D. (eds.): *The Effects of Hospitalization on Children and Models for Their Care*. Charles C Thomas Publisher, Springfield, Illinois, 1973.

Bowlby, J.: "Separation Anxiety." *Int J Psychoanal* 41, 89-113, 1960.

Heinicke, C.M. and Westheimer, I.: *Brief Separations*. International Universities Press, New York, 1965.

Heinicke, C.M.: "Parental Deprivation in Early Childhood; A Predisposition to Later Depression." *Separation and Depression: Clinical and Research Aspects*. Edited by Edward C. Senay, Symposium, American Association for the Advancement of Science, 1971.

Jessner, L., Blom, G. and Waldfogel, S.: "Emotional Implications of Tonsillectomy and Adenoidectomy on Children." *Psychoanal Study Child*, 7:126-169, 1952.

Nagy, M.: "The Child's Theories Concerning Death," *J Gen Psychol* 73:3-27, 1948.

Waechter, E.H.: "Children's Awareness of Fatal Illness." *Am J Nurs* 71, 1168-1172, 1971.

Spinetta, J.J., Rigler, D. and Karon, M.: "Anxiety in the Dying Child." *Pediatr*, 52:841-849, 1973.

Blom, G.E.: "The Reactions of Hospitalized Children to Illness." *Pediatr*, 22:11, 590-600, 1958.

Hofmann, A.D., Becker, R.D. and Gabriel, H.P.: *The Hospitalized Adolescent: A Guide to Managing the Ill and Injured Youth.* The Free Press, New York, 1976.

Kenny, T.J.: "The Hospitalized Child." *Pediatr Clin N Am*, 22:3, 583-593, 1975.

Cameron, N.: *Personality Development and Psychopathology: A Dynamic Approach.* Houghton Mifflin Company, Boston, 1963.

Kübler-Ross, E.: *On Death and Dying,* Macmillan Publishing Co. Ltd., New York, 1969.

Lidz, T.: *The Person:* Basic Books Inc., Publishers, New York, 1968.

Stacey, E., Dearden, R., Pill, R. and Robinson, D.: *Hospitals, Children and Their Families.* Routledge and Kegan-Paul, London, 1970.

Harvey, S. and Hales-Tooke, A.: *Play in Hospital.* Faber and Faber, London, 1972.

Petrillo, M. and Sanger, S.: *Emotional Care of Hospitalized Children: An Environmental Approach.* J. B. Lippincott Company, Philadelphia, 1972.

Klinzing, D.R. and Klinzing, D.G.: *The Hospitalized Child: Communication Techniques for Health Personnel.* Prentice-Hall, Inc., Englewood Cliffs, N.J., 1977.

Van Eys, J.: *The Truly Cured Child: The New Challenge in Pediatric Cancer Care.* University Park Press, Baltimore, Md., 1977.

Hoffman, I. and Futterman, E.H.: "Coping With Waiting: Psychiatric Intervention and Study in the Waiting Room of a Pediatric Oncology Clinic." *Comp Psychiat* 12:1, 67-81, 1971.

McCollum, A.T.: *Coping With Prolonged Health Impairment in Your Child.* Little, Brown and Company (inc.), Boston, Mass., 1975.

Morrisey, J.R.: "Children's Adaptation to Fatal Illness." *Soc Wk* 8:81-88, 1963.

Piaget, J.: *The Language and Thought of the Child.* Meridian Books, The World Publishing Company, Cleveland, Ohio, 1955.

Goggin, E.L., Lansky, S.G., Hassanein, K.: "Psychological Reactions of Children with Malignancies." *J Am Acad Child Psychiatry* 15:2, 314-325, 1976.

Waechter, E.: "Children's Reactions to Fatal Illness." *Death and Presence.* Edited by A. Godin. Lumen Vitae Press, Brussels, 1972.

Spinetta, J.J.: "Communication Patterns in Families of Children with Life Threatening Illness." Paper presented at a postgraduate symposium.

"The Child and Death," University of Rochester, Rochester, N.Y. September 15, 1977.

Dafoe, M.: *The Effects of Hair Loss on the Body Image of Children with Cancer.* Clinical Study, Master of Health Sciences Program, McMaster University, Hamilton, Ontario, December 1977. (unpublished)

Anderson, J.M.: "Health Care Approaches to Hair Loss in Children with Cancer." *Home Care for the Dying Child: Professional and Family Perspectives.* I.M. Martinson (ed.), Appleton-Century-Crofts, New York, 1976.

Bluebond-Langner, M.: "I Know Do You? A Study of Awareness, Communication and Coping in Terminally Ill Children." *Anticipatory Grief.* B. Schoenberg et al. (eds.). See Chapter 3.

Erikson, E.: *Childhood and Society.* Penguin Books Ltd., Harmondsworth, Middlesex, England, 1965, p. 253.

Kagan, B.: "Use of Denial in Adolescents With Bone Cancer." *Health and Soc Work,* 1:4, 71-87, 1976.

Karon, M.: "The Physician and the Adolescent with Cancer." *Pediatr Clin N Am* 20:4, 965-973, 1973.

Kikuchi, J.: "A Leukemic Adolescent's Verbalization About Dying." *Mat Child Nurs J* 1:259-264, 1972. Also see Kikuchi, J.: "An Adolescent Boy's Adjustment to Leukemia." *Mat Child Nurs J* 6:1, 37-49, 1977.

Moore, D.C., Holton, C.P. and Marten, G.W.: "Psychologic Problems in the Management of Adolescents with Malignancy." *Clin Pediatr* 8:8, 464-473, 1969.

Plumb, M.M. and Holland, J.: "Cancer in Adolescents: The Symptom is the Thing." *Anticipatory Grief.* B. Schoenberg et al. (eds.), Columbia University Press, New York, 1974.

Holmes, H.A. and Holmes, F.F.: "After Ten Years, What are the Handicaps and Life Styles of Children Treated for Cancer?" *Clin Pediatr* 14:819-823, 1975.

Van Eys, J.: "Supportive Care for the Child with Cancer." *Pediatr Clin N Am* 23:1, 215-224, 1976.

Sutow, W.W. and Sullivan, M.P.: "Childhood Cancer: The Improving Prognosis." *Postgrad Med* 59:2, 131-137, 1976.

Timmons, A.L.: "Leukemia: Is It So Awful?" *J Pediatr* 88:1, 147-148, 1976.

Kulemkamp, E.: "Eric: A Mother's Recollection." *Home Care for the Dying Child: Professional and Family Perspectives.* I.M. Martinson (ed.), Appleton-Century-Crofts, New York, 1976.

CHAPTER 6

CHILDREN AND DEATH

U P until the last few years many malignant diseases of childhood led to the death of the patient. For example, in their study of 655 children who developed malignant diseases in the period from 1944 to 1963, Holmes and Holmes (1975) found that 79.6 percent of the children died. Although the length of survival has improved markedly in many cancers, we must recognize that even today some children die. For instance, in acute lymphoblastic leukemia 50 percent of the children diagnosed may die within five years; and in the sarcomas, neuroblastomas and some cranial malignancies even higher percentages of the children will die. When a child dies, we, as hospital staff, often have great difficulty facing the death. The physician in particular is prone to interpreting the child's death as a personal failure, and the nurses and the rest of those who participate in the child's care feel the emotional pain of losing a person for whom they have cared. The death of a person at any age brings us face to face with our own mortality. Death in childhood and the anxiety it generates can be carried over to our family members, particularly when we have young children at home. Those of us who have not had the experience of working through the meaning of our own death and the experience of facing the loss of a number of children in our clinical practices, find ourselves in a similar situation to the child's family. For the family, relatives, neighbors and most of the general populace, death is not usually associated with children. Fredlund (1976) points out that in 1900, 53 percent of all deaths in the United States were attributed to children under the age of 15. Children in the family were part of the death experience as most people died at home. By 1974, only 7 percent of deaths in America were children under the age of 15. Today, children are expected to live and most people have not had the unfortunate experience of having a child die. Consequently, when any of us as parents are forced to face the death of a child, we lack the knowledge necessary to help the child and to cope with our own feelings as we prepare for and face the death.

As staff who are caring for dying children, we can benefit from the specialized knowledge found in the literature as an adjunct to the personal growth which is generated through helping the child and his family cope with the actual death experience.

The Child's Concept of Death

In our efforts to understand the impact of death on children, it is helpful to briefly review the literature. Share (1972) in her extensive review noted that Anthony (1940), Nagy (1948), Safier (1964), and Gartley and Bernasconi (1967) found in their studies of children and death that the child's concept of death evolved developmentally. Children under the age of five viewed death as being reversible and as a type of separation. Children ages six to nine saw death as resulting from the acts of others, often as a type of punishment for wrongdoing or thoughts of wrongdoing. Beyond the age of ten death was viewed as being personal and universal.

Children Under the Age of Six

Adler (1969), by combining the works of Alexander and Adlerstein (1958) and Wahl (1958) with his own experience, concludes that children under the age of five years have difficulty distinguishing the difference between life and death. They associate death with immobility and sense it to be unpleasant. In addition, they often associate death with sleep and view a dead body as being able to function the same as a live body. They feel that they can still communicate with dead people even when the dead are buried or thought to be in heaven. Benoliel (1975) reminds us that Bowlby (1961) and others found that children under five years of age responded with separation anxiety rather than considering their own deaths. Bowlby describes separation anxiety in relation to the phases of protest, despair and detachment. In our experience, when children have suffered from pain and malaise as they approach death they become more difficult to manage. We have often seen a child rebel and resist treatments with all of his might. Similarly, we have seen that young children can be very demanding and particularly unreasonable with their mothers or fathers. Mothers have been commanded to remain in the room, to make specific types of food available instantly or to play the same game over and over. When children have remained in hospital for long periods and have been subjected to repeated treatments, they have often become sad, sometimes tearful and cry even when faced with minor changes in their daily routine. When children have experienced much suffering we have seen that they sometimes tend to withdraw and become almost totally mute, rejecting any attempts to communicate with them. In respect to the dying child, protest, despair and detachment are not usually clear-cut phases. The child's behavior often fluctuates in a manner which closely parallels his physical state and his security.

In other writings, Zeligs (1967) notes that children ages three to six years fashion their ideas about death from their parents' behavior toward it. In addition, they tend to associate death with darkness. Gartley and Bernasconi (1967) state that children can accept death in a matter-of-fact manner but acquire a fear of death through observation of adult behavior.

Children Ages Six to Nine Years

Plank (1964) suggests that children in this age range associate death with being man made. Adler (1969) points out that the child relates death to injuries caused by violence. The child recognizes that death can happen to him, but only if it occurs by accident. In keeping with the magical thought processes of this age-group and fears of mutilation, death often becomes mysterious and related to evil or wrongdoing. Gartley and Bernasconi (1967) and Koocher (1974) found that the concept of personification of death described by Nagy (1948) in relation to children in this age range was not found in their studies. Gartley and Bernasconi (1967) attribute this attitude to knowledge gained through television and to religious beliefs of the

Roman Catholic children in their study. Koocher (1974) suggests that the difference was due to cultural variations between Nagy's Hungarian subjects and the American children used in his study. I believe that the difference can be attributed to the influx of knowledge to children through television and other media. This influx has suddenly shifted the way children have attempted to master their feelings about death over the past twenty years. I agree with Koocher (1974) when he suggests that American children have tended to find mastery through knowledge of detail related to the causes of death.

In our experience, dying children in this age range combine both the separation anxiety found in younger children and the mutilation anxiety attributed to their own age group. We have seen eight-year-olds who have responded with the protest, despair and detachment described by Bowlby along with the development of an intense, almost symbiotic relationship with their mothers. In addition, we have seen children become intensely concerned about their limbs or about specific injections. They have responded with such physical protest and irrational anxiety that the carrying out of medical procedures has been rendered almost impossible.

In this age range as well there is a tendency for the child to reason and to seek a resolution of death in his own mind. For example, six-year-old Gail, a child who was suffering from a fatal blood disease, told the child life worker how she wanted to go to heaven to talk with God to ask him to end her suffering.

Siblings in this age range who lose a brother or sister often respond to the death with an intense emotional reaction. There is a need to carefully examine the child's belief about the death as the child may feel that the death of his brother or sister has been precipitated by something he has done or wished would happen. Children tend not only to attribute death to the acts of other people but they tend to blend fact and fantasy. At ages six and seven in particular they tend to have difficulty separating fantasy from reality.

Children After the Age of Nine Years

By the age of ten and sometimes earlier, children see death as an event which is primitive, inevitable and affecting all life. The nine or ten-year-old may talk about his own death and incorporate into his own understanding the loss of neighbors, friends of the family and sometimes the death of one of his grandparents. If he suffers from the loss of someone close to him, he can grieve with the full knowledge that the person will never return and that he personally cannot ever again participate in life experiences with the deceased. In order to understand children in this age range and into the remainder of preadolescence, Benoliel (1975) stresses the importance of recognizing that the child can suffer from guilt feelings. He has learned that at times he has behaved in ways which have been unfair to the deceased and suffers from the fact that he has been unable to apologize. In some instances, he may bear lasting feelings of guilt. I have seen this occur when a child was in constant conflict with his father and the father died suddenly from a coronary. The boy felt that he had caused his father's death and could not resolve his ambivalence about his father. The guilt he suffered thereafter was so severe that it was necessary for him to receive psychiatric help.

Portz (1972) emphasizes the fact that although the preadolescent sees death as being inevitable, he may not see death as a life event affecting himself or those close to him. For example, Wayne, a twelve-year-old with leukemia who attended our clinic, had established a close relationship with another boy with the same disease. When he learned about his illness he seemed to take the situation in his stride. After his friend died, however, he became quite upset and for the first time seemed to realize that he might die from his illness as well. When returning for clinic visits after his friend's death, he tended to be more anxious and less communicative than previously.

As children enter adolescence, they tend to experience a great deal of anxiety when they are confronted with the subject of death. They are at a point in their lives when they are contemplating adulthood complete with careers and families. The threat of their own death is often overwhelming (Benoliel 1975). This is one reason why adolescents will often associate death with old age (Green-Epner 1976).

In his work Gullo (1973) attempts to categorize the types of reactions to death which he believes occur after the age of ten years and which are prevalent in the teen years. These reactions include those of the "death acceptor" and "death denier," with each representing a realistic and a nonrealistic approach respectively. Gullo also suggests that some patients are characteristic of a "death submitter" who upon learning about the seriousness of his illness becomes helpless and overwhelmed. He describes other patients as being "death facilitators," people who contribute to their own demise through acts such as refusing treatments or failing to take medications. Other patients may be "death transcenders" who internalize a religious or existential philosophy of life and seek death as a part of a continuum. Still others may be "death defiers" who will not give in to death but express anger and fight to maintain their freedom and dignity. Gullo recognizes that a dying patient may exhibit several of these responses at various points in his experience with death. Gullo's categories are of value when we recognize that often the adolescent will respond with greater emotional intensity than the adult patient. I will discuss the responses of the adolescent patient in more detail later on in this chapter.

Helping Parents Educate the Child About Death

Educating children about death and integrating death as part of the experiences faced in daily life is a problem that parents have seemed more willing to face in recent years. In fact, the general public through the mass media have been helped to rediscover the subject of death. This revival of interest is reflected in the literature for children on the subject of death. Such books were written during the 1800s and then virtually disappeared until the early 1970s (Marshall and Marshall 1971, Aradine 1976).

Although it is useful for children to read about death, the most worthwhile approach is for parents to talk to their children. The most useful advice has been set forth by Wolfe (1958) and later by Grollman (1967, 1971). Grollman (1971) advocates the use of indirect discussion as a means of initiating a dialogue between parents and child. In fact, he provides an example of this in a discussion between a parent and his child which relates the death of leaves and other things to the death of the child's grandfather. In our approach to helping parents to educate their child about death, we have followed Grollman's guidelines. We have learned that it is important to let the child tell the parent about death. When the child asks questions the adult should listen and once he is sure about what he has heard he should answer the child's questions simply and then stop. Children are naturally curious and death should be related to things that the child can understand as part of his everyday life. It is imperative that death should not be associated with sleep, with long journeys or with God's desire to take the person away. It is very easy for the child to fantasize that the same thing will happen to him (Grollman 1967). Similarly, it is not appropriate to say that a person died because he was sick. Instead, it is better to explain that sometimes when people become very ill or badly hurt the doctors cannot always make them well, so they die. Sometimes this explanation can be associated with the death of a cat or dog so that it ties into the child's own experience and may relate to the end of the animal's suffering.

If the child experiences the death of someone close to him, it is important that he does not feel that he has been abandoned or rejected. He needs to know that it is alright to be sad, to cry and to talk about the dead person. If the parent allows the child to see his or her own grief and is secure in sharing the experience with other family members, then the child learns to cope with the experience in a similar manner. When children have been bereaved we have found that the expression of feelings through art and play can be very worthwhile for the child. I am convinced that the more parents can face death and discuss death with comfort, the more children can understand and accept the experience of loss themselves.

Death and the Child with a Malignant Disease

There has been a great deal written on this subject, as many children have died from leukemia and solid tumors. The death experience has taught us a great deal about child behavior associated with death but this has in no way made the emotional strain on us any easier. Instead, an understanding of the child's response facilitates a modification in our approach to make his health care as humane and comforting as possible.

In studying children with leukemia, Richmond and Waisman (1955) and Hoffman and Futterman (1971) describe them as being passive, isolated, depressed and dependent on parents. They did not, however, show open concern about death. Knudson and Natterson (1960) and Morrisey (1963), in observing fatally ill children, paralleled the findings of earlier works by researchers such as Nagy (1948) when they attributed the fear of separation to children under the age of five years, the fear of mutilation to children ages five to ten years and the realistic fear of death as a universal entity to children over the age of ten. In a very important study Waechter (1971) compared 64 children ages six to ten who were in four categories, i.e. those with life-threatening, chronic and brief illnesses and those who were well. She revealed that when the prognosis was poor, the child's body integrity was threatened. Consequently, he was more likely to discuss loneliness, separation and death. Even though the child had not been directly informed of his diagnosis, he was most definitely preoccupied with fantasies of death. Waechter states that children become more isolated emotionally when adults are evasive, especially at a time when a child wants to express his feelings. Waechter's findings endorse Share's bias for an open, honest and straightforward approach to care (Share 1972). Spinetta and his associates (1974) found that children with leukemia in the age range of six to ten related more stories concerned with mutilation anxiety than children who were chronically ill or children who were free of illness. In later studies, his group found that as children with leukemia became increasingly ill they became more remote from their parents and the hospital staff. When parents were open and honest with the child about his illness and prognosis, he became less remote from his parents and the hospital staff than children who were equally as ill but came from families where open communication about the child's illness was avoided. This is true throughout the period of terminal care up to and including the child's death.

In her experience with dying children, Green-Epner (1976) emphasizes the need for communication which will enable the child to release his feelings. She states that the child must not only be able to understand but also overcome his fears and anxieties. Pacyna (1970) suggests that hospital staff inhibit the child's expression of feelings. She emphasizes the importance of allowing the child to continue to work on small projects which he started when he felt well and stresses the value of allowing the dying child to be cared for by one regular member of the nursing staff.

In discussing one example of home care, Etzel (1976) points out how children are aware of death and describes how much Marty, a six-year-old, wanted to remain at home at the time when his physical condition was deteriorating. As death approached he said, "This is it, isn't it Mom?" Etzel emphasizes how he was able to die in peace, where he wanted to be and with those who loved him.

Klinzing and Klinzing (1977) suggest that if a child is told he may die he needs to be assured that there is still hope, that he will not be abandoned and that he will always have access to someone who cares about him and who will talk to him.

I think that there is no substitute for having the parent or parents remain with the child to love, to hold and to comfort him at the time of death. As Hoffman and Futterman (1971) state, "In the face of an actual, impending death, the ultimate separation, the anxiety with regard to day to day separation is universal." Benoliel (1975) sums up the concern most effectively

> When parents are unable to face the reality of the child's forthcoming death, it is the child who suffers — in the pain of social isolation and in the lack of opportunity to make/his wishes known. Sometimes this suffering includes the indignity of dying in the intensive care unit (I.C.U.) surrounded by strangers and with no chance to say goodbye and to share the final moments of separation with those who are dear to him.

Death and the Adolescent With Malignancy

Warmth, comfort and concern are also important to the adolescent. In the literature discussed in the chapter on hospitalization, Moore, Holton and Marten (1969) focussed on the types of problems that adolescents face in malignancy. Karon (1973) in his writings deals more directly with the problem of death and death anxiety in the adolescent with cancer. He states that the older child is always aware of the seriousness of his predicament, is concerned when adults refuse to discuss his illness and prognosis, and is anxious to share his anxieties with a person who is sympathetic. In continuing, Karon adds

> Those who take refuge behind a classical ploy, "He didn't ask, so I didn't tell him," are often trying to avoid their own anxiety about death and dying by misinterpreting the child's recognition that physicians and other adults have difficulty talking about the diagnosis.

Karon (1973) and Kagan (1976) stress the fact that cancer is added into an already difficult period in life and that denial serves as a major means that the adolescent uses to shut out the prognosis. Kikuchi (1976) in presenting the case of an adolescent boy with leukemia, emphasizes how he struggled with the death and how he added to his knowledge about the progress of his disease only when he was ready. By so doing he was able to pace the preparation for his impending death at a speed which he could tolerate. Kagan (1976) also emphasizes this need to allow the adolescent time to come to grips with his feelings. In her work, Lowenburg (1970), in attempting to understand the fatally ill adolescent, sets forth two lists of behavior indices which are based on the works of Lazarus (1966) and Verwoerdt (1966). These lists focus on "manifestations of avoidance coping" and "manifestations of approach coping." Lowenburg advocates the need to direct the adolescent and his family toward "approach coping" behaviors.

Kikuchi (1976), like Karon (1973), emphasizes the fact that the illness made her patient's identity struggle more difficult. She also shows how hospital staff assisted the patient in dealing with his struggle.

> As these significant adults were unlike his parents, they were not a threat to his independence. Thus, they could be utilized in his struggle to achieve independence. By using these adults in his parents' stead, he was able to supply himself with the

support he needed and yet feel independent. Jim used these adults until he became increasingly ill and able to accept support from his parents.

Easson (1968) states that adolescents may view impending death as a punishment for sin. He describes the role that guilt versus anger and love versus rejection plays in the adolescent's struggle with death. He also dwells on the issues related to the dependency and self-sufficiency conflict. Gullo (1973) in identifying "death defiance" suggests that it is found in the adolescent who is aware of the severity of his illness and the waning hope for recovery. The adolescent patient struggles to keep his identity and his freedom at a cost of prolonged suffering. The protracted period, although difficult, enables him to release his anger. Plumb and Holland (1974) indicate that there is very little evidence to suggest that the adolescent accepts death with the "almost void of feelings experience observed by Kübler-Ross (1969)." They suggest that a kind of adaptation does occur which, although it is not peaceful acceptance, is the type of resignation where the adolescent realizes that it is safer to die than to continue to struggle for life.

Approaching the Time of Death:
Parental Concerns and Participation in Care

The Decision to Cease Aggressive Treatment

As the terminal phase of the child's illness approaches there is usually advance warning. As cancer metastasizes or leukemia can no longer be controlled, parents usually become very anxious about how their child will die and how much he will suffer. Since parents play a major role in the child's terminal care, it is important for the treatment team to advise the parents about the progress of the illness and why the physician is switching from an aggressive and curative approach to a more passive, palliative treatment program. The decision to cease administering massive doses of highly toxic drugs should be discussed with the parents, but they should not be left to make major decisions about the regimen. Parents who are struggling with the fact that they will lose their child want to understand the physician's decision; they want to express their feelings about it, but they want the doctor to make the actual decision based on his expertise and the expertise of his colleagues. When the physician can accept that his approach must be to maintain the child as comfortably as possible until the child's death, then his strength in making that decision can help the parents know that every possible avenue of treatment has been used for their son or daughter.

Pain Control

In the terminal stages of illness, the overwhelming concern of parents is the need for their child to cease suffering (Graner 1976). Time after time parents have asked us what death will be like and whether or not it will be painful for their child. Parents have related that there is no greater feeling of helplessness than to watch their child suffer. We have found that parents want to be with their child at the time of death and want to know that they have done everything possible that they could to help their child live a life free from pain and suffering. Physicians who treat terminally ill adults have recognized that bone pain and chronic pain created by metastasis has created a cycle in which the patient's anxiety leads to anticipation and a resulting intensification of the pain. When this happens there is a need to build up analgesic levels in the patient's blood so that the cycle is interrupted (Mount, Ajemian and Scott 1976). In children this need also arises and the preventive nature of pain control becomes even more important in the face of the influence of parental anxiety on the child. This creates a major challenge for the physician, especially when the child's pain symptoms appear to be out of proportion to the clinical evidence to which pain could normally be attributed. In our experience, the control of pain can substantially reduce parental anxiety and have a positive effect on the child so that he can be helped to die peacefully.

Associated with pain control is the parents' need for assurance that their child will not be required to undergo procedures which are unnecessary. We have found that when parents have reached the point of accepting the cessation of active chemotherapy, they want care to be uncomplicated and directed toward keeping their child comfortable. In a university teaching center where the child and his family are exposed to a variety of personnel from many disciplines, reducing the number of personnel who have contact and the number of tests requested by house staff can be a matter of great concern for the parents. In fact, in a few instances we have respected greatly the family's ability to protect their child and raise questions about the care he is receiving. The time of an impending death is not the time to introduce a new medical, nursing, social work or chaplaincy student or to order blood tests which have little bearing on the care being given. In the same context, a death from metastasis or massive infection does not require heroic measures on behalf of the resident or intern, and this needs to be articulated clearly to medical personnel. Young physicians may use such measures because of their own inability to cope with the loss of their patient.

Mouth Care

Parents who remain with their child are usually faced with a demanding and difficult experience in the few days prior to the child's death. If the child is vomiting or hemorrhaging from the mouth or nose he will require intravenous infusion. The child's lips and mouth become visible problems especially if infected lesions develop. The child will complain of the discomfort and the parent is continually confronted with a need to help relieve the child's suffering. The role of the nursing staff in providing and teaching the mother to provide excellent care to the child's lips and mouth at this time is extremely important. The parent, usually the child's mother, can perform a role which is of benefit to the child, to the nursing staff and to herself, as it partially diverts her from the feeling of being totally helpless.

Love, Comfort and Understanding

When the battle is lost and they have time to realize that all that remains is suffering and death, parents usually want the situation to terminate as quickly and as peacefully as possible, without heroic measures or increased use of life-sustaining procedures such as transfusions. Often parents need help to release their frustrations, to deal with reality and to participate in the care of their child until he dies.

It is this parental participation, particularly on behalf of the mother but also on behalf of the father, that helps the child to die in peace. The child continues to need the protection, love and security that he finds in those he trusts and relies upon. As a young child's physical condition deteriorates he may become more irritable and his behavior may regress, but he still continues to need the familiarity of parental figures, even though it may be difficult for a parent or parents to withstand constant demands. Children of older ages can be difficult as well but can communicate with more understanding in regard to their physical condition. As Waechter (1971) points out, children over the age of six often have much more awareness of their prognosis than their parents wish to believe. In the hospital, the continued stress of dealing with the dying child dictates the need to remove the parent from the situation periodically. When parents can alternate in caring for the child the situation can become easier for both the parent and the child. Irritable and sick as he is, the child will often strive to maintain familiar activities, and where feasible he needs this constant diversion. Friends and relatives can be of great assistance for short periods, but no one can supplant a child's need for his parents.

At times when parents cannot deal with the child's irritability and the period of terminal care drags on for several weeks, we have found that parents often have difficulty being objective about their own role in their child's care. They need a person from outside of the family, such as the social worker or the nurse, to help them restructure their approach. They also need reassurance that their desire to see the ordeal end is not an unforgiveable sin but a normal response to a need to be free of the strain of seeing their child feel so miserable.

Death at Home

When the child is cared for at home, the same needs apply as in the hospital. At home, however, parents usually require even more emotional, as well as medical, support. It is frightening for the parents and for other members of the family to await the death of their sick child. For example, in one family in this situation, the parents usually communicated well and worked together in managing family affairs. When faced with the stress of awaiting the death of their young daughter, they were unable to sleep, the mother cuddled the child for most of the day, the father became irritable and uncommunicative, the two older daughters experienced school difficulties and one continually wet her pants. When the family discussed these events with our team we were able to help the mother see how she could manage her sick child differently, the daughters were given an opportunity to express their feelings through doll play and we offered to meet with the total family. In this situation the family again pulled together and solved its own problems. A relative became a sounding board for the father, and following this the parents discussed their problems and began working together with their daughters to help them face the impending death of their sister. From a medical perspective we have found that parents need to know that they can contact our ambulatory team at any time and that if they cannot cope at home they can bring their child to hospital for in-patient care. If the fear of massive hemorrhage is not intense and if a means for relief of anoxia can be implemented, death at home can be more natural and peaceful than in a hospital. At present in our community we have not developed the extensive community support systems described by Martinson and her colleagues (1976). If such a program existed, then death at home, even with anoxia and hemorrhage, might be facilitated more easily. In most situations, we have found that the availability of the hospital as a 24-hour resource and the trusting relationship which has usually developed between our team and the family has worked to everyone's advantage. It must be remembered, however, that we are a relatively small center and that we know our families very well. In most instances, where children have come to the hospital to die, the child has remained at home until he is semiconscious, and the family has felt relieved to have the hospital assume the responsibility at the time of death.

The Dying Child

As discussed earlier in this chapter, children respond to life-threatening situations with anxiety that is age related. It has been my experience that children under the age of ten want to remain a part of the world around them. When they are told or sense they are going to die, their major concern is that their parents will be with them. For instance, just before he died, five-year-old Donald told the staff that he wondered what it was like to go to heaven. He said that he had never been dead before, but he thought there were no needles there. As he continued, he said that he would "get dead" but come back to be with his mother. Another child, Dawn, age six, was seriously ill. She turned to her mother to ask if a person was alive or dead when he went to heaven. She also wondered if her mother could go to heaven too.

In this age range as well, we have frequently seen how children who are approaching death demand to be pulled around and around the ward in a wagon. They seem to be comforted by the perpetual motion and by the fact that they do not miss anything that is happening on the ward.

When children have been overwhelmed by the constancy of medical treatment and by procedures to stop hemorrhage, they usually feel physically ill. They often become irritable and unreasonable. We have frequently seen children lash out at their parents, physicians and other staff and swear at the top of their lungs. Once this has happened, the child has often become more docile and cooperative, as if the release of emotion has helped him return to his ordinary self. In other children, we have seen the development of trust in the staff that has continued right to the end. When Richard, age eight, experienced several nasal hemorrhages, he asked the physicians to please save him if they could and later on when he was close to death he thanked them for trying.

When children are frightened of their illness and their parents are anxious as well, they tend to develop a smothering type of symbiotic relationship that is so intense that if allowed to persist it becomes almost impossible for the mother to leave the child long enough to get dressed or to go to the bathroom.

Many children, like adults, have to deal with "unfinished business" in order to die in peace. For example, one child told his mother that she must pack up his scrapbooks carefully and take home his clothes because he no longer needed them. After his mother complied, the child rested comfortably and died quietly in his sleep. Another little girl begged her uncle to take her to the drugstore to buy her parents a valentine. Despite the fact that she was desperately ill, her uncle did as she asked. After giving her parents the card and being very happy, she died at home later that evening. In another situation, seven-year-old Patsy waited until a friend came back from vacation, and once she had seen her friend and talked to her, she died peacefully.

Another boy, age six, was suffering from a relapse of his leukemia and his physical condition had been deteriorating slowly, but his death did not seem imminent. When his parents brought him the forty miles to hospital over the same route he had travelled many times over the previous two years, he suddenly began noticing many things and incessantly asked them questions about everything he saw. Shortly after coming to the hospital, he died unexpectedly. Strangely enough, his parents reported that for three weeks prior to his death he had been sleeping in their room, but the night before he died he was adamant that he return to his own bed where he slept very soundly.

Listening to the child and helping him die in comfort demands our most humane attitudes and abilities. The child may not want to talk about death or to deal with it directly in any way. He may just want simple questions answered or want to work out his feelings on his own. If he does want to talk it will probably be on his own terms, and it may be that he shares his concerns with a sensitive nurse during the night or with his father or mother as he sits quietly with them. One father who was concerned that he and his son talk about the finality of the child's illness used his religious belief to help him and his son communicate at the same level. Another mother and daughter talked frequently about their belief in God and Jesus. Another mother simply remained close to her daughter in human support, and the child died in peace saying that she believed God was watching over her.

In the final stages of terminal illness, the importance of physical nursing care and a reduction in the number of procedures becomes crucial. The dying child is entitled to love, comfort and understanding. There comes a time for the child to be allowed to fight off the intravenous injections and painful procedures. He has the right to be free from constant poking and prodding.

I believe that the necessity of having the parents present at the actual time of the child's death cannot be overemphasized. For example, when Tony, an eleven-year-old boy, was restless and semicomatose, he could not be comforted by familiar staff but when his parents arrived their calming influence allowed him to die peacefully. Older children have also found it comforting to be able to say their goodbyes to their parents and siblings immediately prior to their death. Another child, aged five, whose parents had separated, insisted that his parents organize themselves so that they were together and touching him. He said that was the way he wanted them to be, and he became calm with both of them there. In situations where children have become sightless in the terminal stages of an illness, the anxiety of the loss of sight can only be reduced by the mother being right there where the child could reach out and touch her.

In all of our experiences what seems to be most important is the degree of warmth, openness and freedom to communicate honestly so that parents, children and siblings can be as close as possible when death occurs. Where the family cannot be helped to support each other emotionally then the staff must try their best to help the dying child.

The long-range implications of the period of terminal illness are intense. Release of guilt and realization of the necessity for death to end pain and suffering for both parents and siblings can be of great value in assisting the family to adapt to life after their child's death. Staff relationships with the child and his family at this difficult time in the course of the illness are of major importance. Inevitably, death that comes after a time of preparation, which can be facilitated by staff who are concerned and willing to communicate with the child and family, can be less difficult than death that occurs suddenly and without warning. In my experience, it is often more difficult for families when children die suddenly from infections, because the parting process is severed and parents and siblings do not have the time to resolve their own feelings and say their farewells.

The Dying Adolescent

I have been told by hospital staff that of all deaths, the death of the adolescent patient is the most difficult for them emotionally. Personally, I find the deaths of all young people to be extremely difficult. The intensity of the uncertainty of death, the interruption of dreams and the destruction of self-concepts and self-image can make the event devastating for them.

In the section on hospitalization, we discussed the need for privacy, understanding and honesty. In terminal illness, these needs are intensified. The adolescent must know about the plans for his care, the procedures to which he will be subjected and the status of his illness. Information about the latter must be timed carefully so that it cannot only be understood, but also accepted. As Plumb and Holland (1974) point out, the impact of the symptoms become a major governing factor in understanding the adolescent, particularly as he nears the end of his life. Inevitably, his illness and his general physical state will become key factors which influence his emotional response. It becomes difficult then for staff and parents to know how much to allow the adolescent to withdraw, how much to prohibit visitors and how much to allow him to deviate from his regular dietary practices. It is also difficult to assess whether or not the resistance of treatment and tests should be permitted. Decisions about whether or not changes in behavior are permissible should not be the sole concern of parents and staff but should involve the adolescent patient who can often speak for himself.

For instance, Edward, a thirteen-year-old with leukemia, suggested that adults were often unfair. He believed that as a person, he had rights which his parents and the physicians tended to neglect. He stated very clearly that he owned his own body and that he had suffered from the injections, the vomiting and the mouth ulcers and had every right to refuse to be treated. He also pointed out that he trusted in God and that he was prepared to face the consequences of ceasing treatment. In this situation, Edward's close relationship with his parents and his trust in the clinic team helped him face his treatment program until the time when chemotherapy was no longer effective. I believe that the development of a trusting relationship with medical, nursing and psychosocial resource persons can be of great value in understanding, comforting and helping the adolescent in an atmosphere where he is allowed to share his beliefs and feelings.

The process of sorting through denial, bargaining, depression and other feelings will most likely be a spontaneous or natural event between the adolescent patient and the person that he selects. Inevitably this individual will be somebody who is honest, concerned and willing to talk with the teenager openly.

In helping the adolescent patient, we have found that coordination of both psychosocial and medical care becomes crucial. Resources, external to the ward or the ambulatory clinic, can be of great value providing they are part of the overall patient-care plan and providing that the patient has the right of selection as to whether or not he will discuss his feelings with these persons.

The dying adolescent needs to have as much control as possible over his mind and his body. As his physical condition deteriorates it becomes extremely difficult for him to rely on others to care for him. The availability and concern of the ward staff can be of great assistance. Hospital staff can help the adolescent patient through his conflict over dependence and independence so that he can rely on his parents as much as possible as he nears death (Kikuchi 1976).

Many adolescents will continue to strive to maintain as normal a life as possible. Mastery over the environment and acceptance by others around them, especially those of their own age, is very important. The terminally ill adolescent must have some personal day-to-day and longer term goals. Something as simple as being able to sit up in a chair by the window or planning to have her hair done can be a very necessary and worthwhile goal for the teenager who is deteriorating physically. One adolescent boy chose to go shopping for a gift for his parents and later worked hard to finish a model airplane.

Karen, age 17, was extremely ill. She had been admitted to hospital many times but had returned this time for terminal care. She continued to want to live each day as fully as possible. At Easter, her classmates sent her a gigantic chocolate bunny, and one major goal in her life was to feel well enough to eat the bunny. Although she never achieved the goal, for a while it represented a hope and another reason for her to live. On a very realistic level, early on in her hospitalization, she worked toward returning home for short periods of time, and even when she became increasingly ill she maintained her physical appearance for those who she allowed to come and visit. Another adolescent kept up his school work for as long as he could and planned for the time when he could go back home and continue his hobbies. It was important for him to achieve as much as possible during the time he had left.

For the adolescent, love, security and freedom from pain are equally as important as for younger children. The more his parents can be with him and communicate with him with openness and honesty, the more the adolescent can be helped to resolve his feelings at the time of death.

REFERENCES

Holmes, H.A. and Holmes, F.F.: "After Ten Years, What are the Handicaps and Life Styles of Children Treated for Cancer." *Clin Pediatr* 14:9, 819-823, 1975.

Friedlund, D.: "The Remaining Child." in *Home Care for the Dying Child: Professional and Family Perspectives.* I.M. Martinson (ed.), Appleton-Century-Crofts, New York, 1976.

Share, L.: "Family Communication in the Crisis of a Child's Fatal Illness: A Literature Review and Analysis." *Omega* 3:3, 187-201, 1972.

Anthony, S.: *The Child's Discovery of Death.* Harcourt Brace, New York, 1940. Also see Anthony, S.: *The Discovery of Death in Childhood and*

After. Basic Books Inc. Publishers, New York, 1972.

Nagy, M.: "The Child's Theories Concerning Death." *J Gen Psychol* 73:3-27, 1948. Also see Nagy, M.: "The Child's View of Death." in *The Meaning of Death.* Edited by H. Feifel, McGraw-Hill, New York, 1959.

Safier, G.: "A Study in Relationships Between the Life and Death Concepts in Children." *J Gen Psychol* 105:283-294, 1964.

Gartley, W. and Bernasconi, M.: "The Concept of Death in Children." *J Gen Psychol* 110:71-85, 1967.

Adler, C.S.: "The Meaning of Death to Children." *Ariz Med* 26:266-275, 1969.

Alexander, I.E. and Adlerstein, A.M.: "Affective Responses to Death in a Population of Children and Early Adolescents." *J Gen Psychol* 93:167-177, 1958.

Wahl, C.W.: "The Fear of Death." *Bull Meninger Clin* 22:214-223, 1958.

Benoliel, J.Q.: "The Terminally Ill Child." in *Comprehensive Pediatric Nursing.* Edited by G.M. Scipien, Barnard M., Chard, M.A., Howe, J. and Phillips, P.J., McGraw-Hill Book Company, New York, 1975.

Bowlby, J.: "Processes of Mourning." *Int J Psychoanal* 42:317, 1961.

Zeligs, R.: "Children's Attitudes Toward Death." *Mental Hygiene.* 51:393-396, 1967.

Plank, E.: "Death on a Children's Ward." *Medical Times.* July, 1964.

Koocher, G.P.: "Talking with Children About Death." *Am J Orthopsychiatry* 44:3, 404-411, 1974.

Portz, A.: "The Child's Sense of Death." *Death and Presence*, Edited by A. Godin, Lumen Vitae Press, Brussels, 1972.

Green-Epner, C.S.: "The Dying Child" in *The Dying Patient: A Supportive Approach.* Edited by Rita E. Caughill, Little, Brown and Co., Boston, 1976.

Gullo, S.V.: "Games Children Play When They're Dying." *Medical Dimensions* Oct., 1973.

Marshall, J.G. and Marshall, V.W.: "The Treatment of Death in Children's Books." *Omega* :2, 36-44, 1971.

Aradine, C.R.: "Books for Children About Death." *Pediatr* 57:3, 372-378, 1976.

Wolfe, A.: *Helping Your Child to Understand Death.* Child Study Association of America, New York, 1958.

Grollman, E.A. (ed.): *Explaining Death to Children*, Beacon Press, Boston, 1967. *Talking About Death: A Dialogue between Parent and Child.* Beacon Press, Boston, 1971.

Richmond, J.B. and Waisman, H.A.: "Psychological Aspects of Management of Children with Malignant Diseases." *Am J Dis Child* 89:42-47, 1955.

Hoffman, I. and Futterman, E.H.: "Coping with Waiting: Psychiatric Intervention and Study in the Waiting Room of a Pediatric Oncology Clinic." *Comp Psychiatry* 12:1, 67-81, 1971.

Knudson, A.G. and Natterson, J.M.: "Practice of Pediatrics: Participation of Parents in the Hospital Care of Fatally Ill Children." *Pediatr* 26, 482-490, 1960.

Morrisey, J.R.: "Children's Adaptation to Fatal Illness." *Soc Work* 8:81-88, 1963. Also see Morrisey, J.R.: "Death Anxiety in Children with a Fatal Illness." in *Crisis Intervention: Selected Readings.* Edited by Howard J. Parad. Family Service Association of America, New York, 1965.

Waechter, E.H.: "Children's Awareness of Fatal Illness: A Literature Review and Analysis." *Am J Nurs* 71:1168-1172, 1971.

Spinetta, J.J., Rigler, D., and Karon, M.: "Personal Space as a Measure of a Dying Child's Sense of Isolation." *J Cons Clin Psychol* 42:6, 751-756, 1974.

Pacyna, B.A.: "Response to a Dying Child." *Nurs Clin N Am* 5:3, 421-430, 1970.

Etzel, B.: "The Role of Advocacy in the Rite of Passage." in *Home Care for the Dying Child: Professional and Family Perspectives.* I.M. Martinson (ed.), Appleton-Century-Crofts, New York, 1976.

Klinzing, D.R. and Klinzing, D.G.: *The Hospitalized Child: Communication Techniques for Health Personnel,* Prentice-Hall Inc., Englewood Cliffs, N.J., 1977.

Moore, D.C., Holton, C.P. and Marten, G.W.: "Psychologic Problems in the Management of Adolescents with Malignancy." *Clin Pediatr* 8:8, 464-473, 1969.

Karon, M.: "The Physician and the Adolescent with Cancer." *Pediatr Clin N Am* 20:4, 965-973, 1973.

Kagan, L.B.: "Use of Denial in Adolescents with Bone Cancer." *Health and Soc Work* 1:4, 71-87, 1976.

Kikuchi, J.: "A Leukemic Adolescent's Verbalization About Dying." *Mat Child Nurs J* 1:259-264, 1972.

Lowenburg, J.S.: "The Coping Behaviors of Fatally Ill Adolescents and Their Parents." *Nurs Forum* 9:3, 269-287, 1970.

Lazarus, R.: *Psychological Stress and the Coping Process.* McGraw-Hill Book Co., New York, 1966.

Verwoerdt, A.: *Communication with the Fatally Ill.* Charles C Thomas, Springfield, Ill., 1966.

Easson, W.M.: "Care of the Young Patient who is Dying." *J Am Med Assoc* 205:4, 203-207, 1968.

Plumb, M.M. and Holland, J.: "Cancer in Adolescence: The Symptom is the Thing." in *Anticipatory Grief.* B. Schoenberg et al. (ed.), 1974. See Chapter 3.

Kübler-Ross, E.: *On Death and Dying.* Macmillan Publishing Co. Ltd., New York, 1969.

Graner, A.: "The Effects of Pain on Child, Parent and Health Professional." in *Home Care for the Dying Child.* Ida M. Martinson (ed.) 1975. See Chapter 1.

Mount, B.M., Ajemian, I. and Scott, J.F.: "Use of the Brompton Mixture in Treating the Chronic Pain of Malignant Disease." *Can Med Assoc J* 115:122-124, 1976.

Martinson, I.M. (Ed.): *Home Care and the Dying Child,* Appleton-Century-Crofts, New York, 1975.

CHAPTER 7

THE FAMILY AFTER THE DEATH OF A CHILD

The Literature: Studies of Bereavement

FROM my perspective it seems that there is still much to learn about the adjustment of the family after the death of a child from malignancy. There are few formal studies in this area. Hamovitch (1964) interviewed parents of 53 children who had died from leukemia, three to 18 months after the death of the child. He found that 57 percent of the families had dealt effectively with the loss and that 43 percent were still working through grief reactions. There was a significant difference between those who had relatively few problems while the child was alive and those who had a large number of problems. Seventy-one percent of the former were adjusting well as opposed to 36 percent of the latter. He also found that mothers adjusted better than fathers, siblings or extended family. A later study by Kaplan and his colleagues (1976) confirms one aspect of Hamovitch's findings. They found that families who coped well at diagnosis coped far better after the child's death than those who coped poorly at diagnosis. Kaplan's group also found that 38 of the 40 families studied reported health problems among the survivors and 35 families reported morbid grief reactions in one family member. These morbid grief reactions included visiting the cemetery daily, "enshrining" the effects of the dead child or not referring to the deceased child following the child's death. Kaplan and his co-workers describe other difficulties in families, including marriage problems (70%), school difficulties in at least one child (43%) and work problems (60%). Eighty percent of the problems reported occurred after the diagnosis.

In a study of parents of 15 deceased children, Oakley and Patterson (1966) found that two families moved because the house became unbearable and two mothers were hospitalized 11 months after the child's death due to "nerves." Two siblings had nightmares, one had school problems and one protected his dead brother's toys. In the latter situation the child's mother had insisted he be subjected to repeated blood counts because of her anxiety that he might develop a similar malignancy. Another mother refused to become pregnant again, because she had been hurt so badly by the death of her child.

These three studies exemplify the problems families encounter. Time, methodology, lack of information about the studies and many other differences make it impossible for us to draw specific conclusions. There is, however, no doubt that the death of a child severely affects the family system and that negative sequelae appear in both parents and siblings. The following two studies and a number of other papers add to our knowledge.

Vollman and her associates (1971) relate their experiences with the technique of crisis intervention in sudden death situations immediately following death and through follow-up sessions. They found that crisis intervention worked in families where no ingrained pattern of coping with real life crises existed. Where nuclear families were isolated and lacking support the potential for physical and mental breakdown was extremely high. Families with open internal communication systems made more realistic plans for dealing with the death of a family member. Families which dealt with stress by facing reality rather than through use of denial coped more effectively with the death. In all families, the importance of the role which the deceased had assumed in the family system influenced the family's ability to reorganize.

In studying children after the death of a family member, Cain, Fast and Erickson (1964) found that a child's personality was sometimes altered for life. When a sibling died, surviving children often experienced feelings of guilt, concern that they had caused the death or that they should have died instead. Cain and Cain (1964) also delineated the need for parents to mourn and stated that when parents do not mourn, children born or adopted after the death may be endangered. This is especially true when the new child is viewed as a replacement for the dead child. In their small study, Cain and Cain found that because one or both parents had been unable to resolve their grief they continually made comparisons. "These parents grossly imposed the identity of the dead child upon his substitute, and unconsciously identified the two." When this happened the new child was forced to adopt the image of a sibling who was unknown to him. He had no chance to develop his own identity and was constantly reminded that he could never match the achievements of the dead child. He was overprotected and restricted because of his parents fear that something tragic would happen to him. If he developed the physical symptoms of the deceased child as part of the identification process he became morbidly preoccupied. All six of the children studied had become emotionally disturbed and two were psychotic.

In his work Goldberg (1973), applies the concept of crisis to death. He explores role reorganization at length including the question of object replacement and scapegoating. He stipulates that there are four tasks required for healthy readjustment in families. These tasks include: (1) the enabling of a family to mourn; (2) relinquishing the memory of the deceased person in daily living; (3) realigning of roles within the family, and (4) realigning of roles outside of the family. Bowlby (1961) suggests that the mourning process is in three phases. Phase one involves searching to recover the deceased object, complete with tears and anger at oneself, the dead person and a third person such as God or the doctor. It is a period of struggling to accept the finality of the loss. The second phase is one of disorganization where the hope for reunion fades. The person experiences despair to the point of being restless and unable to start or organize behavior. Gradually ties with the deceased are loosened. In the third phase, reorganization and the establishment of new relationships and goals takes place.

Lindemann (1944), in discussing acute grief, describes both immediate and delayed reactions identifying "(1) somatic distress (2) preoccupation with the image of the deceased (3) guilt (4) hostile reactions and (5) loss of patterns of conduct" as "pathognomonic for grief." He emphasizes that guilt, emotional distancing from people and the loss of warmth in relationships with others creates such stress that the bereaved feel that they are going insane. He points out how reactions may be delayed or distorted. Distortions include manifestations such as acquiring symptoms of the deceased child's illness, changing relationships with friends and relatives, becoming furious with specific persons and becoming "wooden" and formal with affect and conduct "resembling schizophrenic symptoms." Other behaviors include cessation of social interaction, carrying out actions "detrimental to his own social and economic existence" and development of symptoms of "agitated depression with worthlessness, bitter self-accusation and obvious need for punishment."

When families lose a child it is hard to assess specifically how much intervention with the family reduces the tendency toward maladaptive grief reactions. I believe that assistance in developing open communication patterns within the family, in working through the anticipatory mourning process and in coping with death, both immediately following a death and during the mourning period, is justified.

Parent Reactions

Fischoff and O'Brien (1976) state that, "parents feel the loss of their child as if they had lost a part of themselves, which, indeed they have." They also state that, "The mourning process will last for months or years with some parents, whereas some parents mourn for a lifetime if appropriate intervention is not forthcoming." They suggest that the events related to the child's death are remembered very clearly and that parents often believe they hear or see their child for months after his death. Kulenkamp (1976), after the loss of her son, reflects on how she "listened to the silence during those long nights following Eric's death and longed to hear her son call her."

In order to help parents share their experiences of losing a child, Fischoff and O'Brien formed a couples' group. They believed that the nuclear family often had to face such a death alone and could benefit from additional support. The group helped parents in their search for a "reason why the child died" and their search for "the meaning of life and death." The group also diminshed concerns about unusual or morbid thoughts, and feelings of isolation and helplessness. Martinson (1976), from her experiences with parent groups, suggests that parents who have lost a child have a natural affinity for one another. She found repeatedly that parents felt they had lost a part of themselves when the child died. She also states that "frustration in being unable to help their own child and in the futility of trying to prevent their child's death, lingers with them long afterwards." She relates that parents often believe they are approaching insanity and are surprised to learn that nearly every parent has had the same experience. Schiff (1977) points out how the parent's world stops. She relates that she felt numb and that she cried and cried. The intensity of these frustrations that a parent experiences are reflected in this poem by Claire Mulholland, a mother who lost her daughter from leukemia.

How many times did I come this way
on this same bus to see you,
waking from guilty oblivion
to another nightmare day,
while you lay anxious in your iron cot
feigning sleep, the shutters of your mind
closed tight till I should come.

You trust us who made and loved you
and we betrayed your trust.
How could you understand that
we were powerless to help you?
We promised you the sun
and instead you had darkness
and nameless terror.

Your cries for help were locked
in your poor brain and could not
find an escape. The baby bloomed
and you grew weak. Yes, I knew too
how cruel was the sun and flowers and
children's laughter. I have a lifetime
of memories but I would give them all
to hold you once again.

I see you in every child.
Each leaf and flower brings you back
and makes you more keenly gone.
Death is no end. It is the beginning
of a lifetime without you, a succession of

days and nights and events and at each of them
you will not be there.

Martinson (1976) stresses how parents have intense feelings of anxiety and how at times they believe they see their dead child. Mulholland reflects this belief in the last stanza of the preceding poem and in this poem as well.

There is no one in the garden now,
but the swing is swinging.
The willow leaves are almost gone,
the sycamore's still green and
the swing is swinging.

Rainwater lies on the garage roof,
the sparrows squabble and the fat coal tit
sits smugly on the fence.
The trees are quiet and
the swing is swinging.

I suppose it is the wind
but could it be my child
a phantom child, a laughing child
silently swinging?

After parents learn to cope with the loss and their grief subsides, Martinson (1976) found that many felt guilty. She states, "They feel that somehow they are betraying their dead child in regaining happiness." Schiff (1977) describes her own inability to accept pleasure and how many women have difficulty reestablishing sexual relationships. In my experience guilt feelings are particularly prominent in cases of sudden death. In leukemia, infection or relapse may end life quickly and end the family's predeath preparation prematurely. The family can then be prone to intense guilt feelings which are often associated with the belief that they had not protected their child adequately. For example, they believe that they did not seek medical care as early as they should have or did not have sufficient understanding of the seriousness of the dead child's medical condition. If a couple hold each other responsible and fail to talk, the problem can then disrupt the marriage. Schiff (1977) describes a situation in which the death of a son due to a car accident precipitated twenty years of marital conflict, resulting in physical and emotional breakdown of both husband and wife. In another situation, I encountered a family who had similar problems. When a young child died in the family the father would not allow the other family members to discuss the death of a child. For years the family remained silent, until at the age of 15, a male sibling became severely distressed and required psychiatric help some eight years following the death of his brother. In this case the father had felt intensely guilty about his son's death and the whole family had suffered in silence until his other son reached a point in his life where another loss regenerated feelings that this other son had been unable to release during his first bereavement.

Anglim (1976) stresses the fact that, in her experience, grieving responses following a child's death from malignancy were usually normal, but combined with a feeling of relief that the child's suffering was over. She notes that religious beliefs help reintegrate some families. I have found this to be the case as well. Families need to be able to attribute a purpose to death. Religious convictions help to provide a framework of belief and a source of comfort through the provision of a suitable explanation of the purpose of life and death. People who have strong religious beliefs seem to have additional strengths for resolution of intense emotions following death, providing such beliefs assist in the reduction of guilt feelings. In some instances religion can be a detriment because parents feel guilty and believe that God is punishing them. Of equal importance to religious belief itself is the community associated with the practice of religion. In many instances, the communal sharing of beliefs and the comfort provided by others who share in the religious aspect of the experience adds additional emotional supports for the family. A minister, priest or rabbi who assist the family by providing reassurance and comfort in a personal manner can be a valuable asset. Schiff (1977) cites the importance of knowing the clergyman and being able to rely on him for emotional support. Schiff also stresses the value of the traditional funeral and how important it was for her to see her dead child, to have people around her and in her situation to experience the shiva. In my experience it has been crucial to involve the clergy prior to the death of a child and to encourage the family to relate to a clergyman in whom they trust. I also believe that the funeral service, if it is conducted by someone who cares about the family and knew the child, can be a great support to the bereaved family. I also think that when the family sees the child following the death and goes through the experience of closing the casket, the finality of their loss is reaffirmed.

Anglim (1976) reports that parents often overprotect remaining children and tend to check them for symptoms of malignant disease. The latter is a fairly common occurrence that I have observed in families during the course of a child's disease as well as following the child's death.

Anglim also states that for some bereaved families, neighbors, and relatives were helpful, while others avoided discussing death or were too embarrassed to discuss it. I have found that parents have often been held responsible for the death by relatives and friends. McCollum (1975) has noted that during a life-threatening illness grandparents are often overwhelmed with feelings that inhibit them from providing emotional support to the child's parents, the child and other family members. For example, they often ask why they did not get the disease rather than the child; they feel they have lived a complete life. After death the same problem often prevails. Helping relatives, and grandparents in particular, to accept the reality of the death can be an additional burden that bereaved parents must face. For the past fifty years society has tried to hide death. Death has not been a suitable subject for discussion, and people have not learned to face their feelings about death, let alone discuss it. Some bereaved parents will continue to face difficulties with friends and relatives. Sometimes friends and relatives will abandon the family and fail to visit the dying child prior to death. If the parents can discuss death themselves with or without the help of clinic staff, then they may be able themselves to face relatives, friends and selected neighbors with the facts prior to the death so that these persons can be prepared for it and involved in the process. In some families no problems exist with relatives, friends and neighbors. In most instances if emotional support is forthcoming to the family it is because the parents have openly communicated with those close to them, included these persons in the care of the child and shared concerns with them prior to the death of the child.

When families are invited to return to the clinic after the death of the child, they will usually reminisce about their experiences during the dead child's illness. This review is often very detailed and comprehensive. Anglim (1976), in her paper, states that "review and reconstruction of what had happened seemed tremendously important to these parents." She also cites how important it was for parents to "remember, to judge themselves as competent and to verbalize both good and bad events, thereby putting the past into perspective." She also notes that parents compare children and often discuss "qualities of the dying child or dead child that none of the other children has." She states that several mothers emphasized that the dead child was the brightest of all. Anglim also adds that one mother reported that she had only just learned that her remaining son was more intelligent than she had realized. I encountered a similar situation when a mother recounted how she had just begun to realize how preoccupied she had been with her daughter's illness prior to her death. She had now found that her four-year-old boy was an interesting, creative and intelligent child. She realized that she and her son had much to offer each other. As in many cases, the son's vibrance and natural desire to live and face new experiences had helped both his parents through difficult periods, such as Christmas. In another situation, the death of her son was the stimulus for one mother to volunteer her time and talents in assisting cancer patients to obtain necessary services. Still another mother embarked on a new career in hospital work. As Anglim stresses, post-death discussions and resolutions of the loss are extremely important in identifying family strengths and in helping families develop "a new awareness of themselves as individuals and families."

The Response of Siblings

The remaining child is prone to intense feelings as well. Rosenblatt (1968) describes the case of a six-year-old boy whose sister died from asthma. He was left with preoccupations about death that were reflected in his artwork, in his reading of obituaries and in his experiencing an attack resembling asthma. He had fears of coming into contact with the corpse and was worried that he might go to hell because he wished someone were dead.

Parness (1975) in discussing loss among preschoolers, underlines the importance of the influence parents have on their child. Parents set the tone for adjustment through their attitudes and pattern of communication. She says that:

> Avoidance or denial of sadness and/or anger may become a source of distortion and mystification, entangling the child in the struggle of adults around him in their efforts to sort out their own feelings of responsibility.

Parness also suggests that regression after a loss is temporary and that the most important issue is whether or not the young child moves towards or away from life experiences.

Weston and Erwin (1963) in dealing with children ages two and one-half to five, emphasize the need to recognize how the child struggles to understand death. They also stress the fact that "feelings of envy for the child which the sibling took from the mother or his anger about the intruding child" (an infant) may arouse guilt and anxiety about being punished for causing the death. The child must also understand the parents' grief and deal with their feelings. Weston and Erwin state that if parents can talk about their feelings of loss, grief, anger and disappointment, it will help the child deal with his own feelings. They also suggest that the parent can help the child by telling him realistically what happened to the deceased child, understanding that he will need to develop his own explanation of the death and reassuring him that his thoughts and feelings were not the reason for the death.

In this age range it is necessary to recognize that the inability of the sibling under the age of eight or nine years to understand the permanence of death is a major factor in his adaptation to the death of his brother or sister.

For instance, in our clinic Johnnie, a four-year-old, developed a body rash and burst out crying uncontrollably several weeks after his sister's death from leukemia. He was upset because his sister had not come back to play with him. Up to that time he had talked about her death and the fact that she was in heaven, but he had not been able to accept the fact that his sister would not return to play with him. Parents must understand the child's need to talk about the sibling's death no matter how painful it is for them. They also must recognize that it will take a number of years for the child to achieve the resolution of the permanence of his loss. Children need the freedom to continue to work through their feelings as long as necessary.

In her poetry, Claire Mulholland reflects the words and thoughts of her little son as he works through his feelings about his sister's death. In the first poem he wants to tell his sister that he is still her friend.

> Maybe the wind, my son said,
> will blow my hat right off.
> It will·sail up over the sky
> into Heaven. Then Ciara
> will see it and know
> That it is mine.
>
> And will God see his wet red hat
> and send it back?

In the second poem entitled "Heaven" she reveals the curiosity of a young child seeking to understand Heaven and to undo the finality of the loss of his sibling with magical thinking and a child's fantasy.

> Has God made her better yet?
> my son asked, When
> is my sister coming back?
>
> Is Heaven a very big house
> with rooms for crowds of people?
> Is it very far above the clouds?
> Has she got a big bed there
> and a cupboard for her toys?
>
> Is she wearing her big blue shoes?
> Why does she not get cold —
> is it very warm in God's House?
> Are there carpets on all the floors?
> How did she get in? Where
> are the doors?
>
> I will get a ladder taller
> than a house. I will lean it on a cloud

and climb into the sky
and go and see her.

In children between the ages of five and ten, it is necessary to recognize that feelings of reprisal for ill thoughts or wishes may continue. Fredlund (1976) warns us that magical thinking can be influential in conceptualizing death and that children often say to a sibling "drop dead." Children in this age range will also fantasize about what has happened to the dead child. They will often include him in their play and talk to him. Recently, when his eight-year-old friend died, another eight-year-old came to the funeral home and talked to the body as if he were carrying on a discussion. He apologized and gave as well as accepted, forgiveness for events which had hurt each of them. He talked over things he wanted to know before the deceased boy went to Heaven. Immediately prior to the funeral he returned to the coffin, said some final words and seemed content. His behavior was natural and necessary for him. He needed the freedom to do what he felt he wanted to do.

In another situation children under the age of ten fantasized that the deceased child was planting flower seeds in God's garden, because she was so very fond of flowers and it was springtime. They imagined that she had toys and books there and that she was an angel.

Parents need to recognize that the sibling has been pushed aside, not only during the illness but following their brother or sister's death.

Schiff (1977) stresses how the home is a place of sadness and how siblings are forced to go to the funeral, visit the graveside and conform to the parental bereavement process. In her experience with her own children and other persons, she emphasizes how greatly siblings were influenced by the deprivation of love and affection during the mourning period. She also describes how siblings resented the artificial nature of the funeral. They had feelings of rivalry with their brother or sister and felt intensely guilty about his or her death.

When children reach the age when they can understand the finality of death, they may have less tendency to share openly their fantasies about death. They may be able to resolve their sibling's death by seeing death in adult terms and interpreting it to be an end of suffering. It is, however, just as important to enable the child to talk about his brother's or sister's death and share his grief with other family members as he works through his bereavement. As children approach their teen years a sibling's death sometimes has a profound impact on the direction of an adolescent's career. I recall how the death of a younger brother motivated a boy in his late teens to realistically pursue studies leading to a career in medical research.

Helping the Family After the Child's Death

Relationships with Staff

In caring for the dying child or teenager with malignancy, families and health care personnel usually have warning that death will occur in months, weeks or at least days. In some instances, leukemia may result in sudden death at onset or due to infection but, fortunately, this does not occur in most cases. In tumors there is usually some period of warning. Consequently, the relationship which has formed between health team members and family members prior to the child's death and the supportive role which those who are close to the family have provided throughout the illness is of great significance at the time of death and following. Quite reasonably, families with relationship problems at the time of diagnosis and relapse will usually be those requiring the most intensive attention of the social worker and other psychosocial care givers. Some of these families will not be able to resolve their difficulties regardless of the assistance provided. However, families who can work on their problems may well have made changes which will assist them to cope effectively with the loss of one member. At least they may have established the type of relationship with the health team personnel which will enable them to continue to gain extra support as they work through their death experience. I believe that many families benefit from the security that familiar medical, nursing, social work, child life, clergy and other professional personnel provide at the time of death, or at least for a short period following.

The Impact of Death

For the family, the death experience can be a time of relief from the overwhelming pressures of seeing one member suffer. It can bring families closer together, increase communications and bring into play the helping ability of relatives, neighbors, friends and helping agents from the community. On the other hand, it can be a time of sorrow, anger, guilt and helplessness. It can be the final straw in dividing a poor marriage or precursor of emotional disorders in parents and siblings. It can be a time when friends and neighbors are not helpful. For example, in one situation a close neighbor provided so much mothering that the young couple felt smothered with attention. They also felt helpless because they did not want to hurt the neighbor's feelings. Other families have related that they have found people just did not understand or fully appreciate what they had experienced. Several families have related how acquaintances have made ridiculous comparisons with their own experiences with bereavement, saying "you are so much better off because you had time to plan for a death."

Even for the family with great strength in communications and relationships between family members, death is a major trauma. It brings with it not only the emotion of loss and separation but an intense change in the pattern of family life. The mother, in particular, is suddenly left without the care of a sick child to consume much of her time. The gap in family relationships is felt by everyone. No matter how much the family has been prepared, the actual death, when it comes, is a shock. I remember that one mother said she felt that the end of her child's life was like a dream and that it took her days to realize the finality. Another mother recounted how she had dreamed of her child's funeral and how she experienced the intensity of the sorrow in the dream all over again when the death actually came. Another mother with very strong religious beliefs benefited from the comfort that her child was with God and that he was no longer suffering.

Preparation for death and the reality of impending death has been a difficult area for families and staff. Often family pressures, from relatives in particular, inflict considerable stress on parents to deny the reality of the impending loss. Our team tends to be very realistic and supportive and in most instances counteracts denying influences in terminal stages of a child's illness. This reality orientation is cited by most parents to be extremely beneficial.

Death in the Hospital

Immediately following the child's death parents and families have reacted in many different ways. Some have wanted to stay and talk with the physician and other staff and have appreciated the opportunity to make phone calls and discuss their feelings. Some have wanted to have some time alone with their deceased child to say some prayers, to cry or to talk with each other. Others have lingered as if in disbelief or have left as soon as they possibly could. The latter situations tend to reflect extremes signifying the difficulties that bereaved parents and families are facing in accepting the reality, the finality or the inevitability of the death.

In many instances the nurse can facilitate a positive experience following the death by ushering the family into a separate room and reorganizing the room of the deceased child. Such reorganization includes removal of equipment, packing up of a child's belongings and placing the child's body in a position of rest. When ready, families can then return to the deceased child's room for what is usually a brief but necessary period of privacy.

Funeral Arrangements and the Ceremony

After death a realistic and empathic approach by staff continues to be helpful. Any help that can be offered to parents in regard to telling the other children about death, discussing the funeral and burial arrangements and helping them realign their roles and relationships is usually met with more than positive acceptance. It is important to assess if a particular family needs any continuing assistance. The family physician, minister, priest, rabbi or other family and friends may be able to help in this regard.

Nevertheless, part of the process at our setting has been to continue to pay attention to the family and the family's needs immediately after the child's death for at least a short period of time. When friends or relatives are not close and death has occurred unexpectedly, the nurse or social worker have often helped families contact an appropriate funeral home, memorial society or religious group.

Following most deaths, one or more of the ward or clinic staff visit the funeral home on their off-duty time. When possible, a staff member who has worked closely with the family attends the funeral. In many instances families request that specific team members come to the funeral or to the home following. This is usually a nurse, a social worker or a child life worker. This attendance at the funeral and the home seems to have a marked importance to many families as it provides them with security and understanding. Some families have pointed out how they feel closer to the staff than to relatives, because they have known them for a long time and know that they can really say how they feel without upsetting the listener. Wherever nursing, social work and medical students have been closely involved with a family this follow-through after the death is encouraged as an excellent learning experience. Attending the funeral enables the student to see clearly the problems that the bereaved family must experience. It also provides the student with an opportunity to work through his own feelings of loss and grief.

One bereaved father related how my visit to the funeral home was of value to him because it helped him talk to someone who had seen what the family had endured. It helped him realize that he was not strange in not knowing what to say to visitors at the funeral home. It also enabled him to really share his anxieties and questions with someone who would simply listen and reassure him.

Such follow-through experiences are certainly subject to criticism. It can be said that staff are meeting their own needs, that this is a waste of valuable time, and that it encourages dependency. It can also be said that following through forces unnecessary care on the family and intrudes upon their personal life. In some instances these criticisms may be true. Being with a family through a funeral and burial does help staff resolve their own feelings and provide some self comfort. Speaking personally, I can say that the time spent in direct contact with the family has seldom been a waste of time. In instances when I and my colleagues have not been needed, the feelings generated have not been of rejection but of satisfaction that this family has adequate emotional support. I also feel satisfied that they probably will not be major consumers of health care in the future for emotional or psychosomatic disorders that have accrued as a direct result of this death.

If families clearly indicate their wish to have no further involvement with the clinic staff or feel that they are well supported by friends, family and others, no one has a desire to intrude in any way.

Where families are inaccessible due to distance, one staff member at least telephones the family and rechecks with them in a week or two, just to see how they are coping. In situations where we are concerned about the family and know that we cannot follow through we try to ensure that follow-up care is provided, usually through the family physician or the clergy. In several instances, where children from other communities have died at home or in a local hospital, it has been the family physician who has been a major support throughout the illness, at the time of death and following.

Follow-Up Visits

In almost all situations where the team has been involved in the care of the child at the time of death, a follow-up visit to the clinic is arranged three to six weeks after death, or when the family feels ready to return. Where post mortems have been performed parents usually want to know the findings of the autopsy. A review meeting with the staff such as the resident, pediatric hematologist, nurse and social worker gives the family and the staff the opportunity to discuss both the medical findings and the family's adjustment to the change which the death of their child has precipitated. It is a traumatic experience for many families to return to the ward where their child died and to the out-patient area where they spent so many hours. The staff must be willing to take the time to accompany the family as they enter the clinic or the ward since being with a familiar person helps reduce their anxiety.

The return to the hospital and the review meeting enables an assessment of needs for follow-up care. In instances where no post mortem has been performed, families usually appreciate the chance to return to the hospital just to thank the staff, talk about their feelings and reassure themselves that there is hope for other children. In a small number of situations, families may not be able to return due to the intensity of their feelings about the child's death or for other reasons. No one is forced to return.

In our experience it is worth noting as well that some families have expressed concern for the physician who has cared for the child and have initiated post-death discussions simply to return and share their positive feelings about the care which their child had received.

Additional Help for Parents

Although it is not currently part of our clinic operation, an organization like the Family Leukemia Association can be a worthwhile adjunct to care at any point during malignant disease, including the time of death as well as following the death. Eleanor Pollit (1976) in her paper points out that emotional support, practical needs and information can be provided through a voluntary parents' organization. Like Mrs. Pollit, a parent who has lost a child may find a valuable role in such an organization. This type of organization may also have as its mandate voluntary fund raising for cancer research. This provides another source of comfort for parents in knowing that other children may be helped to survive. The latter seems to be a major concern to many families. In our setting parents frequently have friends and relatives donate to the Cancer Society, to the Clinic Research and Service Fund or to a special cause like outfitting the playroom.

The Grapevine

In our setting, even though we have not had a formal parents' organization, we have at times introduced parents and children to one another or parents and children have become acquainted in the waiting room, in the playroom or on the ward. Because of the design of the out-patient area, spontaneous discussion is common and parents seek out and form relationships with other parents. Informal relationships can be simply waiting room discussions or in some instances relationships move outside of the clinic. When a child dies, parents tend to inform other parents and recent experiences have demonstrated that parents have attended funerals, written cards and letters, telephoned and visited the family of the deceased child.

Remembering and the Anniversary of a Child's Death

Each and every bereaved parent wants his or her child's life to have had purpose and meaning. Some parents perpetuate their child's memory through donations to a worthy cause, others write about their child's life or dedicate their work to an area related to the care of other children. In some instances, several families have taken a poem or a picture of their child and had remembrance cards printed so that friends, family and those who cared for the child have a token to periodically remind them of the child's life and death.

Families need to remember and to work through their loss but sometimes society treats them with cruelty. Parents recount that days and weeks after the death, donation cards continue to be received and some have stated that months after the death they have been approached by telephone, letter or in person by companies wanting to provide them with costly remembrances of the deceased child. Such approaches have been most upsetting and cruel.

Anniversaries of deaths are oftentimes of great difficulty. In some situations where parents have maintained contact with clinic staff, they report that they have been depressed and upset for the week prior to the actual anniversary day and have been tearful on the day itself. In several instances, I and other clinic staff have been contacted by parents around the time of the anniversary of the child's death to chat, to ask about other clinic personnel or to enquire about something unrelated to the child's death. In one very severe reaction to the bereavement, a mother became less upset following the first anniversary of her daughter's death but immediately prior to the second anniversary she reexperienced pseudo-symptoms of the type of tumor which had led to her daughter's death. She required psychiatric treatment in hospital as a result of her anxiety and psychosomatic reactions.

In Closing

The return of a parent or parents to volunteer to help clinic staff with specific projects such as preparation of an educational videotape, or simply to visit with clinic or ward staff, has been a reminder to staff of the value of human relationships in facing illness and death. The determination, strength and warmth of children and families make working in such a vital setting a rewarding experience. All clinic staff truly appreciate the value of life — enjoying its laughter and sharing in its sorrows. As persons who have grown together through life, the hope of illness and the devastation of death, we who care for children and families continue to invest our hopes in medical care, long-term survival and genuine cures for children with malignancy. When a child dies, we must still face death with reality, compassion and an understanding of its impact . . . . .

> "I'll lend you for a little time a child of Mine," He said,
> "For you to love the while she lives and mourn for when she's dead.
> It may be six or seven years, or twenty-two or three,
> But will you, till I call her back, take care of her for Me?
> She'll bring her charms to gladden you, and shall her stay be brief
> You'll have her lovely memories as solace for your grief.

Edgar A. Guest

REFERENCES

Hamovitch, M.B.: *The Parent and the Fatally Ill Child.* City of Hope Medical Center, Duarte, California, 1964.

Kaplan, D.M., Grobstein, R. and Smith, A.: "Predicting the Impact of Severe Illness in Families." *Health and Soc Work* 1:3, 72-82, 1976.

Oakley, G.P. and Patterson, R.B.: "The Psychological Management of Leukemic Children and Their Families." *N Carol Med J* April, 186-193, 1966.

Vollman, R.R., Ganzert, A., Picher, L. and Williams, W.V.: *The Reaction of Family Systems to Sudden and Unexpected Death. Omega* 2:101-106, 1971.

Cain, A.C., Fast, I. and Erickson, M.E.: "Children's Disturbed Reactions to the Death of a Sibling." *Am J Orthopsychiatry* 34:741-752, 1964.

Cain, A.C. and Cain, B.S.: "On Replacing a Child." *J Am Acad Child Psychiatry* 3:444, 1964.

Goldberg, S.B.: "Family Tasks and Reactions in the Crisis of Death." *Soc Casework* 54:7, 398-405, 1973.

Bowlby, J.: "Processes of Mourning." *Int J Psychoanal* 42:317, 1961. Also see Bowlby, J.: "Grief and Mourning in Infancy and Early Childhood." *Psychoanal Study Child* 15:9, 1960.

Lindemann, E.: "Symptomatology and Management of Acute Grief." *Crisis Intervention: Selected Readings*, H.J. Parad (ed.) 1965. See Chapter 3.

Fischoff, J. and O'Brien, N.: "After the Child Dies." *J Pediatr* 88:1, 140-146, 1976.

Kulenkamp, E.: "Eric: A Mother's Recollection." *Home Care for the Dying Child: Professional and Family Perspectives.* I.M. Martinson (ed.), Appleton-Century-Crofts, New York, 1976.

Martinson, I.M. and Jorgens, C.L.: "Report of a Parent Support Group." *Home Care for the Dying Child: Professional and Family Perspectives.* I.M. Martinson (ed.), Appleton-Century-Crofts, New York, 1976.

Schiff, H.S.: *The Bereaved Parent.* Crown Publishers Inc., New York, 1977.

Mulholland, C.: *I'll Dance with the Rainbows.* Partick Press, Glasgow, 1973.

Anglim, M.A.: "Reintegration of the Family After the Death of a Child" *Home Care for the Dying Child: Professional and Family Perspectives.* I.M. Martinson (ed.), Appleton-Century-Crofts, New York, 1976.

McCollum, A.T.: *Coping with Prolonged Health Impairment in Your Child.* Little, Brown and Company (inc.), Boston, Mass., 1975.

Rosenblatt, B.: "A Young Boy's Reaction to the Death of His Sister." *J Am Acad Child Psychiatry* 8:321-335, 1969.

Parness, E.: "Effects of Experiences With Loss and Death Among Preschoolers." *Children Today.* Nov.-Dec. 2-7, 1975.

Weston, D.L. and Erwin, R.C.: "Pre-School Child's Response to Death of an Infant Sibling." *Am J Dis Child* 106, 564-567, 1963.

Fredlund, D.: "The Remaining Child." *Home Care for the Dying Child: Professional and Family Perspectives.* I.M. Martinson (ed.), Appleton-Century-Crofts, New York, 1976.

Pollitt, E.: "The Family Leukemia Association." *Essence.* 1:2, 107-115, 1976.

Guest, E.: "To All Parents." *All in a Lifetime.* The Reilly-Lee Company, Chicago, 1938. Reprinted 1970, Books for Libraries Press, Freeport, N.Y.

INDEX

175